AT G. H. Q.

BY THE SAME AUTHOR
EARL HAIG

Photo: Lafayette Ltd.

AT
G. H. Q.

BY
**BRIGADIER-GENERAL
JOHN CHARTERIS**
C.M.G., D.S.O.
Author of "Field-Marshal Earl Haig"

The Naval & Military Press Ltd

Published by

The Naval & Military Press Ltd
Unit 5 Riverside, Brambleside
Bellbrook Industrial Estate
Uckfield, East Sussex
TN22 1QQ England

Tel: +44 (0)1825 749494

www.naval-military-press.com
www.nmarchive.com

In reprinting in facsimile from the original, any imperfections are inevitably reproduced and the quality may fall short of modern type and cartographic standards.

PREFACE

All of us who served through those four eventful years from August 1914 onwards, have stored in our memories recollections that we treasure. We can hardly expect that any of the years still remaining to us will rival in interest that period of our lives.

Many may have had the good fortune which was mine, that every scrap of writing sent home from the front was carefully preserved. Others also may have sought to frame from these letters for the benefit of their own families, some readable and coherent record of their doings and their thoughts in the years of crisis and strain. Such was my intention when I began the writing which has now developed into this volume. For, as I wrote, I found it necessary to refer to the records which I myself had of my work at G.H.Q. I had not kept a formal diary; but very early in my days at G.H.Q., I found it necessary to keep notes of my views from day to day, and in particular of the conversations which I had with many people in high places. A most careful and painstaking secretary had seen to it that all the letters which I received and wrote, other than those to my own home, were carefully filed.

From these records I have compiled this volume. It is published in the hope that it will serve to give some idea of the life and problems of G.H.Q., and perhaps throw some light on events that are still obscure.

Where the records were incomplete, I have amplified them by my recollections, and I have now inserted names which, for reasons of censorship, were then omitted. But in the main the book is in the words written at the time.

J. CHARTERIS.

WATERSIDE,
    ECCLEFECHAN.
1.1.31.

CONTENTS

PART ONE—1914
CORPS HEAD-QUARTERS

CHAP.		PAGE
1.	MOBILIZATION	3
2.	FIRST DAYS IN FRANCE	9
3.	THE RETREAT FROM MONS	14
4.	THE BATTLE OF THE MARNE	27
5.	THE AISNE AND AFTER	34
6.	THE FIRST BATTLE OF YPRES	46

PART TWO—1915
ARMY HEAD-QUARTERS

7.	PREPARATIONS FOR NEUVE CHAPELLE	71
8.	NEUVE CHAPELLE	81
9.	CRITICAL DAYS AT YPRES	87
10.	THE SPRING AND SUMMER OF 1915	91
11.	PRELIMINARY TO LOOS	104
12.	BATTLE OF LOOS	111
13.	SIR DOUGLAS HAIG BECOMES COMMANDER-IN-CHIEF	119

PART THREE—1916
G.H.Q.

14.	PLANS FOR THE SOMME ATTACK	129
15.	THE SOMME	151
16.	THE SOMME (*continued*)	161
17.	THE SOMME SUCCESSES	168

CONTENTS

PART FOUR—1917
G.H.Q.

CHAP.		PAGE
18.	Discussions and Rumours	185
19.	The German Withdrawal	197
20.	Battle of Arras	207
21.	Messines	223
22.	Ypres Again	231
23.	Passchendaele	249
24.	Cambrai and its Aftermath	267

PART FIVE—1918
G.H.Q.

25.	The Supreme War Council v. G.H.Q.	281
26.	The German Onslaught	289
27.	The Beginning of the End	313
	Appendix A—Note on German Intentions	321
	Appendix B—Note on the Situation from a German Point of View at the End of 1917	327
	Appendix C—The German Peace Proposals	335
	Index	341

PART ONE—1914
CORPS HEAD-QUARTERS

AT G.H.Q.

CHAPTER I

MOBILIZATION

Aldershot, in June 1914, was just recovering from the excitement of the Ulster crisis, and settling comfortably down to normal times of peace. The annual training was about to culminate in manœuvres. A new mobilization scheme had come from the War Office. Some exciting polo matches were impending. Probably nowhere in the Empire was there less thought of the immediate possibility of a great war. The inevitability of a European war sooner or later, was part of the dogma of the soldier's military creed. For years the date had even been correctly deduced, or guessed, as 1914. A belief in the correctness of the deduction had impelled me to leave a Staff appointment in India and accept a much less promising position in Aldershot. The Balkan War of 1912 had shown how delicate was the balance of peace. But the very fact that a European conflagration had been avoided then, made remote the possibility in 1914. The Irish crisis had turned our minds in other directions. Certainly no one in Aldershot in June, 1914, anticipated anything more warlike than manœuvres for the remaining months of the year. Our warning note—strangely prophetic —had come from an officer [1] then commanding a battalion in Ulster, who in a public speech had warned his men not to worry about the trouble in Ireland but "to prepare themselves for a great war with Germany in the autumn." If many at Aldershot read the report of the speech, none paid any attention to it. Nor did the news of the murder of the Archduke at Sarajevo excite any general interest, or arouse ideas of possible international developments involving Great Britain, in many minds at Aldershot. Sir Douglas Haig, the Commander-in-Chief, on whose staff I was serving, was, however, keenly interested. I still have the rough notes of a paper which he directed me to prepare on possible developments.

[1] Lt.-Col. (afterwards Sir Louis) Bols.

I cannot claim for that paper a successful appreciation of the situation. Obviously hostilities between Serbia and Austria were a possible development, yet with a united Europe pledged to seek peace, even this seemed improbable. And if this improbability should occur, then there appeared only the very remote possibility that the Great Powers would be involved.

A few days after the Sarajevo murders we heard of the insertion in an issue of a London daily paper of the notification recalling the German Reservists to the colours. The edition was said to have been suppressed and the notice cancelled. The explanation given was that it was an error. Errors of this nature do not easily occur. At once to our minds the possibility of war became less remote. Then followed the reports of the successive negotiations and their failure to find a peaceful solution. The contingency that at first had seemed hardly possible became a strong probability. But even then it was only a small number at Aldershot who heard from private or official sources of the progress of events, and they were bidden to hold their peace.

Sir Douglas Haig was very preoccupied. He had little more information than that which reached him through the Press. We discussed the situation each day. Did we hope for peace or war? It is difficult to say. We had no delusions about what war would mean. Neither he nor I had ever shared the optimistic opinion, held by many in high official quarters, of the superiority of the French over the German army. We knew that the British Expeditionary Force, perfect though we believed it to be in organization and training, could not play a decisive part in the great clash of the huge armies of those two great powers. We knew that inevitably we should be in the thick of the fighting and that casualties would be enormous. Yet we were trained for war. It was the task for which we had been preparing ourselves for years. We could not but appreciate that it was only in war that we could fulfil our life's work. Sir Douglas Haig knew his own task would be important—the command of one-third of the Expeditionary Force. He had no doubt about his own ability to make good, whatever the outcome of the war might be.

For me, as for everyone else, there were other side-currents of thought,[1] and I hoped for at least a few weeks' delay.

Small personal incidents show how my own opinions became fixed. A nephew was spending in Germany his vacation from the Royal Military Academy, to learn the German language. His

[1] My eldest son was born on August 16.

mother wrote to me about the middle of July for advice, whether to bring him back or not. The boy himself had written that at Hanover, where he was staying, there were obvious preparations for war, but those Germans whom he had met were still convinced that hostilities would be avoided. On July 22 I replied that it was not yet necessary to interrupt his studies, and that the experience of seeing Germany in a crisis was valuable. So long as we ourselves were not going to be involved it was better he should remain; but if we were to be involved, and if the outbreak of war found him still in Germany, he was liable to be interned. I promised to let him know in ample time if and when he should return.

During the next week, there were rapid developments. Already it seemed possible that letters were being examined. I did not care to risk anything more definite than a post-card, dispatched on the 28th, asking him to dine with me on the following Tuesday in London. The sequel was interesting. The lad consulted a German friend (apparently in a position to know) and was told definitely that war between Germany and Britain was impossible. He decided to remain, and on August 4 was still in Hanover. His German friend sought him out and said he was responsible for the awkward position in which he found himself, and would see him out of the country. Actually he conducted him to the frontier, saw him safely across and then returned to join the German army. There were many straight and honourable Germans and he was one of them. Chance put me in a position, three years later, to help this German when he himself was a prisoner in our hands.

On July 29 the precautionary orders reached Aldershot, and on August 4 came the declaration of war. For the next few days my own part was that of an onlooker. There were a few office records to be cleared up. Some of the cases we were dealing with would read strangely now with the knowledge which the next few years were to bring. General Lomax (Commanding the 1st Division) had just been told officially that he had not been selected for further employment. The reason given was that he had had little or no war experience. In a few months he would have retired. The war intervened. He took his division to France and, until mortally wounded in the Salient, he was perhaps the best Divisional General of those early days of the war.

Dr. Simms, the Presbyterian chaplain, had reached the limit of his service on account of his age. We were seeking to get him an extension, but without much hope of success. He had only a few months to serve when mobilization was ordered. He went to France, became Principal Chaplain to the Forces, served until the end of the war and still serves the State in Parliament as a member for Co. Down.

My chief duty in those few days between mobilization and our departure was meeting the reproaches and prayers of those officers who were to stay at home in charge of depots, and could not accompany their units to France. Their reproaches were fierce, their entreaties almost agonized. It was the chance that they had been waiting and working for, and now they were to lose it. It is never a pleasant task to refuse applications. Particularly hard now, because one felt that there might be real grounds for their view. How little we knew! Their chance came later. Most of them now lie in France or Flanders. One officer, a personal friend, greeted the war with almost frantic joy. Of French descent, he longed for the chance to fight for France against Germany. He also lies in France, killed at the head of his unit in the first ten days of the war.

But there was humour to relieve us. The butler at Government House was determined that he too would see war at close quarters. Sir Douglas Haig decided to take him as mess servant to the Corps H.Q. mess. The trouble was to get him into khaki. Regulations were not then relaxed. To enlist, attest and enrol, takes time in normal circumstances. For all we knew the war might be over before his recruit training was finished. I appealed to my friends of the R.E. at Aldershot for their benevolent assistance in short-circuiting the process. All things are possible when a Commander-in-Chief wants things done. After breakfast one morning I took the butler, immaculate in morning coat and bowler, to the R.E. officer, saw him enter the Quartermaster's stores and waited in the car to take him back. In an incredibly short time, less than half an hour, he emerged, in khaki, puttees neatly tied, a full-fledged driver of H.M. Royal Engineers; he gave a somewhat amateurish salute and then lapsed again into the butler and said, "I beg your pardon, sir, but have you such a thing as half a crown on you?" I asked him why he wanted it, to which came the reply, "Well, sir, that Quartermaster-Sergeant has been very good to me, and I would like to give him something." This was too good to be missed. I climbed out of my car and followed him at a safe distance to see the driver recruit of ten minutes' seniority tip a Quartermaster-Sergeant grown grey in service, for civility. And the Quartermaster-Sergeant, to his credit be it related, did not hurt the recruit's feelings by declining the solatium.

A few days later Sir Douglas Haig was called to attend the Council of War convened by the Prime Minister to decide on the best plan of operation for the British Expeditionary Force. All the great soldiers and sailors of the day took part—Lord Roberts, Lord Kitchener, Sir John French, Sir Douglas Haig, Sir James Grierson and Henry Wilson. I accompanied my chief to London. We had discussed at great length what line Sir Douglas Haig should take. He told me afterwards what had occurred. Sir Douglas Haig was already quite convinced that the war in some form or other would last for several years. He did not attempt to meet by argument the contention of those—and they were in the majority both in the War Council and out of it—who considered that a great war would so disturb the delicate international and industrial situation, that means would inevitably be found to bring it to a conclusion in a few months. Whatever might be the outcome of the fighting by sea and by land, now that Great Britain was definitely committed, it was in his opinion a fight for existence between us and Germany. Neither could survive defeat. Neither would give in until beaten to the knees, and in no circumstances could this be accomplished in one or even two years.

For these reasons he went to the Conference prepared to urge, with all the strength in his power, the formation of a great army, based upon the Territorial organization with the creation of which he had so much to do in previous years. Regular officers and men must be kept at home to train the Army. Particularly the War Office must not be depleted. As for the plan of action, our guiding principle for the B.E.F. must be to do all we could to help France. His own view was, I believe, that this could best be done from a flank position based on the Channel ports from which we could effectively threaten the flank of the German Army, now known to be advancing in strength. He took with him a list of questions, on the answers to which depended the actual decision of our plans.[1]

From the Council of War, Haig accompanied Lord Kitchener to the War Office. There he remained in close consultation with the new Secretary of State, still pressing his views of a long war, and the necessity for expanding the Expeditionary Force into a great army. As we now know, Lord Kitchener concurred with him as to the length of the war, but substituted his " New Army " for the expansion of the Territorial Force urged by Sir Douglas Haig.

[1] See "Field-Marshal Earl Haig," by the author, pp. 79 and 80.

On August 13 we left Aldershot. General Gough, the Chief of Staff, offered to motor me to Southampton in his car. I called at his house after dinner. There was a few minutes' wait before General Gough joined me; his first remark was, "These partings—after all, they are the worst things in the whole war." I could sympathize then and many times afterwards, when as the weary years of war passed I recalled his words. Whatever the strain of war may have been in all or any of its theatres, I think for the individual the greatest strain was those periodic partings at the termination of the brief periods of leave we spent at home. The whole tragic poignancy of war was condensed daily in the departure of the leave train from London. The men going back to the war seeking to hide from their womenfolk the knowledge of all it meant; the women striving to hold back their tears until the train had rolled slowly away from the platform.

Those who have served long years in the East know how one develops a sort of dual personality—Eastern and Western—and how each reasserts itself as one voyages backwards and forwards. Unconsciously the mind is attuned to different circumstances. The mental outlook changes with the physical outlook. The absurd becomes normal. The unbelievable is accepted as sound sense. Even the literature that enchants at home loses its charm under the Eastern sun.

And thus it was, I think, during the war. Without conscious effort the mind put on its "war spectacles" on the brief journey of the leave train from London to the seaports. By the time the transport was pulling away from the wharf, home had already become an almost unreal memory. War, with its discomforts and its joys (for it had joys), its humour and its pathos, its horrors and its moments of almost delirious delight, was the only thing real to our minds. Nothing else mattered.

CHAPTER II

FIRST DAYS IN FRANCE

August 16. I had only time to send you a post-card from Southampton, to say *au revoir*. The words mean more in war than as we ordinarily use them. But I am convinced that they are for us more than a wish or a hope or a prayer. These are, as nearly as is humanly possible, what we are looking forward to with reasonable certainty. I wish I could think that all those we see here around us, all our friends of this last year at Aldershot, could be writing the same words with the same confidence. But they are going into very real danger; I wonder if many of them realize how real—I hope not. For us at Corps H.Q. there cannot be anything like the same risk. That is why I am confident that we shall meet again. Indeed, my danger will not be any greater, if as great, as that which by now you yourself will have safely passed. Let that comfort you—when you read this.

Now for an account of our doings. Southampton provided little of interest. Although the Corps Staff is almost all the Aldershot crowd, there are one or two new arrivals, and some shuffling of work among the old hands, and we are busy settling down. One amusing incident lingers in my mind. Colonel X, who has blossomed into a Staff officer, consulted me very confidentially: "You know all about the army—tell me how many battalions are there in a division?"

We crossed in the *Combrie Castle*, a Union liner, with only two available cabins (four berths in all). These were seized by D.H. and Jimmy Grierson and their senior Staff officers. The rest of us bivouacked on deck. We sailed late in the evening. Fortunately it was fine for most of the night, but rain fell in the morning. It was very uncomfortable. There were no arrangements for feeding us on board, but fortunately we had spotted this (quite by accident) and D.H. produced a well-stocked lunch basket. I was one of the lucky ones who were invited to share it.

Havre is in marked contrast to Southampton. Here the whole

air is tense with the atmosphere of a great crisis. Everything is run by the Army. Civilians exist, as it were, on sufferance. I am a little alarmed by the general tone of the French people. They talk much of what they are going to do, and how soon they will have captured Berlin. It all seems rather forced, "whistling to keep up their courage"; perhaps I am prejudiced, but they seem so much less solid than the Germans, whom I know so much better. Still, the French troops seem admirable, cheery, well disciplined and well found in everything. Our own units are transformed. You remember the skeleton battalions of boys you used to watch at Aldershot. Now they are at full strength, and with grown men preponderating; the reservists have shaken down much quicker than seemed possible. I am very confident our army will not fail us.

An officer in from Calais told me an amusing yarn of happenings there a few weeks ago. When there was still doubt about our coming in, the people went mad with disappointment and dislike of everything British. The Union Jack was torn from the Consulate and trampled on in the streets. British officers were jeered at. Then came the official news that we were in. The pendulum swung sharply back. Adoration replaced dislike and was almost equally embarrassing. The womenfolk kissed everything British that wore trousers. Every band seemed to have forgotten all its music except "God Save the King." A queer, volatile people, these allies of ours. But after all, they know they are fighting for their lives. Are we? I do not know. But if we are, certainly few of us realize it yet.

I had a long talk with General Grierson. He knows Germany better than any soldier I have yet met. But he is feeling the strain and complains of not feeling well. D.H. is imperturbable as ever. A little more brusque. A little more dogmatic. Missing a few more words out of his sentences, but gives such a sense of capacity. Of the two men, Grierson is the more clever; Haig the more capable.

Of our own personal friends: B. is still immaculate. His "this-wonderful-world" air is rather more marked; R. is cheery as ever, thoroughly enjoying every moment of it. A godsend to me, for he talks to me of you and relieves all, or nearly all, of the only real anxiety of which I am conscious.

D.H. unburdened himself to-day. He is greatly concerned about the composition of British G.H.Q. He thinks French quite unfit for high command in time of crisis. He fears he may commit the army to decisive battles before we have time to " collect " ourselves. He says French's military ideas are not sound; that he has never studied war; that he is obstinate, and will not keep with him men who point out even obvious errors. He gives him credit for good tactical powers, great courage and determination. He does not think Murray will dare to do anything but agree with everything French suggests. In any case he thinks French would not listen to Murray but will rely on Wilson, which is far worse. D.H. thinks Wilson is a politician, and not a soldier, and " politician " with Douglas Haig is synonymous with crooked dealing and wrong sense of values. Personally I do not think this matters much, as French will be subordinate to Joffre, and D.H. and Grierson can be relied on to pull their Corps through. What does matter, is Joffre. All we know about him is good, but as far as our Corps H.Q. is concerned we know very little.

August 17. (*In the train.*) The postal arrangements for us have broken down or are not yet working, and I have had no news of you. Now we are moving forward and I fear I cannot expect any post for some days. So far that is the only hardship of war. We entrained early this morning, travelling in perfect comfort, just like an ordinary peace-time journey in France. The funny little bugle still blows the train out of the station, just as if neither the locomotive nor the driver can bear the sound for even a few seconds —and small wonder. At most of the stations, people assembled on the platform and welcomed us and cheered us onward. Whatever else we may do, or fail to do, the British Expeditionary Force certainly has heartened the French populace. They cannot know how microscopic our force really is, compared to the great armies of France and Germany. Even Belgium will put us in the shade so far as numbers count. At the little wayside station of Hergieux we unexpectedly pulled up. The stationmaster insisted on D.H. going to the telephone—he hates the telephone—to hear with his own ears that Jimmy Grierson had died. It is a very great loss. He was a very able soldier. The replacement of any commander now must mean some dislocation. Just when we expect to be in battle within a few weeks it is especially serious. D.H.'s comments were characteristic, *first* annoyance at being called to the telephone to hear news that required no action from him, and *second* that it was better that Grierson should have died now than when he was actually in battle. It sounds cold-blooded common sense. Actually he felt the loss acutely, for Grierson was a close personal friend, but as you know, D.H. never reveals himself.

There is already the inevitable suggestion that the Germans have made away with Grierson—by poison or magic. Utter nonsense! He was a very ill man when I last saw him at Havre. You know D.H.'s aversion to the hard-bitten man, and his fondness for Cæsar's "fat counsellors." But there is reason in all things, and poor Grierson was of too full a habit to stand even the comparatively comfortable strain of soldiering at Corps H.Q.

It is strange as one looks out of the carriage window to see the harvesting in full swing in glorious summer weather. There are more women at work than we see in England, but there are many men in the fields. Probably old men, over military age, but we cannot distinguish age from the train. I wonder whether we should hope for good weather or bad for the next few weeks. If our job is to hold off attack, bad weather will help us. If we are ourselves to attack we want fine days.

August 20. At last there is news, and great news, and I feel just as elated as if we had won the war and I was on my way home. But the news did not come by anything so common as the penny post, or even by telegram.

To-day I was sent to G.H.Q. to see the C.-in-C. He was engaged when I arrived, and I was waiting in an ante-room looking at some French daily papers and reading the news of Sir James Grierson's death, when an orderly came in and casually said, "Perhaps you would like to see these," handing me half a dozen *Morning Posts* from August 13 onwards. And there, in the first one I looked at, was the intimation of the birth of our son. I had hardly had time to appreciate it when an A.D.C. burst into the room howling congratulations. Sir John French invited me to lunch and pledged our health in champagne. That's what I call real war! Nothing nasty or messy—just utter relief and joy. Even Dukani[1] seemed exhilarated when I mounted him to ride back.

August 21. The last three days have been days of hard and long marching forward from the concentration area, up to our place in the French line. The reservists have stood it well—for the serving men it was not a serious strain.

For the Corps Staff it has been a pleasant trek. It is curious to

[1] My charger.

note how the mental strain is affecting the few people we see closely. Neither Haig nor Lomax, nor Munro shows any signs at all of strain. One, at least, of the Brigade Commanders shows signs of cracking already. He insisted on marching all day on foot with his troops, which is absurd, as he is far older than they are. But it is probably to keep his mind from worrying. He is very irritable, which is not a good sign.

D.H. is much concerned about the general plan. He has heard reports that the Germans are advancing in strength right round our left flank and have forestalled our own movement. At a conference at Wassigny yesterday he expounded his tactical views—the whole gist was to keep liberty of manœuvre. If we are to attack, we must retain the possibility of breaking off the attack at any moment if required. The country in front of us is very difficult, and we could be held up by comparatively few troops while the Germans worked round our flank. He is particularly emphatic that all German teaching, strategy and tactics aim at envelopment. He fears that they may let us get deeply forward into their general line before developing their flanking movement. Meantime the great French attack is taking place away to the South. It aims at breaking the German centre. If it succeeds our task will be easy enough. The Germans will have to stop their enveloping effort, and seek to withdraw, and we will have to attack them all out. If the French attack fails—and it may fail, although G.H.Q. is very optimistic—we may be fighting for our lives in a week and perhaps retreating.

CHAPTER III

THE RETREAT FROM MONS

August 29 (*Saturday*). You have had nothing but post-cards, and few of them, since I wrote on the 20th. The next day I received your letter giving the welcome news that all was well with you both and that I need have no anxiety on your behalf. Since then I have of course heard nothing. And, to be frank, I have hardly had time to be anxious. You will understand, for the papers will have given you news of our doings, and of our troubles. They are over now for the time, and to-day we are resting. A God's own mercy for the troops, for they are very, very tired. Even we on the Staff, who have had a relatively easy time, are not far from the end of our tether.

I cannot give you a detailed account of it all, for the censorship is strict, but I will try to give you some pictures of it. For the rest you must wait until we meet, though Heaven knows when that will be.

I do not know exactly what view you have formed of the general outline of the happenings of the past week, from the reports you will have read, but the hard facts are that we were pushed far too soon and far too far forward, right into the thick of a great battle. The great French attack that was to break the German centre, failed. The Germans pressed forward their attempt to outflank us. The French on our right gave way, and our Army had to get back as best it could. As regards our own Corps, D.H.'s extraordinary skill and determination has got us out with little loss, but very, very tired. The other Corps has not fared so well and, indeed, has suffered very badly.

Now for my own doings. Late last Saturday—just a week ago, but it seems a year—we were ordered to push forward to Mons. This meant a night march, and coming hard on top of the long marches up to Amiens it took a lot out of the troops, but probably it was necessary. Sunday morning there was a little rain and drizzle. I had been up most of the night and dozed for a couple of hours in the early morning, and I remember being awakened by the church bells; it all looked very peaceful. The rain had cleared off and there was some sun. I could see the peasants in their Sunday clothes coming along the roads to chapel. It was exactly like any ordinary Sunday morning on manœuvres. D.H. had been haled to a G.H.Q. Conference and about 10 a.m. I accompanied him to Bruyère. By the time we reached there, shells had begun to fall about a couple of miles away from us, but it seemed to be desultory firing. At the conference, the C.-in-C. and General Wilson explained their view of the situation. Most of their interest seemed centred at the time on the great French attack. We spent the day after the conference quietly at Bonnet and the night at Batigny Château. We knew the Germans were quite close to us, and the fact that they did not attack set us all speculating. It might be that they had heard of a big French success and were therefore not going to attack at all. It might equally well mean that they were holding their hand to give their flanking troops time to get round us.

The next morning was still quiet, but just after lunch we got news that the enemy was advancing towards X's brigade. D.H. went towards Brigeul at once and sent me on to see X and his brigade-Major. They had a big telescope mounted on a tripod and through it we could see, far away in the distance, columns of troops advancing towards us. But they were very far away and there was no immediate prospect of attack, though some shells were falling on the brigade. It struck me then that X was rather jumpy. He had worn himself out marching on foot with his brigade all the way up. On the other hand, his brigade-Major was quite cool and collected. D.H. sent for X a little later and soothed him.

Just about that time I saw my first German prisoner. He was a Reserve officer, slightly wounded, who had been bagged in some little outpost affair. He had been in the United States for some time, he told me, and yet could not, or would not, speak English, so we conversed in German. He was quite convinced that the war was utter folly. He blamed no one for starting it, but his great theme was that if England and Germany had only come together they could have ruled the world. (*Zusammen könnten wir die Welt herrschen.*) I told him that we British had no desire to "*herrsch*" the world, gave him cigarettes and sent him off to hospital.

A little later, a Staff officer of the 2nd Corps, arrived at our H.Q. to ask for a couple of battalions to fill a gap between the two Corps. I remember him saying, "If you will send a couple of battalions, the battle will be won." So D.H. sent three battalions—to make sure!—but we did not win the battle.

Just before midnight a report came that there was heavy shelling on a hill held by one of our battalions, and that the O.C. wanted to retire. D.H. was very upset and sent a personal written order that the position must be held at all costs. Then we turned in about midnight. That was the night of last Monday, and to-day is only Saturday.

I had hardly gone to sleep, without undressing, when I was awakened and told that D.H. wanted me at once. I went to his room, and he told me that orders had arrived for a general retreat, and that we were to cover the retirement of the 2nd Corps. This was quite impossible, and I was sent to Smith-Dorrien to make some arrangement. I motored over to Smith-Dorrien's H.Q. and found him just as unperturbed as D.H., which was very cheering. He agreed with D.H. and gave me his plans. It took me nearly an hour to find D.H. again. He was at a small inn with a Divisional H.Q. and was busy writing out his orders for the Division.

Then we started off to go round other H.Q.s and very nearly fell straight into the German lines. We missed our way at a cross-roads, and had gone for nearly 1½ miles straight towards the Germans before we discovered the mistake. It would have been a farcical end to D.H.'s career to have delivered himself to the enemy!

We got back to our H.Q. at Bonnet by dawn (Thursday) and stayed there all the morning. There was nothing special to do. The retirement had commenced. It all reads simple enough, but actually the fact that we got started so rapidly and smoothly was the result of good leadership and good training. In consequence we were not placed in the same dilemma as the 2nd Corps. It was anxious work waiting through the day, getting periodical reports of the retirement of our own Corps, and of fighting by the 2nd Corps.

I went over to the 2nd Corps early in the afternoon and ran into a little crowd of officers round the local telegraph office, all trying to get off wires to their respective homes. When I got back, I found D.H. was gone to see the C.-in-C., and that I was to follow him there. I got there just as he was leaving. He told me he had been urging on the C.-in-C. the necessity of a rapid retreat, otherwise we might be cut off by the Germans' outflanking movement. The C.-in-C. had agreed, but apparently S.D. had reported that his troops could not march further and must rest for a day. As soon as we got back to our own H.Q., D.H. worked out with Gough the plans for the next day, and sent me back to G.H.Q. to get the C.-in-C.'s approval of them. We were to start at 5 a.m. and make a long march to Landrecies.

I had some difficulty at G.H.Q. and did not get back until late. We stopped the night at a farmhouse (Vieux Mesnil). I lay down on some straw in an outhouse to get some sleep and was awakened by Secrett[1] to say that D.H. was very ill; had shut himself up in his room, and given orders he would see nobody.

I got hold of Micky Ryan and went in to D.H. and insisted that he must see Ryan. D.H. was at his worst, very rude but eventually did see Ryan, who dosed him with what must have been something designed for elephants, for the result was immediate and volcanic! But it was effective, for D.H. ultimately got some sleep, and in the morning was better though very chewed up, and ghastly to look at. He wanted to ride as usual, but Ryan insisted on his going in a car that day.

The next day (Wednesday) was the first full day of the retreat, and it was a very anxious time for the Staff and terrible for the troops. We started at 5 a.m. and marched steadily until 4 p.m. (seemed much longer than that); steady plodding along a dusty road in a glaring, blazing sun. We only halted a few minutes in each hour's march. Always there was the sound of guns—now distant, now seeming much closer. The Battalion Commanders knew what we were in for, and made the men lie down at every halt. At first the men resented this, but as the hours slowly passed they dropped as if hit immediately the halt was ordered, and were asleep almost before their bodies reached the ground.

At first there was some whistling and singing, but that soon stopped and by the early afternoon there was no noise to be heard save gruff orders enforcing march discipline. But the men were amazing. Practically none fell out. They stuck it. Here and there you could see a man carrying another's rifle for a spell to ease the burden for even a few minutes. All the side roads were filled with refugees; a curious sight, men, women and children struggling along, every known form of conveyance pressed into service to carry the most treasured of the household gods—fear on every face.

We were with the rear brigade, and just about 4 p.m. we reached Landrecies, where we were to stop for the evening and until 2 a.m., when we were to march again. Though I had been riding almost

[1] Sir Douglas Haig's personal servant.

all day, I was pretty tired, for I had been up most of the previous night. As soon as I had got my billet I lay down to sleep. I had just dozed off when I was awakened by a great disturbance in the street. Refugees were streaming in, shouting that the Uhlans were hard at their heels, and some of them flourished Uhlan lances and accoutrements to prove their statements. D.H. told me to get on my horse and, with one orderly, to ride back and investigate.

Just north of Landrecies, where the refugees reported the Germans to be, there is a thick wood. There the two main roads converge on to a bridge over a river on the outskirts of a village. I got Dukani and with an orderly rode about 1½ miles, up one road, and then back to the bridge and up the other. There was absolutely nothing to be seen or heard, and I returned to Landrecies and reported to D.H. that it seemed to be a false alarm, or in any case, an exaggerated report. There could be no large body of troops within some miles of us. It must have been about 6 o'clock, and I lay down again to rest.

I think I was asleep, though it cannot have been more than ten minutes later, when I was aroused by a sharp rifle-fire and some shelling. Almost immediately after reports came in that Landrecies was surrounded. There was a good deal of confusion, and some amusing incidents. D.H. ordered the whole town to be organized for defence, barricades to meet across the roads with furniture and anything else handy, all secret papers, etc., to be destroyed. He sent me off to prepare a big school building for defence, giving me a couple of companies of Guards as a working party. For once he was quite jolted out of his usual placidity. He said, "If we are caught, by God, we'll sell our lives dearly."

Before I went off to my school I thought I would see how the destruction of documents was progressing. There were some that I thought I would like to keep in existence as long as possible. I found an Intelligence Officer trying to destroy the metal censor stamp by burning it on a spirit lamp, which might, under great provocation, have just managed to heat shaving water. I got the papers I wanted, and put them in my pocket.

It was a weird scene in the village street; men were throwing mattresses and chairs out of the windows for the barricades, which others were making as best they could. The few inhabitants left were protesting feebly. The Guards had arrested and tied up a French officer who had lost his head, and was making an ass of himself. I saw one rather pompous and unpopular Staff officer walking towards me, and a man at an upper window taking deliberate aim with one of those great soft French mattresses, and hitting him fair and square with it. Down went the pompous one, buried in the feather mattress, to the immense glee of the men. He was, of course, none the worse for it, but very, very angry.

Then I heard a great rattle of revolver shots quite close, and went to find out what was the matter. I saw an officer, obviously very excited, discharging his revolver down a street. I asked a military policeman who was near by what was in the street. "Nothing, sir," he said with a smile, "but some officers' horses." So I asked him, "Why the —— don't you stop him?" "Well you see, sir," he said, "he is a full Colonel, and his own horse is there with the others, and besides he's very excited and it may ease him." So I asked the "full Colonel" if he would care to come and help me with my job instead of shooting horses, and he quite amicably agreed. So off we went together.

The job at the school took a couple of hours, and then I went to D.H.'s billet to report. The attack had died down a bit, and I found him just on the point of getting into his motor-car to try to get through the enemy line, which must obviously be thin, to join the main body of the Corps. He told me to get in front with the driver and take charge of the car and choose the best route. I asked for five minutes to study the map. Then off we started. It was rather eerie work, quite dark and of course no lights on the car. There was a little mist, which was helpful in one way, but made it more difficult to find the road. There was still a good deal of firing, and it looked rather a forlorn hope to try to get through. But anyhow it was better than staying in Landrecies and having sooner or later to surrender, which seemed the alternative.

Actually it panned out very easily. Either the German line was very much thinner than was thought, or we struck it lucky in finding an unguarded road, or perhaps they were as tired as we were and all asleep. Personally, I was more concerned with memorizing the road—for there were several turnings—than with the possibility of running into German sentries. Owing to the ground mist, we could not see anything other than the road-sides. When you are up again, try some evening to drive the car by memory along one of the Surrey lanes with lights out; it is not easy. Once I came to a dead halt; the road I was on was at right angles to another road and did not cross it. I had no recollection of this being marked on the map, and had no idea whether to turn right or left. I took the left—pure luck—but it turned out to be correct, and a little afterwards we ran into some of our own men of the 1st Division.

We went at once to their H.Q.[1] and D.H. gave orders for an attack next morning to extricate the Guards from Landrecies. He sent me off at once to the French H.Q. on our right to ask for their co-operation. I arrived there at dawn, and was taken to the local Divisional Commander, a delightful man, very courteous and sympathetic. His command was chiefly French Territorials. He listened to all I had to say and then sent for a Staff officer and dictated orders for 12 battalions to work with us, moving at once. This was much better than I had expected, and I burst into somewhat effusive thanks. He checked me at once. "No thanks, please. I have ordered the move, good, but I don't think they will go. You see they are Territorials." As a matter of fact they did not move, but, equally as a matter of fact, we did not require them, so honours were easy. Apparently the Germans were never as strong at Landrecies as we had thought, and the Guards marched out without any difficulty next morning and rejoined us, but having to leave a lot of wounded for the Germans to capture. All the same it was a close shave; it might have ended in us all—including D.H.—being prisoners!

When I got back about 6 a.m. D.H. had gone to the —th Brigade. I joined him there, and found the brigade engaged in a sharp little fight—a good deal of shelling, but not many casualties. Shell-fire is rather nerve-racking at first, but it is extraordinary how many miss. The Brigade Commander was very rattled and nervous, and D.H. was walking him up and down, holding his elbow and soothing him, just like a nurse with a nervous child. It was an interesting study in psychology. D.H. was showing no signs of his customary curtness with anybody who fell short of requirements. He was adopting the attitude that "bogy men" did not exist, that everything was quite normal, the Germans much more tired than we were, and so on. All this after a night without sleep, and heavy with great anxiety. But when we left the brigade he was very incisive in his criticism, and I fancy the Brigade Commander will be sent home very soon.

There is not much to tell of the other days of the retreat. It was curiously monotonous, but I cannot give you any idea of the ghastly depression and anxiety of it all. The worst moments were when an officer from G.H.Q. arrived with a message that we should jettison ammunition, put exhausted men on the ammunition wagons

[1] La Grande Fère.

and make off with what speed we could. Gough tore up the message. I pray God we have now done with retreat; the long, long marches with no rest to look forward to, and the gnawing fear that we might not escape. The men growing daily less resilient, almost sullen in their dogged determination to carry on—the roads double-banked with transport, the refugees crowding in on us, the sound of guns behind us and, now and then, imagination playing pranks with us and making us hear them ahead of us.

One day, indeed, (I think it was Tuesday) the whole column halted and a message came back from the leading Division that they were held up by a force of the enemy in front of us, and that it was deploying to attack them. D.H. sent me forward with orders to push them on, and break through at all costs. When I reached the head of the column, I saw a few riflemen firing at us on the skyline, but there seemed to be no artillery and I could not hear any machine-guns. So I wrote an order to the officer commanding the leading units to march straight on without deploying, and signed it as coming from D.H. I went with them myself and found there was nothing in front of us at all—probably just a stray patrol of German cavalry who had worked round and perhaps only a few German agents or spies. It was an enormous relief to get the column going again.

But even in the strain of the retreat there is some humour. One of the Staff delights in being in the position of always having a get-away for any error he may make. So he likes to go to every possible source of information and ask what time we move next day. Sooner or later he gets two contradictory replies. Then he is perfectly happy and retorts, " Order, counter-order, disorder! How can *I* give my orders ? " The joke is he has no orders to give to anyone except the mess servants, and they generally find out elsewhere! One day some bright young spirits got their own back on him by not wakening him when we left our bivouac. He is a heavy sleeper and did not stir until the rear-guard coming along shook him up. By that time we were some miles off, and as we had taken his horse the poor devil had to foot-slog it after us. He did not overtake us for two hours, when he staggered in at our next halt, covered with dust, and foaming at the mouth with rage.

It is easy to write light-heartedly about it all now, for I think it is over, and we have successfully brought off a most difficult military operation. Soon, I hope, we shall be attacking instead of running away. Soon—perhaps to-night—we shall have sleep; long sleep, real sleep, not snatches of 20 minutes, and soon we shall forget this nightmare of retreat. But war is a very horrible thing, beastly and palpitatingly cruel. I thank God it is not being waged in our own country. I look at the children and wonder if they are like D. God help the ones I see—homeless fugitives, panic-stricken, fear fixed on their faces, fleeing blindly, anywhere to get away. The French have the memory of 1870 always with them. All their vainglory has gone from them. They are frankly afraid—and I cannot blame them. The Belgians were different. They did not seem to regard the war as belonging to them at all, and both going forward and coming back we saw again and again great hulking young men lounging in the homesteads, looking on as if it was a drama staged for their interest. Now they will suffer as the French suffered in '70.

The really nasty thing about it all is that I cannot rid myself of the thought that the French army morale is affected by those same memories of 1870. An initial defeat is an enormous disadvantage in war. Will they ever fight again with the will to win? I don't know. But how one wishes now that our own country had had some form of universal military training, so that we could have thrown into the fight more of our manhood. If it is to be a short war, it will end before we have pulled our weight, but I cannot think that without us the Germans will be beaten. I am sure now that it will not be a short war, though I do not agree that it will last for three years.

Thomas Atkins is altogether admirable, but his kind-heartedness is troublesome. He persists in helping the fugitives in all manner of embarrassing ways that interfere with military operations. The only thing he is more wholesomely selfish about is cigarettes—they are hard to come by. I have had none for days other than a packet of Petit Caporals that I found in a billet I was in. Billeting is such a lucky bag—sometimes one is in an inn or a farmhouse, lying on the floor in an outhouse, eaten by fleas or worse. Other times (as tonight) at some great château, deserted of course, where we make free with the rooms, but taking nothing except by request from cellar or pantry. The day before yesterday I had a stroke of luck, chanced upon a pretty country house about midday; the concierge invited me in, gave me lunch, delicious omelette and Burgundy—it was good.

September 5. I was premature in my last letter in thinking we had done with retreating. We have had another week of it—in some ways more trying than the first week, for the men are more tired, the heat more intense, and the anxiety about the present situation even greater. On the other hand, though we have had some fighting, there has been no real risk that we would be cut off.

You will have heard about the Munsters, it was our only bad reverse in the 1st Corps. We have not got—perhaps shall never get —complete news of all that happened. All we know is that they were part of the rear-guard, and that orders issued telling them when to retire did not reach them. They hung on too long, and could not get away when they finally tried to withdraw. From the little we hear it is certain they fought most gallantly, and only a few lived to be taken prisoners. Poor Charrier[1] died with his men. How keen he was to fight the Germans, and revenge his beloved France for 1870. I hope he died with the knowledge that he had killed many of the enemy, and done his part of the common task.

To come to my own doings. My last letter told you of a day of rest just beginning, and the hope of a long night's sleep. I had just finished it when a French Staff officer called from General Lanrezac, commanding the French army on our right, asking for assistance. Almost immediately afterwards streams of French fugitives came back through a town (La Fère) just north of where we were billeted, and told us of the failure of a French attack from which we had hoped much. Then later in the afternoon D.H. was haled to a conference at G.H.Q. I went with him, and had my first glimpse of General Joffre. He impressed me. He is very stout, with rather a slow, heavy manner, but very alert eyes, and very decided in his speech. He does not look as if anything could excite him, much less disturb him, and he seemed full of confidence. But anything less like the typical soldier leader cannot be imagined. If "fat counsellors" are really an advantage, he is more than qualified, and I am quite sure that the "lean hard-bitten man without an extra ounce of flesh" cannot stand prolonged strain, and I draw faith from Joffre's avoirdupois.

I was not present at the conference but hung about outside chatting to G.H.Q. Staff officers, whom I found very much more depressed than we are in the 1st Corps, which is strange, for they have had a fairly easy time. I do not think they are pulling together, and they are frankly incredulous of the French fighting powers. Another curious thing is that they are the same lot who, a couple of months ago, were so sure that the French would take Berlin almost before we reached France. Truth probably lies midway between these extreme views. The French will fight just about as well as the

[1] Commanding the Munster Fusiliers.

Germans, and when we are in force alongside of them, we shall be so much superior in numbers that we cannot well be beaten.

When the conference broke up, it was reported that the French army on our right was retiring. In consequence we had again to get moving. D.H. sent orders off, from the conference, for the transport to move at nightfall and the troops at daylight; we ourselves were to start at 3 a.m. so there was the end of my hope of a night's sleep.

The next day (Sunday) we trudged along once more, the men more tired and gloomy than ever. But it was a quiet day, no enemy, not even the sound of guns. On Monday we got more serious news; the French told us that a large force of German cavalry was coming down on our right flank, and besought Haig to turn and fight to protect their flank. It looked very serious, so bad indeed that D.H. emptied some of the ammunition wagons to provide transport for the exhausted men, but he would not fight unless we were forced to battle. The French were very indignant, D.H. adamant, and he was right. The troops were very, very tired. If we had fought, we could not again have disengaged, and there was more than a chance that both we and the French could get back without fighting.

On Tuesday it looked as if even that hope was to be disappointed. We marched again at daybreak, after two hours' halt in heavy mist, through the forest of Villers-Cotterêts and in the early forenoon the rear-guard was heavily attacked. D.H. sent me back to keep in touch. I found the Guards having a very hard fight. Morris, who had worked with me preparing the defence for the school at Landrecies, had been killed and the Brigade Commander wounded. It looked very serious and soon we had the whole of the division fighting. It lasted until late in the evening, and we lost nearly 100 men, but the great thing was that we did get away. I got back to H.Q. very late, and found them in a château belonging to M. Waddington, who at one time had been French Ambassador in London. It was a beautiful house, but we had not much time to enjoy it, for we were marching again by 2 in the morning. But we did do one good thing. The Waddingtons had left behind two signed pictures of King Edward and Queen Alexandra—we did not want the Germans to have them, so we took them with us.

Late at night D.H. sent me up with orders to one of the divisions. When I reached the division I found the whole of the Staff fast asleep in one room. I tried to wake one Staff officer after another, but could not, and eventually the Divisional Commander himself took the orders, and wrote his own orders for his division while his Staff, utterly exhausted, slept on. That gives you some idea how tired men can get. And if it is thus with the Staff, what must it be for the rank and file! It is literally true that men fell asleep marching and tumbled to awaken, and that mounted men were asleep in their saddles.

We who have been in India are accustomed to heat, and probably do not feel it as much as the youngsters; but it is very severe and beats up fiercely from the roads. We passed through Soissons yesterday—almost a deserted city, pathetic in its emptiness; there were two small shops still open, one selling cigarettes and the other selling picture post-cards—of all things in the world. Saddest of all inanimate things is the harvest rotting in the fields. The corn in stooks in many areas. A squadron of our cavalry had gruesome fun prodding some Germans out of the stooks in one field in a little counter-attack. B., by the way, had a narrow shave the other day. He was acting as galloper to the commander of a small force, and was sent to reconnoitre. He saw some horsemen on the skyline, thought they were our men and galloped gaily in his semi-Oriental garb of the Indian cavalry towards them; when he was within a few hundred yards he discovered they were Germans and had a merry gallop for his life.

Another incident has amused us greatly. Two senior administrative Staff officers, far behind the front, were motoring on one of their " various occasions " when they espied an unmistakable armed Uhlan coming towards them. Thinking discretion the better part of valour, and with a just regard for their own importance to the British cause, they manœuvred their car round and fled incontinently. Then shame seized them. They were two, there was but one Uhlan jogging patiently after them. So they halted, took positions behind some roadside trees, and when their pursuer approached called to him to halt and surrender. Whereupon he cast his lance and carbine on the road, held up his hands and said, " Thank God! I have been trying to surrender for the last 12 hours—but everyone who sees me runs away." He was a stray man of a German patrol who had lost his way and his unit, and wandered far ahead of his own army behind our line.

Then there is the story of the " Angel of Mons " going strong through the 2nd Corps of how the angel of the Lord on the traditional white horse, and clad all in white with flaming sword, faced the advancing Germans at Mons and forbade their further progress. Men's nerves and imagination play weird pranks in these strenuous times. All the same the angel at Mons interests me. I cannot find out how the legend arose.

I am almost afraid, after my last effort, to say again that " the retreat is over." Yet this time I am sure it is. This morning at breakfast we had a message from G.H.Q. that the French are really going to stand and attack. The German enveloping movement has been discontinued. Heaven alone knows why, unless it is that they have outrun their supplies. There was confusion at midday, and D.H. sent me to the French army on our flank to find out what they were actually planning. I found that there had been a change in command. D'Espérey has succeeded Lanrezac, who is said to be in jail, but this is probably untrue. I hope so, for if the French are beginning already to jail military scapegoats, it is a very bad look-out. Lanrezac's chief failing was that he distrusted everybody and hated the British. He let us down badly on the first day of the retreat. The new commander seems a determined man, who is really out for business and is going to fight. Le Cateau, and the knock that the 2nd Corps gave the Germans there, have heartened the French up enormously. They no longer regard the Germans as invincible, and I think they will fight well. When I told D.H. this he was very sceptical—said, " That's all very well, but there are two *IF*'s and big *IF*'s : *if* the French advance and *if* the Germans do not attack them before their own attack is organized."

Anyhow, our own orders have just arrived. The British Army is to advance eastwards with a view to taking the line Château Croiselles, and the retreat is over—13 days of it, and 160 miles covered in 12 days' marching without any serious check, but with constant rear-guard actions, and still in good fighting trim. D.H. is very pleased ; he calls the retreat a " tremendous ordeal " and says morale that has stood that will stand anything. It is his own skill and strength, as much as anything else, that have carried us through—that and the training we had at Aldershot. What a tower of strength he is, and how all in the 1st Corps, and I think in the whole Army, wish he were Commander-in-Chief. Some day I will tell you of incidents at G.H.Q. that make one doubt our present leaders. But anyhow I pin my faith on Joffre, for though he is a Frenchman by birth and by his clothes, he is more like a dour, determined low-land Scot in everything else, and that is the salt of the earth. I must qualify that. He is not altogether Scot in temperament and outlook for his criticism of kilted warriors was, " Pour l'amour, magnifique. Pour le guerre, P—— l——," giving that inimitable expression of contempt that Frenchmen alone can make.

CHAPTER IV

THE BATTLE OF THE MARNE

September 12. I last wrote to you quite a week ago, when we were waiting to advance. What a relief it is to be attacking with a definite objective, and not running away with nothing to look forward to but escape. The men felt it and showed their feelings. The last few days of the retreat they were very glum, they marched silently, doggedly, never a whistle or a song, or even a ribald jest, to help weary feet along the road. Staff officers moving up and down the line with orders were glowered at gloomily. I think it was a tribute to our discipline that there was nothing more than dumb resentful looks. Then, after only a few hours' rest, we were moving again, the marches no shorter, the heat no less intense. But it was forward and not backward. Everything was changed. The men were whistling and singing, and as they passed up and down the ranks Staff officers found a cheery greeting and smiling welcome everywhere. D.H. himself was cheered several times each day, as some unit caught sight of him for the first time since the retreat. All thought of anything untoward seemed to have vanished from everyone's mind. It was a happy army, and still is.

Now that the retreat is over, some amusing yarns—I could not vouch for the truth of all of them—are going the rounds. I will tell you some of them, before I give an account of our doings this last week. You remember Rice, our senior Sapper at Aldershot. He has been really great during the retreat—cool, unflurried and full of energy. Haig has begun using him as an extra Staff officer. We were handing over some roads to the French last week, and on one of them there was a bridge prepared for demolition, to be held to the last moment. Rice was told to supervise the handing over. The French detachment were our old friends the Territorials, under a fairly junior officer. Rice thought that the French dispositions were not all that they should be, and summoning all his meagre knowledge of the French language ventured some gentle advice for their betterment. To which the French officer replied in perfect English,

"Of course you are right, sir, but what can one do with these old blighters, they don't know what to do, and can't do what I tell 'em." Rice, somewhat taken aback, said, "Who on earth are you?" To which came the reply, "I am the French master at Harrow" (or some public school) "and this is my vacation."

Seely, who came round a few days ago, has an admirable yarn of coming upon G.H.Q. at Dammartin late one evening, to find a deserted château with dinner laid, and the only human representatives of G.H.Q. a few imperturbable lorry drivers trying to start some overloaded lorries. Seely asked them where was G.H.Q. and got the ironic reply, "Bunked! Grind her up again, Bill!" But the lorry refused to start, so according to Seely he had a good dinner to the accompaniment of renewed objurgations from the driver and further appeals to "Bill" to grind her up.

D.H. was very amusing about one of our Staff officers, on whom the strain had produced the physical result that his voice went into a rather high pitch. This upset D.H., and when the officer had gone said, "What's the good of a S.O. who *squeaks*? If he *squeaks* like this now, what'll he do if there is real fighting?"

D.H. has been very complimentary to me myself on the retreat, though I really had little to do except keep going, and help him on odd jobs. But he has got me the Legion of Honour and, what is far more important, has made me G.S.O. for Intelligence. That means that I have to keep track on the Germans, and try to keep him informed about what they are doing opposite us, and especially what they are likely to do for the next few hours or days. It is rather making bricks without straw, for there is no organization or system for collecting and collating the few scraps of information we can get ourselves, and we are not told much by G.H.Q. The French on our right have a better system running, and I am trying to get some scheme devised for ourselves. D.H. is very dissatisfied with the information he has been provided with so far, and very critical of G.H.Q. who he says are not trusting their Intelligence service sufficiently. He says French relies entirely upon Wilson, and Wilson is full of preconceived and incorrect ideas. He says that Macdonogh, the head Intelligence man at G.H.Q., is very good, but cannot make himself felt against Wilson. Certainly, *most* of the forecasts made by G.H.Q. to us have been wrong, and *all* the French forecasts.

Now for the events of the last few days. I have not time to give you more than a bird's-eye view of them, and to tell you of my own doings.

We started off on the 7th (last Monday) before orders had reached us from G.H.Q. and then got orders about noon to move forward 14 miles—rather a change from the retreat—and of course quite impossible to carry out, for though we were told that the Germans were in full retreat, there was still opposition from rearguards. Actually, our own troops, though the men were very keen, moved absurdly slowly, and D.H. spent the day going from one Divisional H.Q. to another to try to urge them forward. The cavalry were the worst of all, for they were right behind the infantry. This was gall and wormwood to him, for he had always been first and foremost a cavalry officer. Personally, I could not help feeling a little unholy joy, for I have never thought cavalry, or indeed any form of horseflesh, would be of much use in war.

That first night we slept in houses which had been occupied by the Germans in their advance, and it makes one rabid to see the senseless and useless damage they had done to property. Everything that could be damaged had been—historic furniture smashed; one swine had apparently spent his last few minutes driving his foot through the doors of every wardrobe. The next day we crossed a small river—the Petit Morin. There was some shelling in the early morning, and quite a smart little fight developed. In the afternoon D.H. went forward, and took me with him, to watch the attack on a small force of Germans who were holding us up. While we were watching the fight fairly close up, the Germans tried a small counter-attack, and we came under machine-gun fire, and there was our Corps Commander and his Staff, taking shelter behind the nearest cover, which happened to be in a churchyard. It was not really dangerous, but it seemed very curious for a man so valuable as D.H. to be risking his life needlessly, so I expostulated and was cursed for my pains!

The fight was soon over, and for the first time we had the delight of seeing German troops (cavalry and artillery) running away from our fellows. But the Germans had fought very bravely and well, and there was then no signs of disorder; that was to come later.

We bivouacked that night at a little place called La Tretoire.

Although the Germans were retiring on the 8th, it seemed likely that we might have a big battle the next day, for there was a big river, the Marne, just in front of us, which seemed to offer a very strong position. The weather had broken, there were torrents of rain and we expected to find the rivers in flood. But actually we had very little fighting. We moved very early in the morning, and rather to our surprise we heard by 9 a.m. that the Queen's were over the river. A little later the King's reported that they were over, having been just in time to clear off some Germans who were trying to destroy the bridge. So there were the Kings and Queens taking tricks, just as in a game of cards. By the early afternoon the whole Corps was over the river and we were reasonably sure that the Germans were legging it for the Aisne. *Why* they should be doing so seems quite inexplicable. They have not been defeated anywhere that we know of. Indeed, we heard that night that on the extreme left they had had a considerable success. As far as we knew, they were nearly right round our flank. The French had not been fighting well (they are now very cock-a-hoop and will, I think, do much better when they are moving forward); our own British force is too small to have had much effect on the huge German Army. I can think of no reason except that they may have outrun their supplies, and that does not seem probable, though possible. Perhaps there has been a big Russian success of which we have not heard. Perhaps they have made some great miscalculation—but it's all *perhaps*.

The next day (Thursday, 10th) we were off at cockcrow, with orders " to continue the pursuit and attack the enemy wherever met "—nice general orders, but giving no information *where* the enemy was likely to be met. There was a good deal of mist and we could not see much, but early in the morning (about 9, I think) we heard heavy firing, and got reports that the leading troops of both divisions were engaged. But at the same time a message came from the French on our right (from a particularly good French general named Maud'huy) that a great column of German heavy artillery was retiring from near our front, and wanting us to try to round them up. It seemed an excellent chance, but we could do nothing until we had driven back the Germans in front of us. And when we had done that it was too late. D.H. enlarged upon the chance it would have been for cavalry, if he had had enough of them, and rather got his own back on those of us who had been belittling the quadrupeds.

Although the Germans had, as always, fought well, there was no doubt this day about it being a general retreat. The road was littered with equipment they had thrown away, and there was every sign of disorder. We captured a lot of prisoners. At one place two bunches, one of 400, and the other of 1000, threw their hands in and I was busy examining them for most of the afternoon. There was a mixed bag of cavalry, infantry and Jäger. But they threw no light on the reason for the German retirement. One thing seems quite certain. The German Army *retreating* is a very fragile weapon. It will break quickly if we keep it on the run.

The day ended a little unfortunately for me. D.H. went forward late in the afternoon, taking Gough and myself with him, to make a personal reconnaissance, and get out his plans for the next day. Then he sent me round the Divisional and Brigade H.Q.s to issue the orders and collect men. The roads were blocked with transport and, as the distances were considerable, I thought a motor-bike would be the best and quickest way of getting through. I had not learnt how to ride a motor-bike (I did the next day !), so I started off *en pillion* on a dispatch rider's vehicle, just like a flapper on an afternoon out, except that there was no cushion and saddle for me to sit on, nothing except the luggage carrier. My driver was a young Oxford undergraduate, and whatever other faults there may be in that admirable educational establishment, they certainly train them to steer motor-bikes through traffic. Speed was of importance; my sit-upon relatively unimportant. He covered the distance at a satisfactory speed, swung in and out of vehicles and animals, shoulders just grazing all manner of obstacles. And now I take my meals at the mantelpiece !

I got back about 8, and spent another couple of hours with the prisoners, but elicited nothing of importance; then another couple of hours working on a scheme for reorganizing our transport arrangements, substituting more motors for horses, and then lay down, long after midnight, for a few hours' snooze.

On Friday, 11th, we had a " peace march." We had changed our direction, moving to the right of Soissons—a great mistake I think, for we had the Germans well on the run in front of us, and could have forced them back and through Soissons without much difficulty. This morning we started off with orders to seize the crossing of the Aisne—a little depressed by the news that Maubeuge, which we had seen on the first day of the fighting, and had hoped would hold out until we could relieve it, had fallen a few days ago. Our orders still are to continue the pursuit. But we have another river in front of us, and it may well be that we shall have a big battle before we get over it and onward to the frontier.

What a change has come over the whole face of the war this last week. Indeed, as one thinks back—but we cannot, and indeed, should not, think back any more than we can help—what a kaleidoscope of crises it has all been since we left home less than a month ago. First the march up to battle full of hope of victory and advance. We had only maps *forward* from the frontier, none *back-*

ward towards our base. Then that first stunning blow, the French defeated, ourselves running for our lives. The long-drawn horror of the retreat, with the fearful thought that we should end the war in captivity, and that our failure would bring the Empire down in ruins. This last week of advance, first tentative and cautious, then in the full cry of pursuit of our enemy fleeing in front of us—and now, who knows? We cannot hope to win without a battle—and a big battle. The results of that battle do not rest solely, or even mainly, on us. Will the French hold? Will they win? If we lose the next battle, shall we again be in retreat? Can we rally again if we are defeated? How heavy with doubts the future must be. Yet I am sure we shall win, though I cannot justify my faith by any logical process. If all the army were British and all the leaders were Haigs, there would be no room for doubt.

Whether we win or lose, if the war were to end to-morrow, the 1st Corps has no cause to hang its head. It has marched by long forced marches to battle, has fought and, though undefeated, has retired 160 miles in 13 days, with but a broken day of rest; then it has turned and in five days it has advanced 70 miles, fought two engagements and captured more than 1,200 prisoners. These are deeds that will not be forgotten.

I am proving self-centred and selfish. I am writing as if I thought of nothing but these great events we are living through here, and had forgotten you and all your anxiety. Indeed it is not so. I think I know what you must be going through, and you are seldom long absent from my thoughts. It must be awful for you to read of our casualties, and to read of the death of so many of our Aldershot friends. And if I were in a regiment or battery I could not offer much solace. But the risk we run in the Corps H.Q. Staff is not great, and you need have no great anxiety on that account. I think you will have Findlay's[1] death in your mind. But that was almost an accident. He was selecting a position for his artillery, when by pure chance some of our infantry passed near him and drew, on themselves and him, heavy German shell-fire.

I cannot tell you there is no danger, for of course there is, and you would rightly not believe me if I told you there was none. But I do assure you it is not great. I wish all our friends were in as little.

D.H. is the stand-by not only of this Corps, but of the whole Force. He had a slight cold this week, but it has quite disappeared, and he is now perfectly fit and well. All in our Corps wish that he were C.-in-C.

[1] Brigadier-General Findlay, R.A.

I had nearly forgotten to tell you of one rather amazing coincidence that happened two days ago. You know that no correspondents are allowed anywhere near the front. On Thursday a messenger came to me to say that a spy had been captured, and that he had mentioned my name. I went to investigate and found a man whom I had known as Press correspondent in Persia and in the Balkans. He had come out from Paris without any papers, determined to do a " scoop " for his journal. He had been captured and rather roughly handled. Why he should have thought of my name I do not know, for he could not have heard that I was doing Intelligence work anywhere near. Anyhow he did, and it saved him from a very nasty situation, and just possibly from real trouble. For the rule is that spies of all nationalities have to be dealt with by the French so long as we are in France, and the French are brusque in their methods with spies. Anyhow, I released him with a sound cursing for breaking rules, and sent him back to Paris. I felt a hypocrite while I was cursing him, for I had played the same game myself so often before.

CHAPTER V

THE AISNE AND AFTER

September 13. We have been in full cry after the Germans for the last three days, with the 2nd Corps on our left and the French on our right. G.H.Q. tell us that the Germans are in full retreat and urge us forward. We were ordered to cross the Aisne yesterday and seize the high ground on the north bank. The weather stopped us—a regular monsoon downpour all afternoon. To-day has been very stormy and wet, with high wind. We have got over the river and attack to-morrow.

September 18 (*Friday*). When did I write to you last? I cannot remember, but I think it was before we crossed the Aisne, and began the big battle that is now nearly over. This has been a success—and a disappointment. A success because we have done well, tried and proved our little army in attack, and shown them better than the Germans. A disappointment, because we began it hoping to make great headway and drive the Germans far back towards the frontier, and we have gained little or no ground. But so far as we can make out, the Germans commenced the battle equally hoping to drive us back, and that they certainly have not done—not an inch anywhere.

The first day of the battle was last Sunday (the 13th! if you care to let superstition weigh with you) when we crossed the Aisne at two places without much opposition. There had been wild storms the whole of the previous night, and the men were wet through before they started. But it cleared up by morning and the troops were very cheerful. Although there were signs of more enemy in front of us, we did not think there would be very serious resistance, and that night we made plans to advance early the next day and seize the ridge lying just north of the River Aisne.

The ground we had to attack on was not unlike the Pirbright side of the Hog's Back. There was a long ridge parallel to the river and along this runs the Chemin des Dames road. There are a series of spurs jutting out from this ridge to the river, with fairly deep valleys between them. So far as we knew, we had only cavalry with a small number of guns opposing us, and we hoped to be able to drive them back with our advance guards, and march the bulk of the troops along the country road up to the ridge. The fighting on the 13th was not heavy, but there was a good deal of delay in getting over the river. Still, by nightfall we had the whole of the 1st Division and part of the 2nd Division across, and we heard that the rest of the British force had also managed to secure their crossing, and that the French were over on either side of us. So on Sunday night it all looked very hopeful, and D.H. ordered the advance to be continued at daybreak.

I went with the advanced troops of the 1st Division (General Lomax). We started at 3 a.m. It was raining heavily and very unpleasant. At first there was no opposition, but at 5 a.m. we came under heavy rifle-fire, and we were in the middle of a sharp fight. By 8 a.m. we had taken some 200 prisoners, and I was busy examining them to find out what troops were in front of us. They were men of a new unit, which we had not expected, so I went back to report. Just after I got back a young officer came in with a report that he had seen one of our guns and some British infantry retiring in the 2nd Corps on our left, and D.H. sent me off to find out what was happening there. Stragglers from the 3rd Division reported, incorrectly but very definitely, that the whole division had been driven back to the river. Our own Corps was doing quite well, but any retreat of the 3rd Division was serious for us, as it left us rather isolated and quite unprotected on our left. I went back and reported to D.H. who sent a Cavalry Brigade to close the gap, and protect our right flank. Then I went forward again to see how our own troops were getting on. I got right up to the Chemin des Dames, where I found some of the Guards and some of the Queen's apparently quite happy, but unable to see much owing to the heavy mist.

It was now about midday and I made my way back to H.Q. to report. The whole situation was very mixed up—but D.H. was quite determined to push on. Soon afterwards we got two reports —one that the French on our right had advanced up to, if not ahead, of us, the other, that we were being counter-attacked ourselves. All the same, there did not seem to be very strong forces of the enemy in front of us, and D.H. ordered another attempt to be made to advance the whole line to the Chemin des Dames ridge. He went himself (taking me with him) to see General Lomax (Commander, 1st Division) whom we expected to find in the village where he had told us his H.Q. would be. When we got near the village, we saw that it was being heavily shelled, and found General Lomax himself had moved his H.Q. to a house outside the village. Lomax was very cheerful, but very tired. He told D.H. that all his troops were engaged, that he had no reserves, and that he could not make much of an attack—but he was quite willing to try. Nothing came of it. Without fresh troops we could not get forward, though the 1st Division did make a very gallant effort. D.H. is very critical of the 2nd Corps. He still thinks Smith-Dorrien should not have fought at Le Cateau, and believes that the Corps could have disengaged from there without fighting.

That night I slept at Bourg on the Aisne. There was rather an amusing incident there. We were sitting round a camp table, with one candle on it, having some food late at night, when a shell dropped a few hundred yards away. Immediately one of the officers blew out the candle, apparently thinking the enemy had spotted the light! As the shell must have come well over two miles they would have needed damned good eyes! Nevertheless, it required quite a lot of argument before we could prevail on him to let us relight it and go on with our meal. Of course the Germans were shelling the bridge and not us! But nerves play us funny tricks.

All the rest of the week we have been marking time, hoping that either the 2nd Corps or the French would fight their way forward and that we would get a chance of going on ourselves. Actually the 1st Corps is well in front of the rest of the British line and rather in front of the French on our right, so we cannot hope to get forward until one or other comes up alongside of us. The Germans have been shelling us a good deal, and we have been converting our position into practically a field fortress, digging trenches and making bridges.

Although we are all quite convinced that our infantry is better trained and better stuff than the Germans, there are some very disappointing things. The Germans have far better heavy artillery than we have. They are using high explosives and trench mortars—we have little of either and that little not much good. We tried yesterday a new method of directing our artillery fire with aeroplanes and there seems to be a lot in it. Lewis[1] was in the aeroplane and did splendidly. D.H. is very dissatisfied with the general artillery work, and thinks if we had more guns and better work from them we could push on, on our own, without waiting for the French. I do not think so, for the Germans must be strengthening their

[1] Captain Donald Lewis, R.E.

positions as much as we are, and they have all the advantage of the ground.

D.H. is also very scornful of the French on our right, and certainly they do not seem to have much punch in them. They are mainly Colonial troops. He sent me over yesterday to try and impress this on G.H.Q., but it was very coldly received.

Our mess is now broken up into two parts. I am with D.H., Johnny Gough, Marker and Neil Malcolm. We are in a little mill nestling in the hollow of the hills south of the river. Away to the north of us stretches a wonderful panorama, where our troops are in the trenches. By day we see the shells bursting almost continuously—queer, pretty little puffs of white smoke from the shrapnel, and great, thick, nasty dirty columns of yellow thrown by the high explosives. The dull boom of the heavy guns and the harsh crack of the high explosives is punctuated at intervals by the rattle of musketry and machine-guns. It is a marvellous experience.

To-night I am on duty—that comes every second or third night. To-night promises to be quiet—so I am writing this screed, though the Germans have been making some strange new rocket signals which may mean some new devilry.

The last night I was on duty was very disturbed. A German attack was reported about midnight. Telegrams kept pouring in and for a time it was rather critical. I woke up Johnny Gough. He took a very serious view and shook up all the Staff except D.H., who was very angry when he heard of it and talked of " nerves." Gough, by the way, is very far from well. He has violent attacks of sickness which he tries to conceal. I only discovered it by accident and he forbade me to mention it to D.H. I hope it will pass off, for though he is a bit jumpy at times, he is altogether excellent and quite cool when things are really serious.

I wish you could see me now, sitting in a little office in the mill. The faithful Kearns is fast asleep, literally at my feet, so that a gentle kick will serve to wake him if I want a clerk. It is all so peaceful—just an occasional very distant shell to remind one that we are in battle. Through the window I can see the sky lighted up by rockets every now and then, like distant summer lightning. By the way, I hope you will see the panorama photograph of the battlefield which D.H. is sending home. It will give you more idea of it all than any description I can give.

My new job is highly interesting. There is not only the task of " taping " the Germans immediately in front of us, but D.H. demands a general review of the whole situation and forecasts of the future—"forecasting" with little or no knowledge of the facts. And I suppose everyone at home is doing the same. General Rice, our senior Sapper, has made the most original one of all. He predicts that neither we nor the Germans will be able to break through a strongly defended and entrenched line, and that gradually the line will extend from the sea to Switzerland, and the war end in stalemate. He bases this mainly on the Russo-Japanese War. There may be something in it, though D.H. will not hear of it. He thinks we can push the Germans back to the frontier, and after that it will only be a matter of numbers, and has started me off on an attempt to see how many men Germany and ourselves can finally put in the field, and when.

M. is full of stories of Russians passing through London; says his sister saw them, and when I said I didn't believe it, retorted, " Do you mean to say my sister is a liar ! " So *that* ended *that* discussion. I asked at G.H.Q. about the Russians, and was told, of course, that it was rubbish.[1] They could not get there and would have nowhere to go, if they did. But a lot of men here have got hold of the idea—all from home letters.

My own idea is that the Germans will hit at the Channel ports. I can't imagine why they have not done so already. The Belgians could not stop them, and we should be in a real bad way if they got hold of them. But G.H.Q. told me that we are sending troops to help the Belgians—if we have them.

There was a nasty affair yesterday. A report came in that we had found some of our men mutilated by the Germans. I went to investigate and found some men who had been captured by the Germans and had escaped with nasty cuts on their faces. They said a German officer had swung a jack-knife by the lanyard and snipped bits out of them. This may be true, but the injuries look just like ordinary German student " duelling " wounds, and I rather think some half-drunken German officer has been amusing himself by trying to repeat his student exploits. None of the men is badly hurt, and I did not think it serious enough to report officially.

You ask me how I am myself. I am really perfectly fit, and can hardly believe that I was in Millbank two months ago. I had a tooth stopped by a wandering dentist yesterday—rather a painful experience. He tucked my head under his armpit, and never let up until it was finished. Do you remember my story of the dentist

[1] Actually the rumour started by a telegram from a commercial firm reporting the due arrival of 20,000 Russian eggs (or some other such commodity), and worded " 20,000 Russians arrived to-day."

at Quetta, who said he hadn't been trained, that it just "came to him"? This fellow was much the same, and I expect I shall have to get the tooth out. Micky Ryan is itching to have a go at it.

September 28 (*Monday*). It is more than a week since I sent you anything much better than a post-card. It has been a very hard time for the troops, though there has been little fighting. There have been cold and wet almost continuously, and the men in the trenches have had no rest and not many hot meals. But as far as our own front has been concerned, it is rather like Rice's stalemate. The Germans have made a series of small counter-attacks, all of which have been driven back. We have made no serious effort to advance, indeed we cannot until the French on our right come forward. Then we might all attack together with some hope of getting forward.

The French are full of good intentions, and are always on the point of attacking—but it never comes off. It is not to be wondered at really, for their rationing arrangements and their clothes are miserable. The Colonials next to us are still in their cotton uniforms and must feel the cold frightfully, for it freezes now almost every night. A couple of days ago we had to give them 10,000 rations of tinned beef for their Zouaves. They said they had had nothing but soaked bread and raw meat for nearly a week. But even the tinned beef could not get an attack out of them. D.H. is very caustic about the French Staff of these units; says they do nothing but talk, and do not mean business. But actually I am sure it would be impossible to attack with troops that have been in the trenches so long, and nothing will happen, unless, and until, new and fresh troops are moved up.

All the same there is a very great difference in the appearance of our troops and the French. Our men, in spite of everything, are full of go and in excellent fettle and amazingly healthy.

Bulfin was really almost peevish when he was told that his brigade was to be pulled out for a short rest and replied, "We never asked to be taken out—we can hang on here quite well."

The 3rd Division on our left gave us a jump last week by reporting that they were being heavily attacked—but there was very little firing to be heard and we did nothing, and it all settled down very quickly.

You remember that in my last letter I told you of our preliminary efforts at working artillery by air observation. That has progressed greatly and promises to be a great factor. Also we have now got some more heavy guns.[1] They arrived from home out of the blue, and were offered all round, rather put up to auction among the Corps Commanders. Nobody else wanted anything to do with them, so our Corps got them and we have put them in the canal, and are using them a good deal. It is something to be able to send back heavy stuff in answer to the Germans.

We hear reports of heavy fighting far away to the north, where apparently the French are trying to get round the German flank. If they succeed it will mean the whole German line in front of us will have to go back. If they fail, we shall be within measurable distance of Rice's prediction that I mentioned in my last letter. But it seems rather absurd that the British Army should be sandwiched in here, in the middle of the French, when we began on the extreme left. I cannot help wondering what would have been the situation if our forces had been put into the Channel ports in August and kept there. We should have been just in the position now to go for the German flank. But then probably the Germans might have been in Paris by this time. Anyhow, it is no use speculating on what might have been.

We are getting the Intelligence work much more systematic now. Johnny Gough was very indignant when I asked for better stuff, so that we could reproduce sketch maps and issue information regularly to the divisions and brigades. He said that all through the South African War the Intelligence only had one office box, and he didn't see why we wanted any more. But I insisted and D.H. backed me up, so now we have got quite a good little show running, and have all the German units opposed to us fully " taped." Last Thursday we found a new Corps in front of us, located it within 12 hours of its arrival and predicted an attack, which came off the same night but was fairly easily driven back.

Letter begun October 1, finished October 14. There are changes afoot. The 2nd Corps has been withdrawn from the line—we have extended our front to take over most of their area. We shall in turn be taken out of the line, either to rest or to go to some other area.

We have accordingly changed our Head-quarters and are now in a farmhouse (Monthuis Sart) on a small hill about 3 miles behind the front line. I am tied to the office a great deal as there are masses of captured documents to be gone through. But the battle is really over, and there is not so much of interest in the trenches. In spite of our siege howitzers we are still very short of heavy

[1] Heavy siege howitzers.

artillery, and our high-explosive shells are miserable. The shells burst prematurely. It seems incredible that Great Britain with all her resources cannot give us sound and efficient high explosives for our small army, while Germany and France can both provide ample for their large armies.

We have given the Germans in front of us a real bad time, though we have not gained our objective on the Chemin des Dames. We have lost heavily in the 1st Corps and the worst of that is that so many are our own personal friends. I am, however, reasonably sure that we have accounted for far more Germans than we have lost, and we have taken many prisoners and have lost few. Best of all, the German prisoners and the captured letters and diaries show that the Germans are getting depressed, and that they have a very healthy dread of the British Army. Thomas Atkins is the finest fellow in the world, only beaten perhaps by the regimental officers. Men and officers draw very close together in war. Discipline does not slacken—it adapts itself. The only units that maintain full peace-time discipline and still make shift at Aldershot spit-and-polish, are the Guards, and they are marvellous. Even the Queen's cannot compare with them.

You may have seen of poor H——'s death. He came out so full of delight at having got a Staff job, and called to see me on the way to his unit. The next I heard was that he had been killed that same evening. Apparently he missed his way, and his car drove straight through our front line towards the Germans. He must have realized his mistake either before, or with, the first shot the Germans fired at his car, for apparently his driver tried to turn it. It had got half-round, and both the driver and H—— were shot dead—the driver still at the wheel and H—— alongside the car, about 50 yards beyond our front line. I went down to see the place. Our men had made an attempt to get back the bodies, but had been driven in by machine-gun fire, and there poor H—— and his driver still lie.

We have a young Prince of Orleans attached to us as a sort of unofficial interpreter, also a French banker with a magnificent car. Both are very anxious to do anything for anybody. They drove me into Paris one afternoon, and I sent you a small present from there. I wonder if it reached you?

Paris is an amazing place. I think I told you that I went there with D.H. on the last day of the retreat, when they were still expecting a siege. It was then a city of dreadful fear. Herds of cattle were being collected in the parks to provision the place for the siege, and numbers of workmen were hard at it improving the defences. Everyone, man, woman and child, that one saw had that dreadful look of impending doom that one reads of in books, but seldom sees. I can imagine London in the Great Plague being much the same. But now it is as merry and happy as if there were no war; lots of uniforms, of course, but the cafés are crowded; places of amusement are in full swing and all their tails are in the air. I wonder what signs London shows of war—very little I should imagine, for it is still, thank Heaven, very far from the battlefields, and there is, after all, only the Regular Army fighting and losing casualties.

I went to railhead some 6 miles from here yesterday (September 6) and saw a hospital train with a poor tired sister in charge of it. She had been having perhaps the most depressing time of anyone, travelling up and down the railway line, seeing no one but sick and wounded. But it was such a relief to see a well-found hospital train for those who are wounded. The last train-load of wounded I saw was the day after Landrecies, where a train of open trucks was packed with injured men lying on straw—their wounds still undressed and many of them in great agony. Fortunately the modern rifle bullet makes a clean wound which heals readily. But the high-explosive shell makes nasty gashes and gives septic trouble. The medical arrangements are generally admirable, I think the most successful of all of our administrative efforts. I wish the postal arrangements were half as good. But even they, I hear, are about to be greatly improved largely as the result of some vitriolic letters sent from here.

We had an enteric scare a few weeks ago, with over six cases in one battalion. Luckily it was taken in time and did not spread.

We were greatly cheered yesterday by news of the German defeat by the Russians in East Prussia. Apparently 5 Corps were badly beaten. Splendid! But it leaves 45 still to be accounted for, and I fear, before this reaches you, Antwerp will have fallen, and though that cannot of course affect the ultimate issue, it may cause the Germans to try to reach the coast. It would be disastrous if they did reach Boulogne.

This battle, though it drags on, is getting positively dull. There are a few small attacks every night, but they are very easily repulsed. The guns fire away all day, but do astonishingly little damage, and otherwise there is little to show that the biggest battle the world has yet seen, is drawing to an indecisive close. Following the example of Wellington's officers at Torres Vedras some of the Staff who can find time, go out and shoot partridges with shot-guns borrowed from the inhabitants—it provides a welcome change of diet and the sportsman has the excitement, additional to that of shooting little feathered birds, of having shrapnel dropped near him every now and then.

The prevailing ailment is spy-fever. Everyone sees a spy in every un-uniformed human being, and a spy-signal in every inanimate feature of the landscape. So long as we are fighting on French soil, there is not much chance of successful German spying. But when we get into Germany it will be very different, and suspicion is a healthy atmosphere to encourage against that time, so when the spy tales come to me, as most of them do, however ridiculous they are, I do not pour too much cold water on them—indeed, yesterday we had a pleasant interlude in our monotony. Some German spies were reported to be hiding in some caves in a wood near our Head-quarters, so we organized a hunt and drove the woods. It proved a blank, of course, but it was quite amusing and greatly encouraged our amateur Sherlock Holmeses.

Basil has arrived. He dined with me last night, and has gone to the trenches. The Queen's is one of the best regiments in the army, and he will be well taught and well looked after.

It is curious how inaccurate the French are. D.H. went to Chassemy yesterday (10th), on the extreme right of our line, and got hold of a report from a French unit that the Germans had thrown a bridge over the Aisne, and that the French were preparing to destroy it the same night. He gave orders for some of our artillery to co-operate—the artillery came to me to get the position as to the site of the German bridge. So I went out to have a look at it, and found that there was no bridge at all on the Aisne—but one on the Vesle built by our own people in our own area.

I suppose there never has been a war in which the strain has been so heavy and so continuous. Since August 17 we had first the march up from Amiens, then the fighting at Mons, then the retreat, then the advance to the Aisne, and since September 13 the 1st Corps has been in actual battle with only two days off. The men in the trenches, of course, get far the worst of it, for they are in continuous danger and have the greater physical strain, but at H.Q. we have a great deal of strain in a different form, and perhaps the responsibility is almost as trying as the greater physical strain. But we are all fit and well, and though I should like to have a week-end at home to see you and D. I do not feel any the worse for this first two months of war.

Looking back on it now, I think we have been very lucky. I always expected that the Expeditionary Force would be eaten up in the first few weeks of the war. I had no belief in the French and very little in our own War Office. I can honestly say that I expected the first clash of the armies would find the B.E.F. isolated and surrounded by great masses of Germans. Now that danger has been passed. The French have found their feet; the German plan has been completely upset. They have thrown overboard one C.-in-C. and that in itself is an acknowledgment of initial defeat. We have not won yet—far from it—but these two months, hard though they have been, have been far better than I had dared to hope.

One very strange fact is emerging quite clearly from the captured correspondence and from the prisoners, and that is that the general run of Germans are quite honestly convinced that the war has been forced upon Germany, against every effort and wish of the German Government. I could write screeds about this, but I won't. The important part is that it makes them, of course, far more formidable, and there is far less chance of a break in their " will to fight " than if they thought they were trying for conquests at the behest of their Government. For now Social Democrats will be as strong patriots as any Junker. I wonder if it is quite impossible to start a propaganda campaign inside Germany to counteract this fixed opinion. But that is a G.H.Q. job and not ours. There is, of course, just the chance that the Germans are right, and that they *did not* wish the war, though that is hard to square with their invasion of Belgium.

I am beginning also to revise my ideas of the French; they are better fighting people than I thought, and their peasantry are altogether admirable. One sees such strange sights here—farm hands working, quite accustomed to shell-fire, and unconcerned when shells fall near by. The women work as hard as the men, indeed there are more women than men to be seen, for all the young men have been called to the Colours. Shops are open, plying a diminished trade, in towns which are shelled every few days. Fields are being ploughed alongside a battery in action which may at any time draw hostile fire. It is all absurdly like manœuvres— except that the ambulances are full.

I have had some more outdoor work lately, a very pleasant change, doing a reconnaissance of our whole front line. Although I do as much as possible at dawn and dusk, it means traversing a good deal of the shelled area by day. R. came out with me one day and we got caught in a village by some shelling. We took cover while it lasted, and though there were a good number of men in the village, no one was hit.

Later, 15*th*. As this letter contained information I kept it until the news was stale. We are out of the line and moving north to-morrow. The 2nd Corps has preceded us. We shall be together, where we really belong, on the left of the Allied line.

Antwerp has fallen. It held out three days longer than we had anticipated. I hear it was short of heavy artillery. Krupp was said to have held up heavy guns due last February. I wonder if this is true. If so, it finally disposes of all doubt about Germany's guilt or innocence of designing the war for this year. But I think we should have heard of it before if it were true, and I cannot remember any mention of such a delay until now. Anyhow, the fall of Antwerp can make no difference to the final result.

I have been busy these last few days drafting the dispatch for D.H. of our doings since the Retreat. Very interesting work, as reports are now available and one is able to check up actualities with what we thought at the time.

CHAPTER VI

THE FIRST BATTLE OF YPRES

October 19 (*Wednesday*). We are moving forward to-morrow, and shall probably be battle fighting, so this may be the last chance of writing for some time. D.H. came up here last Sunday by car, the Staff following by train. The journey took 26 hours—simply crawling along. There was a nasty little accident on the way—the coupling of the train broke on a steep ascent, and the rear portion, in which I was, rolled off backwards. Eventually 13 coaches left the line, and there was the deuce of a to-do. Luckily, no one was killed, as we derailed in a cutting and the carriages did not overturn. We reached our destination at 2 a.m. and I motored to G.H.Q. which is located in a little town about half the size of Guildford. The most interesting thing I noticed was the Air park—a very great increase in planes on what I fancied we had. D.H. saw the C.-in-C. and I had interviews with the Intelligence Staff.

The C.-in-C. told D.H. that we seemed to be in a position to turn the German flank, and possibly break off one whole German corps and round it up. He said there is only one corps in front of us and the Belgians, who, with some French troops, are on our left and stretch up to the sea. It is interesting that we are now fighting near the Channel ports, where I always thought we should have gone. The Germans apparently did eventually make a push for the ports. But we have forestalled them, and if all goes well should drive them back in the next few days.

One of the Intelligence men said there were signs of at least two more improvised German corps, as well as the corps to which the C.-in-C. referred. But there seems no certainty of this. However, I mentioned it to D.H. and he seems rather impressed and cross-examined me closely. Our Belgian liaison officer, who has very good information, is emphatic that there are more troops than one corps. So we are going to move forward cautiously. But I think we are strong enough to deal with all we can meet; the men are in excellent spirits and full of fight.

An old Indian Army friend of mine came to see me, and told me that a division from India has arrived. Interesting news, as they came according to one of the schemes we had prepared at Simla when we were there in 1910, and which the Viceroy and Whitehall ordered us to destroy as "dangerous and useless."

D.H. went to-day to Poperinghe, a village on the main road up to the front. It is rather like a Scottish village, but dirtier. The roads are all *pavé*, very uncomfortable for man and beast, but serviceable. We met General Rawlinson there, just back from Antwerp way. There is a good deal of the melodramatic about Rawlinson. He was flying an enormous Union Jack on his car, and D.H.'s first remark was rather caustic—"I thought only the King and the C.-in-C. are permitted to fly the Union Jack." Rawlinson's reply was that it helped to encourage the inhabitants. I shall be interested to see whether he is still flying it when we see him again!

I am writing this in my office in the Palais de Justice of a very ancient town in Belgium (Ypres), interrupted every few sentences by messages. The town is wonderfully picturesque and the Palais de Justice really fine architecture. But it is very depressing to see the miserable refugees, who are crowding into the town. Every class of society is represented and all are miserable. They had all fancied themselves so safe under the protection of their treaties and their allies. I shall be glad when we go forward from it to-morrow.

The suffering and hardship of the war on the country people is really terrible. Somehow it hurts more than the casualties to the armies—for it is their job and they get a chance of giving as much as they get. But the country-folk cannot hit back. They lose everything, and even when the war is over will only have the skeletons of homes to return to.

It seems to me that however great our successes may be in fighting, it will be the distress and suffering of the people, more than defeat in battle, that will make a nation give in. But one comes from the other, and they cannot be separated. Anyhow, our people in Britain are not suffering as those of Belgium and France and Germany must be, and we can bend our whole energies to winning battles. How one longs for the time when there will be a great British army in the field. It seems so discreditable to be using only our small Regular Army while France has all her manhood in the ranks. A curious thing is the number of Belgian young men we see in civilian clothes. Their conscription must be much lighter than that of the French.

It is 3 a.m., I am tired and sleepy and we go forward at 6 to-morrow to attack. If G.H.Q. is right and there is only one corps in front of us, we should make good progress. But the first battle on the Aisne showed one thing very clearly, and that is that steady infantry, well entrenched, cannot be turned out of their trenches by artillery or infantry. Masonry forts, such as Namur and Antwerp, are simply targets for heavy artillery. If the Germans are entrenched, we shall have our work cut out for us. I am glad that we are advancing cautiously to-morrow, and not rushing on as G.H.Q. wanted.

October 25. We have had a very considerable success, in a three-days' battle—taken 700 prisoners, and killed not fewer than 2,000 Germans. Our own casualties in the 1st Corps are over 1,000, but allowing a proper proportion of wounded and killed, the Germans opposite us must have had total casualties of over 6,000. But the battle is not over yet; things to-day are quiet and everything looks very favourable. The chief work fell on the 1st Division under Lomax, and the 2nd Brigade under Bulfin. The fighting has been over very difficult country, cultivated, with many woods of all kinds of trees, and many villages, and with high hedges and deep ditches. Fortunately, the Germans are not entrenched, but we had a good deal stronger force against us than we expected. It was very fortunate that we got that warning of the possibility of there being three corps and not one corps as G.H.Q. told us, for three corps seems to have been, if anything, an under-estimate.

I cannot give you an account of all the fighting. Indeed we do not ourselves yet know exactly what happened. We have been much mixed up with the French troops. But I can tell you something of my own doings.

Our original plan was altogether upset by the French cavalry, who were on our left coming back from a big wood,[1] which was at once occupied by the Germans. So that by the early afternoon of the first day's battle, we were in a deep salient again, well driven into the enemy's position. But it looked all right, as the French had plenty of troops coming up and were ordered to attack alongside of us. They have been trying to do so ever since, and though they are under an extraordinarily good general [Dubois] they have not succeeded. By the end of that day we had prisoners from two different German corps, so that it was evident that Sir J. French had been wrong in his estimate of the German strength. D.H. ordered

[1] Houthoulst Forest.

the line to halt and dig themselves in until the French could come up.

The next day he sent me to the left flank, to see what was happening there. When I got there I found that the Germans had attacked and driven back a part of our line near an inn and that there was a big gap in the line. It looked very serious and D.H. ordered the inn to be retaken, and the inevitable Bulfin had to do the job. There was a very sharp fight and a night attack, but we got the place back by early next morning. The Queen's were in this, and lost pretty heavily, but Basil came through all right.

The next day, 23rd, there was another very fierce attack by the Germans on a village we had taken (Langemarck). I got there just after it was all over. The Germans had been beaten off with enormous loss. We could see their dead lying all along the front of our line—a gruesome, but very pleasing sight. On my way back, when quite a long way from the firing line, I had a strange adventure. I had got into a car—a curious sort of body, not quite a saloon, but with a top supported on wooden pillars. A shell burst close by, and the whole top of the car was lifted off by the rush of air. Neither I nor the driver was touched, nor was the car as far as I could see, but it almost stunned us both and the driver nearly landed us into the ditch. That brought me round and I cursed him freely, and I think restored his nerves thereby.

W. Kedie gave me his impression of war the other day—long periods of boredom punctuated by moments of extreme fear! I think this was one of the extreme fear moments. Yet really it was trivial—more frightening than dangerous.

The next day (yesterday) the centre of gravity had moved to the other flank, when another German attack very nearly succeeded. It drove in a big bit of our line and for a time it was very critical, so bad that D.H. called for help from the French. They sent up some cavalry, Cuirassiers. They arrived looking very picturesque and warlike in full peace-time uniform, a great contrast to our men, who are now rather weather-beaten. Gough was very scornful of them, and called them " those damned fellows with their hair down their backs."

That is a very meagre description of a battle, but it must suffice. Such a lot of my time is taken up with routine and office work.

I do not see much of the Corps Staff. D.H. has his advanced H.Q., where I am writing. He has with him only Gough and myself and the A.D.C.; the remainder are all back in Poperinghe, 6 miles away. Whenever I am at H.Q. I am busy with captured documents and examining prisoners. But I have now got a couple of youngsters who know German well and whose job is to help with Intelligence work, and they are doing most of the spade-work with both prisoners and documents. We get very little information from G.H.Q. Indeed, we actually know more about what is happening on our own front than G.H.Q. does. But there is an admirable Belgian officer who comes daily and gives us all the information that Belgian H.Q. has, and they seem very well informed. There is also an accommodating German Corps Commander who sends out constant messages and orders to his units by wireless, without coding them. I suppose he thinks we do not know any German! Anyhow, it tells us a great deal of the German troops both actually in front of us and coming up, and even sometimes gives us warning of their attacks. God bless him! I'll give him a drink if ever I see him when the war is over.

Seely is doing a sort of attaché to G.H.Q. and comes round pretty often. He seems determined to get killed, and is always going where the fighting is most fierce. But he generally gets out somewhere quiet for dinner, and he gave me an excellent meal one night, and told me some of the hairbreadth escapes he had had. He also told me there is a good deal of friction at G.H.Q. and that French will not listen to his Intelligence people, which accounts for that big mistake about the number of divisions we were likely to meet when we advanced on the 20th.

Another interesting man working more or less with me is L. S. Amery. He is an extraordinarily cute little man, with a very good knowledge of Germany and the German Army, and very easy to deal with. J. Baird[1] is also in the neighbourhood, wearing the musical comedy bonnet of the Scottish Horse. D.H. hates all politicians, and does not even like to see me talking to them. Says, "You can't trust anyone who has ever been in Parliament," whereat I remind him of Haldane whom he reveres, and he grunts, and that is the end of that.

November 1 (*Sunday*). I must write something while my recollection of these last days is clear, though it is not yet over. But we have come through where for many days it seemed almost impossible that we could stand, and we have not lost ground. I cannot remember when I last wrote. The fighting has been terrific. Yesterday we lost almost all the Staff of both the 1st and 2nd Divisions. Worst of all, Lomax, who has been Haig's main stand-by, was

[1] Now Lord Stonehaven.

wounded and has had to go. Yesterday everything seemed lost. We have won out at frightful cost, but we *have* won out. It has been a week of great crises. Each seemed worse than what had gone before. Each seemed so fierce that it must be the worst, until yesterday made all the rest seem insignificant.

I can hardly remember the beginning of it all. Early in the week—I think last Sunday—we first got news that columns of Germans had been seen on the roads behind their lines, and knew they were being reinforced. But at the same time the French told us that *they* also were bringing up more troops. The next day was a day of surprises of all sorts. First we were told that we were going to be attacked shortly, then a few hours later, that the Germans were calling for assistance in front of us and that we should attack them. Then, on the top of that came definite news that the 1st Division on our right had been driven back, and we had to send troops to restore the situation there. Then late in the evening came final orders that we were to attack the next day, and that the 7th Division was put under the 1st Corps—a great relief that, for it meant far easier combination. The next couple of days were not very eventful—there were continuous attacks and counter-attacks. But generally we were still waiting for the French to fight their way forward to us and hoped then to push on.

On Thursday there was a great attack in thick fog on our front and I was sent forward at 7 to see what was happening. It was very serious, the road was full of stragglers coming back—not running away, but just not knowing what to do. Lomax, when I reached him, was quite unmoved. The line was holding, though there had been one very fierce infantry attack.

D.H. had authorized me to order up some more troops if Lomax wanted them. Lomax refused them, saying, "More troops now only mean more casualties. It is artillery fire that is wanted. We should keep our reserves until the infantry attack develops and then counter-attack." He was right.

About midday the Germans came at us again and it became very critical. We lost ground and our last Corps reserves were sent in. By nightfall that attack also had been beaten back. G.H.Q. orders were that we should attack again the next day. We were told that the French were going to deliver a frontal attack and that we were to co-operate. But by this time we had located two more German divisions in front of us. The Germans were at least twice as strong as we were, and D.H., very wisely, did not order an attack until the morning showed what the position really was. It was just as well.

On Friday the Cavalry Corps on our right swung back, leaving a great gap in the line. The Germans were nearly round our right flank. We had not enough troops to fill the gap and D.H. asked for French troops. We had a splendid French general working alongside of us —Dubois—who never fails; a great soldier and most loyal ally. He sent help at once, the gap was filled, and that crisis was safely past. By nightfall we began to hope that the worst was over. It was only beginning.

The next day (yesterday) we were awakened very early by the sound of another bombardment, all along the front, heavier than any previous one. No news of any sort came back to us from the front —all the telephone lines were cut. A Staff officer was sent out to get news and we could only wait. Just after he had gone General D'Urbal, commander of the French Armies near us, came to see D.H. and told us his information was that the whole of a German Army Corps was attacking the 1st Division. We could do nothing except hope. There were no reserves of any sort available. Then about 11 the Staff officer returned with the news that the 1st Division had been almost overwhelmed by the bombardment, but that our artillery had retrieved the situation and the line still held. A few minutes later came a definite report that Gheluvelt had fallen, and that the 1st Division line had been broken. D.H. sent me forward to find out what was the situation. You cannot imagine the scene. The road was full of troops retreating, stragglers, wounded men, artillery and wagons, a horrible sight. All the time there was the noise of a terrific bombardment. It was impossible to get any clear idea of the situation. Nobody knew anything except what was happening on his immediate front and that was always the same story. The Germans were attacking in overwhelming strength and our men were being driven back but fighting every inch of the way. The only glimmer of hope was that a counter-attack was being organized.

When I got back to our own H.Q. (at the White Château) I found that D.H. had ridden forward himself and Gough was organizing the mess servants for fighting it out in the château. Gough was quite unruffled, and amused me by saying, "It don't matter a damn what happens here. God won't let those b—— win." I wish you could have seen E.'s (my soldier servant) face when ammunition was handed out to him, and he was told he had to fight. I never saw fear more clear on any man's face—sheer stark staring fear.[1]

[1] Subsequently the man did extremely well with his unit and was given a commission. Then he was killed.

Gough was anxious for more information, and sent me back to 2nd Division H.Q. When I got near them I met a medical officer of the division white as a sheet. He held up a tiny piece of cloth in his hand and said, "Do you know —— ?" I said "Yes." "Well," he said, "that is all that is left of him." I asked him what the devil he meant, and he told me that a shell had hit 2nd Division H.Q., had wounded Lomax and killed seven Staff officers. Munro had been knocked out, but not badly hurt. Whigham was the only one not wounded. Soon after I got back to our H.Q., D.H. came back, rather surprised to find me there, apparently they thought I had been killed. D.H. then sent Rice forward to collect information.

A few minutes later the C.-in-C. himself arrived on foot. His car could not get along the road. He had a few minutes with D.H. and left to go to see Foch. D.H. had ordered his horse to go forward himself when Rice came galloping back, as red as a turkey-cock and sweating like a pig, with the news that Gheluvelt had been retaken and the line re-established.

Can you imagine what that meant? It was just as if we had all been under sentence of death and most suddenly received a free pardon. It had all seemed so hopelessly bad, defeat staring us in the face and then this news that meant, at least, a good fighting chance. I remember shaking Rice's hand, as if he himself had retaken Gheluvelt. Everyone else was just as excited as I was, except D.H. who pulled at his moustache and then said, he "hoped it was not another false report." Rice was certain his information was correct, but I don't think D.H. was quite convinced, although he sent an A.D.C. after the C.-in-C. to tell him. Then he went off up to the front to see for himself.

I was sent off again to see General D'Urbal and General Foch. The scenes on the road back to, and through, Ypres were indescribable. They were covered with transport and ambulances and stragglers, all moving backwards. No panic, but just congestion and confusion. I was first with the news that the line had been re-established, and was very popular! But there were no reinforcements anywhere. When I got to the French H.Q. I found them quite ignorant of what had happened and quite unconcerned. General D'Urbal obviously thought I was exaggerating and talked of the fighting as "fluctuations of the combat." I had great difficulty in controlling my temper. I am not sure I did, but sarcasm in a foreign language is difficult and ineffective. The French had not attacked because of artillery fire, nor could I get any promise from them of action that evening or night.

Foch treated me to some play-acting. When I was shown into his H.Q. he was gazing moodily towards the north, and took no notice for some time. It was probably only a few minutes, but it exhausted my patience. After trying a cough to attract his attention without any result, I butted straight in and spoke to him. He shook himself with a start, as if awakening from a day-dream, and said, " Ah, pardon, I was thinking what we should do on the Meuse." Utter nonsense. He was doing no such thing, but was, I suppose, trying to hearten me, and through me D.H., by pretending that the fighting at Ypres was relatively unimportant, and that we must win anyhow. But once he did apply himself to the problem he was excellent. He said that more French troops were being ordered up, that he would throw them in as fast as they came.[1] That there must be no withdrawal, that the enemy were certainly as tired and worn out as we were, that attack was the best defence and so on. All commonplaces—but he spoke as if he meant them and with real driving power behind his words. He told me he was himself going to see French, and would send a senior Staff officer to see Haig and discuss the best course for the next day ; but he said he thought the German attack would not be renewed that day— nor was it.

I got back to Ypres about 10 p.m. and found D.H. had been there for dinner, and then gone back to his battle H.Q. (at the White Château) for the night. I followed him there, arriving very tired about midnight.

There was one rather peculiar personal episode in the day of great crisis. My Legion of Honour had arrived at our H.Q. some time last week, and with other decorations was awaiting an opportunity for a formal presentation by some big French general who might happen round. When things looked very black, Hobbs (the senior administration officer) who had the decorations in his charge, thought he had better get rid of them. He called me in and threw my " Legion " across the table saying, " You had better have this d——d thing now ; it don't look as if there will be another opportunity for you to get it." So I slipped it into my pocket and have it with me now. I'll send it back to you as soon as I get a chance. Rather a different way to receive a medal from the formal ceremonial procedure of peace time !

Your book of " Sonnets " has arrived ; many thanks for it. I have only had time to read a few of them. They are beautiful. It is the greatest rest to free one's mind, even for a few minutes,

[1] Actually, they did not arrive until the crisis was safely passed.

from all thoughts of war. I know nothing that does this so effectually as reading poetry.

Meantime, there are great dissensions at G.H.Q. French has at last lost faith in Wilson and acquired confidence in the Intelligence.

It is all probably exaggerated, but there is no doubt the Intelligence has been warning Sir J. French for some time that the Germans were much stronger than Wilson would admit.

Amery brought off rather a good bit of Intelligence work, getting the first authentic news of the new German formations that we have been engaging. He saw some German prisoners being brought in by French cyclists. He followed them and heard them being examined by a French Intelligence officer, who asked them nothing but as to the state of Germany, the whereabouts of the Kaiser, and such-like stuff. He got nothing out of them. Amery then asked if he might put some questions. He knows German perfectly, and very soon had discovered that they belonged to an entirely new formation improvised since mobilization, and now arrived at the front. He actually got the definite location of every unit of the new division, and indications of some other similar divisions. He sent the information post-haste to G.H.Q. and was told not to be stupid, that there were no such formations, and that the prisoners must have been pulling his leg.

Later in the day, however, our own Corps got prisoners from the new formation, and also reported to G.H.Q. who were still sceptical, and asked for any prisoner to be sent on to G.H.Q. for examination there. To which Amery replied that we now had seven hundred of them, would they like to see the whole lot!

November 9 (Monday). We have had another week of very severe fighting though never so critical as on the 31st. I am not going to try to give you any description of it; the two worst days were Monday and Friday. On Monday the Germans came at us again in great strength, and with great determination, but the line held everywhere. I wrote the orders for the Corps at the end of the day's fighting. There was nothing to say except to hang on. You remember Kipling's " to hold on when there is nothing in you except the will that says to you hold on "; that is what our men have been doing all this week. There are no reinforcements. We are short, horribly short, of ammunition. Every unit has lost most frightfully. We have beaten off the German attack and we are all confident that we are better men than the Germans,

I could never have believed that any troops in the world could have stood what our men have stood, and still fight on. I wish I could put into words all I think about the regimental officers and men. It makes me feel that I ought to be with them. I asked last night to be allowed to go to a unit in the front line, but D.H. would not hear of it. One very curious fact I notice, and that is, that men under shell-fire get sleepy; it may be utter exhaustion—but I do not think so, for when the fire slackens they become alert at once; it must be some curious physical reaction.

On Tuesday we heard that large French reinforcements were on their way up, and that as soon as they arrived, Foch was going to deliver a very strong attack. This news was too good to keep to ourselves so we passed it on to the troops. I wish we had kept it to ourselves, for no French attack has yet materialized—nor seems likely to materialize, and the effect of hopes raised and not fulfilled is worse even than bad news. That same night our H.Q. was struck by a shell and D.H. sent the office part back to a village six miles away (Poperinghe). He himself went to a château near Ypres (Trois Tours) taking Gough and me with him.

The arrival of our little party at the château was rather funny. The proprietor was still in residence and was very concerned lest our horses, which were tethered in the garden, should eat the bark off his trees! A funny fussy little Belgian who did not in the least seem to realize that there was war, and that it was an even chance whether his château would be existing in a week's time.

But there are curious side-currents in other minds as well as his. D.H. tells me that at a conference of the Corps Commanders at Sir J. French's H.Q. on Friday, the whole discussion turned on winter leave for the troops! It showed a certain sublime detachment; but meantime the 1st Corps is still fighting for its life, and there seems little hope of any relief for some days more.

On Thursday poor Marker was hit. You will have heard of his death. Four of us had established our Report Centre in an inn at a cross-roads. Horne, Marker, Banning, and myself. The Germans were shelling down one of the roads, gradually getting nearer—but none of us thought it would come right up to us. Then one shell struck the building. Horne and I went out by one door in case the building should collapse, and Marker and Banning went out by another. Horne and I got away scot-free. Marker and Banning walked straight into another shell; Banning was killed outright, Marker badly wounded in the leg. Ryan was near by and was splendid. He went straight to Marker, although shells were now falling pretty thick, and tried to dress the wound. He was thrown right across Marker by the burst of a shell—but still went on with his work. Marker was taken to hospital and seemed to be getting on all right. He sent a wire home that " he had had a quarrel with a shell" and was quite cheery. Then gas gangrene set in and he died a few hours later. He is a very great loss, a splendid fellow in every way, who would have been a great leader had he lived.

Friday was another most critical day, just as critical as October 31. The French were driven in on our right, and our own right units came back with them. The Germans had a wedge right into our line almost up to Ypres. All the afternoon it looked very serious, but by evening we had got the line re-established. D.H. sent me to D'Urbal to try to get him to retake the part of the line he had lost. Foch had just been there and I got a copy of an order he had given D'Urbal that the line was to be retaken, also a personal letter saying, " There is no question of falling back 50 or 100 yards nor yet 25, and the whole French line must be reoccupied." D.H. did not think anything more than the issue of the order would happen, and wired to G.H.Q. that unless the French did retake the line, he recommended that the 1st Corps should be withdrawn to a line N. and S. through Ypres!

Even that did not bring about the French attack, for when early next morning (November 7) a Staff officer was sent to get direct information of the progress of the French attack, the report came back that nothing was being done except a desultory artillery bombardment. Then D.H. sent a telegram to Sir J. French urging that Foch had better go himself and inspire the French to attack. It was no good issuing orders, however energetic, if nothing was done to ensure that they were carried out. He ordered our own Corps to attack at 3 p.m. with or without the French, and went out himself to be on the spot and direct. The attack was successful in so far as we re-established our line; but there was one very ominous feature— some of our battalions were at last showing signs of giving way under the strain, and were falling back under only moderate shell-fire. D.H. took very prompt action. He ordered all men who left the trenches without sufficient reason to be brought before Summary Court Martial, and at the same time gave direct orders that all abandoned trenches were forthwith to be reoccupied, and sent Staff officers to see that it was done. This saved the situation, and by nightfall we were fairly happy again after a very anxious day.

Yesterday I accompanied D.H. to a conference with Sir J. French and Foch at Cassel. There was a good deal of straight talk.

D.H. was very emphatic that the French custom of very high-placed officers issuing energetic orders and leaving it at that, without themselves taking active steps to see that they were carried out, was useless. Practically no French general, and very few Staff officers, were ever seen to go forward to visit the troops in their advanced positions. He urged that they must go forward and take a personal grip of things. Our own G.H.Q. is not very much better. Sir J. French himself goes round Divisional Head-quarters, but very few of the Staff officers ever seem to come as far forward even as Corps H.Q. D.H. himself errs, I think, in the other extreme. He is constantly in considerable danger of being hit; he goes everywhere on horseback. I do not know what would happen if he were knocked out. I do not think there is anyone who could efficiently take his place. All the commanders of divisions, brigades and battalions have such complete confidence in him, and I think every man in the trenches shares the feeling, though he is not a "popular" hero.

The most active of the divisional G.O.C.s, in the way of going forward and sending his Staff forward is my old Staff College Commandant at Quetta, Tommy Capper. I saw him this week, and he said—and I think he meant it—" No good officer has a right to be alive during a fight like this." Certainly he takes as much—and more—risk as any of his own men, and his Staff follow his example. There is a story (probably quite untrue) that he came into the Staff Mess one day and said, "What! nobody on the Staff wounded to-day; that won't do!" and forthwith sent everyone available up to the first-line trenches on some mission or other. It sounds rather brutal—but it's not unwise. It heartens the men and regimental officers enormously to see Staff officers, though the Staff officers can do very little to help them. It is, in the main, a series of little regimental battles, and it is to the splendid training and fighting of the battalions that we owe our success and even our existence.

D.H. himself had rather a narrow escape a day or two ago. He was looking at a map opened on a table under a great glass candelabrum. A shell hit the house and down came the candelabrum on the map, very narrowly missing his head. A couple of signallers were killed at H.Q. at the same time. He was quite unperturbed —but we prevailed on him to change his H.Q., as once the German artillery had got the range of his château it was certain to be struck again. That was how Horne, Banning, Marker and I came to be back at the inn when Banning and Marker were hit.

The horrible thing about all these last few weeks, has been to see our battalions dwindling, and no reinforcements arriving to fill the gaps. What we want here now is more men and more ammunition, but particularly men of *any* training; the better trained they are so much the better, but we *must* have men, even if only partially trained. Our trained army has done far better than even its most enthusiastic admirers thought possible, but the casualties are enormous. We cannot go on for ever, we must have men. Germany is in the same fix. We find mere boys under 19, and old men of nearly 50, in their new formations, practically untrained; they are fine, brave material, but they can make no real fight against our trained men. Nor could our untrained men make a good show against Germany's trained men, but our partially trained men would be at least as good as Germany's new formations.

Germany scores in her artillery, and in the use of every scientific device for war regardless of expense. We are suffering, as England always suffers, for the peace parsimony of the politicians. We pay now in blood for the pennies they saved. I wish those who are responsible were here to take their share of it all.

We were all greatly cheered by the news of the Russian victory; it should have some effect on the fighting here. But it will not be felt for another two weeks, and to-day we hear that Yarmouth has been bombarded.

"Dukani" is very fit. He was wounded a couple of days ago, very slightly by a small piece of shell, but is all right again.

My chief assistant has broken down—nerves and strain—and has to go home. It was really rather comic. He came into my office and burst out, "Can't you stop the guns, boom, boom, booming, it's awful!" For the life of me I couldn't help saying, "No booming fear." However, I sent for Ryan and he took charge and has sent him home. I wonder whom I shall get instead.

Don't believe Captain M. that the war will last another two years. Germany has shot her bolt here and failed, and if the Russian news is true, she has failed there also. As time goes on we shall inevitably become stronger. Our own new K.'s Army must be ready in a few months. If we could get 200,000 more trained men for the B.E.F. now we could drive the Germans back. But this is impossible, and we must wait for one of three things :—

(1) K.'s new army.
(2) The Russians advancing into Germany, and forcing the Germans to withdraw from France.
(3) Italy joining us.

I think (3) is probable, (2) possible, but (1) is a certainty sooner or later.

I have always held that the war would be fought out by the manhood of the two nations, and not by their regular standing armies. Our own Regular Army is now finished.

The Germans, if not so far through their trained men as we, are feeling the strain. We are getting prisoners with less than three months' training. They are feeling the loss of officers far more severely than we are. The officers will of course be the weak point in our New Army, but they will be, at least, as good as those the Germans are now putting up against us.

November 16 (*Monday*). We have had another tremendous battle last Wednesday, and again we have won through. Our kind German general with his codeless wireless gave us warning, so we were not unprepared. Nevertheless it was a very close thing. The Germans brought against our Corps 15 fresh battalions, including 1 Guards division. Fresh troops against our men, worn out in the continuous battle of all this month. But we held them and beat them. Our Guards against their Guards at one part of the fight, and our Guards won. But for two hours our line was pierced, and things looked very bad indeed. I remember very little of it; indeed we at Corps H.Q. had not much to do, for it was fought out by the troops on the spot, and we had no reserves to put in. The first of the Territorial battalions have been fighting (The London Scots) and have done well; one battalion lost heavily, and its C.O. reported that his battalion was not fit to take the field and urgently required a rest. D.H.'s comment was that " The O.C. required a rest more than his men."

Now we are to be relieved, definitely, in a few days. Goodness knows we need it, for we have been fighting continuously ever since August 20. But we established a record. Since September 26 we have successively defeated five German corps—including the Guards. It is small wonder that the ranks are sadly thinned. We need rest and time to reorganize, and also reinforcements. Then we shall be ready to take on and defeat any other five German corps they bring against us.

It is the saddest thing in the world to see the remnants of the units as they come back—just a skeleton, the men unshaven, haggard, worn out and plastered with the accumulated mud of the trenches. But there is pride mixed with sadness. I do not believe any other troops in the world could have done what our men have done. I saw Webber leading his company of R.E.s out: the only officer left. He was cheery as ever, smoking his pipe with the bowl upside down, a spare pipe stuck in the waist-belt of his Sam Browne belt, and told me with great pride that his R.E. company had delivered an infantry attack, and performed great deeds. The Queen's were pulled out into Corps reserves, just after B. was wounded. They have done magnificently. But indeed all the infantry battalions have.

The Guards are a class by themselves. Somehow or other, they manage to maintain barrack-square discipline. There is one battalion whose Colonel even exacts strict mess discipline among his officers. If any of them says anything he disapproves of he orders " Stand up," whereupon the officer has to stand up, sometimes on the chair or whatever is doing service as a chair, and remain standing until the Colonel tells him to " sit down."

November 21. We are at Hazebrouck, a nice, quiet, peaceful Belgian township, licking our wounds and getting reorganized. I expect we shall be out for at least a fortnight. D.H. saw the C.-in-C., and was told that he (the C.-in-C.) had had a severe heart attack, and that the doctor had ordered him to be careful. He has sent D.H. home on a mission to Lord K., to give him a verbal report of how things are shaping here. He has taken with him notes on various and most diverse things to discuss with K. Shortage of rifles, shortage of ammunition, high explosives, boots, supply of officers, correspondents and promotion in the field.

Lord Roberts's death is sad, but it is as he would have wished to die, on active service. He lived to see the truth of his prophecy fulfilled, and that is given to few prophets. He had estimated that we would want 1,000,000 men for the great European war. If we had had even one half of them, there might have been no war, and if there had been war, it would have been over long before this. Now we have to ask for twice the number Lord Roberts had asked for. The wiseacres of politicians laughed at him.

You tell me there are rumours at home that the Germans entered Ypres. That is quite untrue, but they have shelled it unmercifully. I do not blame them, for troops were constantly passing through the town—but it is sad to see the fine old town being slowly battered to pieces.

I had an amusing experience to-day in this place. I saw a man in khaki, whom I thought I recognized as an attaché at the American Embassy in London. So I hailed him by name. " Surely you are ———." With a strong American accent he said, " I am not, I am

Lieutenant Brown of the Canadian Army. Lord K. says I am Brown of the Canadian Army, so I *am* Brown of the Canadian Army, and don't you forget it." So we promised not to and took him to our mess to give him a drink. It appears that K. had stretched a point in the rule that no foreign attachés were to be allowed to accompany our army, and had struck on this simple device to avoid questions.

You ask me about my helpers in the Intelligence work. They are a queer mixture—a diamond merchant, an engineer from Vickers's, and a brewer from Brighton who has never brewed. They have been given commissions for Intelligence work. They are all admirable linguists, expert motor-cyclists, and as keen as mustard. Their chief job is examining prisoners and documents found on them, for information that may enable us to make a picture of what is happening behind the German front line. The diamond merchant is appropriately rich; anyhow, he has placed at my disposal a very fine Rolls-Royce in which I can do my trips behind the lines.

D.H. has put me on to write a draft of the dispatch of the last battle—a tiresome job—but it is a dispatch that records great deeds, great sacrifices, but for great ends; hardships bravely borne by officers and men in the trenches, the deaths of gallant men, but with the object for which they served much nearer achievement by their efforts. They have fought a good fight one and all, so it is not all sad. But as one writes—here, where we really do not share in full measure the hardships and the risks—one feels how hearts at home are grieving with pain at each loss, and how even the great purpose for which we are fighting must be small consolation.

Forgive me writing like this; it is the reaction after the strain. I am most inordinately proud of the Corps in which I am serving.

The dispatch should make clear all we have done. I do not think any body of troops on either side can match our record. Since October 20 we have attacked and beaten two German corps, and then been ourselves attacked successively by four more German corps. We have not given up one yard of the ground we gained in our attack. We have beaten the Prussian Guards. Our losses have been very heavy, but those of the enemy far heavier. Perhaps one's view is distorted by being so near to it all, but I think the story of this last month will live in history as one of the great deeds of our Army.

I slept last night for the first time since August 24 without hearing the sound of guns, and in consequence stayed in bed until nearly 8 a.m. Now I am writing after a delightful breakfast in a comfortable, warmed house. There is a gorgeous sun shining outside, and glistening on the frost-covered fields. It is Sunday and the church bells are ringing. Altogether everything is peaceful, and it is hard to realize we are only fifteen miles from the front-line trenches.

I wish the Government would allow more news to appear in the papers. It is difficult to draw the line, and it is better to tell too little than too much. Still, I think something more could be told without much harm, and it deserves telling.

Later. I have just heard that I am to get a few days' leave on Friday, the 27th. I shall reach London either Friday or Saturday.

December 9. I have been back very nearly a week, and there is very little to add to what I told you at home.

Just as we approached Boulogne on our return journey in the dull greyness of a December evening, we saw torpedo-boat destroyers in station outside the harbour, with only their navigation lights showing. Then out of the harbour came a brilliantly lighted ship steaming rapidly. The destroyers formed line, and the whole procession made for England at high speed. It was the King returning from his first visit to France—a very fine and inspiring spectacle, for it gave one complete confidence in our command of the Channel.

I met Travers Clarke on the way across, and we had a long and very serious discussion—about babies!!

D. Baird has left us. He has a Staff job with the Indian Cavalry. His place as A.D.C. has been taken by Alan Fletcher, of the 17th Lancers.

Life now is very uneventful. I spend most of my time getting maps, etc., in order and organizing the Intelligence Office. We had a visit from a German aeroplane two days ago, which tried to hit the railway station with bombs, and missed it badly. That is the only active sign of war we have seen since my return.

I visited the Indian Corps H.Q. and saw many old friends. But the general tone at the Corps H.Q. is not good. There is much pessimism, even dejection, and they do not seem to be pulling together.

We keep at least two hours each afternoon free for exercise. It is all so different from what we were through last month, and indeed from what anyone would imagine war to be. There are numerous football matches, the ground densely lined with cheering partisans. Then you may hear at any time the sound of shot-guns and come across a party of officers shooting pheasants. There is a pack of beagles run by some cavalry units, and in the evenings there is always some form of smoking concert somewhere or other in the vicinity. All the shops in the town are open and driving a roaring trade. Thomas Atkins's favourite purchase is picture post-cards, the more gaudy and sentimental they are, the greater the demand. The Belgians charge all manner of absurd prices for them.

That is what being in reserve means—a very pleasant life. Every mess is a hotbed of rumours of happenings in all places in the wide world. *Sweden* anxious to join us now—this I certainly disbelieve. *Rumania* apparently determined to join us but not until the spring. *Italy* still hesitating, and Count Bülow said to have gone to Rome to buy Italy's neutrality with a slice of the Austrian Tyrol. *Paris* is now very optimistic, and says Germany is trying to make a separate peace with her. Obviously there can be nothing in this, except a perfectly natural attempt by the Germans to split the Allies' concord.

We are very dissatisfied with the meagre information we get from G.H.Q. and the W.O. Practically nothing reaches us officially, and one picks up what scraps one can from visits to neighbouring H.Q. of Corps and to G.H.Q. itself. It is all wrong. There should be a regular system of disseminating information, and as much of it as can safely be disclosed. I think the reason is that there is still friction at G.H.Q. between the Intelligence and the other branches of the Staff. Neither fully trusts the other. We hear rumours of changes at G.H.Q. Wilson may become C.G.S. I hope to goodness this is not correct, for he is utterly unsuited for that particular post. His judgment is almost always wrong, and he is half in the pocket of the politicians and half in the pocket of the French. There is an extraordinary yarn that the C.-in-C. himself lost his temper with Wilson and told him he " was no Englishman and had better go back to the damned Froggies." Wilson is said to have besought him for one more chance.

December 19 (*Saturday*). Here is an account of yesterday. Up at 6.45. In office from 8 to 10 a.m. Then took a young Artillery officer back to his unit in a small farmhouse. I lunched with him. They had taken the only living-room of the farm for the officers' living-room and mess, and the farmer's wife and daughters, assisted by the men cooks, put up a very good lunch indeed. There were six officers in the mess, and their bedding occupied most of the floor space. The room had a really fine, but low, timbered roof, and a flagged floor. We had a very cheery party. As at all units, they were avid for every scrap of information I could give them of the progress of events. They really hear little more than they read in the daily papers—generally two days old. In this particular mess they were greatly concerned about another great—but quite imaginary—battle at Ypres, described in the *Daily Mail*.

From this unit I went on to 4th Corps H.Q. where I saw General Kerr Montgomery in great grief because of the loss of his son who went down in the *Good Hope*. Then on to the 60th Rifles, where I dined with Howard Bury, an old Indian friend of mine, who told me some inside news of the political situation at home. He is in pretty close touch with some political people, and confirmed what I had already heard of intrigues being started against K. in political circles.

D.H. told me yesterday that the C.-in-C. had informed him that he had sent a Staff officer to London to arrange for Wilson to become C.G.S. in succession to Murray, whose health had broken down. French asked D.H.'s view and got it straight—that Wilson was always up to the neck in intrigue, and so far, seemed always to have subordinated the interests of the British Army to those of the French Army. D.H. said he had suggested *Robertson* (now Q.M.G.) to succeed Murray; he said that the whole Army had complete confidence in Robertson. By the "whole Army" he meant, of course, the commanders, for few of the regimental officers either know or care who is C.G.S. I am still quite sure that K. will never agree to Wilson.

D.H. told me that French had asked him to be C.G.S. but he had declined. He also told me that the B.E.F. was going to be grouped into armies each of two or three corps, and that he himself was to get the First Army consisting of the 1st, 2nd and 3rd Corps. He says he will take me with him to run the Intelligence of the Army, or as one of the "Operations" staff.

December 22. We are in the thick of it again. It began last Sunday. I started the day very peacefully with church at 8 a.m. in a small room at the top of the Town Hall buildings. Saw D.H. about 11 a.m. But there seemed nothing much happening anywhere, so after lunch I turned out to play football for the Staff against a team of cavalry. The Prince of Wales was playing. The ground was very wet, and just after I had sat down, unexpectedly and hurriedly, in a nice big puddle of water, D.H. appeared on the ground, and sent for me to tell me that the Indian Corps had been heavily attacked, that one brigade was to move at once, and that I was to go forthwith to the Indian Corps to find out what was the actual situation, and make necessary arrangements for the divisions. He had ordered a car for me, so I had not even time to change into dry kit, but went straight off. I expected to be back by nightfall, but actually I never got back at all.

I found things at the Indian Corps pretty serious. They had been driven out of their trenches, and an attempt to retake them had utterly failed. There was great confusion and the Indian troops were not doing well. Many of their British officers had been shot down by sharpshooters, and without them the units were valueless. I sent back my report and late that evening another brigade was ordered down from the 1st Corps. Their arrival heartened the Indian Corps, and the German attack was definitely stopped. But the Indian Corps was obviously quite unfitted to hold the line against attack. It is not to be wondered at, for they were quite new at the game. The next day D.H. arrived himself, and at once wired to G.H.Q. recommending that the Indian Corps should be relieved. That was yesterday, *Friday*. We have taken over from the Indian Corps, and we are now in new H.Q. at a largish town just behind the front attacked (Merville).

I am afraid there will be a lot of hard words about the Indians. There should not be. They are not, of course, as good or nearly as good as British troops. How could they be? If they were, we could not have held India with the small force we have there. This kind of fighting is quite new to them. They have not been trained for it. They have quite rightly a high respect for the " white man " and the German is to them a " white man." Besides all this, they have no personal interest in the quarrel. But most of all, Indian troops cannot fight without white officers whom they know. And the Germans shot down the British officers, who are always easy to spot in an Indian unit. I have not lost either my faith in, nor my affection for, the Indian units. They will never be as good as British troops—but they will do much better than they have done in this little show. There will have to be reorganization—blessed word! In this case it means many changes among the higher commanders. They are almost all too old for their jobs in fighting like that which we are having. I was told of one general who insisted on his own guns stopping firing for at least $1\frac{1}{2}$ hours after his lunch-time, so that he might enjoy, undisturbed, his afternoon siesta.

Most of the bitter criticisms we hear now are from those who have expected far too much from the Indians. They talked of the Gurkhas taking Lille at the point of the kukri in a night attack, and nonsense of that sort. I think the old Indian time-honoured proportion of one Britisher for every $2\frac{1}{2}$ Indians will work out very nearly right as an index of their fighting value. Anyhow, they have already done good service, for they filled a gap in the line when we had no other troops to put in. Better luck to them in the future! I am very sorry, indeed, for their British officers just now. They are seeing "the thing they gave their heart to, broken."

The new First Army is formed under D.H. Our H.Q. are at a town on a canal (Lillers). I am appointed one of the G.S.O. 1st Grade Operations with S. Wilson as 3rd Grade. Davidson, from 3rd Corps, comes in as Intelligence, but D.H. tells me he will ask for me to change with Davidson as otherwise there will be two Sappers in Operations, and he wants me for Intelligence work—a disappointment. I would have preferred Operations, but it is something to be in charge of the Intelligence of an army before my 38th birthday.

December 31, 1914/*January* 1, 1915. A line to ring out the Old Year and ring in the New Year.

It is only 11 p.m. I dined with D.H. and am just back. It was a very quiet dinner. Most of the talk was of what might happen in the New Year. No one liked to talk or even to think of all the friends we had lost in these last few months. Our speculations of the future lead nowhere. D.H summed it all up in a very telling phrase: "We can hope and we can wish, we cannot know. But what we must *do* is go forth to meet the future without fear."

PART TWO—1915
ARMY HEAD-QUARTERS

CHAPTER VII

PREPARATIONS FOR NEUVE CHAPELLE

January 8. It is interesting work getting a new head-quarters into being. We stand intermediate between the Corps Head-quarters and General Head-quarters. All orders and all information to and from G.H.Q. pass through our offices. The risk is that Army Head-quarters becomes solely a bureau, and out of touch with things that are happening in the front-line trenches, as G.H.Q. had become. But D.H. is quite determined to prevent this. Owing to the 1st Corps having taken over the Indian Corps line just before the Army was instituted, the Corps forming our Second Army were changed, and it now consists of the 1st Corps, 4th Corps and Indian Corps.

Our H.Q. is at a queer little, overgrown mining village—squalidness *in excelsis*; not a decent street or shop, and only two good houses of the suburban villa type. Our H.Q. is in a Jesuit school. My own office is a large bare schoolroom on the ground floor. There is a large table in the centre of the room covered with maps; more maps decorate the walls, and the children's desks ranged round the walls serve as resting-places for the files; a harmonium forms a book-stand, and a rather indifferent coke stove gives heat and fumes in equal degree. Next door is a smaller room where the Operations section of the General Staff works. Then there is a still smaller room for General Gough's private office. Upstairs there are the administrative offices and the clerks' offices. The mess is in a small house next door, where we have one living-room and a kitchen. But we are never there except for meals. My own bedroom is in the same house as the mess.

I took on myself the organization of the mess, and bought the kit in 15 minutes' energetic shopping, engaged a Belgian woman cook while in the shop, provided her with a Tommy as kitchen-maid and two waiters. After she had been with us two days the cook suddenly surprised us by disclosing a quite respectable knowledge of the English language, on the strength of which I at once handed over charge of the mess to a junior officer.

Ryan comes to us to-day as Medical Officer. We find we cannot do without him. The immediate cause was General Hobbs developing appendicitis. Whereupon D.H.—who believes that the medical profession comprises only Ryan and a few learners—telegraphed for Ryan and now will not let him go. I am very glad, for he is not only the best of companions, but has the quite invaluable faculty of making every patient fully convinced that there is nothing whatever the matter with him. He is also developing a tendency to bully D.H.—which is very salutary.

So far all the efforts of the First Army Staff have been devoted to trying to keep the trenches habitable. The whole country is flooded, and most of the trenches have a foot of water in them, though, strangely, there is surprisingly little illness among the troops. A great deal of my time is taken up studying statistics of rainfall and floods, and trying to foresee the vagaries of water let loose from overgrown rivers and flooded ditches. To-day the weather has taken a turn and is fine and frosty. But local reports tell us that for another six weeks we must expect rain at least every second day. Six weeks bring us near March, when so much is due to happen :—K.'s army to begin arriving, Rumania to come in, Italy to join us, and the North Sea Fleet to come out, and we ourselves to begin attacking again, and Russia—but what will Russia do ? Our news from there is none too good. Russia has never yet fought a war to a finish. Will she hold fast in this one—what will happen if she collapses ? And now it looks as if the U.S.A. were going to cut up rough—it seems incredible. But the U.S.A. are in a very strong position, and are not likely to forgo their claim. I am afraid it may mean a great increase in the price of food at home if the U.S. does deny us supplies. On the other hand it will ruin all American overseas trade, and I cannot bring myself to believe that she will do that.

January 19. Yesterday I went to a French H.Q. about 15 miles from here, and had an interesting talk with an old French general, who was full of inventions of all sorts for destroying life, and demolishing buildings and even hills. He explained his theories in the gentle voice of one propounding the advantages of Mellin's infant food—a dear delightful " old-woman " man with fantastic and bloodthirsty ideas.

Coming back I ran into a convoy of 200 London motor-buses—a strange sight on a country road in a driving snowstorm in France, within a few miles of the trenches. All the old advertisements and posters still adorned them, the only apparent change being that wire gauze had replaced the glass windows, and that both drivers and passengers were British soldiers muffled up in khaki greatcoats.

January 22. My cold has developed into bronchitis, and Ryan has ordered me home for a couple of days' rest. I feel inclined to bless the word " bronchitis." There is little doing here. We have just heard that Robertson is to succeed Murray and Henry Wilson to become Liaison Officer with the French, where he can do little mischief. Repington has been here and confirms the report that Wilson did get the French Government to ask the British Government that he should be made C.G.S. What an intriguer the man is ! For a soldier of his rank to descend to intrigue is mental adultery.

D.H. has heard that his note on the reorganization of the army, which he submitted when at home on leave in November, is to be acted on. The New Army troops are to be mixed with the old army in the proportion of one new brigade and two seasoned brigades in each division. The first new brigade will be seasoned—what is left of them—by the time more new K. brigades are ready to be absorbed.

February 11. Yesterday I was out all day going round the Corps and Division H.Q.—8 hours in an open Wolseley car—a very pleasant interlude in the long office day. I drove myself so as to get to know the roads.

To-day I have been in office all day working at plans for our attack next month.[1] We are to have another Corps, more heavy artillery, and hope to take the ridge overlooking our front-line trenches. It will give us much better ground for our line, and it may lead to a withdrawal from a considerable section by the Germans. It will be our first attempt at attacking Germans in well-organized trenches. Much must depend upon the Artillery.

Meantime we hear from home of a proposal to start a side-show in Salonika, with one French and one British Division. This can have no sort of effect on the military side of the war, except to waste our strength by scattering it. We have certainly not got enough troops to indulge in side-shows, nor have the French, if we can judge by the difficulty they had at Ypres in finding troops required for battle here in France. But it may be sound for policy reasons. The principal danger of side-shows is that they always tend to become bigger, and absorb more and more troops.

[1] Neuve Chapelle.

Our own G.H.Q. is discussing proposals for attacks along the Belgian coast. It is certainly most desirable to clear the coast, and if successful would go far to drive the Germans right back. But the operation would require many more troops and artillery than we have available. If G.H.Q. decides on the Belgian coast attempt, our attack here will not come off. On the whole, with the limited force available, everything would tend to point to our attack (Neuve Chapelle) being better strategy.

D.H. tells me that there are to be changes in the Staff here. Gough is to be promoted and get a division at home. D.H. has asked for either K. or W. or B. to succeed him. I shall be sorry when Gough goes. The Aldershot Staff (except for Marker's death) has been pretty well intact so far, and we all know one another's weak and strong points. Apart from this we cannot well get anyone better or as good as Gough. He has been through the show since the beginning. In many ways D.H. is his own Chief of Staff. He knows so much more about fighting than any of the Staff, and he goes round the divisions and brigades so constantly that his Chief of Staff has little to do, except to see that things go smoothly.

My days are getting into a regular routine. Every second day I go round units, leaving at 11 a.m. and returning for dinner. The other days are to the following time-table :—Office 7 a.m. to 8 a.m. ; 8 a.m. breakfast ; 9 a.m. conference with the heads of branches ; then office to 1 p.m. ; lunch at 1 p.m. ; office 1.45 to 4 ; 4-5 exercise ; 5 p.m. to 8 p.m. office ; 8 p.m. dinner ; 9 p.m. conference with D.H. which generally lasts until 10.30 ; after that, a final hour in office and then to bed.

To-day I had a ride with F. E. Smith—a most amusing companion, very destructive in his criticisms, particularly of his political colleagues. He told me he had a recent interview with K. of K. and gathered the impression that K. of K. thought the war would be over by the autumn. I reported this to D.H. who would not hear of it. D.H. does not think there can be any end until the autumn of 1916 at earliest. He is still very insistent on careful analysis of the man-power problem. His view is that France has now put into the field every man she can. Her yearly quota is much smaller than Germany's, and will not suffice to meet her casualties. As time goes on, therefore, the French Army will decrease. Our own Army will increase rapidly, but Germany will fight to the last, and we shall require great numerical superiority to drive her out of her carefully prepared positions, and then defeat her in battle. But I am gradually being forced to the opinion that we shall not win the war by great victories on land or sea, but by wearing Germany out. I cannot conceive a Sedan in this war in the state it has got into now. It was possible in the early months, only we would have been the Sedan-ed, not the Sedan-ers.

I only begin to realize now, as I study in the comparative peace and quiet of Army Head-quarters, how near we were to that, not only in August, but also in October. In hard fact, the German strategic plan, though it failed, was infinitely superior to that of the French. It was not the French plan that won, or indeed the German plan that was faulty, it was the " unexpected " (which in war always happens). Why did the Germans cease their enveloping advance in August ? Why did they not take advantage of the break they had made in our line at Ypres ? Why did they not strike for the Channel ports earlier ? Why did they not eat up the 2nd Corps at Le Cateau ? We do not know the answer to these " whys." But I remember Bird's favourite phrase at the Staff College : " In love, war, and cards, opportunities once lost do not readily recur." So far as one can foresee—and that is not far—the opportunities will be ours in the future. Shall we lose them as the Germans did ? I do not think so, if D.H. has them offered to him. But no one can be sure.

The impossibility of answering those *whys* as regards the Germans are explained in the easy philosophy of the men by the " Angel of Mons " theory, of which I told you when I was at home. I have been at some trouble to trace the rumour to its source. The best I can make of it is that some religiously minded man wrote home that the Germans halted at Mons, AS IF an Angel of the Lord had appeared in front of them. In due course the letter appeared in a Parish Magazine, which in time was sent out to some other men at the front. From them the story went back home with the " as if " omitted, and at home it went the rounds in its expurgated form.

One other yarn has been traced to its source.[1] The Russians in England (whom poor M.'s sister saw !) were undoubtedly the Territorial units moving through Great Britain on their way to ports of embarkation for the East. One youth here adds the embellishment that at a wayside station one bearded

[1] The " crucified Canadian " story, current in April, 1915, began in a report sent by a sergeant that he had seen Germans sitting round a lighted fire, and what looked like a crucified man. He worked his way closer to them, and found it was only shadows cast by some crossed sticks on other objects. The report was transmitted back without this explanation.

warrior, asked where he came from, said truthfully enough, Ross-shire, which sounded like Russia. Even without this embellishment, the explanation is adequate. We shall have many more such rumours before the war ends. A wise scepticism seems called for with regard to all unlikely rumours.

Intelligence work teaches scepticism, if it teaches nothing else. Nothing can be accepted until it is confirmed from at least two other independent sources, and if it appears inherently improbable, it requires confirmation from at least one other source. The Head Intelligence Officer at G.H.Q. has this scepticism developed to the highest point. His strongest affirmation is that " Something or other appears not improbable," that means it is practically certain. D.H. demands more than this. Everything that goes to him has to be sharply divided into Fact, Probability, Possibility, Improbability but reported, and he holds me responsible that everything is in its proper category. I think he is right. " Not improbable " is rather like the miss in balk, playing for safety. But French, at the beginning anyhow, did not trust the Intelligence, and that " Not improbable " was an obvious and necessary measure of precaution. The fault lies with the C.-in-C., not with the Intelligence.

February 17. So you are " blockaded " in England by a few submarines ? What utter nonsense. I have just heard that the Folkestone boat will not sail to-morrow because of the blockade. Somebody seems to have " nerves " pretty badly. It is such a confession of weakness and will hearten the Germans hugely. They are certain to hear of it. What earthly difference could it make if one Channel steamer were sunk. We shall not win either on land or sea by dodging danger—but by taking risks.

The plans for our attack next month have been approved by G.H.Q.

February 22. Poor Gough has been killed, just when he was getting the dream of his ambition, the command of a division. He went to say good-bye to his own battalion in the trenches. He walked down a rather exposed road and was shot by a ricochet bullet possibly of a sniper. The news reached us about midday yesterday, and D.H. sent me off to get him back. Moynihan, who had operated on Gough last year, was ordered to await him. All we knew was that he had been seriously wounded—shot through the stomach. I reached him in the early afternoon, but it was impossible to get an ambulance to him until after dark. He was quite conscious in the ambulance. His C.B. had just appeared in the *Gazette*. His only comment when we told him was, " I would get that now anyhow, even without war ! " Moynihan operated, and thought there was some hope he might pull through ; his heart failed at 5 a.m. He was buried to-day, in the churchyard of an old and beautiful Abbey, within sound of the rifle-fire of the front line.

It is only one more life lost among so many—but for us at Army H.Q., it is like losing one of our own family. You remember that he and I left Aldershot together for France, only five months ago—but so much has happened since then. D.H. is badly upset, though he shows it very little. He told me Gough had offered to give up the division which he was so keen on, if D.H. wanted him to stay. It was a big sacrifice for D.H. to let him go just now, when we are just on the verge of another big operation.

Gough was at his very best when battle-fighting. He was sometimes very irritable when things were quiet—never when there was a crisis; and he had immense courage and confidence. I shall always remember his " God won't let those b—— win," when things were at their blackest at Ypres. An easy optimism, perhaps. But what is all faith but " easy optimism " ? And what can anyone accomplish without faith ? For courage is faith. Robertson, the new C.G.S. at G.H.Q., has a phrase that " a pessimist is more useless than a coward in war."

February 24. I am on duty to-night. Our offices are in a big school building. Downstairs is the Report Centre where all messages come. A few doors off is the Signal Office with telegraph and telephone, leading out to the front, and back to G.H.Q. and sideways to the other armies on either side of us. In the Report Centre there are two clerks on duty. Upstairs, all rooms are closed except my own, and a small room in which there is a shakedown for the officers on duty. The A.H.Q. telephone is in my room, and we can talk to London quite easily, and as clearly as if in Guildford. My table is covered with photographs taken from aeroplanes. We have just started this method of reconnaisance, which will I think develop into something very important. At present it is a very necessary check on the exaggerated reports and the imagination of air observers. Photographs cannot lie—most air observers do, probably unconsciously, though I am not so sure that it is all unconscious.

There is no sound except the click-click of the clerks' typewriters and the distant whir of some motor-cyclist messenger coming in from the front, increasing into the *puff-puff* as he slows down in the streets of the townlet. Challenge and answer ring out, the puffing gets slower and slower, and then stops opposite the office, generally with the sharp crack of a back-fire. After a few minutes the cyclist comes up to my room, encased in muddy yellow overalls, except for the blue and white armlet and a brilliantly red face. They are keen, intelligent boys these dispatch riders, mostly Varsity undergraduates. We pass the time of day, discuss the weather and the roads, and his own particular adventures of the day. Then the answer is written, and away he goes on his 20-mile ride to his destination. The other day one of them took a toss and tore half his thumb-nail off. He went to the nearest hospital, had the whole nail removed, the thumb bandaged, and continued to his destination some 12 miles farther on.

Sometimes a sleepy clerk has to be haled from his dream of England, to search out some reference. Just now I had to awaken my own shorthand man—a special enlistment; in peace-time in a big railway office, with a wife and child at home, and a horrid stammer out here. His ideas of discipline are rather crude, and sometimes when he gets the rough edge of my tongue, he looks at me in open-eyed and open-mouthed astonishment that anyone should so address a free-born British Socialist. But we get on very well together, and I think that on the whole he has decided to like me.

Not very interesting all this, but it may help to make you understand how unexciting life at Army Head-quarters can be in the long lulls between battles, in a war in the twentieth century. What luxury it all is compared to the man in the battalion with eighteen inches of liquid mud in the trenches and snow on the ground. Tame work too, as regards risk of life and risk of wounds, yet there is excitement enough when things are active at the front and telegrams are pouring in and decisions are being made. Even now, when it is only planning for a big operation, there are so many uncertain factors that have to be estimated. We rack our brains seeking to piece together little bits of information and fitting them into a mosaic of truth that will show what has happened, is happening and will happen over against us there, behind that line of trenches that we shall attack.

March 3. There has been a most exasperating hitch in our plans.

Originally we were planning an attack as an operation simultaneous with, but independent of, three great attacks by the French away to the south of us. Then suddenly G.H.Q. told us that Joffre had decided that the French army under General Maud'huy, immediately on our right, was also to attack in far greater strength than we could muster, so that our attack would only be one flank of a big battle. I went over to consult with the Intelligence of the French army on our right regarding the information in their possession, and discovered that there was a big gap between the left of their attack and the right of ours.

D.H. went himself to see Maud'huy and found that his attack was dependent upon our extending our front line up to the left flank of his attack. If we take it on, we shall not have enough troops for our attack. It looks as if either our attack or Maud'huy's will have to be cancelled—in any case both cannot go on, and that means that there is no chance of a break-through of the German line in this area. Personally, I do not think there ever was much chance of a break-through, although the French are in far better condition and spirit than they were last October. I do not think their troops will ever break the German entrenched lines.

Our own British Army is still far too small to have any chance of doing more than make a small gap, not enough for a big break.

Yesterday we had a visit from six Press correspondents, sent out by the W.O.—the first concession to the quite legitimate demand of the great British Public for independent news served up in a more palatable form than by Official Eye-witnesses. The " Eye-witnesses " are, as you know, E. D. Swinton (Ole Luk-Oie) and F. E. Smith. One would have thought that either of them would have known how to dish up news for the British Public and I am not at all sure that the British Public is really dissatisfied with their efforts. But the newspapers undoubtedly are. News from anyone " official" must be suspect. Sooner or later unofficial war correspondents were bound to come, and I am glad it is now.

Nevertheless, the first batch of correspondents had to be treated gingerly. I doubt whether they will really be much the wiser after their visit. They arrived, accompanied by three officers from the W.O., who themselves were quite as ignorant of what was actually happening as the correspondents. They were in my charge while in the First Army. I gave them a short explanation of the operations of the past and present, not a word about the future. Then I handed them over to the Administration people, Ordnance, Medical and Supply, and finally sent them on up to the front under charge of one of my own officers. There are many well-known names among the correspondents. They were all most amazingly ignorant, but that was the real justification for their mission as opposed to the official "Eye-witnesses." It is impossible for us here to realize how ignorant the public must be, and in writing the copy that the public requires, one must begin with the knowledge of how little they know. Among the correspondents there was one American (Frederick Palmer) with whom I was acquainted when I was in the Balkans, and who really knew much more about war than any of the Britishers. I think he had already been some time with the French armies.

By the way, did you see an article in *Blackwoods* referring to some incidents at Ypres? The yarn about the Duc d'Orléans is quite true—but the author omits one relevant fact—the other actor in the little scene was quite drunk at the time, and was sent home in consequence. I know, because I was the Staff officer that settled the case.

What swine these Clyde workers are with their accursed strikes! It is enough to make one ashamed of one's country.

CHAPTER VIII

NEUVE CHAPELLE

March 12. We have had one battle and the result is a modified success. We have not captured the position on the ridge which was our objective. But we have advanced our line more than half a mile, on a frontage of nearly 3 miles. We have taken a fair bag of prisoners (among them a man who claims to be the nephew of a professor at Glasgow University!). But the really important thing is that we have shown that a German entrenched line can be attacked and taken. We have lost heavily, especially in officers. The disappointment is that we should have done so much better. At one time on the first day we had taken the German trench line, with very slight loss. There was a gap. We had found precisely the strength we anticipated in front of us. We knew that German reinforcements could not reach them for at least 12 hours. D.H. ordered the 4th Corps to push troops through the gap. The cavalry was all ready to go through after them.

Then, for some reason not yet explained, the whole machine clogged and stopped. It was maddening. Exactly the same as had happened at Ypres, but with the position reversed. This time we had broken the line and the attack came to a stop. When the attack did get going again the next day, the Germans had reinforced their line, and no progress was made. The German reinforcements came up and counter-attacked, and the battle petered out.

D.H. was determined to find out the cause of the delay and went to-day to both Corps and Divisional H.Q. to investigate the matter personally. The breakdown was undoubtedly at a Corps H.Q. where D.H.'s orders stuck, and were not transmitted to the division concerned for some hours. Corps H.Q. tried to put the blame on the division, and there was rather an unpleasant incident, which leaves a very nasty taste in one's mouth. It is no good finding scapegoats. The important thing is to find out where the failure took place, and see that any similar failure is impossible in the future. In any case, we were short of ammunition towards the end of the battle, and could not have pressed home our advantage, even if we had secured our objective. But our trenches would have been far better placed and far less exposed than in the low-lying country where they still are. One thing has resulted; D.H. in all future battles will have his battle H.Q. still farther up, so that he will be in closer touch with his Corps and Divisional H.Q.

Our Intelligence show was successful, in that we found the Germans exactly as we had located them, and their reinforcements arrived to the exact hour that we had predicted they would. The Intelligence organization is growing in size, as well as importance. I have now two regular majors under me, and three temporary officers—a barrister, a diplomat, and a stockbroker. They are all good linguists, keen and clever, so my work grows easier—only it never stops. The barrister's especial job is studying air photographs, at which he is getting extraordinarily expert; finding out all manner of things, some very important, from them. The Germans can quite easily cover up gun positions and other defences, so that the observers in aeroplanes cannot detect them. It is next to impossible to conceal them from the camera. There is the negative result also, that these air photos teach us how to conceal our own gun positions, though so far as we know at present the Germans are not using air photographs. The plans for the battle were all worked out on maps, brought up to date from air photographs for the first time in war.

March 16. I went with D.H. to G.H.Q. to-day. He, to see the C.-in-C., and work out plans for renewing the battle on a much bigger scale on the same front; I, to see the Intelligence people. There we heard that instead of getting more ammunition, the supply was being cut down, as more and more was required for the Dardanelles and Salonika. It is exactly what we had feared from these ridiculous little side-shows. They grow and grow, accomplishing nothing that can influence the ultimate decision, and absorbing men and ammunition that we require here, where the final result must be fought out. It means we cannot hope to attack again for some weeks, and D.H. is off home for a few days' leave.

We have been trying to work out the German losses at Neuve Chapelle. We know they lost 2,000 prisoners. We estimate their dead at about 8,000, so that probably their total casualties, including all wounded, will work out at something like 13,000, but many of the wounded will return to duty in time.

Yesterday a dog was caught with a matchbox tied to its neck

containing a cipher message believed to be for the Germans. The message has not yet been fully deciphered. Meantime, the owner of the dog has been handed over to the French, who will probably give him short shrift. But as he is a quite unintelligent rustic the message cannot well contain anything of great value. The important thing is to find out whether there is a complete system of espionage within our area. I do not think there can be; the dog method is too crude, and anyhow we know positively that our attack at Neuve Chapelle came as a complete surprise to the Germans.

March 27. Frederick Palmer, the American war correspondent, came to lunch with me, and we discussed the situation in America. He will not hear of any chance of U.S.A. seriously interfering with us. He says that U.S.A. trade has already suffered much, but that she will not do anything to prevent the Allies beating Germany, and he says that if the worst came to the worst, and U.S.A. saw any chance of Germany winning, she would most undoubtedly intervene actively, and even fight along with us. He is very well informed and may be right, but I cannot see that U.S.A. has any *casus belli* against Germany at present, and unless Germany is foolish enough to provide her with one, I do not see how she can fight. A civilized nation cannot now begin fighting just because it does not want one side or the other to win. But the important thing (if Palmer is right) is that we have the moral support of the U.S.A. We should be strong enough to beat Germany without her active help when we develop all our strength, *if* we cut down side-shows, and if France and Russia hold on. The news of Przemysl is good, but one cannot help an uncanny feeling about the Russians. They have never yet fought a war to a finish.

March 28. The G.H.Q. dispatch about Neuve Chapelle is disgraceful. It reads as if the whole operation had been planned by G.H.Q. As a matter of fact, the whole thing was worked out from the very beginning here at First Army H.Q. and G.H.Q. had nothing whatever to do with it. They did not even get copies of the orders issued until after the battle. C.-in-C. has just been substituted for G.O.C. First Army throughout. All the Staff are indignant. I spoke to D.H. about it to-day. He takes it very philosophically. He always is very contemptuous of those who want to be " in the limelight " and says they are not worth bothering about. All the same I think he will have something to say to Sir J. French when they next meet.

You must not worry about the losses at Neuve Chapelle. I see the papers are making a fuss about them. It is the first time in the war that trenches have been taken by direct assault. The losses were to some extent avoidable—rather they will be avoided next time from the lesson we have learnt, and as the officers and men are now experienced in this class of operation. The long months of trench warfare had clogged the wheels. We have no longer the highly trained Aldershot army. We have to learn to work with different material.

I see Sir J. French has given tongue, and says the war will not be a long one. It depends upon the *neutrals* and upon the *strikers*. I think the Americans are playing up as well as they can be expected to. But the head Ordnance man tells me the men in our munition factories are refusing to do a single minute's overtime, and don't work 60 minutes to the hour when they are working. Is that true? It is perhaps not to be wondered at when Ramsay MacDonald tells them that the reason we went to war was to exercise the Navy in battle practice. I wish the Navy would do some battle practice, and I wish—how I wish !—we had R.M. out here. The men in the ranks would look after him. He did come out for a few days last autumn, but did not come near us. I think he was with the Belgians or French.

The mapping work has grown so big that we have had to take on another building for it, and the Secret Service where the French *Sûreté Générale* and Scotland Yard men work. The Scotland Yard detectives are quite out of their element, and still trying to work on their old police methods. One of them dropped his inevitable note-book the other day. It was duly retrieved and brought to me. I put it in a drawer and waited for a couple of days, then sent for the man and asked him for a report of his doings on the day previous to the loss of his note-book. Out came another note-book, and he began the invariable "At 7 a.m.——." Then I pulled out the original note-book and said, "But this note-book says that at 7 a.m. you were doing something totally different." It was rather brutal, but I am sure he will not leave his note-book lying about again, or if he does that he will report its loss.

April 4. Neuve Chapelle has had unexpected results. It has made the French think highly of our Army. Joffre is sending his Corps Commanders to see D.H. and learn how we succeeded in attacking and ousting the Germans from an entrenched position. That is sufficient answer to the complaints in the Press about our losses. I am afraid England will have to accustom herself to far greater losses than those of Neuve Chapelle before we finally crush the German Army.

Lord Esher has been visiting D.H. He has some kind of unofficial mission in France. He is a most acute observer, and a very entrancing conversationalist. But his chief characteristic is that he is always close friends with those that matter. So his visit probably means that D.H.'s star is in the ascendant. It can indeed only be a matter of time before he takes over the chief command out here. He is so immeasurably the superior of all the others.

D.H. sent Esher on to my office, and I had a most interesting talk with him. I wonder what report he will send to whoever is employing him. Anyhow, he told me very many interesting bits of tittle-tattle. He said the French were very greatly impressed by our success at Neuve Chapelle. He thinks they had only given us credit for ability to defend, now they realized we could attack. I did not tell Esher our own view of the French was much the same as that which they had until now held of us ! He said Joffre had dismissed out of hand a French general who had made the attack which failed in Champagne at the same time as Neuve Chapelle ; the dismissed general had pleaded that the plan was not his, and that he was only carrying out a plan that came to him from Joffre's own Staff. Thereupon Joffre also sacked the Staff officer concerned. All this sounds incredible, and would be so in our army, but the French do indulge in a system of slaughter of those who for any reason do not succeed, the general principle being that to save your own skin you must get someone under you sacked first—a sort of band of fratricides, the modern equivalent of Nelson's band of brothers. Fowke (our witty Chief Engineer at G.H.Q.) says that after every reverse the tumbrils go round French G.Q.G. with the cry " Bring out your dead." The French use the word Limoges just as we used Stellenbosch in S.A. There is some imaginary command at Limoges to which failures are consigned, a kind of military Chiltern Hundreds.

To return to Esher ; he says Joffre is greatly impressed by the fact that D.H. was given an entirely free hand to design and carry out his own plan—a very pretty criticism of Sir J. French's dispatch ! He further told me that an American, recently passing through Paris after a visit to Berlin where he saw the Kaiser, told him that the Kaiser had said the British 1st Corps under D.H. were the best in the world.

Esher tried hard to draw me as to whether we were looking forward to D.H. becoming C.-in-C. *vice* French. I said this was, of course, in everyone's mind and that if Sir J. French's health broke down, then I presumed D.H. would succeed as a matter of course, unless K. himself came out. Esher then said that at French G.Q.G. there were serious dissensions between soldiers and politicians, and that Joffre might not long remain C.-in-C. there. I suggested that K. should come to France as Allied C.-in-C. I had previously discussed this with Gemeau, our French liaison officer, who seemed to think that K.'s prestige in France was so high that the French Army and nation might agree. Esher, very wisely, pointed out that that could only happen when our army in France was as big as the French Army, which postpones it until the millennium. (This is not a pun upon K.'s million men.) Personally, I believe that sooner or later K. will come out as C.-in-C. of the Allied Armies, if Joffre does not get a big success within a year.

I saw G. Wingate with his Glasgow Highlanders a few days ago. He told me rather a good yarn about his company grouser, with the singularly inappropriate name of Tom Bright. It was the first day of spring sun after all the wind and rain of winter. A bright sun, birds beginning to twitter, and everything seemed good, and everyone contented—except T. Bright. Wingate met him in a communication trench when he was carrying rations up to the front line and said, " Well, this is all right to-day ! " To which Bright replied, " *You* may think it all right. *I* can't abide this b——y sun in my eyes ! "

He also told me that the German Intelligence seem to have very good information of our front-line dispositions. His unit went up to relieve an English battalion in a new part of the line, and was greeted on arrival by a voice from the German trenches in a good imitation of a Glasgow tram conductor's voice, " Argyll Street, halfpenny station." Shortly afterwards the Germans put on a gramophone in the trenches playing " Stop your tickling, Jock." Though amusing, it has its serious side, for the Germans may have some source of information—unless some prisoners from the unit which was relieved, gave away the fact that the Glasgow Highlanders were coming up, which is the probable explanation. Even more important is the obvious deduction that so long as the Germans can jest like this, there is not much sign of any crack in their morale.

CHAPTER IX

CRITICAL DAYS AT YPRES

April 24 (*Saturday*). There has been no fighting for the last fortnight in the First Army, but a constant procession of distinguished visitors to G.H.Q. and First Army H.Q. Curzon, Balfour and Foch. Apparently the home Government is very concerned about India, where neither civilian nor soldier seems to be coping adequately with the situation. D.H. is rather afraid that he may be sent to India as C.-in-C., indeed Sir J. French made the suggestion to him. I imagine it originated either with Wilson or Rawlinson, both of whom would, I think, like to see D.H. out of France, with a view to the possible reversion of the Command in Chief should French go for any reason. Both Wilson and Rawlinson are born intriguers, but Rawlinson is a good fighting soldier in addition, which Wilson is not. It would be madness to send D.H. away from France just now, unless K. himself comes out here—such madness that I am certain it will not be done. Indeed, all these visits from Cabinet Ministers to D.H.—they do not go round the other armies—make me reasonably sure that they are weighing up D.H. for the Chief Command.

At G.H.Q. itself things are very unsatisfactory. Sir J. French seems altogether in Wilson's pocket. Wilson lives with French, and Robertson in another mess altogether. I came out in the same boat as Wilson on Thursday, and we talked all the way across—rather he talked and I listened. He is an extraordinarily amusing and interesting conversationalist. I can easily understand how he fascinates those who do not know him well. But it all leads nowhere. His imagination seems to take complete charge of his judgment. He belittled Neuve Chapelle, and said it compared badly with French attacks if you weighed distance gained to losses sustained. This is true enough—but has no real meaning. If there was no opposition you could occupy a county without losing a single life, and be no nearer beating the German Army at the end of it. Measuring the results of battle with a pair of dividers on a map is sheer stupidity.

Wilson told me one interesting thing. He said we had accounted for 17 submarines since February, and that the sting of that particular form of " frightfulness " had quite gone. I hope he is right.

Foch had been sent by Joffre to study Haig's method of attack at Neuve Chapelle. D.H. says that Foch told him that before the war, he and the French Staff had never investigated Flanders as a possible theatre of war. They had studied every part of France and Germany, but had never imagined that the French Army would have to fight in Flanders.

We have not yet got full news of the fighting round Ypres. I am going up there to-morrow to see the Intelligence people. Apparently the Germans used heavy asphyxiating gas, which they released from their trenches. The wind drifted it on to the French line held by a Territorial division and African troops, which gave way very badly. We have had to send up some troops (Indian Corps) from the First Army to help to restore the situation. So far it does not seem to be very serious, but it may interfere with our plans for the battle next month.

D.H. criticized the French command very severely about it, not so much for being surprised by the use of heavy gas from cylinders—for our own Intelligence in this Corps had no more information than the French—but because they had not apparently allowed for the possibility of any attack at Ypres, and had no plans prepared to meet it. He has very little use for French generals; he thinks them very ignorant of the practical side of war, and that they will not face facts. But the particular fact they had to face this time was that the Germans used a new method, which is very near to, if not absolutely, breaking the Hague Convention, and that the French troops panicked.

April 28. Ypres has been a very sad affair. All this week there has been very fierce fighting with very varying results. We were hopelessly let in by some French Territorials, and have had very heavy losses. We have had to take over some more of the French line, and have not yet regained all the ground that was lost. It will take some considerable time before we get things straight again in that part of the line. It does not, however, immediately concern our own army—except that we must now expect to have the same methods used against us; that is mainly a medical job. As far as I am concerned it involves only another thing to look for in air photos—and fortunately gas preparations are easily distinguishable in these photos—and a careful record of wind currents, for this gas depends entirely upon a favourable wind. We shall of course now have to use gas ourselves, as soon as we can get it going.

The horrible part of it is the slow lingering death of those who are gassed. I saw some hundred poor fellows laid out in the open, in the fore-court of a church, to give them all the air they could get, slowly *drowning* with water in their lungs—a most horrible sight, and the doctors quite powerless. We have fitted out barges as " hospital ships " in the canal—a most comfortable way of moving bad cases. The barges look so picturesque and peaceful moving slowly up and down the sluggish Belgian waterways. In the next great war I think I shall try and get a job as a bargee, and spend my time supported by the tiller of a barge, smoking plug.

Yesterday D.H. expounded the plan of attack for the next big push to Corps Commanders. It follows the general line of the Neuve Chapelle attack, but will be made on a much longer front with three corps, and is to be in conjunction with a big French attack on our right. The date is not yet finally fixed. So far as our information goes at present, we shall have greatly superior forces to the Germans opposite us and should do well. G.H.Q. wants us to get rid of the Indian Corps, who did not apparently do as well as was expected of them at Ypres last week. But they did do very well at Neuve Chapelle, and D.H. has decided to keep them for this next show. They have not yet had as much fighting as the other corps, and are therefore still relatively fresh. Their British units have still a high proportion of regular officers.

I paid a visit to the Ypres area yesterday. There was still heavy artillery firing. Officers who were through the German attack there last week, say the shelling was very bad, worse even than in October. Certainly the whole face of the area has been changed. Ypres is nothing but a collection of ruins. You remember the château which I told you of near Ypres which was our H.Q. then? It also has been destroyed by shell-fire. The whole character of the area immediately behind the trench area has totally changed. One no longer sees troops; the men stow themselves away in houses, barns, sheds, anywhere where there is cover. Horses seem to disappear by a Maskelyne and Cook magic. All that remain are the vast number of motor-lorries, and they rest most of the day and work at night. As one drives through the area, all one sees is a few men loitering about the villages, occasionally a stray company marching up to, or back from, the trench area; a few—very few— horse wagons, and motor ambulances bringing back their burden of aching humanity; long strings of motor-lorries waiting until nightfall to go up with supplies.

The countryside is pretty enough. Nature is still trying to convince us that there is no war, or perhaps that war is vain. All the fields are green, the orchards covered with apple blossom, the wild flowers just beginning to come out. The most peaceful, and therefore now the prettiest parts, are along the canals with their grass roadways on the banks, shaded by long avenues of high trees, barges, picturesque in the distance, grimy rather when near by, still lazily rippling through the water. Often for long periods there is not a sound of war, not a shell bursting, nor an aeroplane scraping its way through the skies. You close your eyes and wonder if it has all been a bad dream. Then a little white puff of smoke appears from nowhere in the skies, and there is the sharp crack of shrapnel, or the heavy angry snort of a heavy shell and you shake yourself and realize that it is indeed 1915, and all Europe is seeking to destroy human life. The long journeys to distant H.Q. are the most pleasant change from the incessant office work.

It is not the length of one's day's work in office that tires one. After all, we have all done nearly as long days of work in peace. There is the strain that every minute's work entails and every decision is vital—really vital—for on each decision depends human life. Perhaps the hardest thing of all is that we cannot share the dangers we send others to endure. That is why those criticisms in the Press of needless casualties are so cruel—they hurt like a blow. And they make decisions more difficult and encourage doubt. Even D.H., who carries all the responsibility in our army, and on whom responsibility tells so little, feels this—at least I think he does, though he says nothing. He is amazing. You can awaken him at night to hear unpleasant news and authorize some important order; he is alert at once, clear-headed and decisive, and asleep again almost before one has left his room.

CHAPTER X

THE SPRING AND SUMMER OF 1915

May 9 (*Sunday*). The curtain has rung up on another act in the great drama. It is a perfectly gorgeous morning, and a great battle has begun. I was on duty last night, but got a couple of hours' sleep from 1 to 3 a.m. The artillery were to begin their bombardment at 5 a.m. so were all on duty at 4.30 a.m. Our H.Q. is some 8 miles behind the front line (Merville) so we could see nothing, and even the sound of the artillery bombardment was very indistinct. The infantry were to attack at 6 a.m. It is 8 a.m. now, and we are still waiting for news—an anxious time. There is nothing we can do. The battle has to be fought by the Corps and Division. If all goes well we shall have no active part to play until nightfall. We should succeed, for we are massing greatly superior numbers against the troops that we know the Germans to have, but much depends upon the artillery. We are using the same methods as at Neuve Chapelle—heavy bombardment for an hour, then assault by the infantry. The French on our right, who are also attacking to-day, have been bombarding for three days. They have plenty of ammunition. But we hope to get " surprise." So far as we know the Germans had no idea that we were going to attack, whereas the long French bombardment has prepared them for attack from that quarter.

Somehow it seems strange, on this Sunday morning, to see the French people going to chapel just as if there were no battle, till one remembers that they know nothing of what is going on. The French womenfolk are a curious type ; they dress in solemn black in the early Sunday morning, go to Mass looking as demure as a pack of Puritans. That duty over, they change their raiment with all celerity, and their interest with equal rapidity runs from the religious to the purely secular task of ogling everything in trousers that comes their way. It is human nature of course—all the world over—but it is strange with the guns shaking the windows, and the first wounded just beginning to arrive.

May 11. Our attack has failed, and failed badly, and with heavy casualties. That is the bald and most unpleasant fact. No one is to blame—at least no one in France. We had not enough ammunition, and much of what we had was defective. The bombardment had not destroyed the German wire when the infantry attacked, and they could make no progress. The first news that reached me was not bad; the line had gone forward, and some progress had been made. D.H. ordered another attack for midday. He went round the Corps H.Q. himself, and took me with him. Ultimately the second attack did not take place until the afternoon, and it also failed to make any progress. There was a conference in the evening with Corps Commanders, and arrangements made for another attack yesterday, but these were subsequently cancelled.

Though we failed, we are only part of a great battle, and on our right the French have done well; they have advanced 3 miles on a front of about 5 miles. The battle will probably last some weeks more, and we shall attack again, if we can accumulate ammunition enough for an attack, but even this great battle, the greatest so far of the war, will not be decisive. There will, I think, be no decisive battle in this war. We shall win by wearing the Germans down. So far as England is concerned, we have not yet touched the bulk of our strength.

May 16. Another attack yesterday and good news. We made some progress. To-day we have advanced still farther, about 1 mile on a front of 2 miles; we may be able to enlarge the gap to-morrow. We may have something big to record in a few days' time, but so far I am afraid it is all dwarfed by the Russian defeat in the Carpathians.

May 17. To-day a German battalion tried to surrender *en bloc*. The Germans at once turned some artillery on to them, and practically wiped them out.

May 18. Only 2 hours' sleep in the last 48 hours, since 4 a.m. this morning until now, 6 a.m. We made progress yesterday; it is terribly slow work and expensive in life. We are really only pushing on to assist the big French attack on our left, and not in the hope of accomplishing anything very big ourselves. But we widened the gap a good deal in the main German trench line. One cannot measure results by the amount of advance. Our operations are rather like an icebound ship breaking its way to open waters. Even a little progress may bring her ever nearer the weaker ice.

The weather has gone against us. It has rained pretty continuously the last two days, and the ground is a quagmire again. To-day the barometer is rising.

You say the last casualty list is appalling—and so it is, but I am afraid it is nothing to what England must face before we win through. Remember, we have now nearly ten times as many troops as we had in the stormy days of last autumn. The list must go up as more troops are engaged. In the last three weeks we have lost 50,000. Germany has stood an average monthly loss of more than that since the beginning of the war. We shall have to face and endure as big losses as Germany before we win.

May 25. The battle is over so far as we are concerned, and we can take stock. It is not a satisfactory stock-taking for us in the First Army. We have not done nearly as well as we had hoped to do, and our casualties are heavier than we had anticipated. On the other hand, the essential feature of the battle was that it was only one part of a great offensive. We did our part by holding the Germans down to the ground in front of us, while the French, who had larger forces engaged than we had, fought their way forward on our right. Not a very noble part for the British Army to play, but in the next battle the rôles may be reversed.

Our artillery was ineffective, due to lack of ammunition and faulty ammunition. It is deplorable that a great country like England cannot keep the small army we have here, even now, supplied with ammunition. No one, since the war began, is at fault. It is the penalty of starving the army in the years of peace. The politicians will try to blame the soldiers, to save their own reputations, but it is not the fact that the W.O. have failed. The Master-General of the Ordnance from the War Office was out here in February and told me of what he had done. Now Lloyd George becomes Minister of Munitions—a paradox, for he was the greatest economy-monger before the war—and will do all he can to undo the mischief of his pre-war policy.

The most satisfactory feature of the battle is the way the reconstituted units fought. They are not as good as the old regulars, but they are wonderfully good stuff, and the new officers, if not so well trained, are just as determined and brave as the regulars. The mechanism of the Staff worked well, there was no repetition of the clogging of Neuve Chapelle. If, as now seems inevitable, the war is going to last for a long time, the New Army will be just as good as regulars. The great difference we note, is that orders, instead of being brief and only general directions, have now to be in great detail.

There was a very nasty incident last week; one of our best observation posts was shelled to pieces. This was directly traceable to an article by Repington in *The Times*, when he gave away the situation of the post. His article was not submitted for censorship here; the immediate result is that D.H. ordered that no correspondent is to be allowed to go to the front during fighting. I think this is a mistake. The answer should have been far stricter censorship of the correspondents' writings, and no permission for them to go back to England until the battle is over.

The strange thing is that the only fully trained military correspondent should have been the one who let us in. Repington is a law unto himself, overweeningly conceited, and with a dulled sense of honour. Still, I cannot imagine he did this intentionally, for there was not any purpose to be served. But rumour here says that he is working hand in glove with French—which means Wilson—to get rid of K., who will have nothing to say to either of them.

About the censorship there is one delightful true story. A correspondent waxing poetical quoted Kipling's "The captains and the kings depart." The Censor blue-pencilled the quotation with the note "Movements of H.M. must not be referred to."

F. E. Smith and Neil Primrose, who were "Eye-witnesses" with the Indian Corps, also failed. They wrote an article giving away all manner of information, and were replaced by a dear old Indian colonel, who could not write for toffee. Among the present gang of professional correspondents who are out here permanently, is Valentine Williams, who was working for the *D.M.* in Vienna when I was working for *The Times*. He lunched with me, and I sent him on to the front, where he spent the night in the trenches. He wants to get a commission, and I think he should. He would make an excellent officer. I would like to have him with me for he knows Germany and the Germans, together with their language, very well. But he wants to fight with a battalion—all honour to him for it.

A telephone message has just come in that the London Territorials have taken three trenches in a little attack—a feather in their cap, for some regulars, who are more tired and stale, tried to take these trenches and failed last week. It is very encouraging, for it is units like these "Terriers" that will form the bulk of our army next year. That, and the fact that the French are now fighting splendidly, are the most encouraging things out here.

We should not be worrying out here about what happens at home, and indeed we do not, but I cannot help being glad that Winston has left the Admiralty. The fleet has done so little so far. The Dardanelles seems the blackest spot on the whole war picture. We do not know whether Churchill or Fisher was responsible. We hear that Fisher was nearly off his head a short time ago. But anyhow as you know, I have never had much belief in Churchill. He is so glib, and his judgments seem always wrong. He has always such a perfect explanation, like a child with the inevitable excuse that you cannot break down, but know to be untrue.

June 1. The Prime Minister has been here all day. I lunched with D.H. to meet him, and then D.H. sent him down to my office, and he pumped me about our Intelligence system, and our views of the Germans. I had not seen him since he was at Aldershot as War Minister after the Ulster crisis. I told him about the jest we had when he was upsetting our time-table by an unduly prolonged private interview. Hamilton said nothing would end the interview except the prospect of refreshment and proceeded to make a noise like drawing the cork out of a bottle, which had been immediately effective. Responsibility does not seem to have weighed much on the P.M. Certainly it has not aged him. He gave me the impression of dependability more than of strength. But one thing is certain, he is a Sahib and will never let anyone down. He gave great praise to D.H. and to the First Army.

He was so kind and friendly, that one forgot in talking to him that he was Prime Minister. Generally he gave me the impression of being optimistic about the issue. He had lunched well when he came to me and was smoking a big cigar, which he turned over in his lips whenever he wanted to think out what question he was going to ask, and always before answering any question one ventured to ask him. He invited me at the end of the interview, which lasted an hour, to ask him anything I thought he could tell me, so I asked " Why not conscription to give us the men we need ? " His reply was, " Would men, without arms and guns and ammunition, help ? " So *that* was *that*.

His secretary was very consoling about the Dardanelles. I hope he was right, but I doubt it.

Your respirator has not come. But I have received one from the Empress Eugénie—a handsome swell affair that covers the whole face, with goggles to look through.

French G.Q.G. told me a few days ago that they think the war will end in October, and that after that there will be a long occupation of German territory. If the Germans did not deserve all and more than can be given to them, I could find it in my heart to pity them if France occupies their territory. The French are bitter—no wonder—and will be vindictive in repaying in full measure all their own country has suffered, both in 1870 and in this war. I enclose as a curiosity a French paper published in Lille.

Yesterday, I was examining a German prisoner who had been at Cambridge University. He would, of course, say nothing about military matters, but talked very freely about Germany. He says the Germans hate and despise the French, hate and fear us, hate and laugh at the Russians. I asked him if there was anyone they did not hate, to which he replied the Americans. He said that educated Germans now knew that they could not win the war, but that on the other hand they could not be beaten. When I pointed out that Germany was already using old men in the ranks, he quite fairly answered so were the French, and added even the women will fight rather than let Germany be conquered. I asked him whether Germany still believed in the Kaiser, to which he replied, " Rulers did not matter, it was the people." He would not admit any shortage of anything in Germany itself.

June 5. We have changed our H.Q. (Choques) and are now in a very comfortable château. My office, bedroom and mess, are all in the same building. The mess has started a great flirtation with the two daughters of the household, aged 7 and 8, and you would laugh to see the whole Staff playing hide-and-seek in the garden for half an hour after lunch. To-day, a 15-year-old sister joined in, and presented me with the medal which I send with this.

I had a day of spy-hunting with a Scotland Yard man and a French detective. The Scotland Yard man is a full-faced, rather dull-looking creature, very slow thinking, but quick to act; the French sleuth, a bundle of nerves, sharp-witted, keen as mustard, but not always logical. The two had got across one another, so I went out with them, trying to make myself look as much like Sherlock Holmes as I could. Between us we ran our quarry to earth, a little gang of three, and they are now safely in French hands. They had been making quite elaborate notes of our formations, but had not any means of transferring their information to the Germans, except by the ordinary civilian post to a collecting centre in a neutral country. They had not done much harm, and we got very valuable information from them which the French will have to use. It is out of our hands now.

June 11. The waves of war wash up unexpected flotsam from the wreck of pre-war politics. The latest are two thorough-paced Socialists, Ben Tillett and Bruhl (from Paris). D.H. saw them first, very dignified and correct. The Grand Seigneur personified. He then handed them over to me. We had been warned that both Tillett and Bruhl were strongly anti-militarist, and would be on the look-out for any sign of being shepherded. We never had the least wish to conceal anything, but to enforce this D.H. gave me specific orders, while they were present, that they were to be shown everything they wanted. I took them back to my office, and as it was a very hot day, I suggested we should all be more comfortable in our shirt-sleeves. We soon became quite friendly. I crossed the T's and dotted the I's of D.H.'s orders by telling the officer who was to take them round that the only restriction to their movements was that they must not draw fire on the troops, and that they were to be warned whenever they were going into personal danger, but not prevented from going if they cared to take the risk. Further, that if they wanted to talk to any men without an officer being present, they were to be allowed to do so, and regimental officers were to be told so. I told them I would see them if they wished when they had finished their trip, and they could then let me know if these orders were not fully carried out. When they did see me at the end of their visit, they were both most friendly and impressed by what they had seen. Tillett said the men had nothing but praise to give to their officers, and he himself thought them "the finest fellows he had ever seen."

I hope it all bears fruit when they get back to England. I believe it will. As you know, I have not the least fear that the real working men of England will not play up, and the Labour party and trade union leaders in the main are just as loyal and patriotic as any others. I exclude Ramsay MacDonald and those of his kidney, but these are not working men in the real sense of the term, and not in the least likely to attract a following so long as we are fighting a foreign nation for a great cause. The more we can get representatives of all classes of society, and particularly the "bell-wethers" of public opinion, to see things out here, the better for us all. We have nothing to be ashamed of and nothing to hide. Unless we have the nation with us, and believing in us, we may just as well give up at once.

We are planning another small operation to help the French, who are still pegging away at their big attack to the south of us. It will be quite a small affair, for we have not enough ammunition for serious attack. I went out last night to one of the divisions which will attack, to watch the artillery bombardment and the German reply to it. The beauty of it all made me almost forget it was war. We had been shelling the German line all day, and they were obviously very much on the alert and anticipating immediate attack, and were lighting up no-man's land with a steady stream of rockets and star shells, and an occasional coloured signal. The men extract happiness from little things that under other circumstances would be commonplace trivialities—dry sleeping-place, a good dinner, a song sung in chorus, even the removal of insects from their garments.

Of this latter pleasure there is an amusing yarn. A distinguished general, who inspires terror as well as confidence in those under him, paid a surprise visit to a unit in reserve, and found some elderly soldier performing the necessary but unpleasant operation of delousing his garments. Thoroughly pleased, the general addressed the man cheerily : " Well, my man, picking out the lice ? " To which he got the reply, " No, sir, just taking 'em as they come."

June 18. We have had our little attack, and it has failed. We had departed from the Neuve Chapelle plan of infantry attack after a short bombardment, and adopted the French system of a long bombardment. The Germans were well prepared, and though we got into their line at several places, we could not make progress or even hold what we had gained, and are back in our own front-line trenches. There are three reasons for this failure—not enough artillery, the Germans had excellent deep dug-outs that our fire could not reach, and in the middle the French on our left asked for assistance to meet a German counter-attack. Of these, the vital one was the second, the deep German dug-out. The Germans are admirable military engineers. We must expect better and better defences as time goes on, unless we attack constantly and keep them occupied.

Esher paid us another visit, and I had a long talk with him. He tells me that the French are very optimistic that the war will end in the autumn ; Lord K., on the other hand, says it must last another year at least. As against this a senior officer from French G.Q.G. says the French people are getting tired of the war, and there is a universal desire for a great effort to end it this year. Esher says opinion at home is sharp against the Dardanelles, and that the

French are very bitter about that theatre also. Our own G.H.Q. says that the War Office are very pleased about the Dardanelles, though why, Heaven alone knows.

Esher says that in "political circles" there is considerable speculation as regards the length of Sir J. French's period of command, and as to his probable successor. "Political circles" with Esher probably means K. of K. himself. There has apparently been much more friction between French and K. than we know; obviously K. must resent French's incursion into the Press on the munition question.

Esher's most important statement, however, was his definite view that we must anticipate a total collapse by Russia. He does not appear to have any definite information, but is convinced Russia will not hold out. We have been expecting to hear of Germany sending back troops from East to West, but so far there is no sign of that. Rumania, though still shy of fighting, will eventually come in, and Bulgaria may; that will mean some withdrawal of German troops from one or other theatre. Neither Salonika nor the Dardanelles has drawn away a single division.

Meantime the French are fighting hard and well on our left. We ourselves can do little or nothing until we get more ammunition. That will not be for another month or six weeks at earliest, but we are told that then it will be all right, and that we shall have as much as we can shoot.

June 24. You will have seen that I have been given the D.S.O. I was quite pleased until D.H. entirely spoilt it by telling me he had put me up for a brevet Lt.-Colonelcy, and that he was annoyed that I had been given the D.S.O. instead. General Hobbs supplemented this by telling me that D.H. was still pressing for the brevet for me—so I may get it after all. A brevet would be much more useful to me, for I am constantly dealing with senior officers, and some look askance at a mere major.

The kaleidoscope of war gave another quite paradoxical view to-day. The Indian cavalry, who are well in the back area, staged a Horse Show at a little place with a natural amphitheatre (Estreblanche). It was so utterly out of place—some 20 miles from the front-line trenches, where the infantry are cheek by jowl with the Germans, and the French just finishing off an enormous battle next door to us. And then a Simla horse show with French military bands playing music to us! Every one of the competitors, and most of the spectators, beautifully turned out; all the horses' harness polished till it shone in the bright sun, motor-cars grouped round the ring, subalterns—and even generals—flirting with young women in neat uniforms, a tent with drinks and Indian mess servants. All the same, it was very enjoyable, though it made one wonder whether cavalry that had time for this sort of Tamasha were of much use in modern war. I only had time to stay an hour, as I had to go up to Ypres, where the Second Army had some fighting last week and had gained some ground.

I have a new addition to my staff in the person of Lord Onslow. He will go to the Belgian Army to keep touch there, as soon as he has learnt his job. He was private secretary to Sir E. Grey, and is well up in all political circles at home. He tells me K. is having a very difficult time with the Cabinet. Lloyd George wants to oust him and become the popular War Lord, which is amusing, considering L.G.'s pre-war exploits. He also tells me that Bulgaria may come in against us, and possibly also Sweden.

Meantime we hear that the Cabinet and the W.O. want to send still more troops to the Dardanelles, and even to give up the Channel ports. D.H. is writing to urge that Calais must be held as a bridgehead at all costs. We have also been working out the strength required for a big attack on a 25-mile front, based on our First Army experience. The result is 30 divisions, and 1,100 heavy guns.

July 4. An old Indian friend, Sir Harcourt Butler, has just been staying with D.H. on his way to become Lt.-Governor of the United Provinces in India. I stayed with D.H. during his visit to show him what there was to see. He was mainly interested in the mechanism of G.H.Q. He said that there was no weakening of our prestige in India owing to war against Turkey. We discussed the Mesopotamian campaign, and the risk of too deep an advance there. So long as it was Indian Army, with a sprinkling of British troops, no harm could come of it, but if it involved British troops and much ammunition it was a serious blunder. D.H. was very strong on the necessity of reconstituting the General Staff at the W.O. to prevent wild-cat schemes being adopted to please politicians.

July 9. D.H. saw K. yesterday, and tells me K. went very fully into the difficulties he had had with Sir J. French, and had said that he, K., was ready to do anything even to " blacking French's boots, in order to get agreement." Apparently they are now on quite satisfactory terms with one another and everything points to a big offensive in August, which the First Army will make in conjunction with the French. We have been working at this for some time. The French want us to attack immediately on their left flank, that means well to the south of where we are at present. Some of us have been down to look at this area, and as far as we are concerned at First Army, not one of us likes it.

D.H. is pressing that we should attack near Neuve Chapelle again, and make sure of getting the high ground there. Personally, I am urging an attack still farther north, where the German supply lines are least direct, and ours are easiest, and where they least expect attack, but anywhere would be better than on the immediate left of the French. It is a mining area there, and the Germans have all the advantage of position. They have very strong defensive lines which they are steadily increasing. The decision rests with G.H.Q., but it must be made soon if we are to get ready in time to attack this year.

July 17. The worst of going on leave is that on one's return one finds everything piled up waiting for disposal. Perhaps it is as well, for it prevents too much rumination on leave and farewells. The B.E.F. is again being reorganized. We are forming a Third Army with Sir C. Monro in command. The New Army Staff are coming to us to learn the working of an Army H.Q. D.H. is back from leave. He says he spent most of it playing golf.

Things will be quiet here a little longer, as no definite decision has been made about our next big attack. G.H.Q. and G.Q.G. are still wrangling about it. The big part of the fighting will be by the French; we have not yet got either troops or ammunition to take the main part in any attack.

Esher has been here again. He is very optimistic about everything, except the Welsh coal strike, where the miners seem determined to do their best to ruin us. I cannot believe the men are really unpatriotic. If they are so throughout the country, we had better make what terms we can now and end the war, for we shall not win it unless the country plays up.

August 1. We were visited by the members of L.G.'s Ammunition Committee, who are by way of being responsible for the supply of ammunition. God help us! One of them wanted to know whether we still used much round cannon ball! I told him he would find the last one fired in war in this part of Europe at Lillers, where it had been embedded in a church wall for nearly 200 years;

that settled *him*. He asked no more questions. Another sought information as to the difference between high-explosive and common shell! Still, if they provide the men and the money to make the stuff, and don't interfere with the type of shell that is made, they will help.

Lord Haldane was here yesterday, and came down to my office after lunch. He was most expansive and most interesting about his last pilgrimage to his spiritual home. The gist of it was that Bethmann Hollweg was a genuine pacifist there and wanted peace. Tirpitz was all for war. The Kaiser neutral. He said that all four of them, including himself, realized quite clearly that we were steadily drifting towards war, and Bethmann Hollweg was genuinely trying to find some way to avoid it. Haldane said he knew for a fact that neither Bethmann Hollweg nor his Foreign Minister ever saw the ultimatum which Austria sent to Serbia. The Kaiser and Tirpitz did see it and approved of it. I reminded him of our conversation at Aldershot in 1912, when he had said that it was the task of the statesmen to avoid war, as the excuse for the Government not making more preparation for the war that even then was inevitable to my mind. He remembered this, and said that even then he had honestly expected *we* could avoid it. Actually I suppose it was because the Government could not face the unpopularity of further taxation for the Services. Can *any* Government ever do so, except when war has begun?

Haldane was very optimistic of the issue. He is on a sub-Committee of the Council of Imperial Defence that is engaged in watching and estimating the effect of German casualties, and their available man-power, and tells me their estimate was 2,500,000 casualties out of an available 8 million.

The news from Russia is bad; Warsaw is bound to fall.

To-day I was at the Indian Corps, and then on to the Ypres area to investigate the new devilry that the Germans have introduced—liquid fire. It was apparently very terrifying, but did little harm. The attack was on our old Head-quarters in October, Hooge Château. The fire came like a stream of water out of a kind of hosepipe, with a bright flame, followed by a thick black smoke-cloud. The first use of this, accompanied by very heavy fire, lost us some trenches—but afterwards when the Germans tried them again, the men carrying them were shot down quite easily before they could be used. I do not think they will have much effect in any attack in future—but they would be very difficult to deal with if used from strong points in defence. We have not yet captured one of the instruments and do not know how much stuff can be carried, or how long the charge will last.

The Germans keep the secrets of their various new forms of "frightfulness" very well. We hear from prisoners that something new is coming along—nothing more. And as most prisoners tell us this, often without any foundation in fact, it is difficult to know when the warning is a real one. We have been lucky in both the 1st Corps and First Army and have not yet been caught by any surprise "frightfulness," but it is only by our good luck, for all information is pooled, and either gas or liquid fire might just as well have been found first opposite us.

It becomes more and more difficult to keep personal contact with the troops in the front line. As the size of the army increases there are necessarily more Corps and Divisional H.Q. which one must visit at frequent intervals, and that leaves less time for trips to forward units. I had one long day in the front-line trenches last week, investigating a "spy" rumour. It was reported that there was a system whereby news-runners were getting across into the German lines. There was nothing in the report, but it gave me an excuse for spending a day in the front line. Everyone is so eager to get authentic information.

The problem of what news to send forward to one's own troops, and how to send it, is most difficult. If you tell them bad news, it may depress them. If you tell *only* good news, it is naturally suspect. If you send it in writing, someone may carry it with him into action and it may find its way into German hands. If you send it by word of mouth, it is certain to be distorted. Yet the men in the trenches naturally and rightly do want news. The best thing would be a *Daily Mail* issue, reasonably well informed, but without any official status. Only it would have to be less imaginative, and bear a closer resemblance to fact than does the *Daily Mail* itself.

CHAPTER XI

PRELIMINARY TO LOOS

August 7. There was a big conference at G.H.Q. to-day, at which it was announced that our First Army argument in favour of an attack on Aubers Ridge, instead of alongside the French and south of La Bassée, was overruled in deference to urgent representations by General Joffre. So we are to attack in the latter area. Hill 70, near Loos, is to be our immediate objective. It will be a difficult and costly business, and not nearly so effective as our own scheme. The main fight is to be by the French, and they have the right to ask us to attack where they think it will help them most. All the same, they are wrong. We would help them more by attacking where we would draw most German reserves against us. In any circumstances this attack cannot be decisive. Nothing but a miracle can now end the war before next winter, and our line between Neuve Chapelle and La Bassée will still be in the water-logged area next winter.

After the G.H.Q. conference, I went to the H.Q. of the French army with which we attack, to discuss the available information with its Intelligence man. Their Intelligence system is not nearly as thorough as our own. They have no representative with the smaller units, and nothing like as complete a picture of the German defences as we have of them in our area. They gave me particulars of the whole French plans for the big attack—27 divisions in Champagne, 13 divisions in Artois, with our own half-dozen divisions on their left. The Germans may try to upset this gigantic plan by forestalling it with an attack of their own. I do not think it likely, but if they do, they will certainly strike again for Calais, which, if successful, would be very nearly decisive. We could hardly maintain our present army, and certainly could not augment it, if all supplies had to come via Havre.

I have a very nice new summer office; two large, very light and airy huts, erected under some splendid trees. My bedroom is in the château where D.H. has his H.Q.

War gives pictures of such strange contrasts. Yesterday I was at Ypres. There was very little activity, and I spent an hour going round my old haunts. It was such utter desolation. Here and there a few crops had straggled through, and the men were helping to harvest in the area quite close to the line. Hardly any of our various H.Q.s in the battle of Ypres still remain even recognizable. All the grim, fierce cruelty of war at its worst.

To-day I have been out all day interviewing French mining engineers and mine managers, getting full details of the underground workings of a mine that runs underneath no-man's land and connects with pit-heads on ours and the German side of the country. Then I went on to a gunner observation post, where we had a splendid view of the German trenches. Everything was quite peaceful. Not a gun firing anywhere near. The French farmers were cutting their corn within half a mile of the front line. Over on the German side we could see through telescopes the villagers there working in the fields. You had to shake yourself and make yourself believe that it was really 1915 and we were at war. Then suddenly away in the distance there appeared an aeroplane. We heard it before we saw it. It came over the lines and was followed by some half-dozen German shells at longish intervals of time, spilling great columns of earth and smoke into the air. Some German guns were registering. A few more minutes and the aeroplane turned back, and the shelling ceased. Everything was quiet, and not a peasant had even looked round.

August 20. We have had an official visit from K. He carries his load easily enough, so far as one can judge. There is little outward difference in him since he was in India. He was much more communicative than had been expected. D.H. tackled him about compulsory service, on the ground that men were not forthcoming in sufficient numbers, that we must expect very heavy casualties, that the French Army was getting near the end of its possibilities in man-power, and that from now on the British Army would be the decisive factor. If Russia cracked, the French Army could not keep on attacking much longer, and if there was a long hiatus between the end of the big French attack and the development to its full power of our own army, there would be very real danger of a big German attack achieving great results, and possibly resulting in a compromise peace.

K.'s reply was most interesting. As regards the past, he said that voluntary enlistment had got the best of the nation in as large numbers as could be armed and trained. If conscription had been introduced last year, it would have had to be on an age contingent basis, and would have got men neither physically nor morally the equal of his volunteers. He admitted that the supply of volunteers was necessarily now weakening, and might not suffice, but if conscription were now introduced, the politicians in Parliament would insist on so many exceptions that it would not give the men required either in numbers or in quality. A national register of men was now being taken, and he would not take any action until that was completed. But he seemed to argue the case against conscription without much belief in his own arguments. He said several times that it was a *political* question, which had to be decided on political grounds. D.H. was very emphatic in his view that it should be introduced at once, even if not fully enforced, so as to be ready for eventualities, and the difficulty of exemption would increase and not diminish the longer it was deferred.

All this was before lunch. D.H. had asked me to lunch with him and K., and afterwards K. came down to my office, and spent more than two hours there. He went into every bit of our Intelligence work, and then discussed the general situation. He said that in his own view the Russians had been so badly beaten that it was doubtful whether they would go on fighting if the German pressure were continued, and repeated Esher's argument that Russia had never yet fought a war to the bitter end. He therefore thought it right that both the French and our attack should be pressed to the uttermost, even though we suffered very heavy casualties. He did not seem to expect for a moment that the French and our attack would be decisive, and talked about what would have to be done next summer. But he has no doubt at all about the ultimate result. K. is always impressive, but I think this time he was more impressive than usual. It is ten thousand pities that he is not in supreme control at home. He would know what to do, and would do it. I am sure the country would accept from him far more stringent orders and laws than from any of the politicians, whom they have been taught to criticize from their earliest youth.

At the end of the interview, he told me he was going to make me a brevet Lt.-Colonel at once, as the result of D.H.'s representations. Fitzgerald was with K. He was with me at Quetta and showed me the letter D.H. had sent to K. about me.

In contrast to K.'s' views, there is an extraordinary vein of exuberant optimism running through French G.Q.G. just now. They say that Germany is on the verge of cracking, and that

PRELIMINARY TO LOOS 1915

Russia is very well pleased with the situation—though there seems precious little for Russia to be pleased with. Anyhow, the French are very hopeful—more than hopeful that the big attack next month will send the whole German line back for 50 miles. If so, it will be their attack, not ours, for we have only 6 divisions attacking and not nearly enough guns for even these 6 divisions.

August 24. By some blunder one of our colliers was sunk right athwart the Boulogne Harbour fairway. All traffic is diverted to Calais until she can be removed or demolished. The Navy are undertaking this job.[1]

September 7. Our plans are progressing but changing. There was a big conference here yesterday—38 generals in one room! —at which D.H. expounded his plans. As at all the conferences, the proceedings begin with a summary of what is known about the general situation and the German in particular; this D.H. makes me give. So far as our immediate front is concerned, everything promises well. There are not more than 15 battalions (probably only 13) holding the line that we shall attack with our 6 divisions. These may, of course, increase between now and the attack, but not appreciably, as the Germans will be fully employed meeting the French attack. We are to use poison gas—if we get favourable wind. So far as we know the Germans opposite us have no respirators. Even with our small proportion of artillery, we have more than the Germans on our front. The general plan is to rush the attack—as the Germans did at Ypres, only more so. D.H. is pressing for more divisions from G.H.Q.—reserves to be put at his disposal, so that if we get on well at once, there should not be delay in taking advantage of the success, as appears to have happened to the Germans at Ypres. But G.H.Q. is making difficulties. In theory it should not make much difference whether the Reserve divisions are under us or under G.H.Q. provided they are available, but even with telephone and telegraph, orders are slow to get through and every minute is vital in battle.

At the conference the Indian Corps made difficulties, and were very roughly dealt with by D.H.

We are getting quite a number of deserters from the Germans. I am not quite sure what it means. It may be because they know of the impending attack and cannot face it, or simply the approach of winter. Anyhow, it enables us to check up our information

[1] Eventually the wreck was removed by the Royal Engineers.

of the German units in front of us. The number will probably increase as the attack gets closer. But the strange thing is that they are not going over to the French in anything like the same way. It may be because the Germans know that prisoners are better treated by us than by the French.

A sergeant in the Argyll and Sutherland Highlanders bagged a prisoner a few days ago after a go of fisticuffs between the lines in full view of both trenches; nobody fired at them until they had settled their little personal quarrel, and then the Jock got his man back unscathed.

D.H. was rather amusing yesterday about a certain Territorial colonel, whom he described as a " sad-looking man who only brightens up at the thought of a fight "—and added " that's the sort we want."

The news from Russia is very bad—worse even than we had last year. I hope they may be able to pull themselves together again as quickly as the French and we did, but I am afraid there is very little chance of it, and we must give up all hope of a peaceful spring and summer next year. If Russia collapses, the Germans will bring back their armies from the East, and our task will be far harder. But even then they will hardly have enough to attack in the West with any hope of success. The remainder of the war should be, *us* attacking and finally defeating Germany in the West.

This day last year was the battle of the Marne. I remember it all so clearly. The old army so tired after the retreat—the men's spirits at their lowest. The Staffs dog-tired and dispirited. Then came the order to turn and fight—like a tonic to us all. And all the next week the exhilarating pursuit with little scraps each day, many prisoners, and ever-increasing signs of demoralization in the Germans. We had high hopes then, and they were disappointed. It makes one chary of too high hopes this year, and for this next fight.

The Intelligence Staff keeps on increasing. During the last few weeks it has grown greatly. My chief assistant, Lumsden,[1] is a Marine major, many years older than I am. Then there is Wilkinson, a senior Indian civil servant—" on leave from India "—who looks after the detectives; Romer, a barrister, runs the mapping section assisted by a young civil engineer. H. does sort of secretary to me. His military experience before the war was the charge of a Boys' Brigade somewhere or other, but he has developed a great aptitude for the work, and is becoming most useful. The chief clerk is

[1] Major Lumsden, who subsequently earned the V.C., and was killed when in command of a brigade.

a full-fledged solicitor. A professor from Birmingham University runs the chemical department, which is getting very important, and a meteorological expert, Gold, has now joined up to keep us wise regarding wind and weather prospects. The French detective staff for contre-espionage has also grown, but that is the lighter side of the work and gives me many a laugh. Mostly they are hunting hares. For every unit is prolific in spy scares, and each has to be fully investigated.

All these work at Head-quarters. Out with the units we have a regular officer with each Corps, and most of the divisions, and temporaries with the other divisions. The whole organization is working very smoothly as regards collecting information, but the giving out to our own units is still cumbersome and unsatisfactory.

There are times when all one's mind is filled with nothing but the conviction of the awful waste that is the very essence of war. Waste of everything—waste of lives, of money, of property, most of all waste of time, for the whole progress of the world is at a standstill. Will there be another war after this one? I hope not. Surely the world will have had enough of destruction. But human nature does not change. It will be a chastened world for a few years after the war—a world with less wealth, less luxury, less selfishness. Yet human memories are short. In ten years' time the suffering will be forgotten. There will be new interests, new ambitions, new rivalries, new hates and probably new wars. An Indian frontier show gives peace for a decade. Then the trouble begins again. Will it be the same in Europe?

September 20. (*At Paris.*) These allies of ours have the most amazing vitality. If it were not for the wounded that are everywhere, it would be difficult to believe that Paris was the capital of a country at war, and with a large part of its territory overrun by an enemy. For Paris is still gay. Far more like the normal Paris of peace-time than London is like pre-war London. Hotels, shops, amusements, cafés, show very little change from peace Paris. But a very different Paris from that I saw a year ago, when there seemed a real prospect of a siege. It is not mere light-heartedness, for everyone you talk to knows far more about the war than do our Londoners. Nor is it foolish optimism, for they all seem to appreciate how serious the situation is. It is really just vitality, and a logical course of conduct. The logic that things are not made easier by being gloomy, that is wise to take pleasure in such compensation as offers, that after all the scales are weighted in our and their favour, an immense conviction that justice and France (but particularly France) will prevail. No one but a fool could help admiring them.

But there is a danger in their logic. For if they ever become convinced that decisive victory is impossible or even improbable, they will want to make a compromise peace with what speed they may. I do not think Britain will ever accept a compromise peace. We will fight to a finish. The more improbable decisive victory, the more determined we will become to achieve it. A great defeat in battle would shake France, possibly into a compromise peace—it would shake England into giving her last man and her last penny to win. Indeed, England now *requires* a defeat, and France requires a *success*, to hasten the ultimate effort that will win.

I wish I could see Berlin and judge for myself how Germany is shaping. No other person's opinion can ever give complete conviction to one's mind.

CHAPTER XII

BATTLE OF LOOS

September 21. I got back from Paris just in time to see K. who had arrived very unexpectedly at Hinges. On the way back I stopped at French G.Q.G. (Chantilly) to see their IIme Bureau (Intelligence). They are more interested in the Champagne attack than in Foch's effort in Artois. In Champagne they have a very great superiority both of guns and men, not less than five to one, and the ground is far better for attack; there are no villages. The weak point is that unless *both* attacks succeed, the Champagne attack leads nowhere. It does not strike at the German main communications and, unless the Artois attack makes great progress, will only bend back the German line. It is much the same with the Artois attack; if it succeeds and the Champagne attack does not, unless we reach Valenciennes we do not seriously threaten the German railways.

K. had been impressing on D.H. the political importance of success at the present time. There are apparently grave political difficulties at home. K. is now quite weaned from any idea that success in any other theatre than France can be decisive, and has ordered everything to be done to help the French attack.

Meantime there is very serious friction with G.H.Q. about the reserves. G.H.Q. refuses to put them under First Army, or even to move them well forward. It is too late now to hope for any change. Our bombardment commenced to-day, and then the heavy rumble of distant gun-fire. The aeroplane reports are good, but we cannot tell definitely how successful we have been until the air photographs are developed. Obscure reports are never fully reliable. We have certainly done some good work, for there was a tremendous explosion in the German lines a few hours ago that made the houses rock, even as far back as this place. Probably an enemy ammunition dump has been destroyed.

September 23. I was out most of yesterday going round the

units that are to attack and seeing the preparations. The air photos of the first two days' bombardment show very good results. The German guns were not firing much, and the gunners think they have silenced many of them, but probably a good number are still serviceable and are only holding their fire. The weather has been fine, but such wind as there is, is not at all suitable for our gas. All the men and officers are in excellent spirits; the strength of our bombardment and the small reply of the Germans have heartened them greatly. Some of the divisions have been trying by means of feint attacks to get the Germans to man their parapet and come under shrapnel fire. One of them, at which I happened to be present, was quite successful as far as we could judge. To-day it is misty, but the wind is veering to the direction we want. I hope it continues, so much depends on it.

Indeed, everything seems to point to success; we count and recount the chances, and all seems to point to the same conclusion. I pray it may be so. In war so much is uncertain. Fate, chance, luck—call it what you will—plays such an enormous part. Have we overlooked anything? So far there have been no surprises for us. The Germans have not brought up more units, no guns that we had not marked down have opened fire. Our own arrangements have moved smoothly and up to time. This afternoon some buildings far away in the German lines were set on fire by our guns, and the whole sky is still aglow with the light from them.

Whatever the issue of the battle, the casualty list will be huge. That is the sad part of it. And if any of us have made an error in our work, it will mean more lives. If we have failed it is not due to want of thought or lack of work. Whatever the casualty list may be, the end we are fighting for is worth the loss.

September 24. 11.30 *a.m.* Before this reaches you another great battle—greater than any we have yet been engaged in—will have begun. To-night is the eve of the commencement. At dawn the First Army begins the attack, and by noon the whole line, French and British, will be engaged. If we are successful, it will go far to rid the world of the weight of war. So much is uncertain, we cannot count the chances with any degree of accuracy. We have laid our plans with what care and skill we can; the issue remains with God. It is very solemn and very sad. Yet I am confident we shall win—if not in this battle, yet in the end.

We have been very hard at it all day—revising, going over again and again every little detail. I was with Sir Douglas for a final consultation, after dinner, taking to him the last weather reports that Gold then had. After it was over we went for a stroll in the garden, climbed the Watch Tower [1] and watched the flash of the guns all along the sky-line, and the innumerable flares and rockets turning night into day in the trenches. Sir Douglas carries an enormous weight of responsibility. None could carry it more bravely or better. We of the Staff are, after all, only advisers; he makes the decisions and bears the real weight. He is satisfied that as far as the army is concerned everything possible has been done—except the three Reserve divisions. They are too far back. If our first attack gets through we shall want them at once. It is the first real break between him and Sir J. French. Last week D.H. might have asked Kitchener to overrule French, and I am sure K. would have done so. I wish he had. It is so vital. But, after all, it *may* go all right.

When I left him the weather reports were bad. The wind had changed and was blowing from the enemy's trenches. Gold says it will not last; there will either be no wind or one favourable to us. That was only an hour ago. Now D.H. has turned in and I am back in office waiting for better news of the wind. We have been testing Gold's forecasts for the last few weeks by measurements in the army area, and he has generally been dead right. Now his work is over, and we are depending upon actual reports from the line for the decision whether to postpone the gas attack.

September 25. We have had a great fight and a great success so far. There was not a breath of wind until 5 a.m., but before that Gold's reports had become pretty confident that the wind would be favourable. I went to D.H. at 2 a.m., when we had just received a report from distant station that made Gold reasonably hopeful. Our own report from the line was that it was dead still. At 3, when the decision had to be made, I took Gold to Butler and then to D.H. Gold was then more confident and D.H. ordered zero hour for 5.50. Both at 2 and 3 D.H. was fast asleep, and had to be awakened to take the reports.

At 5 he came to our office with Fletcher. There was quite a faint breath of wind then, and Fletcher's cigarette smoke moved

[1] A wooden scaffolding tower had been erected on the top of Sir D. Haig's Head-quarters, from which the front line could be seen.

quite perceptibly towards the Germans. But t died away again in a few minutes, and a little later D.H. sent down a message from the tower to 1st Corps to inquire whether the attack could still be held up.

Gough[1] replied that it was too late to change. I was with D.H. when the reply was brought in. He was very upset. Actually I think Gough was quite right. There would have been great confusion if any attempt had then been made to postpone the attack. Some units would certainly not have got the order and would have attacked; others would have held back. Anyhow, by 7 a.m. we were getting very encouraging messages from both 1st and 4th Corps. Both reported that they were well across the enemy's front-line trenches and pushing on. The question of the Reserve divisions became urgent. At about 9 a.m. a Staff officer brought Sir J. French's congratulations, and was sent back post-haste to urge that the reserves might be handed over to him.

Meantime, there was no sign of the French on our right attacking, and at 10 D.H. sent an urgent message to Foch urging him to attack at once. Actually the French infantry did advance their attack, but even then they did not move until nearly 1 p.m. About noon Sir J. French himself arrived, and said he would go personally to the Reserve divisions and put two of them under First Army, keeping the third and best (the Guards Division) under his own orders. It was not until 2 p.m. that we heard definitely that the Reserve divisions were available, and then it was too late for them to be used to-day. It is such a huge blunder—not ours, thank Heaven—but that is of less importance than the fact that we have lost the best chance we have yet had of getting through. Some of the 4th Corps had penetrated $2\frac{1}{2}$ miles into the German lines, and were then only stopped because there were no fresh troops to support them and carry them forward. Later in the afternoon we heard that our line had not gone as far forward as the first report had said—that always happens; at least it has happened every time we have attacked. Still, we have made a greater advance than has yet been made in France against an entrenched position. We go on again to-morrow with the two new divisions. They are K. divisions fresh from England, and will have a chance of distinguishing themselves.

September 27. Yesterday was a day of most bitter disappointment. In the morning all seemed well for another big advance.

[1] Sir Hubert Gough.

The new divisions were to push through between the two corps that had fought on the 25th, and attack the German second line of defences. Not much opposition was expected. The French were to attack on our right. There was a conference at 9 a.m. I had been down to the H.Q. of the new Corps (XIth) arranging their Intelligence and got back about noon. Soon after, most alarming reports began to arrive. The new divisions were reported to have broken and were retiring in great disorder. A little later an even worse report came in that the infantry of both divisions were in complete disorder, and that guns had been abandoned. D.H. went forward at once to take charge on the spot. It was only late at night that we heard the facts.

It was the old story, "too late." During the night the Germans had reorganized their line. The new divisions were worn out with their long march up during the 25th, and they had never been in action before. The Divisional and Brigade Staffs had each some experienced Staff officers, but most of the regimental officers went into action for the first time. They went forward with great gallantry—there is no doubt about their courage. But they came under unexpectedly heavy fire, and did not know how to act. They broke and came back. Even now the whole story cannot be disentangled. The broad fact is that we failed to make progress and lost very heavily. The French on our left attacked, and late in the evening we heard they had taken the Vimy Plateau, but were short of troops. To-day's report makes this doubtful, but the original report caused D.H. to release a French division which Foch had offered to help us.

To-day's fighting has been just readjusting our line. The Guards brought off a very fine attack to rectify the line near Loos. Later in the evening an intercepted German wireless message said the British Guards had broken through the German lines. I went up to Loos to find out the actual situation. I got as guide a young officer who had been out all the war and done exceedingly well. There was very little shelling. I noticed that my guide was under some very great strain. I made him sit down for a few moments under cover, and asked him what was the matter. He broke down altogether and told me that for the whole of these three days he had been in an agony of fear, and even now could hardly make himself go forward. Poor chap, his nerve had gone entirely. Small wonder, for he had been in the very thickest of the fighting since August '14. I sent him back with orders to go sick at once, and I am arranging for him to be sent home.

It made one realize what these youngsters are going through. I am very glad to hear that C.[1] is not very badly wounded. I saw him the night before the battle. He was in great spirits. He is now on his way home.

We will attack again in a few days, but there is now no hope of getting through this time. The French on our right are finished, though they too will attack again. In Champagne things are reported to be going well. The report mentions 20,000 prisoners and 45 guns captured. But a success there cannot give great results.

Our own battle in spite of yesterday's set-back has been important. We have captured 2,400 prisoners and 20 guns. We have not done nearly as well as we should have, the principal reason being the lack of the Reserve divisions on the first day of the battle. But even with them, we would not have been strong enough to have gone right through unless the French Artois attack had succeeded—and it failed. Looking at the battles as a whole (including Champagne) we have done well: 29,000 prisoners and 140 guns. We must now await spring for another big effort.

D.H. has sent home the whole story of the reserves. He is very bitter and says French remains impervious to all the teaching of the battles we have fought, especially the handling of reserves. Certainly there is one big fact that cannot be blinked. We captured Loos at 6 a.m. The reserves that should have been available to drive home the success did not reach even our front-line trenches until twelve hours later.

Sir J. French is played out. The show is too big for him and he is despondent. There is a report that he has said we ought to take the first opportunity of concluding peace—otherwise England would be ruined. It would be better to win and be ruined than to give in and be prosperous, even if this were possible, which it is not. I do not think that after Loos, D.H. and French can work satisfactorily together. One or other will have to go elsewhere.

October 1. On my way to examine a captured German aeroplane, I happened to find myself near Ryan's hospital, and looked in to see him. I meant to spend half an hour and ended by being there 2 hours. He insisted on showing me over the whole show. His record of work during the battle is something to be proud of. The nurses worked without a break for 72 hours—just eating biscuit

[1] Capt. Clarence Hodgson, subsequently killed on the Somme.

in the wards as they carried on. One surgeon operated continuously for 19 hours, then had to rest. The theatre sister carried on with the new surgeon for another 10 hours—she looks about 25 years of age. The matron wrote a note to the relatives of every one of the 369 officers who passed through the hospital, and made the sisters write to the relatives of every case that was reported "Serious" or "Dangerous." Amidst all the grouses and grumbles that one hears, there is never a word against our medical service. They are really magnificent—and there is no other word—in their efficiency.

October 8. The German counter-attack that we have been watching for, was delivered to-day. They attacked in the late afternoon, after a long bombardment, and were driven back with very heavy loss. It was the early days of Ypres over again. Almost everywhere they were shot down before they could get near our lines. At one point only they got into the trenches, but were eventually driven out of them by the Guards. The ease with which they were repulsed at most places makes it all the more remarkable that both at Neuve Chapelle and Loos we were able to overrun their trench line with our first assault.

October 9. The friction with G.H.Q. regarding the reserves shows no signs of abating. In the weekly report of operations the First Army made two definite statements of fact—that our leading troops, unsupported by adequate reserves, suffered heavily and were subsequently either killed, captured or driven back out of Loos, and that the IVth Corps asked for reserve troops and none were available. That started the ball rolling, and there has been a very acrimonious correspondence couched in perfectly courteous official phraseology. G.H.Q. accuses First Army of having misused the reserves. To this First Army gave chapter and verse of the various stages of the laborious process of getting the reserves out of G.H.Q.'s claws. Finally G.H.Q. sent a rebuke and a delightful editorial addendum, "This correspondence must now cease." So there it stands at present. But Haldane was out from home to-day to look into the matter and got the facts:—

1. That inexperienced divisions should not have been used for what was a vital part of the whole plan.
2. That the divisions were held back and not even concentrated.
3. When required, they were pushed forward without adequate arrangements for their food.

4. From the beginning the vital importance of the reserves was not realized.

The really maddening thing about it all is that now that we are really getting the German side of the show disentangled by examination of prisoners and captured documents, it becomes clear, without any shadow of doubt, that we had in fact broken the German line as clean as a whistle. For 4 hours there was a glaring gap; then it was gone. At the time, I realized this gap, and urged that the whole thing should be put to the hazard and the cavalry sent straight forward to replace the divisions that could not possibly get there in time. They would have suffered enormously, but they might have got the line moving again. Still, that was only a makeshift for the missing Reserve divisions.

It seems doubtful now, after the experience of the 26th, whether the new divisions, even if close up, were highly enough trained to have exploited the success. One thing is certain, officers cannot be made in a year's training at home. The material is excellent, just as good as the raw material of the regular officers for fighting purposes, but it must be wrought into the finished article. The quickest and best way to do that is out here, with seasoned units. All men in the ranks, whether Regular or New Army, are, consciously or unconsciously, very sensitive to the capabilities of their officers. Unless the officers are competent the men do not respond.

October 19. Poor Sandy Wingate was killed yesterday, fighting his trench-mortar battery at one of the most dangerous parts of the line. He and I were friends from the age of 10 onwards. Do you remember that great argument we had, in 1912, about the possibility of the war and the necessity of everyone joining the Territorials? Soon afterwards he joined. I do not know whether it was due to that discussion or not. I saw him at Hazebrouck when he had just come out with his unit as a sergeant. I have seen him several times since, both here and with his unit. He was doing well. It is the best of the nation who are called to die. He was one of the best. Only one name in the list of the killed—but a name I have had in my mind from my earliest youth—the name of a dear friend of my whole life. " The oldest friends are the dearest friends, and the new are just on trial."

CHAPTER XIII

SIR DOUGLAS HAIG BECOMES COMMANDER-IN-CHIEF

October 24. The King has been doing a tour of inspection. His visit was kept a dead secret. No one was told he was coming before he arrived. To-day when I was driving, a lady in another car made vigorous signs that she wanted to speak to me. She opened the conversation by saying, " Tell me where is the King." For want of a better lie I said, " Probably at Buckingham Palace, but he may be at Sandringham." To which she said, " Oh ! Colonel Charteris, don't be stupid. I want to see my husband who is with the King out here." It was ——, now managing a Y.W.C.A. hut at Abbeville. So that was that. I gave her lunch and sped her on her way.

This time last year we were at Ypres, and all our anxiety was lest we should be pushed back. This year our anxiety is not less, but it is lest we should not be able to get forward when the time comes. Anyhow, that is a great improvement. There will be little more fighting this year, for winter has set in—a steady downpour of rain all day, and very cold and dreary.

The troops are far better off than last year. We have enough to give frequent relief, and when not in the trenches they will be reasonably comfortable. Even in the trenches, we are far better prepared. There will be hardships, but nothing like last winter.

The C.G.S. was here to-day, very concerned about a proposal from home to send more troops to Salonika, and enlarge that side-show into a considerable operation. Apparently this particular folly originated with the French and not in our Cabinet, and the old argument is used that the forces required will—like the housemaid's baby—be only a small one. Like the housemaid's baby, it will in due course grow, and again like that estimable child, it argues an extraordinary lack of foresight.

October 29. You will have heard of the King's accident. It looked horribly serious. The whole thing was over in a few seconds. The charger he was riding had been schooled to stand every form of noise that could be foreseen. B. had been doing nothing else for a fortnight. It would rest its head happily all day long against the big drum of a band playing "God save the King". Gunfire did not make it even twitch an ear, I think it would have sat in an aeroplane doing stunts. But what had not been foreseen was the extraordinary noise emitted by 20 flying men trying to cheer. The wretched animal reared up like a rocket and came over backwards. No one had time to do anything. It looked as if H.M. must be seriously injured. He was carried into a small village home. The news now is that no bones are broken and there is no internal injury.

October 30. Now that things have settled down for the winter, D.H. has called for notes on the problems in the various other theatres. The Dardanelles is simple enough. We have failed and must break off there. The only argument against that is the possible effect on India, where we shall lose prestige. Mohammedan India may revert to the view that Britain has been beaten by Turkey. But though rumours fly quickly in India, deductions are made very slowly, and I do not think any active ill-effects will result for many months. Meantime, we must have here next spring every man and every shell that can be made available.

Serbia is a much more difficult problem. Here it is prestige again, but with neutral powers, not with India. Even if Serbia is crushed and Germany joins Turkey, it would do Britain little direct harm. Egypt is quite safe. No enemy army can reach her. Germany will certainly not be foolish enough to send her own troops there. But the effect on Russia will be very bad. It will be even worse on the neutrals.

Germany is nearing the end of her resources. She can only keep up her strength against France, ourselves and Russia, by one of two methods: (1) by forcing or inducing one or other of us Allies to a separate peace and then moving against those that remain or (2) by bringing in the neutral countries on her side. The problem is, can we stiffen Serbia to effective resistance without weakening unduly our strength for the decisive fighting here? We have four or five months in front of us in which there can be no very heavy fighting. If we can keep Serbia on her feet and fighting for these months, without too much expenditure of men and munitions, it will help us greatly in the spring. Then we shall need everyone and everything here. We have not the information here to judge whether this is possible. D.H. very wisely is refusing to commit himself to any definite opinion without full knowledge of the data. But he is urging that Robertson should go to the W.O. as Chief of Staff, to give the Government the strategical advice they need so badly. He and Robertson are the only two men big enough to take this task on. One of them must remain in France and the other go to the W.O.; it does not much matter which goes and which stays. K. could work with either.

There are rumours, too strong to be ill-founded, of grave trouble in both the French and British Cabinets. That is where our real weakness lies. The fall of the French Government makes Joffre's position difficult. If Gallieni goes to the French War Office it will be very difficult indeed, and L.G. is biting at K.'s heels.

November 11. The dispatch on Loos has put the fat in the fire, and we are in for a first-class squabble with G.H.Q. It is worse even than the Neuve Chapelle dispatch. This one makes definite misstatements. D.H. has demanded officially that it should be corrected as regards the use or misuse of the reserves. It is amazingly stupid of G.H.Q., for all the facts are on record, with timings of the messages. As long as the squabble does not get into the Press it will do no harm, but it will make it impossible for D.H. to serve under French. It is ten thousand pities that we should have squabbles like this in the Army—it reduces us to the level of the Cabinet—but I do not see that D.H. could have let the dispatch pass without strong objection. G.H.Q. had refused to thrash the thing out at the time. What is more important is to prevent any chance of its recurring.

November 16. Esher has been with news of the intrigue against Kitchener in the Cabinet. Apparently L.G. made a strong bid a short time ago to oust Asquith. The House of Commons was canvassed and L.G. only got 30 votes. Now Churchill has thrown his hand in. I don't think he is much loss. His apologias are extraordinarily well done. His great fault—and a big one—was to try to do everyone's work. The real trouble is that a Committee like the Cabinet cannot run a war. It is impossible to get a strong policy strenuously carried out. There appears to be no hope of that from this Government; but there seems nothing to put in its place.

The whole body politic at home festers with intrigue and make-believe. The leaders are so impregnated with the opportunism which passes for statesmanship in peace, that they cannot rid themselves of it even in this crisis of our history. If words were deeds, the Government would be a paragon among Governments. It seems certain that it will fall soon. Heaven knows what we shall get in its place. Our greatest danger is not in Serbia, or the Dardanelles, or here in France, but in Westminster.

Esher and D.H. agree that the best solution at home would be for Robertson to be made C.G.S. and advise the Cabinet direct, not through K., and to have part of the W.O. transferred to him and form a real Imperial General Staff. K. should remain responsible only for the business administration of the W.O. I cannot see how this would work. There would be inevitable friction between K. and Robertson, and the Cabinet would have the best of excuses for wobbling between divergent opinions. I think K.'s position should be strengthened, not weakened. Give K. the best General Staff available, not the present emasculated W.O., and leave K. and Asquith in supreme control of the war and the country. Bring back Haldane into the Cabinet, and get rid of everyone (including L.G.) who is intriguing against K.

I went to see my old Sapper and Miner company to-day, and had a great reception. Many of the older men had been with me in 1910; they seemed very contented in spite of everything. They did not know, and I did not tell them, that they would be off very soon to the East again.

November 19. John Redmond came to our H.Q. yesterday. A striking-looking man and very pleasant to deal with. His view is that we need have no fear regarding Ireland if she is treated rightly, by which he means in exactly the same way as the rest of Great Britain as regards all war measures. He went right into the front-line trenches and would not hear of stopping outside the danger zone. In point of fact, though, there was practically no firing.

D.H. goes home to-morrow. He has been preparing himself for interviews there. If his view is asked, he is going to urge that there should be an Imperial General Staff under Robertson, independent of K., which means presumably that he becomes C.-in-C. here. He also is going to press for a homogeneous army—all distinction between Regular units, Territorial units and K.'s army to be done away with, and the units to be kept at full strength. All very sound, except that I think the C.G.S. should be under K. D.H. thinks K. is so obsessed with Egypt that he would not accept Staff views of the force necessary there.

We are all very amused at Lord St. Davids' effort.[1] G.H.Q. is very touchy on the subject, and is unmercifully ragged by everybody. Of course it is all utter nonsense.

I saw Winston Churchill at G.H.Q. to-day. I wonder what mischief he is up to now. He is said to be green with jealousy of Seely, who has mounted the badge of a Brigadier-General with the Canadians. We shall have Haldane commanding a Corps soon!

December 1. Things are very quiet and dull. Even the stream of visitors has dried up during D.H.'s absence. I went for a walk yesterday into Béthune, and had tea at a shop filled with young officers and a sprinkling of French maidens. My arrival acted as a blight on their enjoyment. The young officers stood up—the maidens became demure and hardly smiled all the time I was there. I hastily gulped down one cup of tea and fled, feeling mentally the penalty of even the modified glory of being a Lt.-Colonel with red tabs.

To-day, I was out at a Corps and surprised one mess amusing themselves making a photo screen of pictures of members of the Cabinet and French ladies with " nodings " on. Very improper, but very amusing. Afterwards I went through the trench line. Winter has set in much earlier this year than last, when all our bad weather was in February. This year the trenches are already heavy with mud. The men are much better off, with good dugouts, and seemed cheerful and happy. There was hardly any firing anywhere on the whole front. We have had a good number of deserters from the Germans lately, mostly Alsatians and Poles —queer disgruntled creatures without much " guts "—but a fair proportion of real bullet-headed Prussians. One cannot judge by deserters, but these give the impression of feeling the discomfort of the weather more than our men.

One of the strangest things of the war is to see men who have spent all their lives in towns, and probably slept always in comfortable beds, enduring the life in the trenches, quite contentedly and without any ill-health. Man is an adaptable creature. Of course the ration arrangements are perfect and they get plenty of good food. I lunched at an inn quite near the front line, within easy reach of the German guns, doing a roaring trade. A vivacious

[1] The suggestion was that there were lady visitors to G.H.Q.

French girl in charge of this made obvious advances to the subaltern I had with me, which he rather sheepishly tried to fend off. The character of the French still surprises me; they laugh at misfortune and hardship. They are in the depths of depression at some quite trivial incident, and then back in the seventh heaven of optimism. Their peasants have a very keen eye for money, and fleece our men unmercifully. It does no harm, for our men have far more ready cash than they know what to do with. There are not many pubs open and the money burns holes in their pockets. The French have stood far more as a nation than we have as yet. Until we have equalled their efforts we have no right to criticize. Indeed, any criticism one could indulge in would be of their leaders, not of the rank and file of the nation or of the army. Fits of depression pass without ill results in the lower ranks, but in the leaders they are very dangerous.

December 6. D.H. is back. He had interviews with Asquith, K. and Bonar Law. Apparently it is all settled that he will succeed French, and Robertson go home as C.I.G.S. The immediate cause is the Loos trouble. But it would have happened in any case. K. and D.H. have got into full agreement. D.H. is not at all impressed by Bonar Law; thinks him an "honest, feeble man." He says the whole Government at home is terrified by the Balkans and Egypt, and can think of nothing else. K. apparently expected an attack by 200,000 men on the Suez Canal! I suppose they would feed on sand and emulate the camel for drink on the march there. All the same we cannot do without K. at home.

December 11. I had a very interesting day with the French Army, looking into some new schemes they have introduced, including one for locating the position of German guns by sound. It is still in its infancy and requires improvement, but it has great possibilities. I am going to try to start a similar show here at once. When I had finished with that I went to a French 75 which was in action against the German guns. The French artillery is most efficient, and the 75 is, undoubtedly, the best field-gun of the war.

I find the French are just as full of "troopers' yarns" as our own army. That of the bombs stuffed into the trousers of an unpopular N.C.O. was in full swing. I suppose it was the invention of some nimble mind, as a hint to unpopular N.C.O.s, to become popular.

SIR DOUGLAS HAIG BECOMES COMMANDER-IN-CHIEF 1915

December 12. The great change has been made, and D.H. becomes C.-in-C. He told me to-night that he has asked for Butler as his C.G.S. and that he intends to take me with him as head of the Intelligence of the army in France. This is not quite certain yet, as it depends upon Macdonogh (at present at G.H.Q.) going to the W.O. as head of the Intelligence there. It is very characteristic of D.H. that this is the first time he has mentioned this, though it has been in both our minds ever since it seemed probable that he would become C.-in-C. Rawlinson takes over the First Army. I wish it had been Munro. Rawlinson is very able and has been in the thick of all the fighting, but I am never quite sure that he may not try to supplant D.H. Apparently there is great difficulty in placing Wilson. Neither D.H. nor Robertson wants him anywhere near them. He has been instigating articles recommending that the British Army should be put under Foch, and has been belittling everybody except himself and Foch.

December 25. I take up my new job on New Year's Day, and meantime am going round making unofficial inspection of the other armies' Intelligence, and the innumerable side-shows that come under G.H.Q. I went first to the Ypres area—a most sad sight. In Ypres there is now literally not a habitable house. It is like one of the ruined cities of old Delhi.

There was a small gas attack, the first I had seen at close quarters. Little damage was done; the infantry did not attack as if they meant business. But I was unfortunate enough to get a whiff or two of gas which has touched up my bronchitis a bit. I had to go on later to a village close up to the front to interview some of the remaining inhabitants on some Secret Service work. The Germans took it into their heads to throw over some couple of dozen shells, and I heard again—probably for the last time for many weeks—the crack of shells bursting near at hand. There was plenty of cover in the town, and no one paid much attention. No one was hit. Only a few more bare walls thrown down—a little more debris to be cleared from the road.

From the Second Army I went back to the First Army and began the handing-over there to my successor. Then on to Paris where we have a small office, and back via G.Q.G. to meet and confer with French Intelligence. I was introduced officially to General Joffre, and had a few minutes' talk. He is pleased at the change at G.H.Q., though he does not know D.H. personally.

There never was anyone less like the ordinary conception of a great soldier, than Joffre. He is very big in person, very placid in appearance, almost benevolent, slow in his movements and in his speech, and has remarkable eyes—very steady and still. He keeps his eyes fixed on you all the time you are with him, not glaring, or unfriendly, but just as if he were determined that no change of expression should pass unnoticed. He wanted to know what was to become of Wilson. I had nothing to tell him, and replied that either at home or in one of the many theatres of war he would find his place. He said I was the first of the new G.H.Q. Staff to visit him, and presented me with one of the pipes of which he keeps a stock to give to favoured visitors.

To-day I paid a last visit to the First Army trenches as a Staff officer of that army. The Germans said farewell by a single shell blobbed at the observation post where I was standing. It burst about 30 yards away and did no damage. Now I am back at G.H.Q. and have begun to take over. It is a huge show with branches everywhere. In addition to ordinary Intelligence work it has the censorship, the Press correspondents, ciphers, all communications with foreign Governments' Secret Service and contre-espionage so far as France is concerned, all map work and distinguished visitors. There are about 50 officers altogether employed on the work.

I hear there is a good deal of criticism of the new Staff—and especially of my own appointment—on the ground of youth. But those whose opinion matters seem genuinely cordial in their congratulations. Most of the heads of the General Staff are the First Army team, Butler,[1] Davidson[2] and myself. Kiggell[3] comes out from home as C.G.S. D.H. had originally asked for Butler, but he was considered too junior.

December 31. To-night we all dine with the *Chief*—thus beginning a new common task in traditional British fashion.

[1] Now Lieut.-General Sir R. H. Butler.
[2] Now Major-General Sir J. H. Davidson.
[3] Now Lieut.-General Sir L. E. Kiggell.

PART THREE—1916
G.H.Q.

CHAPTER XIV

PLANS FOR THE SOMME ATTACK

January 1. Dinner last night was a regular New Year's beano, more like a London New Year's Eve festival than a war one. There were present the Duke of Teck, General Macready, Sir A. Sloggett, General Butler, General Trenchard, Colonel Hutchinson, Dr. Simms, Alan Fletcher, Sir P. Sassoon and myself. It was quite a merry party, crackers and all the rest of it. I do not think any of us spoke about the present war all through dinner. There was much reminiscencing of other wars. Sloggett was the life and soul of the party with his yarns, some of which were libellous and few of which would have passed muster in a drawing-room.

D.H. never shines at a dinner, but he was obviously in very good spirits, and kept silence merrily. When it was all over and the others had gone, he took me into his own room to discuss matters. He is quite satisfied with the new arrangements at home, and showed me his instructions from Lord K. promising wholehearted and unswerving support from the Government and from himself. D.H. is quite independent of the French, but of course, has to co-operate in every way with them. He wants an appreciation of the whole situation in all theatres prepared for his personal information, which I shall have to do. The general lines of the grand strategy for this oncoming year have already been settled between Joffre and Sir J. French, a combined and practically simultaneous offensive on the Russian, Italian and this front. Kitchener is doubtful whether France will stand more than another year of war, and thinks unless we win this year, the war will end in stalemate, with another war in the near future, and therefore urges that we must force the issue this year. Much depends upon what reserve of fighting power the French still have. They have borne the brunt so far, but they cannot go on for ever. This next year the big effort must be ours. D.H. wants, from the Intelligence, a very close estimate of German man-power and French fighting power, and periodic complete appreciations of the situation from the

German point of view, with forecasts, not merely records of what is known.

January 2. The Intelligence offices are in a large house, all of which has been taken over for its work. My own room, originally the dining-room, overlooks the garden. I have had all the furniture taken out and the pictures taken from the walls, to get space for the big maps. There is one long table, a roll-top desk for secret papers, and a stand-up desk at which I work most of the time, and another table at which to interview people. Next door is a large room for conferences. My second-in-command, with his assistants, works in a room just across the lobby. The Secret Service section is on the same floor, with four officers. Upstairs, on the first floor, are two more sections (six officers in three rooms) and the register clerk, a stockbroker by trade. Farther up still are the other clerks.

My billet is in a very delightful bourgeois house belonging to a wealthy merchant, a very big comfortable room with a bathroom leading from it, which I share with my hostess! That is to say her room has also a door leading into the bathroom. So far we have not collided! My hostess is a very pleasant woman. Her eldest daughter (16 years of age) is at school in England. The youngest is a baby. The husband is a semi-invalid who seldom appears.

I have been in the office all day—it is now midnight—getting hold of the new work. The whole morning was taken up with visits from people to make my acquaintance, and friends coming to congratulate me. In the afternoon I placarded a notice "Out" and locked the door.

January 4. I dined with Sloggett[1] last night and found Winston Churchill there. He talked very freely and showed all his good and weak points. He holds very strong views on military as well as political matters. He talks and argues brilliantly. When he makes a clever phrase—and he constantly does—there is a sort of pause as if he relished it like a glass of good port. His lisp disappears after the first few minutes. He is most bitter against Asquith. It is a personal vendetta more than disapproval of a policy.

His most striking phrases were "You cannot combine politics and war. Politics require popularity, and the direction of war means inevitable unpopularity. The fighting men got all the

[1] Lieut.-General Sir Arthur Sloggett (Head of the Medical Services in France).

popularity of any success; the statesmen, the unpopularity of any ill-success." I suppose that is why, to us, it seems that the politician will stick at nothing to reverse the process. He likened politics to a game of football, the politicians always trying to beat the other side and score goals. When an election came the public totted up the goals and decided by their votes who had won. He was quite frank about the attraction that power had for him. He is all out for it. He could not lead a party but would be an admirable second-in-command.

I told Churchill that Raymond Asquith was coming into one of my branches. He will work with Onslow. Churchill himself wants to get a brigade, or higher command.

January 9. Joffre has written suggesting that the Germans may attack the French near the Somme, and wants proposals for a counter-attack by our troops near that front, or alternatively a scheme to move British troops to help the French in resisting the attack. I do not think the Germans will attack there; there is nothing to be gained except by a very big advance, for which they have not enough troops. As far as we know, there are no signs of an attack being prepared there, nor indeed anywhere on or near our front. If there were, we could easily move troops to help the French, if they were needed.

Our wandering soldier M.P.s, who went home to vote, are all back again. They say that Simon has done for himself by his opposition to this Compulsory Service Bill. His speech has neither caught the country nor increased his influence in Parliament. It is a pity he has taken this line, for he did admirably as Home Secretary in the early days of 1914, backing up the contre-espionage people in their somewhat drastic methods.

January 20. This work is absorbingly interesting, but it is never-ending. I have not been to bed before 2.0 a.m. since I took over. Joffre was here this morning to discuss details and date of the great offensive. Apparently the idea that Germany would attack on the Somme has petered out—if it ever really existed except as a reason to get us to submit a scheme for a counter-attack. Joffre says Russia cannot attack before June. He wants us to make a preliminary attack in April with a limited objective north of the Somme. He thinks the Germans are very depressed.

January 21. C.I.G.S. (Robertson) has been here. Men and

ammunitions will be plentiful by May. He thinks the Russians will be ready to attack in May, but that Germany will forestall them.

January 24. There was a conference of Army Commanders this morning, to arrange for the April preparatory attack near Arras. The Third Army Head-quarters, where the conference took place, is 60 miles from here. My driver—a man from the Glasgow Corporation Tramways—covered the distance in one hour fifteen minutes; good going. I had to give a summary of the situation to the Conference. Afterwards I went to inspect the Intelligence at the Corps Head-quarters, then drove back here to meet some Allied and neutral correspondents. I did not get to my office until after dinner, and worked until 4.0 a.m.

January 26. Yarde-Buller, Military Attaché with the French, has been here. He says the French nation are quite steadfast and that there need be no fear that they will not fight on, however long the war lasts, but says there is a great deal of intrigue in political circles and that Joffre is having as hard a time on the home front as K. in London.

Joffre has now written that if the big offensive does not come off until late in the summer, he wants another, in addition to the Arras one, at the end of May. He agrees to Flanders for our final big attack, and promises French help in it. He is going much too far. We would be bound to have heavy casualties in the preparatory attacks, and the main attack would be weakened. But it is a great step to have got the plan for the big attack to be in Flanders. Strategically there is no doubt about that being the best place for us to attack. It strikes direct at the main railway communications of all the German armies. The Germans could not even make good their retreat. A victory, however great, on the Somme would still let them get back to the Meuse. Tactically the ground is more difficult. Most important of all is the weather. An attack in Flanders must be delivered early in the summer. June at the latest. Farther south it can be much later.

January 28. There are amusing interludes even in this work. The censorship discovered some young officer advertising in the *Vie Parisienne* for a " marraine." The advertisement met with quite a voluminous response from a variety of females. As it was possible some of them might be enemy agents, the contre-espionage had the replies taken out of the mail-bags and brought here. One of my young men says he spent an amusing hour working through them—fortified by a gas mask to protect him against the scent used by some of the ladies. " Marraines " are taboo for our army, so now we are following up the possibility of agents working this scheme by putting in our own advertisements for " marraines," and also by answering any advertisement for " marraines " that looks as if it might emanate from our army. It is sad to interfere with any profession striving to carry on " business as usual," but war is war.

January 31. There has been an invasion from home. Yesterday Lloyd George, Bonar Law, and the C.I.G.S. arrived. I dined with D.H. to meet them, and sat next to Bonar Law, a mild-mannered, gentle little man, quite overshadowed by Lloyd George who was opposite, and who set himself to fascinate everybody. He certainly was most attractive. D.H. alone seemed quite impervious to his allurements. To-day the pair of them came to my office for a couple of hours and went through all the Intelligence work. Lloyd George led the cross-examination, and it was very severe. He is astonishingly quick at grasping points, but, curiously enough, could not read a map. Bonar Law said very little, but when Lloyd George had left, he lingered for a minute and said he wanted to sympathize with me at having been put into the witness-box. I said if things went wrong, we should all be lucky if we escaped the dock. He asked me what I thought his job in the war was. I said I had no idea. Then with a twinkle he said, " Hanging on to the coat-tails of that little man, and trying to hold him back." But whatever else may be said of the " little man," there is no doubt he has genius. He dominates. One strange physical feature draws one's eye when he is not talking—his curious little knock-kneed legs. When he is talking one would not notice if he had no legs or no arms, his face is so full of vitality and energy, and after all, it is from the chin upwards that matters. One of the Staff called him " an intriguing little Welshman," but he is much more than that.

D.H. dislikes him. They have nothing in common. D.H. always refuses to be drawn into any side-issues in conversation, apart from his own work. Lloyd George seemed to think this meant distrust of him. It is not so much distrust of him personally as of politicians as a class. D.H. hates everything but absolute honesty and frankness and it is only when he knows any politician intimately and long that he can find it possible to give him credit for these characteristics. But can anyone in politics be really honest and frank ? Asquith is the only one I have yet met who gives that impression. And his frankness seems always to be *de haut en bas*, not condescending, but simply Olympian.

Robertson was tongue-tied at dinner, neither agreeing nor disagreeing with anything anybody said. He likes to write his opinions, not to discuss them. But he is very sound and very much master in his own War House. He and D.H. see absolutely eye to eye, and D.H. tells me that K. holds the same views; together they make a very strong triumvirate to run the war.

The Intelligence has brought off our first success since we took over. We were able to warn the troops of an attack—time, place and strength—and punished the Germans rather heavily. It was a small thing but it gives confidence, and brings the whole team up to their bits. They are an excellent team, but naturally a little uncertain of the new regime.

February 1. More politicians! Lord Derby is here and I had to give up a good part of the afternoon to explaining our part of the show to him. He was very pleasant, a change from the ordinary run of public men. He knows much more about the Army and fighting than most of them; not very quick-witted, but with a delightful gurgling laugh. I think we could count on every support from him, even if the fighting brings disappointment and difficulties at home.

The general routine now with these distinguished visitors is that D.H. gives them an interview, either half an hour or an hour, and then hands them over to me. Sometimes I am present at their interview with D.H., then it is easy. Sometimes I am not, and then one has to be very careful, for one does not know what may have passed at the interview. Sooner or later they, one and all, bring the conversation round to the Eastern *v*. Western front problem. That is easy argument, but leaves an uneasy feeling that there is some very strong leaning at home towards easy victories in unimportant theatres, with small casualties and no real results. How on earth one can hope to beat Germany by killing Turks or Bulgars passes comprehension. It is like a prize-fighter leaving the ring to trounce his opponent's seconds. Germany would ask for nothing better than to see us " spread-eagling " over the Balkans to Mesopotamia, while she took Paris.

I dined with a batch of neutrals last night; an interesting lot but rather a strain, for they are neutrals, and when they go back to their own countries can write and tell anything they may pick up. You cannot censor their memories. Generally they give the impression of trying to prevent themselves being convinced that Germany is going to be beaten. The sabre-rattling of Germany in peace has made most of the world believe she is invincible. As soon as the neutrals are convinced that Germany must lose in the end, they will tumble over one another to join the Allies. None of them except America can affect the real issue between the Armies. I can see no reason at all why America should join either us or Germany. She stands exactly where many of our own people wanted us to stand, with a front seat on the ropes of the ring and drawing all the gate money. It is utter nonsense to say she should join us out of kinship and friendship. There is not much kinship, and besides, relations always quarrel; as to friendship, "Business is business," and the U.S.A. is the U.S.A. Ltd., doing a very thriving business, with a big bonus to shareholders piling up.

February 2. There has been a most amusing little interlude in monotonous official life. F. E. Smith came out without having taken the precaution to provide himself with the appropriate pass. He jumped a Staff car at Boulogne, bluffed all the sentries at the various inspection posts, and proceeded gaily to the front-line trenches. As no one could be quite sure whether it was really F.E. or someone impersonating him, the A.G. issued orders for the individual—whoever he was—to be sent to G.H.Q. The orders went by telephone and in their course were transformed into " Arrest the individual and send him to G.H.Q." So the great F.E. was duly arrested by some Assistant Provost-Marshal and brought in a prisoner—the embodiment of offended dignity and vowing vengeance on all concerned. He had an interview with D.H., who pointed out that F.E. had only himself to blame, and that if he *did* make a public matter of it, he would appear in a rather ludicrous light and be thoroughly well laughed at. F.E. eventually took it very well and peace reigns again. But it looked at one time as if we were in for a fine little fracas.

February 5. Curzon has been here, overwhelming as ever. It must be bitter for him to see the Army, which he always disparaged in India, playing the leading rôle and K. controlling it. D.H. got on extraordinarily well with him. But both should have been in eighteenth-century costume, with perukes and frills. D.H. is always dignified in manner, and Curzon's pomposity accentuated it. I always see Curzon preceded by two A.D.C.s walking backwards through the doors at Viceregal Lodge in Simla to usher in His

Excellency, and two girls, who had been reproved for not treating him with proper respect, throwing themselves on the floor full length and touching the floor three times with their foreheads.

Curzon did not give much time to Intelligence work. I fancy Military Intelligence to him is a contradiction in terms.

February 8. D.H. has sent an official reply to Joffre, that he does not agree to our doing a series of preparatory attacks in April and May, if the big offensive is not coming off until late in the summer, and saying that preparatory attacks should be within one or two weeks of the main attack. Meantime we go on with preparations for one big preparatory attack at Arras, which may become the big attack, if required to relieve pressure in Russia, where the Germans are reported to be massing their troops. Joffre is coming to discuss this, presumably to try to get D.H. to change his view. He will not succeed. But it may result in our main attack being elsewhere than in Flanders—a great pity if it does. I am sure Flanders is the right place to hit. I think D.H. agrees, but the Operations section (or some of them) are all for the Somme, on account of it being much easier ground to attack over.

There are beginning to be signs that the Germans may forestall our attack by themselves attacking in France.

Yesterday a batch of Russian officers arrived on an official visit. They had their own conducting officer with them to take them round the front area. I only saw them at dinner and gave them their interview afterwards. They knew nothing about happenings on the Russian front, less than we already know here. Knox's [1] reports are very full and very disquieting. Generally, these Russian officers seem quite untrained and ill-educated—which agrees with Knox's reports. There seems no doubt about the lack of everything—guns, rifles and all technical stores—in the Russian Army. All of this points to the correct plans for Germany being to overwhelm Russia this year and not to attack here. On the other hand, if Germany is really near the end of her tether, she must seek decisive victory this year, and that means in France a gambler's throw. For if she failed in 1914 she cannot well expect to win here now, when the Allies are relatively much stronger.

My bag of visitors to-day included Hunter-Weston,[2] back from the Dardanelles where he did so well.

February 9. K. has been here again with Fitzgerald in attend-

[1] Now Major-General Sir A. Knox, M.P.
[2] Lieut.-General Sir Aylmer Hunter-Weston, K.C.B.

ance. He arrived last night. I dined with the Chief to meet him. He looked very worn and old and tired, and was sombre and gloomy all the evening. He went to bed immediately after dinner. I stayed with D.H. after K. had retired. D.H. told me that K. is being very heavily attacked at home in the Cabinet, and that although Robertson and K. are working together excellently, the hostile element headed by Lloyd George may succeed in getting rid of him. Curzon is apparently siding with Lloyd George, while Asquith is backing K. The real thing that matters is what the nation thinks. I feel sure they would stand by and for K. against any or all of the politicians.

K. came to my office again with Fitzgerald this morning, and stayed for two hours. He was quite himself, went into all the work and discussed everything regarding our possible action. His great point is to work with the French in every way this year, although he did not seem to think we should end the war this next campaign. He was very emphatic against any talk of breaking through the German lines. He said someone from G.H.Q. had been talking about a break-through, and that it must stop. I told him that it probably came from the French, who do believe and talk of it before every attack, but that I did not know of any such idea at G.H.Q.

He then became quite his own self. " It is the German people you are fighting. Your eyes should be on them, in the Intelligence, as much and more than on the Army. There will be no break-through. You must lean against this line, press it, hit it as hard as you can, bend it. Some day you will find it is not there, going back, but you *will not* break through." I pointed out that if we bent the line back in Flanders a relatively small distance, the rest of the German line must go; he agreed, but said the French would not consent to any big effort there.

K. is right enough, but it is really a distinction in terms: for to bend the line you have to break through the defences. Of course, given time, they can form another line behind unless we reach their communications, which we can only do in the north.

Immediately K. had gone I motored straight to D.H. and reported the whole conversation to him. D.H. was, as always, quite unperturbed. I fancy he himself has been using the term break-through to some of the visitors, and it has reached K.'s ears!

February 11. There are definite reports showing that the Germans are going to attack on the Western front, and G.Q.G. say it will be at Verdun. Meantime Joffre's plans have reached us.

The main attack, French and British, is to be astride the Somme, us to the north, they to the south, only a preparatory attack in Flanders, just before the big one in July. The Arras show to go on in April.

There is to be a Conference to-morrow at G.Q.G. to which I am going.

February 15. Back again from the Conference. I left on the 13th, visited the Third Army about the Arras show, then on to Amiens, where I lunched, then to Senlis where I spent the night at the Grand Cerf. Senlis is a perfectly delightful old French country town. The Germans were there in the early part of the war, and shot the Mayor and burnt many houses on some very slight pretext. The people are very bitter, much more so than in Amiens or Béthune.

Yesterday morning I went to the Conference, which lasted until 1.0 p.m., then lunched with General de Castelnau, and on to Paris to see our office there. Left Paris at 6.0, stopped the night at a small inn, and returned here in the early hours this morning.

At the Conference the date of the big offensive was fixed for July 1, the Flanders attack a week or two earlier. If, meantime, the Germans attack the Russians, everything to be advanced in date. But it now seems certain that the Germans are going to attack in France, probably at Verdun, possibly elsewhere. There are indications of preparations at other parts of the French front, but none on ours. But they have not moved away any troops from opposite us.

February 16. Dined with the foreign attachés—a mixed lot, one Serbian, two Russians, one Italian, one Belgian, three Japanese— to tell them as much as can be told. They have their own conducting officer to take them round the front, and they are, of course, mainly concerned with details of administration and tactical arrangements, which they can investigate to their hearts' content. Only a few of them talk English fluently, so conversations and explanations were in French and German. My job is to ensure that they are getting every facility and to let them ventilate any complaints. There were none, except that they wanted one and all to see and talk to D.H.

People pester me with applications to do some job for them, Jack Cowans worst of all. I hate asking favours; I hate people who ask for favours for themselves; I hate people who ask for favours for other people.

February 23. The Germans have attacked at Verdun. The French are not sure whether it is a big attack or only preparatory to a big attack elsewhere, but want us both to take over line from them and to attack. I go to London to-morrow for two days.

February 27. A line to tell you of my safe arrival back. We left Charing Cross at 9.0, reached Dover at 10.45, embarked on a destroyer at once and reached Dunkirk at 12.45. As we left Dover we saw some three or four other destroyers making for a P. and O. liner which had been mined, and was obviously in great difficulties. Our skipper would not join them. He had his orders, he said, to deliver us as quickly as possible at Dunkirk! We had a roughish crossing. I spent most of the time in the charthouse on the bridge, until we were close to Dunkirk, then went to the Wardroom, immediately over the propeller and very uncomfortably unsteady, for refreshments. The T.-b.-d. people do not have as much risk as the Army, but it is a hard life; they get little rest.

There is little more news of the Verdun battle than you see in the papers. It will go on for at least ten days more. The French seem to have been surprised in the actual attack. Why this should be so is not clear, for there was ample warning at G.H.Q. Anyhow, it means the beginning of the fighting for the year, and we shall be at it continuously until summer is over. Meantime we are taking over more line from the French, to free more troops for Verdun. But the real help we can give them will be by our own Arras attack, which will effectively prevent the Germans sending more men there and probably bring many back from Verdun. It is only playing the German game to try to regain ground already lost at Verdun, or to make them stop attacking by pouring in more troops there. An attack elsewhere is the proper answer. The Germans are not bringing troops from Russia, so far as we can find out. D.H. is still away.

March 4. We have had our first lady visitor (*pace* Lord St. Davids!), Mrs. Humphry Ward and her daughter have arrived on a more or less official visit. Roosevelt, who is a real friend of ours, had urged that she had great influence in U.S.A. and that if she wrote with first-hand knowledge of our doings, it would be helpful in forming public opinion in U.S.A. and counteracting German propaganda. I gave Mrs. Ward dinner at the Press château. She is altogether charming, but I am afraid too gentle-hearted to bear the sight of some of the cruelties of war. I am sending an officer round with her. She must, of course, go into no dangerous area, but I am arranging for her to see artillery observation posts, and have some meals with units close up to the line. She has been touring England, looking at munition works and seeing how far women can replace men. If what she tells me is the truth, and I am sure she could only speak the truth, we should be able to comb out many men from the factories. We shall need them all.

March 4. Joffre writes hopefully of Verdun. The Germans are attacking very vigorously, but the French have still 10 divisions available in reserve. He estimates Germany may make available twenty-two more divisions for another attack. This can only be so if Germany brings back ten or more divisions from Russia, and so far we can only trace the movement of *one* division. Joffre wants us to attack all out, as soon as possible. That would be in six weeks' time at the earliest.

It has been a very busy day. There was an Army Commanders' Conference at which I had to explain the present situation, as we know it. Then D.H. expounded his plans. In office all afternoon. Then an official dinner with the Belgian representatives. Then interviews with three Russians, and then back to office work until now—1.0 a.m. One of the Russians was very frank about his country. He said the main difficulty, or one of the main difficulties, was that every official was corrupt and added, " You could buy every Colonel and most of the Generals with a case of brandy."

March 8. Just back from Paris, where I went on Sunday, stopping at G.Q.G. for the latest information regarding Verdun. It is a very fierce battle there, much like Ypres in 1914, and shows no sign of abating. It is difficult to see exactly what the Germans hope to gain by it. I do not think they can hope to break through. Certainly there is no chance of their succeeding. It may be that they only want to bleed the French fighting force dry and thus prevent them attacking, or perhaps then make a bid for peace. But they are using up their own troops at least as rapidly as those of the French, thereby making things better for our own attack.

Yesterday I was busy all day in Paris, including an interview with the Ambassador, who had complained that the Army took no notice of him. I do not know why we should, for we have nothing really to do with him. He spoke a lot about Sir J. French whom he knew well, and liked. He has not met D.H. He seemed to resent Esher's presence in Paris as an " unofficial ambassador from the War Office." He had no knowledge of any French military matters, and I imagine now that Paris and London are communicating direct he has very little to do. He wanted to know our plans for the summer, which was easily answered by saying, quite truthfully, that it all depends upon Verdun.

Paris is very quiet; the streets are almost empty and everyone is very serious. There seemed no sign of lack of confidence or of weakness. The Verdun casualties are very heavy, and Verdun is very close to Paris. It has been snowing for the last two days, and that may cause the German pressure to ease up, anyhow for the time. The Verdun attack does seem to make it probable that the war will be over by the end of the year. The Germans are clearly seeking decision. There is no other explanation of their attack in this form, and at that place. If our big attack gets even reasonable success, and if Russia holds fast—and it now seems probable she will—and *if* Italy attacks with force, we should win. These are big "ifs," but each in itself is a probability. The next few months hold very big events in the history of the world.

March 14. Paris again! This time with D.H. There was a Conference yesterday at G.Q.G. Joffre is really great in this crisis. He is firm and unrattled, pressing us to take over more line, which is quite natural and proper, but determined that he will not allow Verdun to alter his main scheme for the year. There is certainly a great advantage in Head-quarters being well away from the actual fighting. I remember Ypres, and realize how difficult it is for any commander close up to the fighting to keep his judgment of the whole picture unaffected by the immediate problem. Joffre has to hold back his reserves, only doling out the very minimum that can hold the Germans in check at Verdun, and await the time for the big blow. If our whole resources were available now we could attack sooner, but the longer the Germans hammer at Verdun, the better our chances. That is easy for us to see and urge. It must be very bitter and difficult for Joffre, who sees his own army and countrymen enduring hell in a great attack while we are apparently idle. There will, of course, be far fewer French troops available for the big attack; but as their numbers diminish ours increase. The Germans are not so fortunate. So that, steadily, the scales weigh down more and more on our side.

After the Conference we came on to Paris, where D.H. wanted to see the Ambassador. We lunched at the Crillon, and afterwards went for a walk, finishing up at the Invalides. It was closed to visitors, but the guardian made an exception in D.H.'s favour and took us round. Napoleon's tomb is always impressive, but doubly so seeing it with the C.-in-C. of a British Army fighting in France against Germany. If Napoleon's spirit was near his tomb, did he wish to pull D.H.'s ear and wish him luck, and tell him the secret of victory? Would he have had any magic of strategy in these days of trenched positions, without any flank, and guns that range 10 miles? This gigantic war is far bigger than any that Napoleon can have ever conceived. Yet he had conquered continental Europe when he was twelve years younger than D.H.

From Napoleon's tomb we came back to earth at the British Embassy, where D.H. was received by the Ambassador. After dinner I started back for G.H.Q. It was very late and snowing, and I stopped the night at Beauvais, returning here before breakfast this morning. Since then, office.

March 17. Verdun is still the centre of activity. The Germans are exchanging new divisions from our front with tired divisions from the Verdun front, but they are not reducing their strength opposite us.

We have a delightful, nice-looking, elderly Russian general with us now. He speaks some half-dozen languages quite fluently, claims to have been in six wars and, like Napoleon's mule, seems to have learnt very little from them. But his view of political events seems sound, if cynical. I cannot spell his name, but it is pronounced "Duke o' whisky." Like our previous Russians he has no illusions about his own country or its Army.

March 30. A long and very important communication from the French, giving details of Joffre's proposal for the big attack. He wants no preparatory attack, but everything available devoted to one big effort. There are many further details to be fixed up, the chief being that both infantry attacks must be simultaneous and not like Loos.

April 2. Rather a sharp go of bronchitis; the doctor says it means a few days in bed. D.H. has telegraphed for Ryan!! I am in the Duchess of Westminster's Red Cross Hospital, Casino, Le Touquet, and very comfortable, but I get little sleep and am tired out.

(*April* 2 to *April* 30 absent, ill with bronchitis and pneumonia.)

May 1. Back again and in the thick of it. Had a long interview with D.H. Verdun has still further reduced French divisions available for the big attack. Probably now not more than ten will be available, or about half of our attacking force. Thus we become for the first time the chief partner in a big attack. But the attack cannot now be decisive, even if the Italians and Russians make a big effort. D.H. looks on it as a "wearing-out" battle, with just the off-chance that it may wear the Germans right out. But this is improbable. Joffre still thinks a break-through just possible. There is no material alteration in the strength of the Germans opposite to us. The Flanders preparations¹ are still going on.

My own office is quite satisfactory. There is some trouble about *communiqués* not being full enough. A—— has now joined us here and will be in charge of drafting them. Press correspondents quite happy.

May 4. The Lord-Provosts of Edinburgh and Glasgow were here to-day. Dunlop of Glasgow very emphatic about Churchill, who happened to pass when I was saying good-bye to the Provosts at my office door. "That's one of the   who did all the damage with their blethers about peace and economy in Glasgow in 1913." Rather unfair on Winston, who did do a great deal to get the Navy efficient, and was *not* War Minister. But it is true enough of the Cabinet of which he was a member.

Our new H.Q. (Montreuil) is certainly much pleasanter than St. Omer. The town itself stands on a hill. There is an old wall with distinct evidence of ancient war round it, and a very picturesque old citadel. In peace-time, artists congregate here, and there is one who still remains. He claims relationship with R. L. Stevenson. What is certain is that he is a relative of an ex-Provost of Glasgow who was remarkable for his Little-England sentiments. My own billet is all that could be wished. My host and hostess cannot do enough for me. My host was an officer's servant for fifteen years, and knows exactly what is required. A small child of five is staying with them, the son of a major at Verdun.

D.H. lives at a château some 2 miles off. The routine is changed from St. Omer. My daily interview is immediately after breakfast, when I take him the railway map showing movements of German divisions, and the position map showing location of German troops on the whole front, and mark up his map. As soon as that is done,

¹ Mining at Messines.

there is the discussion about general intelligence and plans. The C.G.S. is generally present at the latter. But, as the general lines for the big attack are now settled, it is chiefly the other section that is concerned. If there are any important visitors to see him who are coming on to me, I stay on to be present at the interview, but for the moment there are none about. Generally, D.H. has some problem on which he wants a note prepared. He holds weekly conferences at each Army H.Q. in succession, to which I go to explain the German situation. They are in the forenoon, and I spend the rest of that day going round the particular Army. I can get round all the Corps H.Q. but seldom can get as far as Divisional H.Q., unless there is something especial to make me miss out a corps and go to a division.

Once a week I have a conference at my own office of the head " I " officers at Amiens. The daily Intelligence Summary is prepared in each section at my own office, so far as its own work is concerned. I finish it off in final form after dinner, rather like a newspaper editor.

I have a weekly visit to the Press château where the correspondents are located, to give them an official statement of the situation. They play up absolutely loyally to all restrictions, and it works far better to tell them frankly as much as one possibly can, differentiating clearly between what they can use and what they must keep to themselves. The foreign correspondents are more difficult, and require greater discretion as to what one talks about. The Press censorship works very smoothly, mainly owing to the loyalty of the correspondents and the tact of the censors. Very seldom a point of issue between them is referred up to me. War photographs and cinema films take very little time so far as I am concerned, though I myself see every film before it is passed. The photographs are quite harmless. The Secret Service takes more time and requires much thought, but I cannot write about that. The postal censorship is automatic, under an excellent man, and only disciplinary cases and espionage cases come to me. When we are actually fighting it will be more difficult. The only letters that are not censored are those that go with the King's Messenger, and D.H. has given me discretionary power to open any of them that I wish. Letters can, of course, be opened without any visible sign. The mapping section runs itself. The reproductions of big maps are done at Southampton and is one of the most efficient side-shows of the whole Army.

The censorship department has had one amusing case. A

letter signed with a fancy name was found written to a young lady in Paris, disclosing important information.[1] All letters to that address were collared and there followed a regular stream from the same correspondent posted at various parts of the area, getting more and more amorous and each giving a little more prohibited information. As the letters were never posted in the same area twice and often in the French local post, it took some time before the writer was traced and sent home. His last and most amorous letter was signed—" ton Richard, cœur de Lion," and he was an elderly amorist too!

May 30. Esher has been here all morning. He says all France is waiting for our counter-stroke, and getting captious about delay in its delivery. He does not think there has been any leakage of plans, but the logical French minds have deduced that there will inevitably be a counter-stroke, and that it must be by our Armies. It is probably inevitable that the Germans have some agents in Paris and also in London. I do not think they could have any inkling of plans from London, for even the Army as a whole has no idea of the time or place of the attack, but Paris is more militarily-minded than London and there is a real danger of leakage there. The prisoners we lost at Vimy Ridge can give nothing away, for they know nothing.

June 1. Hughes, the P.M. of Australia, has been here—a most interesting study in personality. He is that queer combination, a Socialist and Imperialist. No one could be more determined than he is that we must endure all things for victory in the field. He is frankly scornful of the Cabinet, calls them a lot of old women, and says they should have but one aim and purpose—to back up the soldiers and sailors. He is very deaf, with a squeaky voice and a most charming laugh. Always moves at a trot, which, however, is not much quicker than a fast walk. I took him round the ramparts and he jogged along quite happily the whole way, nearly a mile and a half. His hero is Kitchener, so far as soldiers are concerned. He quite realized that big though Australia's effort is, that of England is proportionately far bigger, but says Australia is only beginning. His optimism was cheering. He takes an interest in peace terms. He says his only concern after the war is the fate of the soldiers maimed and whole, and talked of the difficulties of ex-service men after the South African War. Hughes committed

[1] About the Tanks.

the offence, unforgivable to us here, of being late for dinner with the Chief, and did it in a very thorough manner, by about a quarter of an hour. D.H. was very impatient and grumpy during the wait, but he *did* wait, much to my wonder. Hughes, quite unabashed, hardly even apologized, and his personality carried it off successfully. He is a magnetic little man, not in any sense great, but magnetic to an extraordinary degree.

June 4. There are going to be difficulties with the Press. The official *communiqués* are being criticized as incomplete and bald; the correspondents' dispatches as too heavily censored. The first criticism is true but inevitable, the second is not. I shall endeavour to put a distinguished imaginative writer to try his hand at sensationalizing the *communiqués* and the result will be interesting to watch. About the Press correspondents we can do nothing more than we are doing. They can write up incidents as much as they like and are given every facility for collecting them, but they must not disclose either our intentions or the location of our troops. Most of the trouble is probably from the newspaper people, not from the public. It should cease when things become active. Both *communiqués* and Press stuff should be exciting enough then.

June 9. It is sad about Lord K. and terrible as well as sad, for there is literally no one who can take his place and do the work that he was doing as a soldier chief in the Cabinet. K. and Robertson and D.H. working together were impregnable to politicians. There is no one big enough to take K.'s place.

We got the first news from an intercepted German wireless, and I took it at once to D.H. after confirming from home. His comment was, " How shall we get on without him? " I cannot understand how the Germans got the news so soon, unless by wire from London.[1]

Lord Roberts died with the Army, K. with the Navy, both in harness, the two great soldiers of the Empire. I had always believed that K. would become C.-in-C. of the Allied Armies; and unless the next great battle brings decision, which is now unlikely, I think that would have happened next year, when our Army will be bigger than the French Army.

Lord Newton came to-day to discuss " Press " and " Propa-

[1] It subsequently transpired that the correspondent of a neutral country telegraphed the news to his paper, whence it was at once telegraphed on to Germany.

ganda" with me. His theme is that our part in the war wants "boosting" both at home and with neutrals. All we can do here is to provide material, and that we shall do next month. The "boosting" must be done at home, where Foreign Office, War Office and Admiralty are playing with it. The Admiralty have not much to boost at present. So long as the boosters confine themselves to boosting what has happened and not what they hope may happen it can do no harm, but if they raise hopes too high and then get disappointment, it will do much more harm than good, and might bring D.H. crashing in the commotion. Newton is very sensible about it all and very witty. I told him what we were already doing in the way of facilities and offered to improve them in any way he could suggest, subject only to censorship requirements. He suggested a free-lance man from his own department[1], to which I agreed.

Meantime all goes well with our preparations for next month.

June 15. I was present at the very impressive Memorial Service for K. at St. Paul's. I arrived at the War Office from France early in the morning and was told that I was to go to the Service, as the representative of G.H.Q. I found myself occupying a pew all by myself in an embarrassingly prominent position, but embarrassment was soon lost in the beauty and solemnity of the Service. One did not, could not, think, one simply *felt*. It was utter peace, unconscious of everything, the war, one's own little troubles, the great assembly, though everyone who mattered was present. One was close to the great beauty of the dimly lighted Cathedral and the beautiful music, made even more beautiful by the modulated voices of the clergy. It was only at the end of it all, when the "Last Post" rang out, that one realized one was there to mark the passing of a great man, from a great work well done, into eternity. I stayed until almost everyone had left, then got away alone and walked back to the War Office through streets nearly as busy as in peace-time.

Everything looks well for our attack. The Russians are doing well in Galicia. The Germans are continuing to hammer at Verdun, where the French are holding admirably. There is no strengthening of the German lines opposite to us.

It has turned into summer here. The farmers are beginning to cut the hay. The spirits of our own men are at their best, and munitions are coming in well.

[1] Col. John Buchan, M.P.

Rumour has it that Lloyd George will succeed K. at the War Office. I suppose it is inevitable that we have a civilian there, but nobody could be less welcome to the Army than Lloyd George. He knows nothing about the Army, and has no sympathy with it. He dislikes D.H. and I cannot imagine that he likes Robertson. The first thing he will do will be to look about for somebody to succeed one or both of them.

June 21. Lord Crewe is here, very much the old school of statesman. He spent the whole morning in my office. He told me that Asquith always supported K. in the Cabinet, but that all the rest were hostile to K., particularly Lloyd George, for whom Crewe has a mixture of admiration and personal dislike.

I went to-day to see Gavan Pagan—a sort of cousin of mine. He was minister of a big church in Edinburgh before the war, which he left to enlist in the ranks. D.H. wants him to take up padre's work again out here. Good padres are not easily found, and there are plenty to do the work Pagan is now doing. I went to urge this on Pagan, but he would not hear of it; he sat on a box in his tent looking like a crusader, and quoted, " There is a time to pray and a time to fight." I think he is quite right; if he becomes a padre he could pray but not fight, now he can both fight and pray. By the way, D. found rather an immature and priggish padre with his battalion and turned him into a most human and useful padre by making him go over some jumps every morning on horseback, and sending him to fetch *La Vie Parisienne* for the Mess, so as to get in touch with their failings I suppose. Ryan at Loos used one of the padres to give coffee to the wounded as they arrived and another to write letters home, and two more to help to dig the graves!

But the padres out here as a whole are admirable. Sectarianism has almost, but not quite, disappeared. The padres are no longer the class apart that they are in peace-time. Men are more ready to listen to padres of any sort in war, and the right sort do immense good. War has made France a deeply religious country again, anyhow so far as religious observances are concerned. The churches are crowded all over our area.

June 27. My latest recruit for Intelligence work is Lord Crauford. He was working as a stretcher-bearer in a R.A.M.C. unit. He had some scruples against becoming a combatant. He has a good knowledge of languages and will be useful. I am getting him a commission.

By the time this arrives we shall have begun. There must be heavy casualties, but everything looks well for success.[1]

June 28. We have arrived at our Advanced G.H.Q. to-day. Up to now things have gone quite well, but it is too early yet to make any forecast. So far as I can see, the Germans have no real idea of any attack in force being imminent. The movements behind their lines appear to be only that of resting battalions up to the front line. The chief danger I fear is that they should leave their front-line trenches practically empty and hold in strength their second and third lines. Evidence to-day tends to show that this has not been done as yet. Gas appears to have been only moderately useful.

Newton's emissary, John Buchan, arrived this morning. I have sent him on, meantime, with the Press people, but have told him he can do exactly as he wishes, and go where he pleases. I have written to ask for him to be given a commission at once. He has not got uniform at present, and runs some risk of being arrested and suffering some measure of inconvenience if he leaves the Press.

The correspondents are divided into three parties, each with one officer attached. They will be given full facilities for seeing whatever can be seen. The officers with them have authority to interview Staff officers to get detailed information. The G.S.O. in charge of Press as a whole will come here every day to get the latest information available, which the Press correspondents can embody in their articles. In addition to their articles, they will be allowed to send over the official wires in time for the morning papers a joint cable which they themselves will prepare.

The weather has cleared. There has been no rain to-day, but the sky is overcast most of the time, but with intervals of sunshine. I do not expect to be able to leave G.H.Q. much during the next few days, and went forward this afternoon to see the preparations. It is impossible to describe the scene. We have been bombarding for five days, and the Germans replying. The whole area is torn with shells, trees stripped to skeletons, villages just heaps of ruins. The noise is terrific, with the continuous roar of our own guns and the crack of enemy shells. Our observation balloons hang in the sky like great gorged leeches of the air. Our aeroplanes are

[1] Weather caused postponement until July 1.

entirely masters of the air, and are circling like sparrow-hawks over the enemy lines. I went up in one and across the line. Except for the flash of the German guns one could see no sign of life. In our own trenches we could see men moving about, and away back, the column just beginning to move up. And all this over an area 22 miles long, from the left of our attack to the right of the French. From the air the rivers and the canals are the most noticeable, after them the defensive lines; one cannot see the rise and fall of the ground which means so much to-morrow.

Late in the evening—after dinner—I went to one Corps where the preparations had not been so thorough, to advise whether that part of the attack should be held back. I had been given power to countermand the attack of the Corps if I considered it advisable, a most unpleasant responsibility, for it had little chance of complete success and there was a certainty of many casualties. But even partial success might mean much to other parts of the line. The Corps Commander was more than satisfied. He was convinced of a very great success. The Divisional Commanders are almost equally confident. Eventually I decided to let the attack go on, and came back feeling very miserable. The Corps Commander said he felt "like Napoleon before the battle of Austerlitz!"

CHAPTER XV

THE SOMME

June 30. Once more the eve of battle. We do not expect any great advance, or any great place of arms to fall to us now. We are fighting primarily to wear down the German armies and the German nation, to interfere with their plans, gain some valuable position and generally to prepare for the great decisive offensive which must come sooner or later, if not this year or even next year. The casualty list will be big. Wars cannot be won without casualties. I hope people at home realize this. We are *winning*, even if we do little more than we are doing this time. But it will be slow and costly. If we face losses bravely we shall win quicker and it will be a final win.

It is always well to disclaim great hopes before an attack. The rumours [1] which have been current regarding the taking of Lille, give now a good opportunity of pointing out that at the present stage of the war, and with the present strength of the Germans opposite the British—which has not been affected by events in Russia—it is not wise to consider as even possible an advance through a large area or the capture of important places of arms. You have been told of the arrangements for special telegrams by the Press correspondents. I hope that there will be no delay in getting them passed straight to the Press.

July 1. We attacked this morning at 7.30 a.m. and have done well on the main part of the attack (Fourth Army) where we have penetrated to the depth of one mile. On the left we have not done well. We took the German first-line trenches, but were driven back in the evening with, I am afraid, very heavy loss. The present situation offers great possibilities, if we can grasp them to-morrow. The Germans are reported to have had warning, apart from the bombardment, of our intended attack from French deserters, but

[1] These had been started with a view to drawing German attention away from the Somme, and seem to have succeeded.

this requires confirmation. Our bombardment was very effective against the trench line, but ineffective against villages and concreted casemates. One German unit (2nd Guards Reserve Division) put up a first-class fight, but generally the morale of the Germans was low. Progress was hampered, and in some cases prevented, by lack of training. Troops failed to take advantage of situations offered to them, because they had not been ordered to carry out the particular operation. This must happen with a new army; we improve daily.

As regards the German troops, " milking " is in full progress near the Somme, and to the south of it. North of the Somme there is no " milking." I am not certain why, but it appears probable that they did expect an attack as far north as Lille. This, anyhow, is according to captured correspondence. It may, of course, have this other meaning, viz. that they propose to press on us should a suitable opportunity occur. Ypres, of course, always offers itself. There is not enough definite informatiou yet to form a logical opinion. On the whole, our interpretation of the information received has been fairly good.

July 4. Joffre and Foch were here yesterday. D.H. tells me the purpose of this visit was to get him to change his plans, and attack again on our left flank. It is difficult to see why they should wish to interfere. Anyhow, no change is being made.

July 5. We have captured the whole of the front system of German entrenchment, on a front of 6 miles. This means a depth of one mile throughout. Their next entrenchment line is a mile ahead of us, not nearly so strong as the first. Captured documents show that the Germans have made great use of their apparatus for overhearing telephone messages and, in spite of all our precautions, got information of the hour of attack through this means.

We captured at the H.Q. of a unit several letters addressed from Germany to soldiers at the front, and held up by their censors as giving away too much about the internal state of Germany. The total of prisoners is 15,000. A whole battalion surrendered yesterday, twenty officers and six hundred men.

Repington comes to-morrow. I do not look forward to his visit with either pleasure or confidence. He is so untrustworthy. But he can write, and I am sure it is to the interests of the country that he should be allowed to come out in spite of all he has done.

Lord Crauford has been promoted from "Lieutenant in the

Intelligence Corps " to " Cabinet Minister " ! He asked me if I could not keep him here. But as Bonar Law wrote saying he was indispensable, or nearly so, for the Government, he had to go. We have had ex-Cabinet Ministers coming out here to junior jobs; but promotion of a Lieutenant in the Intelligence Corps to Cabinet rank is unique !

July 8. Repington sought to ingratiate himself by much gossip from home. He is not a pleasant personality, and will no doubt gossip equally about us here when he goes home. But he is very well informed about the German Army. I do not know where he got his information, but it must be from some official source, probably French. I was present at his interview with D.H. (as a witness). D.H. was very polite, but very frigid.

Esher is here to-day and says France is much impressed by our success, but that the French papers are giving all the credit to the French attack, which was a relatively small affair, but which goes on under our shadow with relatively very little loss. If it heartens the French, that is all to the good, but Esher is insistent that we should get more said of our doings in the French Press. That is a Foreign Office or War Office job—Lord knows which—but, anyhow, not mine. All I can do is to give facilities.

The following are the arrangements for the French Press :

(*a*) We have Tison, formerly editor of L'*Illustration*, an accredited French correspondent, who telegraphs at least twice each day to the French Press Bureau at G.Q.G.

(*b*) Buchan, sent by the Foreign Office for Press and propaganda, communicates his stuff to London, whence it goes to Paris.

(*c*) All our official *communiqués* are posted at every French P.O.

(*d*) I have arranged for a party of French correspondents to be sent as soon as the situation demands. Probably I shall call them up to-morrow. All preparations have been made.

(*e*) A résumé of each day's operations will be telephoned daily to Paris for Esher and the French Press there.

Esher says that in spite of Verdun, the French are more determined than at the beginning of the year, but that Joffre is being sniped at.

Muirhead Bone is out doing pictures of the back areas. Now the newspaper proprietors want to come out, and each paper wants to have its own representative, instead of six shared by them all. It is quite impossible. We could not control a crowd of correspondents, nor could we ensure that all of them would be as responsible as the present ones are. The War Office is very anxious to do nothing to offend the newspapers, naturally enough. " He who lives by the river must make friends with the crocodile." The proprietors could do nothing good out here except amuse themselves. They can come when the battle ends, not before, but I *should* like to have some of the editors here; that would be helpful.

July 10. The Russian C.G.S. was here to-day lunching with the Chief, and his Staff officers came to me. I took them out and motored right into some of the villages which we took from the Germans in this battle. The Russians are doing well in their fighting, but their officers never impress one favourably. One of them gave an interesting comment on the administration breakdown there. He said that up to the war, not only all the civil businesses, but also most of the Government departments had Germans in responsible positions, who really ran the details of administration. Most of them have gone, and there is no one trained to take their place. Others remain and are not helpful, if not, indeed, deliberately making difficulties. He said that French and Russians, in spite of the Alliance, never work well together.

An extraordinary situation has arisen about a man whom I sent up for a commission in the Intelligence Corps. He was recommended with most glowing reports, had been Sergt.-Major of a battalion, an excellent linguist, and was in the Intelligence police when he was brought to my notice. He had a son holding a commission in the Army. When his name went home, a very important firm of bankers wrote that the man had committed an offence in his youth while in their employ. They had not prosecuted him, but had stipulated that he must leave England and not return. The bank now objected to his getting a commission. On the face of it, if the man was not convicted, he is still innocent. In any case it seems vindictive now to drag it all forward again. But the W.O., or rather the Government, seem frightened of the bankers, so the poor devil will have to go.

July 14. The battle has entered on a new phase with a very brilliant bit of work by Rawlinson, an advance over no-man's land on a three-mile front *by night*, to within a few hundred yards of the German trenches, and a surprise attack at dawn. It has been completely successful. The Germans have been thickening up in front of us and it means a long and fierce fight, which will last many more days before we can hope to finish the battle. We have already accomplished one thing; the German attack on Verdun is over, or practically over. All their available troops are being sent here.

July 18. Another stage of the battle is over; we hold 4 miles of the crest of the ridge. One cannot help comparing this battle with the Aisne, when for nearly a month we strove to gain the Chemin des Dames ridge and made no progress. In this battle, in three weeks we are on the ridge. How different it all is from 1914. Then we had no heavy artillery, little ammunition for our light guns, no hopes of reinforcements. This time, ample artillery, and reinforcements coming out regularly. Even more remarkable is the progress on the scientific side of war. Observation balloons, aeroplanes, air photographs, sound ranging, listening-in apparatus, Secret Service. On the Aisne each corps only had one officer for " I " work. Now there is one with each brigade and division, and altogether seventeen at Army Head-quarters, and every Corps is asking for a larger staff. It is the same in every other branch. War is a science. G.H.Q. are now controlling a far bigger and more intricate business than any industrial concern in peace-time. As time goes on it will get bigger still. Not only will the Army expand, but we shall inevitably have to take over the railways from the French.

There is still very considerable trouble with regard to the information reaching London and neutral countries. The papers themselves are largely to blame; the war correspondents' special telegram is given exactly the same prominence as the official *communiqué*, and as they are not necessarily similarly worded, or contain even precisely the same information, there is confusion.

Northcliffe is coming out, so that he can see for himself that the arrangements for the Press are suitable.

Lord Derby has been here, and the Chief put the whole problem of the Press before him. He seems satisfied, but says that there is a strong demand from the newspapers for a Special Correspondent for each paper. I think this would be very dangerous. We cannot conveniently control more than six correspondents. The Armies that are carrying on the battle would object to more or larger visits than they get at present. There are difficulties about accommodation. Every article has to be signed either by myself or one other Staff officer, and it would be quite impossible to read through twelve dispatches. If the War Office overrule us, and we have to take more, the only result would be they would have to be housed still farther back, and the facilities would have to be curtailed.

July 19. The Germans have counter-attacked, and taken some ground; not serious, but we shall have to retake it either to-day or to-morrow. The weather conditions are all against us now.

July 21. Lord Northcliffe has been here, and I think good will result from his visit. He is very dramatic, and requires gentle handling. His first request when he came into my office, after shaking hands, was to be allowed to send a telegram, direct and immediately to London. The only line on which this could be done was the G.H.Q. line. He then walked to my stand-up desk and wrote his telegram in great printed characters. When it came to me to be countersigned—which was necessary before it could go on to the direct wire—I found that it was to his mother to say that he had arrived safely, and sending her his love.

So far Northcliffe has been quite easy and pleasant, and full of satisfaction at the treatment he has had here. A great deal depends on how he and D.H. get on together; they have very little in common. The last time I saw Northcliffe his whole mind was filled with distrust and dislike of Kitchener. I do not think his tirades against Kitchener affected public opinion much, but Kitchener's position in the public mind was much stronger than that of D.H., and Northcliffe could do immense harm.

The battle is going on normally. The French have done well, taking 3,000 prisoners and 20 guns; we, ourselves, made only a small advance, with 200 prisoners. The most interesting points are the excuses which the German Staff is now making.

There is some concern about the German offensive in Russia in the late autumn, and I have to prepare an appreciation of the possibility. It does not appear probable that there will be an offensive on any great scale for the following reasons:—

1. The exhaustion of German personnel, both at Verdun and in this battle.
2. The fact that the 1917 class is now being used, and that after it the 1918 class is the only reserve.
3. The exhaustion of Germany in resources, continued reports of which are reaching us.

July 22 (*Sunday*). I spent the whole day with the newspaper people, first with Lord Northcliffe and then with Lord Burnham, and finally presided at a dinner given in their honour by various journalists out here; a strange proceeding in the middle of a battle.

Northcliffe is definitely favourably impressed by D.H. and we can count on his support until some new maggot enters into his brain. He is amazingly outspoken in his comments on people at home; he regards Asquith as quite played out, Lloyd George as only out for his own career, but says that the latter has more vim than all the rest put together. Burnham is very non-committal. Both seem thoroughly satisfied with the arrangements for their people. Actually we have had no difficulty at all, so far, with the correspondents themselves. The War Office want Gibbs[1] to write up some special articles for Australia to soothe the feelings of people there, as I had to refuse permission to come here to one of their own representatives, who had been very difficult on a previous visit.

Northcliffe is very interesting with regard to Repington, and told me an interesting incident when he bought *The Times*, but before it was publicly known. He says that Repington came to him with the story that *The Times* regarded him as so invaluable that they were willing to pay any figure for his services, and wanted to sell himself at a higher figure to Northcliffe for the *Mail*. Northcliffe now regards Repington as valueless, and said that if there was any more trouble he would be prepared to sack him out of hand at any request from us.

Donald of the *Daily Chronicle* has expressed himself as very satisfied with the existing Press arrangements, and says that if *The Times* does not get a correspondent of its own none of the other newspapers will press any further for special representation, but that if *The Times* does so all the others will. Northcliffe is quite prepared to share the *Daily Mail* correspondent with the *Manchester Guardian*, at our suggestion.

Both the Foreign Office and the War Office are worrying a great deal about propaganda, particularly in France, and there seems to be great confusion at home as to who is responsible; our own responsibility here is only to give facilities for the collection of material. Crauford was to do this for the Foreign Office under an arrangement made with Lord Newton, but their scheme was that he should have full access to all documents and official reports which would be of use for two purposes :—

---

[1] Now Sir Philip Gibbs.

(a) To provide the propaganda offices at home with material, treating them rather as a journalist treats his editor.

(b) To provide stuff for the French Press, acting in conjunction with the Maison de la Presse, and the G.Q.G. providing articles also for the *Bulletin des Armées*.

When Crauford was taken home by the Cabinet I employed a temporary man, C. E. Montague, who is in every way suitable, except that he is himself a Press man, and the other journalists view him askance. I would much prefer to have Onslow for the work.

The trouble about propaganda work at home appears to be that while the Foreign Office wants to publish favourable news, the War Office wants to withhold anything that tends to show that the Germans are hard hit. There is no doubt but that the German Army is affected by the internal conditions of Germany, and that their resistance to us, stout though it has been, is suffering to a certain extent from the effects. To this extent the publication of definite information regarding the internal conditions of Germany could only have a good effect. In England it is no longer a question of trying to get recruits, therefore, from that point of view, there seems to be no reason why we should paint the picture any darker than it is. To the outside world there is no doubt that we have tended to discourage confidence in ourselves by always holding back that which is favourable. We here, therefore, are in favour of the publication of favourable news regarding the internal position of Germany. We quite realize, of course, that the final decision as regards the policy whether to publish or withhold must rest with those at home, and we shall not cavil if we are overruled, only we think the decision will be wrong.

July 29. All the troubles regarding the Press and the correspondents seem to be satisfactorily settled. The only small difficulty now outstanding is that there is a threat to take away Perry Robinson of *The Times*, who has throughout acted as doyen of the Press correspondents, and been most helpful. Actually he has been allowed to see more of our plans and intentions than most Staff officers. Even with the best of intentions, he might let something slip out in conversation at home. And he knows so much that the risk is too great, during a battle. If he is to be relieved I shall ask Northcliffe to send him to somewhere in the south of France to write up our bases, etc., and keep him from the risk of contamination until the battle has developed a little further.

Both Esher and Briand are pressing for better film propaganda in France.

One of the Secret Service systems has temporarily broken down and there is a gap in our information. We know that a large number of exhausted German divisions have been withdrawn from our immediate front, so as to avoid the depressing influence on the morale of troops coming up and passing through exhausted divisions resting in the battle area, but we do not yet know where they have gone.

Air reconnaissances for information have failed us; the aeroplanes have to go too high now for good observation. The number of reconnaissances is very limited and the information given is meagre and amateurish. The best material is coming from prisoners' letters and the examination of prisoners. We now have two thoroughly competent Intelligence Corps examiners at each of the prisoners' cages to sift out those with information, which is easier got when a prisoner is still under the stress of battle. So far, this is working very well. Intercepted German telephone messages have not given great results, although we now have two intercepting apparatus in each corps area. The Germans, knowing from their own experience how valuable this source is for small tactical information, must have taken very great precautions about our using the same methods.

As regards the general strategical problem, the situation on the whole is quite satisfactory; there seems to be very little doubt but that the morale of the Germans in front of us is not so good as it was. For instance, their counter-attacks during the last few days have been very mild affairs compared with those we experienced at Loos. Of course our barrage has been better, both as regards direction and volume.

At present, owing to the rather contracted front on which we are operating, the Germans can get sufficient troops to oppose us. As the front enlarges, and it will shortly, I think they will be hard pressed to find troops, and we are hopeful of a fairly big result. The great difficulty is between cramping the initiative of subordinates by giving them difficult objectives on the one hand, and the lack of perspective by inexperienced commanders on the other hand. Even Divisional and Corps Commanders are at present inexperienced in their new commands. After another year's war it will be possible to leave to them a much larger measure of initiative, and they themselves will feel much less cramped by such orders as they do get and they will know when they can exceed them. We are still paying the penalty of an Army which has grown rapidly into a formidable force from a very meagre beginning. The type of orders which have been issued now are utterly different from those which were required when we were dealing only with the old Regular Army.

A very hopeful feature is the new young officer, who, apart from his lack of experience and training, is every bit as good in battle as the old Regular type. He is just as brave and self-sacrificing, and just as willing to lead. Regimental officers tell me that when these juniors are not fighting they require more supervision than the old officer; the sense of duty for monotonous routine is not so great.

July 30. The stream of visitors is unending, and takes up much valuable time. Yesterday we had a party comprising Lord Bryce, two Americans and a Swede. To-morrow we have the Prince of Monaco, who is said to be interested in nothing but zoology and biology. Fortunately the Army is big enough now to find several tame zoologists and biologists to go round with him.

Lord Bryce is covered with white hair and gives the appearance of a fox looking through a hedge. His strong subject is, of course, America. He told me that he was convinced that sooner or later America would be fighting on our side. It seems to be very unlikely at present, but Bryce is an acknowledged expert on our transatlantic cousins. There is, by the way, a good story going round here about an officer on leave, who found himself travelling in a railway carriage with an American. The American pored over the newspaper accounts of the fighting, then threw the paper down and said, " Some fight," to which the young officer dryly commented, " Some don't."

CHAPTER XVI
THE SOMME (*CONTINUED*)

August 2. There is a little war within a war on in London between the War Office and the Foreign Office, all about films! Newton and Esher both pressed for films of our fighting to be shown in France. French films are being shown on the London stage, but no British ones on this side of the Channel. The French G.Q.G. offered to take films and show them within a fortnight in twenty French towns, and apparently this made quite a flutter at home, where some funny little Foreign Office committee, represented by Masterman and presumably independent of Newton, has made agreements with the foreign countries, and is very upset at anyone getting ahead of them. It is more like peace rivalry and jealousy than war. On the other hand, the Foreign Office have written to the War Office that our news service to America is admirable and that German news has been swept out of the American papers. They say that their papers comment on the swift flow of news from G.H.Q. Most of the brunt of the trouble falls on the Intelligence of the War Office, who point out that the great difficulty is that if the Press are upset in any way the particular paper proprietor goes at once to the highest authority—either the Prime Minister or the Secretary of State—and that the War Office is put in an awkward position.

August 5. A very good little success yesterday. The Australians, together with one of our own divisions, took 2 miles of front-line trench and some 500 prisoners. Among the documents was one very interesting appeal printed in Germany to the German people to rise in revolt and enforce peace on the German rulers, and thus avoid starvation in their country. In itself it may not mean very much, there must be in every country at war some people who want peace at any price; the important thing is that it should have been found in the possession of and treasured by, one of their soldiers.

The curiosity of the female sex is stronger than the fear of danger. Yesterday I was motoring up towards a Divisional Headquarters, when I overtook two young women on foot going the same way. I asked them what their destination was, and they said they wanted to walk to a unit in the front line and see what it was like to be under fire. I put them into a car going the other way and told them not to be naughty. They were both nurses at one of the casualty clearing stations having their day off. One of them was under twenty and said that she was at school in August, 1914.

August 9. A committee has been formed at home to examine the available man-power of the Germans. The War Office have arrived at the following figures for all fronts :—

In main line depots	150,000
Available in Germany to refill front-line depots	250,000
Total available up to the middle of October	400,000

After October the 1918 class will become progressively available, 350,000, making a grand total of three-quarters of a million ; if this is correct it would mean that there would be no hope of exhausting the German reserves of personnel in this year's fighting. There is a movement of German troops eastward from Mons, either towards Russia or possibly to the south. It seems very probable that it is towards Russia, where the Germans appear to be having as much as they can do.

Although the number of men available is the most difficult factor to estimate, the question of morale is even more important. I cannot see Germany fighting on with her depots depleted and with no hopes of reinforcements from any neutral country joining her. She cannot now have any real hopes of America siding with her, and there is no other neutral country with sufficient men to matter. War is a thing of surprises and it is easy to be too optimistic. Probably in London it is difficult to appreciate as strongly as we do here the relative loss of morale in the German Army. They are still fighting well, but there is a marked difference between this year and last year, and we have still some months' campaigning in front of us before the winter sets in.

August 12. His Majesty's visit has been a great success. We took him into Fricourt and even a bit farther forward than that, so that he was very close to the fighting line. The visit will do a great deal of good, at home as well as here. He has been followed by cameras everywhere, and the whole visit is being well written up in a series of articles which will appear as soon as he is safely back in England.

The German wireless is becoming more and more laughable each day. I see that they now announce a very big attack by the whole of the Allies on the Somme, as having taken place yesterday. Actually on our part there was no attack, we went forward a few miles north of Guillemont. That was all in that part of the line. On our extreme left we advanced very considerably. The best part of the news came from the Australians fighting the 16th German Division. They seem to have established just as much superiority over them as they did over their old opponents, the 117th Division.

Vimy Ridge is asking to be retaken, and the Germans on the Ypres Salient are weaker than they have ever been before. Yesterday the 4th and 5th Ersatz Divisions behaved in an extraordinary manner at Ypres. After a bombardment from the German guns a few patrols got up and walked about, and were duly knocked over; they were in turn followed by a few more, who suffered the same fate. It was all very foolish. It may be that the Germans intended an attack and could not get going.

The air reconnaissances are beginning to do good work; we have them out as far as Maubeuge and Mons and they are valuable in confirming our agents' reports. The Flying Corps will not take up seriously the question of dropping agents behind the enemy's lines. We tried with X. a few days ago and I am afraid that X. has been done in; it is a great pity, for he was quite our best man for that work.[1]

---

[1] Subsequent adventures of X. formed one of the most remarkable incidents of the war. The aeroplane which took him behind the German lines would not rise from the ground for its return journey. The pilot, a boy of nineteen with no knowledge of French or any other foreign language, urged the agent to leave him to be taken prisoner. X., however, said that he could get him away in safety, and took him into some caves which he knew of in the neighbourhood, where they remained until the hue and cry was over. Subsequently he was provided with a suitable disguise, and the pair of them made their way towards the Dutch frontier. Passing through Brussels they became separated, and the young Air Force officer, in spite of a good counterfeit pass, came under suspicion of a German contre-espionage officer. He was on a tramway car at the time; he knocked the officer down, jumped off the tram-car and fled into one of the by-streets of Brussels. While still running away from the commotion, by a most extraordinary coincidence, he was picked up by another of our agents, who concealed him in his house until the hue and cry had died down, and then took him on to the frontier, which he crossed safely and returned to England.

The reports from agents regarding troop movements are distinctly good and very prompt. I cannot help thinking that the Germans are moving further troops to the Eastern frontier. Things appear to be very bad there, and they must try and do something to rectify the matter. On the other hand, it is difficult to see what troops they can hope to spare from here. We are jostling them hard, and they must know that they are going to be jostled harder in the future. The actual units are getting thick on the Somme front, though many of them are only mere cadres of their full establishment. I think the opportunity for a German counter-attack is past. Certainly it will not have as good a chance now as it would have done ten days ago, though it is of course a possibility. If it does come it will be on the Guillemont-Trones Wood line, and I think the 16th or 17th the most probable dates.

Lloyd George has been out here; he was very cheery and optimistic this time, quite different from his last visit. Whatever his faults, he has amazing energy and a great flow of words. Lord Reading was with him, very learned and clever, but utterly dwarfed by Lloyd George's vitality. Neither of them seemed to be worrying much about our casualty list, at which I was greatly surprised.

We are attacking again to-morrow, and I am hoping for great results.

September 6. The Prime Minister has been here again. There was one most amusing incident. D.H. has some excellent old brandy, which, however, he only sends round once at each meal; after that it stands in solitary grandeur in front of him on the table. The Prime Minister obviously appreciated it very much and wished for more, but did not feel that he could ask for another glass. His method of achieving his aim was to move his glass a little nearer the bottle and then try and catch D.H.'s eye and draw it down to his glass and then to the bottle. The glass advanced by stages as small as those of our attack, until, last of all, it was resting against the bottle; then, overcoming all his scruples, the Prime Minister, with a sweep of the arm, seized the bottle and poured himself out a glass.

I was sitting opposite and the by-play was indescribably funny. D.H. did not notice it at all. When I told it to him afterwards his comment was, "If he has not enough determination to ask for a glass of brandy when he wants it he should not be Prime Minister."

September 16. The tanks have been a very great success. I do not know if they would have accomplished so much against infantry that was not at a low point as regards morale. There was much discussion as to their use—whether we should wait until we had built up a bigger form of them, and had the personnel more highly trained. The main argument in favour of their use was that the Germans did definitely know we had some new instrument, but had not yet found out what it was. If we waited, they would find out and might—we do not know—have found a suitable reply. Also we learn more by one day's active work with them than from a year's theorizing. When we use them next time we shall have improved by this experience; it is still not too late to make alteration in design if necessary. Above all, this is a vital battle and we should be in error to throw away anything that might increase our chance of success. We have still a month's fighting ahead of us.

The name "Tank"[1] came into being to avoid leakage. There had been much correspondence and telegraphing regarding "water tanks" from Flanders and Belgium that were coming to us, just when these "Tanks" were beginning to become important. So we carried on with the old word, meaning the new thing, as being less likely to attract attention than a brand-new word. On the whole the secret has been very well kept so far, in spite of stupidity in England,[2] and the tanks have contributed very freely to our success in this fight—a mile forward on a six-mile front, and more to follow.

I have just had prepared for the Press an analysis of German *communiqués*.

On July 3, after we had captured 7 miles of German trench line and four strongly fortified villages, Montauban, Mametz, Fricourt and Le Boissel, with 4,000 prisoners, the German *communiqué* said: "The Anglo-French attack secured no advantages north of the Somme."

[1] The idea of a mobile armoured strong point, out of which the tank developed, probably occurred to most minds after our first experiences of attacking strongly entrenched positions. I first heard it suggested by an Intelligence Corps Officer as early as the battle of the Aisne. His idea took the form of a group of men carrying a section of bullet-proof shield. Very elementary calculations of weight proved that idea impracticable and the suggestion of using the "Caterpillar" tractor, which had been experimented with at Aldershot in 1914, immediately arose. I remember discussing the possibility of this with Colonel Swinton (now Sir E. D. Swinton) in 1914. But it was so obvious a development that it must have occurred simultaneously in many regimental and Staff messes.

[2] A party of M.P.s were taken to see the Tanks in England and there was immediate leakage of information discovered in the censorship.

On July 7 we captured the Leipzig Redoubt, and advanced 500 yards on a front of 2000 yards, routing a Prussian Guard unit in the process; the German *communiqué* says of this: " The heroism of our troops caused the enemy a day of complete disappointment; his attacks were repulsed with heavy losses."

On July 8 we captured a large part of Trones Wood. The Germans called this " six unsuccessful attacks."

On July 14, after our capture of 4 miles of trench line and the villages of Bazeutin le Petit and Bazeutin le Grand, and Delville Wood, the Germans said: " The English attacked in the Mametz-Longueval section. Their first attempts have been driven off with heavy loss."

It is all very gratifying. For if the Germans have to resort to lying *communiqués* to keep the people up to the mark they must be in a bad way.

We go on again to-morrow, but you must not expect any decisive battle yet. It is possible—but no more than barely possible —that the Germans may collapse before the end of the year, if the weather holds and we can go on attacking them. It has cleared up again after a bad spell, just in time for this attack, and to-day is fine and clear.

I wonder if people at home realize either the magnitude or the importance of this battle, or think it all waste. I heard—at the Foreign Office—last month from Lampson[1] that people at home take no interest in war films. He called it " incredible and discreditable "; he says all the public want to see is Charlie Chaplin. But to-day Faunthorpe writes that the Somme film is " a record boom in the history of cinematography." I don't know which is right, nor do I care so far as the film is concerned, but I do hope that England realizes what is being done out here by her troops, that we have effected already more than any previous attack either by the French or ourselves, that we have beaten a great portion of the German Army in battle, and that we may still force them to peace this year.

September 19. Lord Esher has been here again, very concerned about propaganda. He says there is " conflict and confusion, and the absence of responsibility that inevitably comes from the employment of too many cooks. The Germans, with their radio and their misrepresentations, will manage to keep up the morale of Germany long after the time when it should have been forced down to the

[1] Now Sir Miles Lampson. Then in charge of film propaganda.

lowest point of the scale." He is right. Northcliffe writes much the same from Italy. He says, " They do not appear to know that we are bearing the burden of the Somme."

The trouble is that the Foreign Office, Home Office, War Office, Admiralty and Masterman's absurd committee are all working separately and each is jealous of the other. After all, the actual matter must be collected out here so far as the military information is concerned. We are doing direct propaganda here in a small way, by dropping stuff from aeroplanes behind the German lines—leaflets, facsimiles of German prisoners' letters, showing their good treatment in England.

What we have to do in propaganda is to seek to defeat the German censorship; that is, to tell the Germans precisely that which their censor is trying to prevent them from knowing. It does not now much matter what happens in neutral countries, except America, and there we are already well served by the correspondents here and by our American visitors. For propaganda in enemy countries we want one co-ordinating authority for all such work, for propaganda, like advertising, must be continuous, persistent and co-ordinated. We should employ the expert, not the amateur. The expert is either a newspaper man, the company promoter or the organizer of some of our big amusements. This authority should have his own agents out here, so far as this area is concerned, and should not have to get stuff filtered and doled out from either the War Office or Foreign Office. As a matter of fact, half the trouble now probably is that the War Office do not want things to look too rosy; it may queer their pitch in their attempts to get what the army needs.

CHAPTER XVII

THE SOMME SUCCESSES

September 20. The full results of the attack on the 15th and 16th show that it has been the biggest success we have yet had. The casualties are relatively small, we have made a very deep advance, and taken over 4,000 prisoners. Most important of all is that the fighting power of the enemy seems definitely decreasing. A good deal of this fall in morale is no doubt due to the tanks, but not all. The Germans increased, rather than decreased, the moral effects of the tanks by warning notices which they had issued to the troops. They knew that something was coming, but not enough to foresee absolutely their effect. The result of the warnings to their troops was that their nerves were strained with anticipation of some new very powerful instrument of war, the full effects of which they could not know.

Actually, the tanks, though very good, have marked defects and are vulnerable to direct artillery fire. Several broke down mechanically, but that was to be expected. The tanks were led in one place by an officer on foot carrying a red flag, just as in the pre-motor days, and by a marvel he escaped unwounded.

D.H. has presented me with one of the gold chronometers given by Mr. Leo Rothschild a year ago to commence sound ranging—when the War Office could not issue suitable chronometers—which has been in use in the trenches for over a year. It will be a very interesting trophy of the war. The Chief, when giving it, reminded me that I was the only Staff officer who had been with him continuously throughout the whole war. The runner-up is Rice, who came out with him and is now back with him again, but he had been away at Salonika for some time.

Sound ranging has become most valuable; we have improved on the French system, and now every part of the line is covered by sound-range sections, and armies are asking for more.

September 25. This is the anniversary of Loos, and we have attacked again to-day, and made another considerable advance—a great difference between this year and last year. Our army then was fighting only as an adjunct to the French attack, and though Loos gained much ground, yet it was a great disappointment. This year, we carried almost all of the load, which is quite right from every point of view. We are gaining ground steadily. There has been no serious set-back. If we had another two months of summer in front of us we might well get near a decision, but that is impossible. Already the weather is breaking badly. At the best, we can only hope for one more month.

The French on our right are disappointing. I am afraid they are played out for this year. It is not to be wondered at, for they had almost all of the fighting in 1915, and a tremendous doing at Verdun. D.H. tells me that Foch quite realizes this and used the expression, "L'infantrie française n'existe plus." This is an exaggeration, of course, for it means only at this period and this portion of the line. All the same, it is serious, for it means that we shall have to take over from them part of the task which should be theirs.

When the fighting stops I hope to get away for ten days. I have not had a day off for five months and want rest very badly.

Ryan came into my office this afternoon and told me he had the Chief's order to take me out for a walk; we did three miles in forty-five minutes. Ryan is the only man who can bully D.H. He sends him to bed like a naughty child if he tries to stay up too late at night, but as a matter of fact D.H.'s day is mapped out with the regularity of a public school. So many hours' work, so many hours' exercise, so many hours' sleep. He is very upset if anything interferes with it, and distinguished visitors have to conform. I wish junior officers could have the same discipline with visitors, for they take up a very great deal of time. The only visitor who made the Chief break his rules was an American with an immense flow of interesting anecdotes, which fascinated the Chief. He sat on at dinner for half an hour longer than he generally allows himself, and then took his guest into his private room, where they talked for another hour and a half, upsetting the whole programme of some heads of departments who were waiting with routine business.

We have had quite a little success in deceiving the Germans by a little "Chinese" show on the coast. Agents' reports, and the observations of railway movements by French air services, and road movements by our own Naval air service, show that we got their troops moving about quite merrily. The great advantage is that if ever we try and do a real show on the coast the Germans will be so accustomed to bluffs that they will not take fright too readily.

The writing of official *communiqués* has been handed over to me on the grounds that they are too bald. I am getting John Buchan over to-day, that is if the Foreign Office will part with him. I feel sure it is better to get a man who is accustomed to phrase turning more than is a mere soldier, and no one can quarrel with Buchan's literary taste.

The Bavarians opposite are fighting very well, and put up a remarkably good show all last month.

We have been very lucky in spotting all the probable movements of the enemy during the fighting of the 15th onwards. We have foreseen the whole of their movements, with the exception that the 6th Bavarian Division came up instead of the 6th Bavarian Reserve Division, which we had foretold. I think the Germans are pretty far through now, and if we had another two months before the winter set in I should have no doubt at all about making them conform to our plans. As it is, I am afraid winter will forestall us.

I quite agree there is very small chance of the Germans falling back voluntarily, that is until we make them, and certainly there is no direct sign of it at present. The optimistic Foch comes round now and then with some cock-and-bull story of the Germans being on the move. On September 12, he was convinced that he only had a rear-guard in front of him; on the 15th the rear-guard gave him a very severe set-back. The Germans have, of course, massed most of their artillery opposite our troops, and our front is still much more thickly held by infantry than that of the French, but there are still quite a number opposite the French, necessitating a very prolonged artillery preparation. I do not think the Germans can move many more divisions, if any, from West to East until the winter has set in, and I do not see how, with the divisions they have at present in the Eastern theatre, they can get great results through Rumania, though they will give her her fill of fighting in the next few weeks.

One of the curious things about the Somme battle has been the very slow rate at which the 1917 class has appeared. We have now got a very full and thorough examination of *Soldbücher*, both of prisoners and of dead, with a view to identifying their classes.

In most cases where we have found a man of the 1917 class he has turned out to be a volunteer. Still, the 1917 class is now beginning to appear, and if the weather holds we shall have worked through them pretty quickly, though I still do not think we shall get the 1918 class in the front line before December at the earliest, and probably not before the end of the year.

Muirhead Bone's work has greatly impressed the Chief. The Foreign Office—I suppose Masterman's committee—seems to have forgotten all about it, as nothing is being done so far as I can make out at present. Sir Douglas's idea is that this work can best be made the most of by publishing it in either journal or book form, either fortnightly or monthly on the style of Raemaekers' albums of drawings.[1] As regards the letter-press required, we could easily do this with our present staff here; to my mind three points are essential with regard to this, viz:—

(*a*) Bone's work should not be mixed up in any way with camera work; one spoils the other entirely.

(*b*) The letter-press must be provided here, and it is essential that whoever writes it should be in constant touch with Bone himself.

(*c*) Issue should be made as rapidly as practicable after the incidents described by the drawings and letter-press.

I am sure that work of this sort will have a great propaganda effect, particularly in America.

Bone is not deterred by difficulties. He was arrested by some over-zealous military policeman one day in Amiens, and incarcerated in a garret, lighted by a small skylight. Bone discovered that he could just get his head through the skylight and catch a glimpse of the spire of Amiens Cathedral. So he spent some of the time of his imprisonment making a very beautiful sketch of the Cathedral spire: one of the best of his sketches out here.

October 1. We are getting very optimistic here with regard to the fighting. There is no doubt that the German is a changed man now when opposed to British infantry. His tail is down, he surrenders freely, and on several occasions has thrown down his rifle and run away. Altogether there is hope that a really bad rot may set in any day. Do not think that this means I am very sanguine. Nobody can be who sees the ground over which the men are fighting here. Still there is a possibility.

[1] This idea was accepted at home and carried into effect.

The trouble at the present time is that we are not quite so well off as regards artillery positions as we would like. We have gone over the ridge, and the Germans are now able to put their artillery at such ranges that we cannot reach them behind the ridge, whereas they can reach our infantry in front of it. This will improve after we have made about another mile of ground, and that should not be long now.

I am concerned about the possibility of the Germans bringing back tanks against us, and am warning our agents to look out for this, but of course it is more in the purview of X.'s fellows. There are grave objections to introducing any new type of artillery, weapon or ammunition. But I think this will be necessary if we get definite information that the Germans are producing tanks to use against us.

October 2. A horrible wet day. Is it the beginning of winter? I hope not. If it is we shall be robbed of the result of much of our success, but it looks very wintry to-day, lowering skies, pouring with rain, and no signs of breaking. I remember this day last year, it was just such another; we were then in the middle of the battle of Loos. The year before that we were at the end of the battle of the Aisne, and things looked very black indeed.

If the weather is really breaking we shall not be able to do much more fighting this year, and shall have to wait for the spring. Six months that means (or five at the very least), and the Germans will get stronger in the meantime.

October 5. Burgess, who was formerly private secretary to Lord Esher, is coming to me as secretary.

It has been a full day with visitors; Lord Esher, Clemenceau, Geoffrey Robinson, the editor of *The Times* and Mr. Munsey, the American publicist, as well as an official visit from a War Office officer.

Esher prophesies that Clemenceau will be Prime Minister of France if the war goes on; his reputation is more that of destroying other ministries than of building anything big himself. He knows English perfectly, but does not seem to wish to speak it. He got on very well with Sir Douglas. I sent Alan Steward round with him and am awaiting his report.

October 7. Clemenceau had a narrow escape of getting into considerable danger. He was being taken to a H.Q. very far forward and just approachable with reasonable risk in a car. They managed to miss the turning that led from the main road to the H.Q. and ran straight forward on to a road in full view of the Germans, and kept by them under continuous observation and fire. S. discovered the mistake and, in spite of Clemenceau's protests, turned the car and got back without misadventure.

The editor of *The Times* was very helpful; he quite realizes the importance of full accord between Northcliffe and Haig. He made three suggestions for improvement in the Press work here :—

1. There is a risk of the six correspondents getting on one another's nerves, and that, therefore, leave and change of personnel are desirable.

2. That they are too much shadowed by junior Press officers.

3. That they badly need some competent military authority for advice and guidance to whom they can refer when writing their articles.

The first of these is not possible during the battle; the second is being looked into; and the third is the most important, but difficult to arrange. The ordinary Staff officer dislikes the Press correspondents, and does not get on well with them. There is a risk also lest any military opinions the correspondents advance would all dance to the tune of their bear-leader.

October 11. The weather is still dead against us. I have been studying the weather records of this area for the last hundred years and find that October is the wettest month of the whole year.

Lord Newton is staying with me. He is very amusing in his comments and conversation. He is obsessed with a dislike amounting to fear of Northcliffe.

I was up in the front line yesterday—an awful scene of devastation, and now almost impassable. The roads have been smashed by shell-fire; the trenches in the area over which we have been fighting are now deep in thick mud. I do not think that even if the weather improves we shall be able to fight forward during this year.

October 19. The impending list of visitors is portentous: A. J. Balfour, the Duke of Connaught, the King of Montenegro, the Duke of Devonshire, and Ben Tillett. I give them in the order of arrival and not of importance, but D.H. will have to see the whole of them.

Esher has prevailed upon the Chief to allow John Masefield to come and write up our fighting, not for propaganda purposes, but—in Esher's words—"for work of a permanent value in the domain of high literature." I have not seen his book on Gallipoli, but Esher puts it on a level with Tennyson's "Charge of the Light Brigade." One can take that according to one's own particular sense of literary values. Esher himself wants to produce a "Chronicle of the Somme." I think he means by this only that he should edit it, and Masefield and others write it. The position will be curious. If Masefield writes now it will have to be censored, even if it is not for immediate publication, in case it should fall into other people's hands; and if he is to be censored he will probably not write.

October 21. We have had another attack and have done well, taking more than a thousand prisoners. Our own casualties are not much more. The weather for the time is glorious, cold and bright, but it does not look settled.

Balfour has been here for two days. He has been through the whole of the Intelligence work rather dreamily, and at the end of it fairly took me aback by asking what were my views on what would happen if we did not win the war, adding pensively, "It seems to me always possible that we shall not win." I do not know what he had in mind, unless it is the possibility of France accepting a compromise peace during this winter, and that I do not think is possible. Certainly, for any of the Allies to think of making peace now, when we have given Germany the heaviest blow that she has yet had, but still not beaten her, would be utter folly. It may only have been Balfour's "philosophic doubt." Perhaps he thinks we are too optimistic and wished to apply a corrective.

October 25. A letter from the War Office throws a good deal of light on the difficulty with regard to propaganda. They do not wish anything published which would make the public think the German morale is broken, and that, consequently, the task of the British Army is easy, on the grounds that it offers opportunity to politicians and others who are seeking to criticize our operations, to run down the technical handling of the troops and minimize the efforts of the British nation. The line of argument is that if the German morale is broken we should get on quicker than we are doing. This, of course, loses sight of the fact that the lowering of the German morale is as much a step towards victory, in fact a longer step, than mere progress on the battlefield. The War Office objects strongly to Montague's articles, which in point of fact are quite correct in the incidents they relate. Anyhow, propaganda is their business and they can fight it out with the Foreign Office. But there is a real danger that if the public is not told of the effect of the fighting on German morale they might weigh the casualties against the progress on the battlefield only, and round on the Chief. The War Office (and its new C.-of-S.) themselves would then be in clover, for they could say if they wished to, that battle fighting was not their task, and that any failure had been here. The real explanation is probably that Lloyd George is dissatisfied with the results. Montague's articles were written for the neutral Press.

October 28. Of course everyone must agree that undue optimism either in Press or in Council is unwise. I think there is a distinct risk, however, lest we go to the other extreme. There was a tendency at one time in certain papers—most marked in one paper—to belittle everything that the Army had done and give exaggerated reports of everything the French Army had done. This, of course, was ludicrous to us, for we know the facts, but it was none the less galling. I hear also that some of the politicians who came out here seem to have got rather a wrong idea of the effect of the offensive. *All* our captured documents, *all* prisoners' examination, more important still, *all* reports from our own Commanding Officers in the front line, do actually point the same story, viz. that the German, though he is very far from being a demoralized enemy, is most undoubtedly not of the same calibre as he was this time last year. The offensive has shaken him up in a way that it is difficult for anyone not out here to realize. He is trying to conceal this from neutral countries; I have certain fears that he may succeed in concealing it from our own people.

October 30. I dined last night with the Duke of Connaught and his equerry, Sir Malcolm Murray, at Amiens. It is wonderful how much knowledge he has assimilated about the fighting and the army out here, far deeper and more to the point than that of almost any of the other distinguished visitors. He has, of course, had great opportunity of meeting officers from the front line whom he knows personally, and who talk to him freely. Still, it is very remarkable, and his influence at home will be valuable.

We are arranging to try a new scheme to give a few selected artists a chance of getting impressions of the war, that they may either use in their work now or after the war. The idea is to have them out for about a week, and give them as much liberty as possible. We are making a beginning with Kennington, and after Kennington are going to offer the same plan to Orpen and Sargent and one or two others. It is rather on the lines of Esher's idea for Masefield. It is not for propaganda, it is in the interests of art after the war. Sooner or later, someone will have to paint the big picture of the war, as well as someone write the big book of the war. It seems even more important that the artists should see than the authors, for authors can get their information later by their ears, but eyes can only be used at the time.

October 31. The King of Montenegro, accompanied by a "general," according to his pass, has just been here. The King is a very picturesque old brigand. His reputation is that he borrows money from everybody and forgets to repay it. The Army will not be able to help him much in that. He brought with him a great collection of impressive-looking Montenegrin orders and medals. The "general" appeared in a rather shabby antiquated black frock-coat, carrying a small black bag and looking for all the world as if birth control were of more importance to him than war. Investigation made subsequently brought to light the fact that he began life as a doctor; if so, he has reverted to type. But the black bag only contained medals. He lunched with me at my mess and dished out one medal, just like a tip, to the conducting officer who had been taking him round.

The weather, I think, is changing at last. It is a fine clear day and the barometer is rising.

November 2. Back at work after two days in bed with a bad chill. D.H. is insisting on my going home for a week, partly to recuperate, but also for some work with the War Office.

November 13. Another great success to-day; the attack was helped by a thick fog. At one place we had more prisoners than the number of men who were attacking, and on the whole day we have taken more prisoners than we had casualties; altogether there are more than 6,000 prisoners.

D.H. has gone to Paris for a conference about the plans for next year.

We have had an American here who, when discussing Wilson and Hughes, said, " There is no more difference between them than a barber would remove in ten minutes " ; whoever is President will have a much freer hand with regard to the American attitude towards the war than before the election. Germany seems to think she can do what she likes with America.

There has been direct correspondence from here with the Chief Censor (Sir Frank Swettenham), at home, about the Press correspondents' work. The points the Chief Censor urged were that :

(1) The reports of depreciation in the morale of the enemy cannot help us and may help the Germans to take steps to remedy any rot which has set in.

(2) That writing about tanks may take away from the Germans the fear of the unknown.

(3) Publication has few advantages and many disadvantages.

This is not direct criticism of us, because we do not use war correspondents to enunciate our views, nor are we responsible for their articles, except to see that no valuable military information is given away. The articles are the general impressions gained by the correspondents by their own observations.

It is rather absurd to think that the German General Staff will rely on the reports in British papers for information as to German morale, though as a matter of fact the correspondents have almost always, on their own, qualified the report of any very favourable incident by saying that any lack of morale which has come to light can only be regarded as local, and should not be taken as a symptom of the whole German Army.

About the tanks : one of these was for several hours in German hands, and we know that it was examined and parts of its fittings taken away. Several more are lying out of action in full view of the Germans. Full information also has already been given in French newspapers, far more than any we have published.

The political effect of the correspondents' articles in England is not our concern, our censorship is not final. The Chief Censor at home, if he wants to counteract any effect of the correspondents' articles, should do so by inspired leading articles, or by an official caveat. From a military point of view, soldiers confident of their own superiority fight better than the soldiers who think the enemy is superior. So do nations. It would certainly be a great mistake if we did agree to prompt the correspondents to be pessimistic.

In actual fact there is deterioration in the morale of the German Army in this battle, although people at home will not recognize it. Surrenders are more ready than they were at the beginning. Though far from being demoralized as an army, the Germans are not nearly so formidable a fighting machine as they were at the beginning of the battle. Our New Army has shown itself to be as good as the German Army, and it is difficult to see why the public at home as well as the Army should not be given confidence in the New Army. Nothing can be more inclined to inspire the Germans to renewed and further efforts than the belief that the British nation did not think well of what the Army had done during this battle, and were not confident that we were winning.

If the censor's views are really those of the Government or the nation, we have a hard task in front of us, but I do not think that the nation is as frightened of itself as the censors are.

While undue optimism is admittedly unsound, such statements that have appeared in the correspondents' articles cannot have any military disadvantage to the army in France, and may have even a distinct military advantage in its effect on the fighting powers of our own troops, and exercise a good influence in maintaining confidence of the nation at home.

I would like to hear Northcliffe's views of the censor.

November 15. We have just been saved from a most extraordinary blunder. Some time ago the Fourth Army brought to notice a medical subordinate warrant officer who claimed to have a ray which could do things that no other ray has ever been able to do. That it could kill animal life, that it could photograph the internal economy of the human being, showing the actual organs, lungs, etc., and that it could take photographs of things that were out of sight. Medical people, after investigating something of it, seemed to think there was a great deal to say for it for medical purposes. The man was given a little hospital to experiment in, with a special medical officer looking after him, and a tame scientist to look into the electrical part of the work. All reports seemed favourable, and we had just recommended that he should be given a commission, paid £2,000 for the exclusive use of the apparatus during the war, when a patent expert whom we had sent for from home exploded the whole thing as a fraud.

November 24. The battle is over and we shall not know the actual effect it has had on the Germans for many a long day, but it has certainly done all, and more, than we hoped for when we began. It stopped the Verdun attack. It collected a great weight of the German Army opposite us, and then broke it. It prevented the Germans hammering Russia, and it has undoubtedly worn down the German resistance to a great extent. If it had been begun earlier—but that was impossible—or if the weather had kept fine for the whole of October, it might have done more.

Somebody at home tried to saddle us here with a man for Intelligence work who was said to be an excellent German scholar. I had him examined, with the most amusing results. He translated "*mit Rücksicht darauf*" as "in marching order," probably with some idea in his mind about rucksacks; and better still, that "*bei der Aufstellung der Colonnen*" meant "by order of the colonel." We do not often get schoolboy howlers in war.

December 2. Now that the battle is over we are not so tied to Head-quarters. I celebrated this release by going to a St. Andrew's Night function at Paris. They had asked D.H. and he sent me to deputize. Buchan made the speech of the evening. They put me in the chair, and all I had to do was the ordinary "two or three words" to introduce speakers. The meeting was enthusiastic; all St. Andrew's Night dinners are. War restrictions did not impede the flow of either beverages or words. If words won wars, this war would have been over long ago.

December 6. The cat is out of the bag about all the censorship squabbles. At least I suppose it is reasonable to conclude that Lloyd George at the War Office, wishing to oust Asquith for lack of success, took every precaution (and I suppose that was one of them) lest people should think that under Asquith we had not done so badly. So I suppose the British public will not have it impressed upon them that their army has won a great battle and taken in four months nearly 40,000 prisoners and 100 guns. Anything that goes for a more whole-hearted and energetic conduct of the war is to the good, and if a Coalition means that political rivalries cease, then we can be well content. But there is something paradoxical as well as ominous in Lloyd George becoming a war Prime Minister. I suppose no one was more directly responsible for our lack of preparation than he. They say nobody is so zealous as the latest convert, so perhaps all will go well. All the same, Asquith was a Sahib; he may have been a tired-out Sahib, but he was, is still, and always will be, a Sahib, and he has been very scurvily treated. And from all we hear of Lloyd George from the War Office he will not be very inclined to listen to soldiers' advice.

Curiously enough, the general opinion out here is favourable to the change. Meantime, now that the Army is having its time off, the Navy should be up and doing. This submarine menace seems to be getting very serious. Are we going to lose the war at sea before we can win it on land? Is that what Balfour meant?

I shall be home on the 9th for a week.

December 10. (*At home.*) London is extraordinary in time of political crisis; it is like a melodrama. St. Loe Strachey compares it with what Disraeli described in his political novels—everyone full of the wildest stories and canards. He quotes John Bright with regard to the negotiations and intrigues that brought Asquith down—" a pure and honourable ambition would not have aspired to them." Asquith's speech to the Liberals was wonderfully generous. Nobody seems to have any real confidence in the new Government. Strachey points out that people who get power by intrigue are apt to suffer the same treatment from their enemies. He writes, " They have taught them the trick by which they were themselves discomfited. The strange thing is that Asquith never appears to have had any suspicion of what was going on, until the knife was stuck in his back. That in itself may be evidence that he was played out.

"It is only when at home, that these political evolutions interest one. How small they are compared to the struggle in France. For one cannot really believe that it is only, or mainly, the national interest that makes these creatures strive to oust their colleagues. And it is not as if the struggle were going against us in the field. They know, however much they may try to conceal the knowledge, that 1916 is ending with real progress made and the goal in sight, if still distant."

Strachey warns me that in his opinion Lloyd George, however excellent his intentions may be at present, is likely to interfere with the soldiers. He says, " if things do not go right, or if we get into serious difficulties, even temporary ones, he will try short cuts to victory." Heaven forbid! " Short cuts to victory " lead straight to disaster and defeat.

December 14. Just back from a conference at G.Q.G. on next year's operations. Surely it will be the last year. The Germans have a breathing space and will make full use of it to strengthen their defensive and reorganize their troops, but they cannot make men. We have still ample reserves of men to draw on. Certainly they could not stand another Somme. The only really important principle settled for next year was that this is the decisive point and that troops for it are not to be detached. I wish it had been that every available man and gun was to be massed on it and a really great combined effort made.

I am sorry that Joffre has fallen. In spite of the original big blunder by the French, he has done wonders. He has borne the heat and burden of the day and now that we are definitely on the offensive—for there is no question of Germany attacking us here—next year his task would have been easier. Any change in chief command upsets the troops. We know little of the new man (Nivelle). He brought off a big attack at Verdun; but, according to our information, he has got the job more because of what he claims he can do than for what he has hitherto done.

December 20. Just back from a conference at Cassel, where D.H. saw Nivelle. Nivelle certainly sees big! The French are to do the main attack, *not* alongside of us. We are to attack to help them. This means a complete change in all our schemes. We have to take on a great deal more front-line trench, so as to set free French troops for their big effort. The French think Germany may attack us before they are ready. I think this is nonsense. There are some signs they may go back a bit, not that they will attack. They are certainly preparing very formidable defensive lines in their back area; things look as if they were going to await attack, and that would be their soundest strategy.

D.H. is sceptical about the French being able to deliver a decisive attack. If it fails we shall be back at the position of a year ago, with all the advantages of the Somme thrown away.

Wilson's peace proposals are rather ridiculous, but dangerous all the same, with all this talk at home of no more Somme battles.

December 26. Another interesting letter from St. Loe Strachey on the political crisis. He says, " Asquith and his immediate friends in the Cabinet had not the slightest idea that the thaw was coming until the ice actually broke under their feet. And yet, outsiders, like myself, could see quite clearly what Lloyd George was doing, and that for many months past their doom was sealed." Is that why the censorship wanted to belittle our progress here? It looks like it.

December 27. Northcliffe has been here again. He was very friendly and said he had cracked us up at some City banquet at which he was speaking. I had to pretend I knew all about it, and that I was duly grateful. Northcliffe regards himself as having put Lloyd George into power, and appeared to think he could make him do anything he wanted. He seems a little off his head —what the French call *folie de la grandeur*—but anyhow, so long as he supports D.H. it does not matter how mad he is on other subjects.

A very breezy, amusing sailor-man called Gaunt was here with him.

December 31. The last day of the year. A fortnight ago I would have added " and certainly the last New Year's Eve of the War." Now I am not so sure, but I pray it may be so.

PART FOUR—1917
G.H.Q.

CHAPTER XVIII

DISCUSSIONS AND RUMOURS

January 2. You will have seen in the *Gazette* that I have got my brevet as full Colonel which is the best reward that I could have from my own point of view. What I am really pleased about in the *Gazette* is that we have managed to get C—— his D.S.O. He has done extraordinarily good work for the Secret Service, but there were many difficulties in getting him rewarded.[1]

January 3. The strong points in the new Government are Curzon's and Milner's administrative abilities, and although I have always been an admirer of Asquith's, still I think that the change can do no harm. I think we should have been very anxious if the German peace proposals had been addressed to the late Government.

We are all rather aghast at Wilson's note, it seems so purposeless, yet he has been logical in most of the things he has done previously, and I think there must be some reason which we cannot fathom behind the note. The wording of the note is, of course, atrocious; the curious point about it is that he should have chosen to say that "the aims of the two opposing groups of powers were identical," then specify those aims as the ones for which we have always, admittedly, been striving. Germany has only claimed these ends for the last few months.

As regards Germany herself, evidence grows that she is very hard hit. She will make every sacrifice of concrete advantage to

---

[1] The case of this officer is unique in the whole of the records of the British Army. Early in life he had to leave the Service owing to a sentence by a civil court. He had refused to defend himself, lest his defence should incriminate others. He served in the Secret Service and by sheer good work, great personal courage and most valuable service, he was eventually and most deservedly reinstated in the Regular Army and received both British and foreign decorations. He had risen to a responsible position at the time of his death some years ago.

retain her halo, for she knows that very soon she will have to give up both the concrete and the halo. It is pitiful to think that there is even a chance of the Allies not seeing the thing through. All we want is a few more months—I do not think more than twelve at most if there is no set-back—but you remember what Napoleon said, "Ask me for anything but time."

The examination of prisoners of war and investigation of parcels which the German soldiers are receiving from Germany, are giving interesting results. The information is too meagre to form any definite conclusion, but it generally looks as though further examination will enable us to say:

1. Clothing forms a very inconsiderable item in the parcels received.
2. Tobacco is the main item.
3. Fats form a small item, and appear to be issued by a central agency, though this is not quite certain.

On the question of shortage in Germany, I heard when I was at home last month that some very reliable correspondence emanating from very responsible people in Germany, and passing through a neutral State, had come into our possession. Evidence in this correspondence was very distinct that the position of affairs in Germany showed greater strain that even the most optimistic of us had considered possible. The relief afforded by Rumania is not considered to be very marked; the estimate varies at from two to four weeks' supplies for Germany. There is also very good evidence that some form of epidemic has appeared in Prussia and notably in Berlin, which is causing considerable loss of life. The exact nature of it is not known.

Our captured documents do not confirm the epidemic noticed in *The Times* at Hamburg, which they call "marmalade cancer," and I am inclined to disbelieve this at present.

Paris attaches very great importance to the news which they consider Mr. Gerard must have taken from Germany to the President of the United States. A study of dates shows that immediately after Mr. Gerard arrived in New York the President appears to have entered into negotiations with Switzerland with regard to his peace note. Apparently Norway and Sweden were also included, but this is not certain. So far as we are concerned here, it is pure speculation to attempt to divine what information Gerard took with him, possibly you can throw some light on it. I hesitate between three explanations, viz.:—

1. Information as to the internal state of Germany both eco-

nomic and political; but each of these must have been affected by events in Rumania which took place subsequently to Gerard's departure from Europe.

2. The actual terms which Germany is prepared to concede. These were no doubt much more liberal than we in England envisage, and it is possible that the knowledge of these terms may have toppled over the balance of Mr. Wilson's judgment.

3. There is a possibility that Germany may be contemplating some new frightfulness of which Gerard has cognizance, and the danger of which may have influenced Wilson. I do not think this is probable without our getting to know of it.

The interesting point is, that whatever Gerard carried with him must have been something which the Germans were not prepared to communicate even by their code, or in writing by one of their submarines.

Of course, it is quite probable that there is no connexion whatever between Gerard's visit and Wilson's effort, which may be a pure coincidence, but the French General Head-quarters hold a very definite opinion that there is a close connexion.

Esher writes from Paris wishing to be made Lieut.-General, and wants to have an officer under him attached to Lyautey's head-quarters. What with Geddes as General and Admiral, and all the munitions Field-Marshals, we poor soldiers had better become simple " misters."

January 3. Can you let me know in a private letter, and with due regard to all the interests which you have to consider, what is the state of mind of the people in America with regard to the President's note? We are all a bit at sea about it here. As you know, I have always defended Wilson's attitude and action so far, but it is difficult to answer the criticisms now directed at him both by our newspapers and in private, but these criticisms all turn on the same point, that he has failed so completely to appreciate our views. There is, of course, no sort of resentment at his sending a Peace note, that is quite clearly within his rights and probably within his duties, but it is difficult to believe that America as a whole does not realize our attitude as a nation.

The French connect the note with Gerard's visit and the information which he no doubt took from Germany to the President, but we are quite ignorant of what aspect that information took. Optimists and pessimists give different versions.

It is not an exaggeration to say that the whole army is looking forward to the fighting in the spring with the utmost confidence.

January 3. There is a pretty little brawl on with the Embassy at Paris over an absurdly trivial affair. One of my young men is employed there on very responsible secret work, and he wants to marry a young woman who is employed at the Embassy. I have told the young man that there is no objection whatever to his getting married, but that if he does I will remove him from Paris without loss of pay, position and prospects, to some other area of activities, or that alternatively his wife must leave the Embassy and go to England. The Military Attaché was very upset and cannot realize the danger of a man employed on confidential work living in the married state in Paris. The same problem has arisen at French G.Q.G. I was amused to see there the other day a notice that officers were not allowed to receive visits from their wives. A French friend of mine with whom I discussed this, told me the restriction, anyhow as it was at present worded, did not extend to their lady friends. I asked him whether visits from ladies, whether casual acquaintances or intimate friends, did not tend to disturb work, to which he replied " You English look at these things so strangely; with us it is not a distraction only an *apéritif*." What would Lord St. Davids say?

January 4. Sometimes it does one good to meet a good hater. We had a visit a little time ago from Leo Maxse, a tremendous patriot, quite convinced that the motives of everyone who does not agree with him have their origin in personal self-seeking. He has a very acute mind, and a great gift of stinging phrase. He was a very strong advocate of all those measures which were required to prepare the country for war, and for that he deserves every credit, but his bitterness makes one involuntarily see the other side of the question far more clearly. It weighs one's judgment against his own views, however valid they are. Like all journalists that I have met here, he has an abiding horror of Northcliffe, who, by the way, is coming back to-morrow from Paris.

January 6. Northcliffe was here yesterday, after he had seen the Prime Minister and Milner. He told me that he had warned the Prime Minister that he would " withdraw his support " if the Government continued to scatter forces in the Balkans.

The change in the Government has made Northcliffe consider himself more nearly omnipotent—if that is not a contradiction in terms—than he did before the change. We have no means of knowing here what power he wields, but in the meantime he is a whole-hearted supporter of D.H. and, to a lesser degree, of Robertson.

Northcliffe made one most extraordinary remark when we were talking together away from the Chief's château; he stopped in the middle of a sentence about something totally different, and said very emphatically, " What an enormous advantage it must be to be a gentleman, like Sir Douglas." Heaven knows what was in his mind! It had nothing whatever to do with the subject-matter of our conversation, but it is quite literally true. D.H.'s greatest asset is that nobody can conceive that any action of his is not prompted by the highest motive.

Northcliffe said that the great change with the present Government was that Lloyd George revelled in making a decision, every problem is disposed of on the spot, whereas with Asquith the tendency to let difficult questions solve themselves by lapse of time had become an obsession. Certainly it is true that any decision, even a bad one, is better than no decision in war.

Meantime, we are having a very sharp conflict with the French, who are pressing us to take over more and more front line from them. It means emasculating our attack, both as regards the number of troops we can employ and also with regard to the amount of training they would have. I do not think that there is any chance of the Germans attacking us, but they still have a formidable number of troops opposite the Ypres Salient and in the Somme area, and if we weaken our line unduly the possibility of an attack would certainly arise.

January 10. Rain, snow and wind, and before this reaches you we shall have made a small attack to-morrow.

D.H. tells me that the C.G.S. has had a very alarming interview with the Prime Minister, who disparaged all our efforts on the Somme, and said that much of the losses had been unnecessary and useless, and that the country would not stand any more of it. The general idea is that he wants to emulate Napoleon, cross the Alps and dictate peace with Vienna—I suppose at the same time as the Germans will be entering Paris.

January 12. Yesterday's operation, though quite a small show, was very successful. We took something like 200 prisoners, and the inevitable counter-attack by the Germans came to grief badly.

January 14. I was at the Belgian Head-quarters yesterday, and came back through a blinding snowstorm very late at night. The Belgian Intelligence seems to be very well informed as regards what is happening in Paris, London and Rome. Their report is that the proposal to mix up the British and French armies emanates from London, and is not seriously backed by France. This seems incredible, but all things are possible now. Lord Newton, who has been here for two days, laughs at it and says that the country has complete trust in the Army and very little trust in politicians or amateur strategists. I hope he is right.

Meantime, the discussion as regards the extension of our front and other points, has been referred home for decision, a great mistake. I do not think it would have happened last year. I go to Paris to-morrow, and after that hope to get home by the end of the month.

January 15. I went up to the Second Army area to look into what appeared to be rather a threatening sign round the Salient. The conclusion I have come to is that the Germans are doing exactly what we should expect them to do if they were going to put in a small attack with five or six divisions. It does not follow, of course, that the attack will come off. If it does it will probably be near Boesinghe. The Belgians are convinced that no attack is impending either in their area or at Ypres.

A prisoner states that the Germans have got a new form of *flammen-werfer*, giving out an acid which eats away barbed wire. If this is correct they have got ahead of us.

G.Q.G. are concerned about the possible collection of troops in Alsace, but as we have definitely located in our own area the units which they mentioned, there can be nothing much in it. All our information shows that an operation through Switzerland is not in the least probable.

January 18. Gemeau has just returned from Switzerland. He told me that on the day of his arrival he found the whole of the people in his part of the world packing up, on the grounds that the Germans would be through in a fortnight. He saw a good many officers of the Swiss Army and has given as his final conclusion that although there had been very great excitement and general alarm with regard to the intentions of Germany, the danger, if any, had passed off.

January 20. I have just had a visit from four miners' agents, sent out by Lord Derby with his special recommendation that they have helped him very much since the war began, two of them having helped to raise a pioneer battalion in August, 1915. Their visit is to counteract the resolution which has been proposed by the Labour Party Conference at Manchester, that Labour should withdraw entirely from the war.

They have been all round the front, and I had them to lunch at the end of their visit. Each of them insisted upon making a speech, so that lunch lasted for nearly two and a half hours, but all the speeches were of the right sort, and I think their visit will certainly send them back strongly in favour of carrying on the war, if they ever had any doubts on the subject.

Conan Doyle is rather upset about the censoring of his account of the battle of Loos. Actually it contained a very great deal of stuff which would be of help to the German Intelligence. I am asking him to come out here so that we can talk it over and I can go through the debatable points with him himself.

January 24. D.H. returned yesterday. The Government has not supported our views against the French; we have to take over more line, everything is to be secondary to a big French attack, which is to start not later than "the 1st of April." Rather an unfortunate date. If the French fail we shall have to take up the burden. Meantime, we are to attack (Arras) to help the French big effort.

D.H. says that the War Council meeting had a paper in front of them putting French divisions as totalling 99 and with a strength of 7,700 each. This excludes 10 Territorial divisions. The French base their argument on the length of line held by French and British in comparison with the strength of the armies, taking no note of the dispositions of the Germans, who are generally much thicker in front of us than in front of the French. Apparently the Cabinet did not go into the merits of the case, but decided that we must conform to the French views, on the general grounds that we were fighting in France and the French Army was still bigger than ours. If the French Army is really able to bring off the big decisive attack it is quite right that they should concentrate every available man for their effort, but if it fails, and if the Germans then put in an attack elsewhere, it will become very awkward. Meantime, all the signs go to show that the Germans will not attack in the immediate future, and may be, and probably are, going back to their defensive lines in the Somme area.

January 28. If war does nothing else it does bring celebrities in touch with the Army. Our latest is George Bernard Shaw. Do you remember Lord Lytton, who when he was asked what he thought of the Taj Mahal could think of nothing else to say but that " the Taj Mahal is very like the photograph of the Taj Mahal." I feel rather inclined to say almost the opposite about G.B.S. He is most unlike what I expected him to be. The conducting officer who took him round was very frightened of him at first, but soon became an adoring admirer. He tells me that the name of Shaw caused much more terror to the officers of the Army than the Germans have ever succeeded in doing. Every officer was apparently straining his mind to find some deep and subtle meaning in every phrase that Shaw uttered. Actually, he said nothing that might not have emanated from his butler, if he has one, or even from his housemaid. I only saw him at dinner, and certainly there he was entirely delightful, unaffected and natural. He seemed rather surprised, or anyhow affected surprise, to find that most of us knew his books quite well. He told me he was immensely impressed both by the organization in the Army and by the officers and men that he had met.

A batch of foreign correspondents have had their first interview with the Chief. Esher and Newton have both been pressing for this for some time. Neville Lytton, who has taken over charge of the foreign correspondents' work and is doing admirably, has also been at me about it; it was intended as only a formal presentation, but D.H. took the opportunity of giving them his view that the Germans were hard hit, and that this year's big attacks should be successful. It may do good; the Chief is quite unknown to the French except as a name.

February 15. Back again, and saw the Chief this morning. The news from Russia is better. Henry Wilson has reported that the Russian reorganization is complete, and that they will be able to attack in the spring. D.H. also tells me that the railway difficulties are being solved, and that the people at home are supporting him in this matter.

The interview with the foreign journalists seems to have been reproduced in a rather garbled form in the London papers; they are telegraphing about it from home, but the papers are not yet in.

February 16. D.H. has had a meeting with Nivelle, and has come to a tentative agreement about dates for the attack; the ruling factor is the railway arrangements.

There is the deuce of a mess-up about the D.H. interviews. They are sensationalized, but not really very different from what the Chief actually said to the newspaper representatives or indeed to many other people not Press correspondents, at previous interviews.

February 20. Both Newton and Lampson of the Foreign Office, when they were out here for the first time, urged us most strongly to get foreign visitors seen by D.H. This was confirmed by almost every Foreign Office representative who accompanied Foreign Office parties. Paris has sent the same representation to us several times, sometimes through the Military Attaché, and sometimes through Lord Esher, also we have received several letters from the War Office indicating that the French wished that distinguished visitors could be presented to D.H. and in one letter urged this in so many words.

The whole show was really very unfortunate and is a strong reminder that the B.G.I. should not go home for anything more than two or three days. The sequence of events is that the foreign correspondents pressed for and obtained permission to see Sir Douglas just before I left for England, the idea being that it was to be a courtesy visit, as they put it—"*pour serrer la main.*" This of course, has happened several times before, notably with Palmer, and with our own British correspondents last year, and all that we allowed to appear was the customary "Union Jack over the door, cow grazing in a meadow, strong, silent man, blue eyes, white moustache, raised maps" and such-like drivel. Unfortunately at the end of two or three pages of this type of rot each correspondent enlarged upon various remarks that had passed. The articles were actually sent home to me, and I had them in my possession for nearly ten minutes. They were sent with my attention drawn to one or two paragraphs marked with blue lines which the censor had put on them; these I looked through and censored from a military point of view, and gave them back to the messenger who was waiting, in the full expectation that permission to publish would be obtained from the C.G.S. or Sir Douglas. By some error this was not done, and the articles appeared in France.

The letter asking for permission to make reference to these articles in the British Press was not referred to me. If it had been I should, of course, have required to see what was being put in before I could pass it. As it appeared in the British Press it was a frightfully garbled account; the various interviews were put together rather badly, the translation was indifferent, all the "cow-in-the-meadow" touch was cut out and several bold statements were made. So far as we can see here, the statements were perfectly harmless from a military point of view, though the taste was unpleasant.

The net result, so far as France is concerned, has been extraordinarily good; that is rather a curious point about it all. The French Press has never been so pro-British as for the last few days, even the military criticisms, for the first time, were favourable, and I received letters by several mails to the same effect from French people. All this, however, is beside the point. The really ridiculous thing about it all is that here, in the middle of a big war, the whole of the time and energy of many senior officers, and a good many members of the War Cabinet, have been absorbed by a perfectly puerile question. I suppose these things appear larger to politicians at home than they do to us out here.

Lytton[1] was sent home to explain matters and his account of his interview with the War Cabinet is very interesting. L.G. was furious. Curzon out for D.H.'s head on a charger. Balfour was helpful and rather laughed at the whole thing and eventually won the day. Robertson was silent throughout, but as he came away with Lytton, said to him, "Now you see what I have to put up with." The other members of the Cabinet might as well not have been there. They did not count.

Max Aitken writes very nicely about it. "I hope you will not let the C.-in-C. take the matter too seriously. A sort of attempt has been made to take advantage of what slipped through in the Press, but this has been frustrated entirely because no decent paper would touch it. As far as the House of Commons is concerned, there is a unanimous opinion, apart from Peace cranks, that the whole matter should be dropped." Northcliffe writes in the same strain and accuses L.G. of wanting to stir up trouble.

February 21. Paris is concerned about the possibility of a big

[1] Major Hon. Neville Lytton. He has since published an interesting account of the episode in his book "The Press and the General Staff."

attack at Ypres. The position is much the same as regards hostile troops as it has been for some time, but the ground is now pretty soft, and I do not think active operations on any large scale can commence north of the Salient for another three weeks, even under the most favourable weather conditions. Meantime, evidence goes on accumulating that the Germans may withdraw to the Hindenburg Line if they are at all pressed by us, or even without pressure. The French disagree with this, and one cannot be quite certain.

February 22. I went up to the Second Army Head-quarters for another personal investigation with regard to the Ypres position. Although there are some distinct symptoms of activity, particularly from the front line, the information obtainable cannot be said to point definitely to attack, indeed the evidence to my mind is rather the other way, as if the Germans expected us to attack. But I am not quite happy about it. The Second Army is taking a very serious view about the whole thing and I do not think there is any risk of us being surprised.

The most pleasant feature of the whole Army out here is the extraordinary high morale of our own men. All the little raids for identification have been most successful, and they are getting the people we want with very little loss. The Germans are on the alert for any attack. Their barrage came down an hour before the assault on the 17th (on the Ancre), and the counter-attacks, both on the same day and on the following day, were easily driven off, and we have gained valuable ground and over 500 prisoners.

Lord Northcliffe sent a very interesting letter with regard to the interviews in which he stated that when he saw the announcement in one of the papers that the Government were going to repudiate the interviews, he communicated with the Prime Minister's office and when he found that this was true, he then spoke to the Prime Minister and told him that repudiation would have three effects :—
(1) It would depress the whole French nation; (2) It would affront the Commander-in-Chief before the whole world and his army, and (3) It would gain the hostility of the correspondents involved, including that of the Havas Agency.

The Prime Minister sent for Northcliffe for an interview with Curzon and himself. Of this meeting Lord Northcliffe wrote that both of them took what he considered a ridiculously exaggerated view of a trifling incident. He read aloud to the Prime Minister the Havas interview, and asked what fault the Prime Minister could find with it. The Prime Minister said there was none, except that it gave the Germans evidence that we were going to concentrate on the Western front, which as Lord Northcliffe pointed out, the Germans must have known for the last two years. Lord Northcliffe added:

"The general attitude of both was that of birds with ruffled plumage. I suppose that the relations between generals and politicians have always been difficult, but the interview with these two men made me wish that Milner was back. I am sure in that case we should not have heard anything of the incident, little as the incident matters.[1]

"I was discussing my visit with one who knows the C.-in-C. as well as these two politicians; he summed up the situation by saying that Lloyd George does not like the soldiers' point of view, and that Curzon, who had known Haig for many years, is jealous of his rising position."

[1] In a letter to Lord Northcliffe I wrote: "Everyone here is most grateful to you for the line you took about the interviews. I am quite content that the War Cabinet and War Ministers, and anybody else who wishes, should consider that all the blame of this is attributable to me. In point of fact in a sense it is, because the arrangements which were made when I went on leave were made by me, and these arrangements broke down. The long and the short of the matter is that the Head of the Intelligence out here has no right to go on leave. Actually, I only saw the articles from the point of view of containing information for the enemy, and needless to say I did not give permission for them to be published without submission to the Chief. The net result in France is undoubtedly exceedingly good, that is the irony of the whole thing."

To this letter Lord Northcliffe replied:

"The French reporters are bad enough, they embroider everything, as you know, but the Americans, with the exception of a few, are the extension of the limit, to use their own phrase. If the censor had had any knowledge of French ways, he would have made these interviews agree, and taken out the frills in the English version. I never allow an interview with myself to appear in a French newspaper until I have signed it. That does not stop them inventing. The *Figaro* had a column and a half of me the other day, written by a man I had never seen. Now that we have Buchan in charge in London, things, I think, will gradually improve in the Press Bureau."

CHAPTER XIX

THE GERMAN WITHDRAWAL

February 25. The German retirement has begun. Yesterday his front-line position was found empty, and to-day although there is strong opposition, he seems to be definitely on the move, back to his main line of defence. We have pretty good information about the German defensive line at Arras, St. Quentin and Laon, both from reports and from aerial reconnaissances. The evidence as to the intention of withdrawal on this line has been accumulating slowly, and is still very vague.

Early in the Somme battle a captured order indicated that the Germans at that time, envisaged a withdrawal at least as far as Cambrai. Reports in January gave gossip current in Cambrai, and to a lesser degree in St. Quentin, that a withdrawal was possible, and a prisoner captured this morning, apparently well informed, stated definitely that the Germans intended to withdraw as far as the Hindenburg Line, which they hoped to reach by the 25th of March. A severe cross-examination failed to shake this evidence. The deduction is that the man absolutely believed what he said, and that his statement of the information coming from an officer is true. It is, however, not yet proved that the officer knew what the German intentions were, nor is it clear why, if he did know, he should have divulged them to the prisoner.

From other prisoners there is an impression, though a definite statement cannot be obtained, that the retirement would be to a line farther rearward than the Loupart line.

Withdrawal from the front line of trenches in the Ancre area is now known to have begun about five days ago. While it is feasible that the number of prisoners taken during this month, and the correspondingly heavy losses and other casualties, may have induced the Germans to withdraw from their immediate line of trenches, it is most improbable that these casualties alone would cause them to withdraw as far as the Hindenburg Line. The lines held by the Germans at the commencement of the present withdrawal places them at a distinct disadvantage with regard to observation and of gunfire on our troops, and this is more probably the reason for this particular withdrawal.

The Hindenburg Line is very strongly defended, though the site does not give the Germans particularly good command. The withdrawal would set free twelve German divisions, until such time as an attack can be launched against the Hindenburg Line.

The strategical reasons which may have induced the Germans to retire voluntarily to the Hindenburg Line would appear to be the following :—

(*a*) To gain time for training new German divisions now being identified, or for the development of an offensive elsewhere.

(*b*) To place at a disadvantage any attack on a large scale by the French and British on the Arras–Somme front.

(*c*) To draw us from our present prepared trenches over ground in which communications would be bad and supply arrangements difficult.

(*d*) To obtain a larger striking force for decisive action elsewhere.

Any, or all, of these would be sufficient to justify a strategical withdrawal, but against them must be weighed the great moral disadvantage of a withdrawal, even when voluntary, over a space of from 20 to 30 kilometres unless the withdrawal is accompanied by a striking success elsewhere, or followed by a successful counter-stroke in the same area.

So far the enemy have only retired to the Bucquoi–Loupart Wood line, and there is every indication that they intend to hold this line with a considerable measure of resistance.

February 26. During the past two months there have been many rumours from political sources, from agents, and to a lesser extent from prisoners, regarding Germany's intentions. These rumours group themselves round two objectives (*a*) Flanders and (*b*) Alsace-Lorraine.

With regard to Flanders, some vague confirmation of the rumours is obtained from the train movements; there has been activity on the coast, and new guns have been installed there apparently for coastal defences.

There has been an increase of artillery and artillery activity round the Ypres Salient; the number of divisions in Flanders has increased by two. As against those, we have a constant supply of prisoners in this area, and none of these has any information of an intended attack. Moreover, ground conditions are such as to preclude the possibility of any large attack for another month.

As regards Alsace-Lorraine and the Swiss frontier, evidence points to these rumours having been circulated by the Germans for the purpose of deceiving us. The French Intelligence at one time inclined to the opinion that there was much concentration of German troops on the Swiss frontier. We do not agree. Gradually fuller information has enabled us to eliminate every division from the proposed concentration. At the present moment it can be definitely stated that there is no sign of any concentration at all. It is very noteworthy that for the first time since the beginning of 1915 there are three active divisions in line side by side with their flank on the Swiss frontier. German documents have indicated that the Germans attached importance to the fact that General Foch was somewhere in the Nancy area, and that there was known to be grouping of French divisions there.

The attack by the Germans in Champagne in February was of no strategical importance. It is difficult to see any reason for it except to raise the morale of the people in Germany.

The grouping of German divisions on the Western front gives large blocks of reserves at (1) Flanders, (2) Valenciennes and Maubeuge, (3) Somme area, (4) Montmédy, (5) Saarbrucken. This has all the appearance of being a defensive organization awaiting events. Information from Germany itself indicates the possibility of an offensive against Russia in the Riga area. This, however, cannot begin until the end of April. Such an offensive would be in accordance with the known inclination of von Hindenburg, and it would follow the plan which apparently Germany has adopted throughout the greater portion of the war, in striking in greater strength at the weaker of the Allies.

D.H. has gone to a conference at Calais with the Prime Minister and the French to discuss transportation problems. I am going up to-morrow to the front where the Germans have been withdrawing, to see if any more information is to be gleaned there. It is the first time the Germans have really retreated since the Marne; we are not quite sure yet why they have started so soon, or how far they will go, although we have known for some time that such a move was "not improbable."

March 1. The Chief is back from Calais, where there have been extraordinary doings. The net result is that the British

Government has handed over the British Army in France, lock, stock, and barrel, to the tender mercy of Nivelle, anyhow until the end of the forthcoming campaign. The only saving point is that we are still to be allowed to fight such battles as the French may tell us to fight in our own way; even this concession was apparently only wrung from the Cabinet after a great deal of dispute.

It is all utterly wrong and unnecessary. If the French do get a great success and end the war in their next big attack, which is very unlikely, not much harm will have been done. They will claim all the credit for the whole war, as well as for this attack, but that does not matter. If the big French attack is indecisive in its result, then inevitably, as the war goes on, our army will become the biggest on the Western front (unless Lloyd George sends everybody off on side-shows), and there is bound to be interminable friction. If the French attack fails altogether, we shall have the whole weight of the German Army on the top of us, and the position will be even more difficult. If Joffre were still in command of the French and they were putting the British Army under him there might be some justification for it, for he has all the experience of the war behind him, but Nivelle is new to the game, with far less experience of actual fighting than D.H., and, according to what we are hearing from French officers, he does not seem to have the confidence even of his own generals. Whatever there has been in the way of difference of opinion between the French and ourselves, until the present time, it has always ended in a pretty fair compromise.

The whole thing is exactly what many people warned us to look for from Lloyd George, but it has come sooner than any of us expected and with less reason. One could have understood it, though even then it would have been wrong, if we had failed out here. I suppose the real reason at the back of it all is the hope that we shall win the war without many more British casualties. If that is so, it is an amazing error of judgment.

It is difficult to see why, if the Cabinet wanted to have one supreme military authority, they did not press for somebody, either French or British, who would have been over both D.H. and the commander of the French troops in France.

Personally, I think D.H. should have refused altogether to accept the position and resigned; it would have resulted in the end in something much more workable being hammered out than the present arrangement.

March 5. Mrs. Humphry Ward has been out again, and has made a trip round the French front, as well as our own. She is very enthusiastic about everything that she has seen, and she says that she has little doubt but that America is speedily becoming more inclined to take her share of the war.

I wish it were possible to let the public know how well informed we have been on the whole matter of this retreat, and how accurate we were in our forecast of what the Germans were going to do. But that is impossible at present. As soon as things have developed a little more, I propose to let the Press correspondents write articles to show how much even they knew about the various stages of the retreat, and of course, though they were told as much as was possible, there were things we knew that we could not tell them.

We have been trying to form an opinion of the strategical reasons which have actuated the Germans in this withdrawal. It is now certain that the pressure which the Allied armies have exerted during the last few weeks, since the weather conditions have permitted a resumption of active operations, is not sufficient to account for so extensive a withdrawal.

The strategical situation which is presented to the German Higher Command would probably be governed by the following main considerations :—

(*a*) Germany has been unable to obtain a decisive victory in the field, and her resources both in men, material and money are admittedly weaker than those of her enemies. Should the war continue until 1918, the superior numbers and superior weight of metal would therefore in all probability necessarily lead to the military downfall of Germany.

(*b*) The submarine campaign, whatever success it may attain during the next few months, can at best only force England to a Peace Conference, it cannot lead to Germany dictating terms of peace to her enemies.

(*c*) On the other hand, by super-organization, by better use of available man-power, Germany, in the present year, may still hope to meet her enemies on the field of battle which she herself can select. By a decisive victory in the field she may still succeed in dictating terms of peace.

(*d*) A decisive victory in the Eastern theatre, while less difficult to attain than in the Western theatre, can at best only result in the detachment of Russia from her Allies.

A decisive victory in the Western theatre, on the other hand, combined with modest success in the submarine campaign against England, would clearly mean that Germany could dictate her terms to Europe.

If Germany, either by leakage or by careful observation, has obtained information of our intentions, then the withdrawal to the Hindenburg Line from the sharp salient on the Somme, and possible preparation for a further withdrawal if and when the Allied attack develops, comes as a logical sequence. By such a withdrawal she sets free no fewer than 19 divisions. If she can force the Allies to commit themselves to an attack in considerable strength, from which it would be difficult to disengage, then these 19 divisions become available as an asset for possible operations elsewhere.

March 14. You will have seen in the papers that we have made another good advance. It brings us within easy reach of Bapaume, and I hope that that little town will soon be in our hands. From what we hear, people at home are still trying to belittle the work of the Army here; nevertheless, we have retaken a big slice of ground. As I write, a report has come in that we are in Bapaume, but it is not yet confirmed.

The news from Russia is very bad indeed. I hope it does not mean that they will break off the war altogether, but as you know that has been a possibility in our mind for more than two years now. The curious thing is that most people you meet here, and apparently most at home too, are all rather pleased with the revolution. They say that the Tsarina was a pro-Boche and had gradually got the Tsar round to her way of thinking. Revolutions always leave a country unstable. The Germans will certainly make capital out of this and try to get a counter-revolution.

N——, who is no longer in any official position, is rather concerned about the effect that Bernard Shaw's visit has had in the Argentine, and calls him a " literary mountebank." I should like to hear Bernard Shaw's opinion of N——. What Shaw actually wrote was, " I must confess without shame that I enjoyed my week at the front better than my week's holiday at the seaside." I have no idea what he does at the seaside, but he certainly fully appreciated every moment of his time out here, and said that he had never spent more interesting days.

We have been trying to work out where the Germans can attack here, if they do decide to venture an attack. On the Western front there have been constant rumours ever since December of concentration in Belgium, and the possibility of an offensive there. In January, the Belgian General Head-quarters reported that the Germans had taken steps to lower the water in the canal, and in the same month the strength of their artillery round Ypres, which had been decreased during the Somme battle, was brought back to the strength it was in June, 1916. There has been more aeroplane activity, and some new wireless stations have appeared.

On the 6th of February the War Office sent us out news, from an authority which they said was generally reliable, that the Germans would commence operations in the middle of February, and deliver the main offensive about the 10th of March. Ypres was mentioned as one of the points of attack. In the middle of February the French General Head-quarters received news from a Polish source that an attack would be delivered at Ypres. Yesterday there was a very heavy artillery bombardment at Wytschaete; now, there is news that the Belgian frontier is closed. All the same, all our information from the front line, and our photographs, do not show any of the signs which we generally get prior to a large offensive, and weather conditions this year have made the ground quite unsuitable for operations, or for preparations for operations, any time this month. More than that we cannot say at present.

March 25. Things have straightened themselves up a little better than they were immediately after the Calais mess-up, chiefly I think, owing to the fact that Nivelle's own position is very insecure. He is not having an easy time with his politicians. He deserves it in a way. He appealed to Cæsar and Cæsar now seems inclined to cuff him. Our own particular Cæsar at No. 10 is for the moment not so unfriendly. D.H. had to refer home some very impossible demands of Nivelle's, going even beyond the powers given to him at Calais. There was a conference in London last week, and there has been entered this caveat, that we are *allies* and not *subordinates* of the French, and that the British Army remains *as a whole* under the British C.-in-C.

D.H. tells me he did offer resignation " in the proper quarters " and was told that there must be no such thought in his mind. He also told me that Lord Derby was most sympathetic.

Nivelle has been insistent upon Henry Wilson as head of our mission at G.Q.G. and D.H. has agreed. I think this is a great mistake, and urged that X. should be appointed. Esher, who knows Henry Wilson well, says he is always quite loyal to the man he is serving, and that as long as he is at G.Q.G. he will be helpful, and if anywhere else very dangerous.

Paris is in the middle of another political convulsion. Lyautey has decided to create a Chief of Staff on the lines of Robertson at home, and I am told de Castelnau's appointment had actually been signed. Briand is said to have approved of this before Lyautey's speech, and then to have deserted him afterwards. Anyhow, the whole Government is very much shaken, but a change of government in Paris is not so serious as in London. Lyautey's speech was resented more on account of his manner in making it than because of the matter in it. The " Representatives of the People " thought he was treating them as he did " the Kabyles of Morocco." It is a pity Lyautey has fallen. He was a sound, straight man. It seems pretty certain that he had nothing to do with the Calais Conference proposals, and knew nothing about them until just before the meeting. Nor did Nivelle! They emanated from our own Cæsar, and, I suspect, Henry Wilson!

We are near the end of the German retreat. They are right back to their entrenched lines in most places. The next great change is to be the big attack next month.

March 26. Our cinematograph people rival our cousins on the other side of the herring-pond in hustle. I have just been censoring films showing the entry of our troops into Péronne, which we took from the Germans just a week ago.

For the moment, things are quiet, and I am getting a walk every day ; down the hill from the ramparts, then a good walk along the turnpike road and through two typically pretty French villages, then across the fields to a ferry operated by an ancient dame. It runs on a wire rope, and the old lady pulls it with one hand, keeping the other extended palm uppermost all the way—in case something might fall into it. But she never asks for anything ! Her only subject of conversation is the weather, and about that she makes the same remark, three times each crossing ; once as you get on board her craft, once during the crossing and once as you disembark. Across the river, my route takes me through some fen country and then along the railway line back to the town, about an hour's walk in all, a very pleasant relief from work. I always go alone, for out here, whenever even two are congregated, the talk is " shop."

There are strong rumours of riots in Germany. If they are even half-true the end may be near. The first signs of the real defeat of Germany will be the fall of the morale of her people, and then the commencement of revolution. But the news from Russia shows a much worse state there than even these rumours, which are, of course, exaggerated, show of Germany. I saw the Russian Attaché at Paris last week. Usually an optimist, he is now very depressed. The Grand Duke Nicholas, he said, though straightforward and resolute, is ignorant and unintelligent. The Provisional Government cannot, he thinks, last. Now that the " dignity " that has always hedged the Tsar has been defiled, he does not think the troops will fight or the nation wish to go on.

April 1. Unless there is a change in the weather very soon, all our plans will have to be altered. It has been raining and snowing all day. Most of our doubts as to the German intentions have been set at rest by a captured document. They have no idea of going any farther back than the main line which they have prepared.

The chances of a German attack on the north are now much less than formerly. Indeed, they appear to be making preparations there against an attack by us.

Rather an amusing incident in the search for information happened yesterday. An Intelligence officer, dressed up as a German and who spoke the language perfectly, was put into a bed in hospital next to Prince Frederick Charles, in the hope that he might elicit something. But Prince Frederick Charles was not in the least deceived and, entering with zest into the spirit of the great game, gave most circumstantial accounts of the Germans being already on the move from Mulhausen to the Rhine, and other similar fantasies. Both the officer and the prince enjoyed themselves immensely, each thinking he was getting the best of the game of wits, and, I fancy, neither got the least advantage except that of enjoyment. All the same, we have got some useful information out of the prince, but not about the military operations.

Both Italians and Russians are now writing that they expect all the German strategic reserves to be thrown at their heads! So far there is no confirmation of any move of German troops, either eastward or to Italy. But both Italy and Russia have fallen out of the combined offensive plan, so the French effort becomes an isolated one, except for our supporting attack.

Personally, I am now pretty well sure that all these German moves are simply precautionary. She has been much harder hit on the Somme than even we thought, and she is awaiting our blow, in the hope that if it fails some opportunity may offer for her to attack ; but she regards the initiative as ours for the time being, and so it is.

Prisoners' letters show much greater stringency as regards food in Germany than there has ever been before. One has to discount these letters a good deal. Still I think there is something in it. We shall know much more about it all next week.

CHAPTER XX
BATTLE OF ARRAS

April 3. Another day of disheartening weather, the country is under a blanket of snow, the heaviest we have had this year. It is as bad for the Germans as for us, but if it continues it will make our advance much more slow and will very seriously interfere with the French.

So America has come in ! That is the best world news we have yet had in the whole war. If there was ever any doubt about the ultimate issue, it must be ended now even for the most pessimistic. The war may be over before America can bring her armies over here; but if it goes on beyond this year, we shall have an almost inexhaustible reserve of man-power to draw on. Anyhow, it secures us from any danger of shortage of food or of munitions, or of money.

The Government is concerned about rumours that the Germans are using our prisoners on work in the battle area. The only news we have here comes from two escaped French prisoners, who say there is a prisoners' camp at Marquion near Cambrai. Russian prisoners are apparently employed near Ypres, and some who escaped in that area talk vaguely about a British prisoners' camp being there. Anyhow, I hope there will be no reprisals. It would be quite unnecessary, for we are in the very strong position of being the only Allied power that has more German prisoners than Germany has of our men, and it should be a case of bargaining, not of reprisals, even if there is something in these rumours, which I doubt.

April 6. Before any attack there is always a spring tide of visitors. Yesterday we had Sir Mark Sykes, off to the East on a secret mission, and to-day Esher and Smuts. Sir Mark Sykes is a very remarkable character. He knows the East with the detailed knowledge that one only expects from men who have spent a lifetime there. He has very high ideals, and is a most entrancing conversationalist; altogether a man who should make a very big name for himself. I wish I could have seen more of him, but I was out all day visiting the front, and only got back at 8.30 for dinner. I had expected Sykes to stay the night and to see him in the morning, but he had to be in Paris to-day. He was with me at dinner and afterwards until 1.0 a.m., then left to drive to Paris through the night.

Esher tells me that Nivelle's position is even more precarious than we had realized. A strong section of the Government wanted to forbid the French offensive altogether. Several of Nivelle's own generals are against it. Nivelle had great difficulty in holding his own. What a commentary on the Calais Conference! Unless Nivelle has a big success he will certainly fall. Some of our gunne who have been to the French front are very doubtful about the French chances. I hope and pray they are wrong. Failure now would throw everything back for many months, probably a year. I should be much more happy if we were carrying out Joffre's scheme, but even that, without the Italian and Russian parts of it, would have been a hard task. Our own plans are very well advanced and everything looks favourable.

Smuts is a fine, straightforward little man. He impresses one as quite honest, very clear-headed and with no axe to grind, and no aim except victory. His Staff officer is a capable, hard-bitten fellow. They gave us a very interesting account of their little war in South-West Africa.

April 7. I am greatly struck by the fact that none of our visitors, even those with whom we have constant communications, have ever realized until they come here what an enormous organization the army in the field has grown into. Each one knows the particular department he has been connected with. No one seems to have had much thought of the other parts of the organization. Here at G.H.Q., in our little town away back from the front-line trenches, although we think of nothing but war and deal only with war, there are few visible signs of war. We might almost be in England. Nearly every one of the ramifications of civil law and life has its counterpart in the administration departments. Food supply, road and rail transport, law and order, engineering, medical work, the Church, education, postal service, even agriculture, and for a population bigger than any single unit of control (except London) in England. Can you imagine what it is to feed, administer, move about, look after the medical and spiritual requirements of a million men, even when they are not engaged in fighting, and not in a foreign country? Add to that, the purely military side of the concern. That we have to concentrate great accumulations of this mass of humanity quickly into some particular restricted area, have to deal with enormous casualties, and have to keep a constant flow of men back and forward for hours.

The amazing thing is that with the exception of the transportation and the postal service, every particular part of the organization is controlled by regular soldiers. Even in transportation, though the head is a civilian, the traffic control and the engineering part of the business are under soldiers. It all runs with extraordinary smoothness. There are no committees to confuse and delay. There are no jealousies. Everyone is out only to win the war. Each department is under its own head, and all the heads take their orders from one man only—the Chief. He does not see any one of the heads of these great departments more than once a day, and then very rarely for more than half an hour at a time. Some he does not see more than once a week. Correspondence is reduced to a minimum; all the formal letters and notes of peace-time have disappeared. The work goes on continuously; office hours are far longer than of any civilian office in peace-time. There are few, if any, officers who do not do a fourteen-hour day, and who are not to be found at work far into the night.

Then, apart from these great administration departments, there is the General Staff Operations, which has charge of all the fighting, and my own department of Intelligence. The Operations section are supposed to keep themselves clear of all administrative work; they are supposed to do only the thinking and the planning, and not to concern themselves with detail, but as everything they have to plan for depends upon administration, they have to know all that goes on. Intelligence is a mixture of administration and policy. Apart from the purely military side, which is by far the most important part of the work, it has the Press, censorship, Secret Service, mapping, ciphers, visitors and various odd little sideshows, like sound-ranging, telephone-intercepting sections and carrier pigeons. It has offices in Paris, in England, and in neutral countries.

All the work in all the departments is systematized now into a routine. Most of it is done in office. One of the great difficulties of everyone at G.H.Q. is to get away from their office often and long enough to get in close touch with the front. Few can ever get much farther forward than the H.Q. of the Armies. All the offices are located here in one little French town.[1]

When a battle is on, the Chief goes forward into Advanced G.H.Q., taking with him some of the General Staff only. Everything else remains behind here, and the administration heads of departments go forward to see him when necessary. All the Intelligence, except myself and one assistant, remain behind.

Forward at Army Head-quarters, one is nearer the fighting, but even they are now mostly in towns or villages several miles behind the front line. Farther forward still are Corps Head-quarters, where there is generally plenty of evidence of the war. They are mostly within distant range of the German guns, but even Corps Head-quarters are now pretty big organizations and are almost always in a village. In front of the Corps Head-quarters the Divisions are mostly in farmhouses, but well in the fighting line. One can almost always get one's car up to them. But that is about the limit, and visits forward of them consequently take up a good deal of time. We all manage, anyhow, to see something of Divisional Head-quarters, but it is only when there is some particular object, more than simply looking round, that one can give up the time to go beyond them. I have not seen even a Brigade Head-quarters in the front line for the last month.

April 8. We are again on the eve of battle; although it is only to help the French it is a big thing. Three corps, each with four divisions, are making the main attack, and the Canadians are attacking on their left. The big French attack is being held back on account of the weather, but will not make very much difference to us, so far as the immediate fighting is concerned, always provided that the French Government does not at the last moment succeed in overruling Nivelle, and stop the attack altogether; if they do that we shall have the whole German Army on our heads here in a month.

I think we know precisely whom we shall be fighting against, and everything looks well. Certainly no attack that we have yet made, not even the Somme, has been as fully and as carefully prepared as this one. General Allenby, who is commanding the main attack for the first time in a big battle, has any amount of determination and go. He has only one severe critic. Allenby's nickname is "The Bull" and this critic says he will rush blindly on like a bull and be pole-axed. Allenby shares one peculiarity with Douglas

[1] Montreuil.

Haig, he cannot explain verbally, with any lucidity at all, what his plans are. In a conference between the two of them it is rather amusing. D.H. hardly ever finishes a sentence, and Allenby's sentences, although finished, do not really convey exactly what he means. Yet they understand one another perfectly; but as each of their particular Staffs only understands their immediate superior a good deal of explanation of details has to be gone into afterwards and cleared up.

I remember hearing Lord Kelvin lecture. He had just the same peculiarity, and had a sort of Greek chorus in the form of an assistant who explained in very broad Scotch exactly what Lord Kelvin meant. The only difference then was that the comments and chorus went on at the same time as the main motif. At these Army conferences no one dares to interfere, and all clearing up has to be done afterwards. All the same, Allenby's preparations are as perfect as anything can be in war, and the Chief looks forward to a very big local success to-morrow.

Byng, with his Canadians, has a very difficult job. He is going for a place (the Vimy Ridge) which quite defeated all efforts of the French last year. If he succeeds, and I think he will, it will be the end of all dangers of a big attack from the Germans in the north. Incidentally, if he succeeds, we shall have very considerable trouble with our Press arrangements. Beaverbrook has already been on the warpath to insist on even more publicity for the work of the Canadians, and urges that it is absolutely necessary to boost the Canadians because of its effect in Canada. At the same time, Northcliffe is sending from America long telegrams that the boosting of the Canadians is affecting not only American opinion, but also recruiting in Canada. He argues that the Canadians are beginning to say that their young men are being sacrificed and the British troops are being spared. We have to hold the balance level between these Press war-lords. It is no easy task. But after all, the great thing is to win the battle; it does not matter much whether any particular part of this great Imperial army gets an undue share of the credit. There is absolutely no jealousy out here in the army itself, so far as I can see, between the Canadians and British or anyone else. There is a good deal of comment on the fact that the Irish divisions are all below establishment, and that the Irish people are not coming forward; perhaps now that America is in, that extraordinary little island will play up better.

The German casualty list shows a total of 60,000 for the month of February. An analysis of this list is interesting. Prussia carries about two-thirds of the whole, Bavaria one-fifth and the smaller states the remainder. Saxony, latterly, has only been carrying two-thirds of the proportion of casualties that she should carry according to her size, while Wurtemberg is carrying twice as many as she should. There might be good stuff for propaganda inside Germany in this. The Prussians, of course, are the backbone of their army, just as the English are the backbone of ours; all the other parts of our Empire, even including Scotland, are relatively insignificant compared with the proportion of the fighting army which England is providing. With the exception of the Guards, who are a class by themselves, I do not think there is very much difference, unit for unit, in the fighting value of any of our nationalities. The same thing seems true of the Germans, although so far as our own experience goes, the Wurtembergers and the Prussian Guards are always the most difficult to tackle.

April 10. The attack has been a complete success. Yesterday we took more than 10,000 prisoners and 38 guns. Our first assault went straight through the German front-line trenches, and captured the whole of them within an hour. It looked as if the cavalry were at last going to have their chance during the afternoon and they were ordered forward, but one miserable hill (Monchy le Preux) still held out, and the cavalry could not go on; they may have better luck to-day.

The one unfortunate thing is the accursed weather. It has broken again, and we are having snow and rain. Just now it is practically a blizzard, but our scientific weather prophets promise better conditions for the next few days. Do you remember this day last year when you were taking me down to Cimiez after my pneumonia? We were caught in a hailstorm and then snow.

Do you remember H.? He had a very narrow escape a couple of days ago. A shell landed very close to him in a trench, and he was buried and when dug out was found to have concussion and shell-shock. He was sent back and told he would be sent home to England. This did not suit him at all, so he broke out of hospital and found his way somehow or other to my office here to make an appeal to be allowed to return to his job.

April 11. D.H. is enormously pleased with our success. Yesterday we made a lot of ground, and have got as far as we had originally intended to go. I have never seen D.H. so stirred by success before, and he has been most kind and complimentary about our little part in the show. It means a great deal to him personally, though I do not think that weighs much with him. After all this trouble at Calais, however, there is no doubt in any of our minds that the Prime Minister would have got rid of him out of hand unless this show had been a success. It is a success, indeed it is more than a success, it is a victory. The one unfortunate thing about it is that strategically it loses much of its value owing to the delay in the French big battle. I do not think they are to blame, though there is much criticism here. The weather has been against them, and from their point of view it would have been folly to have risked any part of their meagre chance of success by attacking in adverse weather conditions. The trouble is that after this Calais Conference everyone is so sensitive and is inclined to look for indications of the French not playing the game by us. That is one of the results of stupidity like the Calais Conference. It tends to set the whole of the two Staffs by the ears. D.H. himself is above all that, and is very severe on any mention of it; all the same, the thing is natural.

April 12. Northcliffe has sent a telegram " Press work prompt and greatly interesting the public," which is very gratifying to the Press department and to the correspondents. Certainly they have played up extraordinarily well, both prior to the attack and particularly for the last few days.

There are signs that the Germans are beginning to go back, which may be the commencement of another big withdrawal. The number of prisoners and guns is steadily mounting and I hope we shall have taken twenty thousand by the end of the month, but we are now nearly as far forward as we can safely go in this area. The information from Paris is rather disturbing. Painlevé is said not to have acquired any very great celebrity, except for always being away from the Ministry "pour commander les troupes." The French information from Russia is also very bad; they say that the troops are starving, and there is only one rifle for every five men.

The Duc de V. has just come back from Germany, where he has been a prisoner for two years, and reports a great lack of food and a great increase of Socialism, but says that their roads are excellent in the lines of communication area.

There seems to be no doubt at all now that our attack on the 9th took the enemy by surprise; they did not expect an attack before the 15th at the earliest, though it is not clear why they had selected that date. They meant to hold on to the Vimy Ridge at all costs, anyhow for the time being or until their back lines were completed. They had begun thickening up their front line on the 28th of March, probably to make secure the hinge on which the further withdrawal would pivot. The bombardment quite overwhelmed them. On Vimy Ridge the ground is more cut up now even than it was on the Somme. The counter-battery work for the first time was thoroughly effective throughout the whole of the battle front, and in consequence, although our batteries were very thick on the ground, we lost practically nothing from hostile artillery during the bombardment.

The attack on the first day went like a show at Olympia; the whole line went forward in one enormous wave and there was practically no loss. As the attack went on, cohesion was lost to a certain extent, and yesterday some of the operations were distinctly disjointed.

The morale of the Germans is still rather puzzling. At some parts whole battalions threw their hands in with hardly any resistance, while alongside of them a group of ten or twelve men would hold out with the utmost determination until the whole lot were killed. On the whole, I think there is a lowering of their morale, but there were very marked exceptions, and one cannot draw any definite conclusions.

The pigeon service has proved most useful, and we are getting very much more valuable information than from agents as regards movements of German troops of importance during the battle.

We have captured some very interesting documents: the most important is "Experiences of the Somme Battle," by von Belou, in which it is distinctly evident that all through the latter stage of the Somme battle the Germans were fighting a losing fight, and were only just able to hold their own. This is most interesting reading and very good confirmation of what we had thought here. Other German official documents refer openly to the weakening of the German fighting power. Incidentally, definite admission is made of the supremacy of our aircraft, which would do beautifully to stuff down the throats of our Pemberton Billings. The German *communiqués* are again lying freely, but that is not to be wondered at, and will probably not do them any good, for the truth is sure to be known very soon, even in Germany.

April 15. We have done our share of the big operation and

the French begin to-morrow. All luck to them; I hope they will have as big a success as we have. We have gone forward more than 4 miles, and have secured every tactical point that we intended to take. We have captured 14,000 prisoners and 200 guns, we have drawn to our attack more than double the number of German troops that were here when we began. So far we have done all we could to make easier the task of the French. The Germans made a heavy counter-attack to-day, but were driven back.

Norton Griffiths,[1] fresh from his exploits in Rumania, is here to-day, an extraordinarily vital and forceful man. His adventures in Rumania, as he recounted them, would make a real thriller of the Stanley Weyman type. He was out to destroy the oil-fields and wheat of Rumania, to prevent them falling into the hands of the Germans, and seems to have accomplished wonders. He was with me for an hour and a half, and I could have listened to him for twice as long if I could have spared the time. When I last saw him he was starting the tunnelling show with the old First Army. I think if it had not been for him it never would have been started, though it is now far bigger than even he dreamed of at the time.

We are still attacking, just to prevent the Germans moving troops from our front to the French front, but practically our task here is over.

April 17. The French seem to have done only fairly well in their big attack; we had hoped for something much bigger. It may all come right. As we know on the Somme, lack of complete success on the first day does not mean that the battle is a failure.

Repington has been here. Mostly his talk was about political fights at home, which was interesting but not of particular importance now after our big success this month. He says that for the first time since the beginning of the war England is really impressed by what the Army has done, which is amusing, because this effort, successful though it has been, was nothing like so great as that which we gained on the Somme, or as that we should have made under other circumstances. He was very alarmed about the submarine menace, and gave it as not only his own opinion, but that of people who ought to know more about it than he does, and whom he had met, that there would be a serious shortage of food in England if the war went on through this autumn. He is very sarcastic about the Navy, and not at all hopeful about what the

[1] The late Sir J. Norton Griffiths.

attitude of the people would be if they are faced with real personal hardship. He thinks that a lack of bacon would depress Great Britain even more than the biggest casualty list. One always discounts Repington's own personal views; he talks more for effect than giving a really serious considered opinion, but he is probably truthful enough in relating other people's views, for he would be found out if he twisted them too much.

If the French attack does really make anything of a success it will have one very important result. I think it will certainly force the German Fleet to come out, and then if our fleet can give a really good account of themselves it will bring the war much nearer an end.

It is extraordinary how correct our anticipation of the German dispositions and intentions before this battle have proved to be. We put up to D.H. a written appreciation on the evening of the 8th of April, pointing out where the German resistance would be greatest, what troops they would use in resisting the attack and what troops they had in support, and when they would arrive, and what we thought they actually had in mind if we did attack. We summed it up, " the attack to-morrow bids fair to find the Germans hesitating between two plans, viz.: (1) Of holding with all their strength their front line, as was their general scheme of defence last year, and (2) A skeleton force in front and the bulk of their troops held back in, or actually withdrawing to, a position so far back as to be out of reach of our gunfire."

April 18. The French are doing rather better now and the number of prisoners is mounting up, but the whole thing has fallen very far short of their expectations and our hopes. D.H. foresees a complete change of plans which would put us in again to play the lead.

April 20. There are strong rumours that the inevitable is happening, and Nivelle will be replaced by somebody else. There is a conference to-day in Paris. D.H. has called for a paper.

The general position is that the Germans have got 26 fresh divisions and 16 divisions recently taken out of the firing-line, available for this front; they have also 7 partially trained divisions in Germany and can probably bring over another 10 from the Russian front, a total of 46; but of the 26 divisions probably at least 15 will be required to replace the troops which have been engaged against the French.

There has been a noticeable falling off in the German artillery fire both against the French in the present battle, and also, though to a lesser extent, on our own front, which probably means some shortage of munitions.

The reports of disaffection and food trouble in Germany culminated in that of the Berlin strike, which is too strong to be disregarded.

Having regard to all these considerations, in spite of the collapse of the French attack, and despite any difficulty with regard to man-power which the Allies may be experiencing, it seems evident that the present is not the moment to withdraw any active offensive operations and adopt a passive policy. For the first time, the enemy shows definite signs of giving way under pressure of our operations.

We are urging that every active offensive operation should be continued, if necessary by artillery bombardment only on the French front and without much expenditure of infantry; if this is done and the German reserve divisions are withdrawn to that front then offensive operations undertaken between the Somme and the sea at our selected point should have a great hope of decisive success. But for this success it is essential (1) that preparations should be pressed on as rapidly as possible, and that the attack should be delivered on the date selected with due regard to the consideration that hitherto every delay, however small, has been a distinct asset to the defence, and (2) that the operations of drawing German reserves to the French front must be so arranged that they *must* extend, not only over the whole period of the preparations of our northward attack, but at least for the first fortnight of the time devoted to that attack itself.

April 21. At the conference in Paris yesterday it was decided to carry on with the French attack for at least another fortnight, which is all to the good, but I am afraid the general position has changed for the worse. This last week the French attack has definitely failed; it cannot now hope to achieve anything really important.

Macdonogh has been away from the War Office ill, which leaves a great gap so far as I am concerned, for his opinion is the only really valuable one with regard to Germany's intentions which I get to help me. He is always very sound, if cautious. French opinions are valueless; they think out what they would like to be happening and then manufacture evidence that it is happening.

To-day for the first time it is real spring weather, a very pleasant change. The trees are bursting into bud and the sun has brought out all the birds; war seems very futile.

April 23. We are changing our Head-quarters; my new office is in a hut, very comfortable and with plenty of room. My billet is in a small farmhouse, not over-clean, but in, at present, a countrified area. I went up to Arras—very desolate and deserted now after all the stir that was there prior to our big attack. A few shells were still falling into it, but nothing to matter and soon they will stop also.

We have been fighting again to-day and made good progress in the forenoon; but in the afternoon very strong counter-attacks developed and we lost some of the ground that we had gained. The German attacks were unusually determined, probably as a result of the ill-success of the French attack; they have taken back a little ground but must have suffered very heavy losses from our artillery. I think it is possible that these counter-attacks are only to cover withdrawal.

A very interesting German captured document says, " since the 15th March the rations of the whole of the army have been reduced by one-third." This is the first direct indication that we have had that the shortage of food in Germany has forced the diminution of rations to the army. There are some indications that the enemy may be contemplating withdrawal in the north; he is preparing a back line, and has been throwing bridges across the canals.

D.H. has asked for another note with regard to Germany's strategical intentions, for a conference on the 26th. The decisive factors seem to be :—

(1) The submarine war, however serious, cannot bring decision before next harvest.

(2) America's entry into the war renders quite impossible any decisive victory for Germany; it follows the only object that Germany can have is to ensure conditions favourable to a compromise peace.

She may hope to do this by a series of withdrawals during the summer and autumn months, avoiding decisive battle and hoping that the approach of winter will induce the Allies to accept a peace conference. Alternatively, she may hope by accepting battle in a strong defensive position and gaining tactical successes in the next few months, to show to the Allies that it is impossible for them to obtain a decisive victory this year, and thus bring them to a peace conference in the late summer or early autumn.

She may seek by a fleet action to put all to the hazard, hoping that if successful she may gain some measure of decision in her favour. This, in my opinion, is her only real hope of a favourable ending of the war for her.

Whichever of these plans she may adopt, it is clear that a vigorous and active offensive on the part of the Allies in the Western theatre is the thing which the Germans themselves will least desire to meet.

April 28. D.H. is back from the conference in Paris and tells me that the notes which we gave him so impressed Ribot, the French Prime Minister, that he grabbed them and asked permission to use them " in a French state paper." The net result of the conference is on the whole good, the attacking is not to stop, nor the general plans be altered. Apparently Nivelle is to go, although D.H. urged that he should be retained, on the grounds that any change now will only mean further dislocation. It is very generous of D.H., considering all that has happened in the past, to try to save Nivelle. D.H.'s view is that Nivelle, now that he has learned that things do not always happen as one would like them to happen, will be a much easier man to deal with than before, and that " the devil you know is better in any event than the devil you do not know."

April 29. We had a regular Scottish Sunday. D.H. took me to church in a little wooden hut in the village. The sermon was to the effect that we all had to believe that God is working in us for a definite purpose; all very cheering if you are quite certain that that purpose is our victory. But it is difficult to see why a German preacher could not preach just such a sermon to Hindenburg and Ludendorff. All the same, D.H. seems to derive an extraordinary amount of moral strength from these sermons. We discussed it after lunch, for all the world as one used to do as a boy in Scotland. Then D.H. suddenly switched off to a paper which he is preparing for the War Cabinet at home, and was back in 1917 and at war.

The general lines of his paper is the same old story—go back to the first principles of the war; wear down the enemy's powers of resistance to such a state of weakness that he will not be able to stand a decisive blow, and then deliver the blow. D.H. does not think that the time has yet come for the decisive blow, and that this was the cause of Nivelle's failure. We have now to go back to the *wearing-down* process, the duration of which cannot be calculated. It all leads to the same conclusion; to keep up our pressure continuously all this summer and then perhaps find Lord Kitchener's forecast fulfilled, that some day the enemy will not be there. We were certainly very near a decision at the end of last year; it may be possible to get it again this year, but there are two big " ifs "; first, *if* Russia holds, and secondly, *if* the French can keep on attacking.

April 30. Fuller information about yesterday's fighting shows that it was much more like one of last year's battles than those of this year. The Germans fought with great determination, and the battle front swayed backwards and forwards, until eventually we got the upper hand and held our objective. The fighting was renewed to-day, and there have been six distinct counter-attacks by the Germans, all of them repulsed. Although only on a small front, we have taken 1,000 prisoners.

May 1. D.H. is back from Paris. It seems more than doubtful whether the French will open another attack or continue with the present one. Exactly what we feared has happened. The French now want us to take up the whole burden of active operation on this front. Nivelle will go. At present Pétain is appointed French C.G.S. with Nivelle under him. The French casualties have been very heavy, and there is great trouble brewing. Poor Nivelle! One cannot help being very sorry for him. With all his faults, he did take a big view of things, and he certainly did not seek to spare his own army. He staked everything on this one battle and has lost.

I have been up to the front to-day, through all the area we have taken this last month. Such a scene of awful desolation and waste! It impresses one so much more, now that one only sees it at longish intervals than when one was in the midst of it all. I wish everyone in England could see it, to make them realize what war really is. It is impossible to describe; and when the war is over, nobody, except those who survive out here, will have any real conception of what war is. If Germany is really the cause of it all, no nation should ever again treat her as civilized. Everything that one associates with the idea of human civilized life is utterly devastated; villages, orchards, cultivated fields, roads, railways, canals, telegraphs. Even the processes of nature are abruptly stopped. The trees, stripped and blasted—where they still stand —are great gaunt skeletons. The only living things that survive are the great swarms of flies wherever there is a dead body; and the birds, which, curiously enough, sing just as merrily and happily as away back behind the line.

I spent much of the afternoon in prisoners' cages, chatting to the Germans and trying to form my own opinion of their morale. Strange to say, the prisoners are not in the least unpopular with our men. There seems no resentment on either side. So far as a mutual ignorance of each other's language admits, they confab together amicably and happily. Indeed, our men fraternize far more readily with the German prisoners than with their French allies. The German has a very great respect now, whatever he had in 1914, for the British Army, and for the individuals comprising it, and our men are completely and quietly confident that we are " the chosen people " and better than anyone else. They do not push it down the German's throat, they just take it for granted that the German realizes it, and as far as the prisoners are concerned, it is on that basis that they meet.

Prisoners are, of course, a very poor gauge of morale. I discount their spoken words, but the written evidence that one collects by the sackload in every successful operation, is of the greatest value. Two very interesting things have been learned from captured German orders. First, they are very short of copper and are trying to find a way of using steel cartridge cases instead of copper ones for their rifles; and second, the German soldier's ration is just about three-fifths of our men's. They get about the same amount of cereals and vegetables, half of the amount of meat (including the inevitable German sausage) and no jam or cheese or bacon. If this is so for their army, it must be much worse for the German in Germany.

May 4. G.B.S.'s visit has cropped up again. This time some ass in the House of Commons wanted to know who was responsible for his visit, and whether the nation paid! This apparently stumped the War Office, who telegraphed out here. Actually it was D.H. who wanted him; but as his name must not be dragged in, I have written that the invitation to him went under the same arrangements as those to Conan Doyle, H. G. Wells, D'Annunzio and the editors of the *Spectator*, *Saturday Review*, and the *Nation*. That will give the War Office something to ruminate about, and if ever I meet G.B.S., I shall ask him with which of these distinguished gentlemen he would like to be classified.

CHAPTER XXI

MESSINES

May 6. D.H. is back from yet another conference in Paris. The result is generally satisfactory. We go back to our original plan (northern offensive), but after a loss of two months of most valuable time. The French are to take over some of our line and are to help in local attacks whenever possible. " Both nations are to fight with all available forces ! " Meantime, there is much better news from the French; they made a limited, but very successful attack yesterday, and got their objective on the Chemin des Dames, for which we fought in 1914.

May 7. Lloyd George, Lord Robert Cecil and Colonel Hankey arrived yesterday, and dined with D.H. The Chief was summoned away during dinner by an urgent message and called me to his chair at the head of the table. So I sat between, and presided over the P.M. of Great Britain on my right, and the acting Foreign Minister on my left. Lloyd George made merry at the situation, but was most charming all the same. He can fascinate in a way I have never known any other man fascinate, and he enjoys doing it ! You have to take hold of yourself, shake yourself and make yourself remember all his misdeeds, or you would become a " chela." He is amazingly sharp-witted, and full of energy, fire and go. At present his line is outspoken praise of everything in the British Army in France, and especially of D.H. He compares us now with the French, very much to the disadvantage of the latter, and says he trembles to think what would have happened if we had been held up with them. I longed to point out that if the Calais Conference agreement in its first form had held, we probably *should* have been held up just the same, but refrained, as I am not supposed to know anything about that most disreputable of all intrigues. Lloyd George finished up by giving an extraordinarily amusing imitation of Robertson at a Cabinet meeting. It was a wonderful bit of mimicry, and kept us all in fits of laughter. Probably it was all done with a purpose—to weaken the bond between the War Office and G.H.Q. If so, it failed, but it was as good, or better, than any music-hall turn.

Lord R. Cecil impresses me very much indeed. He has great brains and imagination, and altogether strikes me as the most remarkable of all this Cabinet. He came back to my office after dinner and we talked far into the night. When he gets interested, he sinks lower and lower into his chair until all you see of him is a great beak of a nose hooked on to the table and a pair of gleaming eyes peering at you. I do not think there is much love lost between him and the P.M., but he has a great admiration for what he called "his fertility of resource" and his power of decision. Very desirable qualities, if he does not use his fertility of resource in thinking out new Alpine adventures and his power of decision in sacking everyone who points out their absurdity. Do you remember Sir W. Nicholson's remark to the Staff College alumni? "You are reported as having great independence of judgment and strength of character. Both of these failings you will, no doubt, in time overcome!"

Hankey, who is said to know more about everything than anybody else in the Empire, preserved an almost unbroken silence all through dinner. Probably that is how he acquires his knowledge. After dinner Lloyd George and he went off together to deal with their own particular business.

May 10. A long day at Belgian G.H.Q. where the German peace proposals are exciting great interest. The Belgians seem to think something will come of them, and certainly they are very different from the tone of the December proposals. But I hope we shall not dream of accepting such terms, anyhow for another six months, and then, if all goes well, we shall be able to exact something very different.

I am afraid my lady clerks are not altogether a success. One of them wants to get married at once; another is engaged; and a third has lost her mother. So I am trying to send them all back and have recourse to the less amorous male.

May 15. I was in Paris yesterday and dined with Esher, who gives most alarming accounts of the situation there. He says the morale of the whole nation is badly affected by the failure of their attack. The Military Attaché confirmed this. The Government cannot, apparently, make up its mind what to do. First they intended to get rid of Nivelle altogether and make Pétain C.-in-C. and Foch C.G.S. Then that was changed and Pétain made C.-in-C. and Nivelle remained. Now they are back again at their original plan, and Foch is to become C.G.S., but the appointment is not out yet. Wilson, who was here yesterday, did not know of the last change, and apparently G.Q.G. thought Pétain was to be both C.G.S. and C.-in-C.

May 19. The news to-day is not good. The French are having very serious trouble in their own army. I was at a conference with the new French C.-in-C. at Amiens yesterday. He is very different from either Joffre or Nivelle; not nearly so impressive as Joffre, or as romantic as Nivelle. He looks just an ordinary, steady-going soldier, who will always do the ordinary steady-going thing. But he seemed a strong, determined man. I cannot think that he and Foch will hit it off, but I think D.H. and he will. Foch, by the way, has amazed us all, by suggesting as one of his first expressions of opinion in his new office, that Henry Wilson is now not fulfilling any useful purpose at French G.Q.G. and should go. I could have understood it if he had followed that up by asking for him at Paris. Not a bit of it! He wants him anywhere except near himself!! These were exactly D.H.'s and W.R.'s feelings when they took over their respective charges, and so H.W. goes home. But he will bob up again, for "Satan finds some mischief still for idle hands to do."

May 25. The news from Russia is a little better this morning, but one can no longer hope for anything really good from there. Things are better in the French Army, but at a heavy price. They are giving every man ten days' leave every four months; that means something like a quarter of a million permanently away from the front line. Our own total on leave is not a quarter of that. It means definitely that we cannot expect any great help from the French this year.

I am trying to get rid of the detail of Press work. It takes up far too much time and energy. The present proposal is to have Lord E. Cecil out in charge of Press. He would have to work under me, but could correspond direct with the Press war-lords.

June 3. Winston Churchill has been out, while I was in England. He lunched yesterday with D.H., who tells me that he was quite humble-minded. He was against any offensive this year. Apparently he did not know anything about the state of affairs in the French Army and nation. D.H.'s criticism of him is very definite. " No doubt he has great brain-power, but his judgment seems to be unbalanced ! "

The pleasure we have been taking in revolutionary tendencies in Germany, and in captured documents that enlarge on those tendencies, have had a rude shock. Our own country seems to be tainted with the same disease. I have just had sent me a circular letter which Ramsay MacDonald and his crew of peace-at-any-price maniacs has issued to all Trade Unions, calling them to a conference " to do for this country what the Russian Revolution has accomplished in Russia." It is signed by—among others—Ramsay MacDonald, Philip Snowden and Robert Smillie. I should have thought Smillie would have known better. The others are beyond all sense of shame. I wish it had come last week, when I had some Labour leaders here—good staunch men. I would have liked to have asked them to get the signatories sent out here to learn something about it all. So far as I know, none of them has ever even tried to come out and see for himself and talk to the men. Of course, this particular effort of our defeatists cannot be taken seriously. The chief thing they want is probably the 2s. 6d. from " each delegate " attending the conference : but it helps one to put a juster value on some similar captured German documents. We have probably been giving them too much importance. All the same, it is disgraceful that there should be such people in England now.

June 8. We attacked again yesterday, and again had a very great success. I went up to see the commencement of the battle. The whole of the main part of the German position had been mined for nearly a year—a very closely guarded secret and apparently successfully guarded. The mines were exploded just before dawn, and the troops went over at the same time. The whole attack went like clockwork. Everything exactly as it was intended and exactly at the time intended; a very great feather in the caps of Plumer and Harington. They are a wonderful combination, much the most popular, as a team, of any of the Army Commanders. They are the most even-tempered pair of warriors in the whole war or any other war. The troops love them. When a division is rattled for any reason, either because of very heavy casualties or because it thinks it has had unfair treatment, it is sent to the Second Army, and at once becomes as happy as sandboys. The two men

Great Labour, Socialist *and* Democratic Convention *to hail the* Russian Revolution *and to* Organise *the* British Democracy
To follow Russia

May 23rd, 1917.

To Trades Councils, Trade Unions, Local Labour Parties, Socialist Parties, Women's Organisations and Democratic Bodies.

DEAR COMRADES,—

The Conference to which we recently invited you is already assured of a great success.

It will be one of the greatest Democratic Gatherings ever held in this country. It will be historic. It will begin a new era of democratic power in Great Britain. It will begin to do for this country what the Russian Revolution has accomplished in Russia.

There is little time for preparation. Action must be taken immediately by every Branch and Society desiring to be represented. It seems not unlikely, owing to the rush of applications for delegates' tickets that the Committee may be unable to give facilities for those who delay till the last moment.

The Conference will be held in the ALBERT HALL, LEEDS, on SUNDAY, JUNE 3rd, commencing at 10.30 a.m.

We now send you the Resolutions which are to be discussed. Owing to the shortness of time for the preparation for the Conference the proceedings will not be subject to the rigid rules which usually govern Labour and Socialist Congresses. It will be a Democratic Conference to establish Democracy in Great Britain.

Russia has called to us to follow her. You must not refuse to answer that appeal.

Send in your application for Delegates' Cards at once. You are entitled to send one delegate however small your membership may be, but an additional delegate for each 5,000 of your membership above the first 5,000, or part of 5,000.

Applications, accompanied by a fee of 2s. 6d. for each delegate, must be sent to one of the Secretaries as under.

ALBERT INKPIN, Chandos Hall, 21A Maiden Lane, Strand, London, W.C.2.
FRANCIS JOHNSON, St. Bride's House, Salisbury Square, London, E.C.4.

In the confident hope that your Society will join in this great event,
On behalf of the United Socialist Council,
We remain,
Yours fraternally,

H. ALEXANDER
CHAS. G. AMMON
W. C. ANDERSON
C. DESPARD
E. C. FAIRCHILD
J. FINEBERG
F. W. JOWETT

GEO. LANSBURY
J. RAMSAY MACDONALD
TOM QUELCH
ROBERT SMILLIE
PHILIP SNOWDEN
ROBERT WILLIAMS

are so utterly different in appearance. Plumer, placid and peaceful-looking, rather like an elderly grey-moustached Cupid. Harington, always rather fine drawn and almost haggard. Neither has ever been known to lose his temper. The nearest approach was in some discussion or other about maps in which they were involved, Harington wrote about " bowing to the opinion of those who had more knowledge of what trench fighting in the Salient required than those who had been there seven months!" D.H. referred to Plumer last night as "his most reliable Army Commander." High praise for both of them, for nobody knows where Plumer ends and Harington begins.

This is the first big attack they have brought off and it could not have been better. We have taken 7,000 prisoners and over 50 guns, and our casualties are less than 10,000; altogether a remarkable day.

I think that after this victory, coming on the top of the Arras one, even the most convinced pessimist at home must realize that the Army can fight and win battles. But one never knows. Even the War Office seems to like discouraging us at times, by disparaging our successes. Perhaps that is unfair criticism, but certainly they will not admit what we *know* here, that the German fighting power is steadily decreasing, and ours increasing. I am sometimes tempted to tell them that although attack may be the best form of defence, it does not follow that defence is the best form of attack !

The one depressing thing is that all this should have been done at the beginning of the fighting this year, and not now when half the year is gone. We are two months later than we should have been.

I spent yesterday afternoon, or a good deal of it, at the prisoners' cages. The prisoners show distinct signs of being fine drawn. Their morale is low, but that may be accounted for by the mines. The 3rd Bavarian Division struck me as rather above the average. I do not think the mines actually inflicted many casualties, but German officers tell me they so upset their men's nerves that they offered no resistance. Our " oil-cans "[1] are also reported by the prisoners to have had a great moral effect. Two officers said it was impossible to stay in any trench within five yards of which an " oil-can " landed. This is very satisfactory.

Another remarkable feature was the rapidity with which our guns

[1] These were 2-gallon tins filled with inflammable oil and projected into the enemy's trenches.

were able to move forward, with the result that whereas we only had one gun for every fifteen yards of trench on the long arc of the circle on which we began, on the shorter chord on which we finished we actually had one gun for every seven yards of front. The news should have a good effect on France.

Paris has been very restive and unhappy for the last fortnight. All leave to Paris from the French front was stopped and the Government were holding a brigade near Paris ready for emergencies. I am told that people in Paris were again beginning to discuss Caillaux seriously. The report of him was that he is obsessed with the idea that he alone could control French finances —Colbert *redivivus*. I remember Asquith speaking highly of Caillaux, on the ground that he succeeded in introducing the income tax into France! I suppose the French people are just about as grateful to him for that as Australians are to the Scotsman who introduced rabbits into their country. The Paris strikes are reported as "hectic but good-tempered."

June 14. It is the lull between storms, and there is little fighting. This morning a little successful show gave us a hundred more prisoners, and a very important position which held up our cavalry in April (Monchy le Preux). It is reasonably certain now that the Germans will not launch any big general attack against us this summer.

Mark Sykes has been here again. All his interest is in the East. He is looking to build a new big empire there. He knows nothing of, and seems not to care much about, events here, nor has he any idea of what is happening in the French Army. There is a very real danger in all visionaries now. For all our minds, like all our material forces, should be concentrated on the one object of beating the German Army here in France. When that is done, it will be time enough to build empires. The first and immediate thing is to make sure we are going to preserve our present Empire, and that can only be done by victory in France.

D.H. goes home to-morrow and we have all been busy getting papers prepared for him.

Muirhead Bone is very anxious to be allowed to sketch the Chief, so by way of a first approach he asked to be allowed to do me. I agreed, provided he did not ask me to stop work for a regular sitting. The result was amusing. I sat at my table writing up notes for D.H. Bone scouted round the room trying first one corner and then another, to see whether from some point of view

I might not present something worth committing to paper. Finally he set to work, but by mutual consent we tore it up afterwards. He said it was not like me, and I devoutly prayed that it was not. All the same, he is a great artist, and I am going to ask D.H. to allow Bone to make a picture of him.[1]

[1] The result was what is, in my opinion, the best picture of D.H. during the War.

CHAPTER XXII
YPRES AGAIN

June 21. The longest day of the year, and we have not yet even begun the really big effort. Six months ago I thought that by this time we should have been near peace. Now it looks as if nothing can prevent another full year of war. In six weeks the "three years" that seemed the extreme possible limit will be passed. Except that America is now with us we are not much better off than, if as well as, we were this time last year. Then, as now, we were getting ready for a big attack, but then, Russia was still hopeful and France was fighting well. Now Russia is out of the picture, and so, for the time being, is France. We cannot hope for much from Italy. The Dardanelles venture is dead. Salonika is useless, worse than useless indeed. Mesopotamia does not matter either way. We fight alone here, the only army active. We shall do well, of that there is no reasonable doubt. Have we time to accomplish?

It all might have been so different, and should have been so different, or, as far as one can judge, *would* have been so different, with better leadership. Our faults and failures are in the Council chamber, not in the field.

June 26. D.H. is still at home and having a difficult time, but we shall not know what is happening until he returns in a couple of days. Meantime, the stream of visitors is unending. We have had Garvin of the *Observer*, who talks just as he writes, that is to say he never stops, and there never seems any reason why he should stop. It just pours out, idea after idea, criticism after criticism, like a tap full on. Every now and then one longs to say, "Stop! I want to remember that point and think it over." But his talk is very interesting. Like everyone else, he is full of criticism of Lloyd George, but like everyone else he says there is no one else to take his place.

Then we had Lord Charles Beresford, a great, good-natured, breezy creature, very emphatic and dogmatic. His mind runs on rails, quite straight, and quite oblivious of everything outside their line. He is still and always a sailor, and has the traditional sailor's view—there should be a yard-arm ready for everyone who does not agree with him.

We have also had Norton Griffiths again, claiming most of the credit for the Messines mines, and, indeed, if it had not been for him, I suppose we should not have had tunnelling well enough advanced to have prepared the mines, eighteen months ago. He is a typical buccaneer of the cloak-and-sword age. I would like to see him sent to Russia just now. He reminds me rather of Gordon, without Gordon's religious inspiration.

The most interesting of all the visitors was Sir A. Williamson, who was on the Mesopotamian Commission, and told me a very great deal about the blunders there.

To-day I have had with me General Nolan, who is to run the American Intelligence. He is here picking up wrinkles. If all the American Staff is of his type, they will do very well. He is precisely the man for the job, clear-headed, and very penetrating in his criticisms and questions. He is the exact opposite of the usual British conception of the American. Very courteous, not in the least assertive, genuinely anxious to learn and not to teach, and very appreciative of the part we have played in the war. He has already been to G.Q.G. and has gone back there from here.

I tested the strength of my Rolls last night in a collision, going at 50 m.p.h., with a French car going at about the same pace. Neither of us had noticed a heap of stones which narrowed the roadway so much that we could not pass, and we took it left wheel to left wheel. My wheel was splintered, but the car kept the road, and we got nothing worse than a bad jolt. The French car, a saloon, did not fare so well. It went rocketing into a cornfield and eventually turned over. Out of it climbed a French officer who, to my very great surprise, came to me, saluted and apologized for any inconvenience he might have caused me! There's politeness for you! We sat and talked for half an hour, until a lorry happened to come along that took me on towards my destination. I left him still on the heap of stones, but sent a car and some refreshments back for him from the nearest H.Q. I have not yet heard any more from him. While we were talking we had a very beautiful little firework display, as if arranged for our special benefit. A German aeroplane was over our area and dropped a couple of bombs. It came under our searchlights and was shelled, unfortunately without being hit. It was a very beautiful sight in the darkness of the night. Somehow I could not help being rather glad that that particular plane got away uninjured; it left one free to enjoy the beauty of it all, without the thought of some poor wretch being killed. If one could only stage a war without loss of life, without wounds, without hardships, there would be very great beauty and little ugliness in it. Not only beauty to please the eye, but the beauty of endeavour and accomplishment in face of difficulties. It is the waste and the suffering that make it ugly, so ugly and so awful that one wonders whether it is not indeed the suicide of civilization.

June 28. D.H. came back yesterday. He has had great difficulties. He tells me that every one of the Cabinet, Lloyd George, Bonar Law, Curzon, Milner and even Smuts, vies with the other in pessimism. They all, headed by the P.M., wanted to stop offensive operations for this year and save up our men and resources for 1918, indulging in Chinese attacks with demonstrations of infantry and plenty of gun-fire. I can imagine nothing that would suit the Germans better. Either they would hit hard at the French, (and goodness knows what the result would be now if they began another Verdun), or they would make a great entrenched line and fight us to a standstill on it next spring. It looks as if the Cabinet wanted to hand the baby of casualties over to the Americans; not a very dignified rôle for Great Britain; to have watched the French fighting the war for the first two years, to fight themselves the third year and then watch the Americans winning it in the fourth or fifth year.

Apparently all this discussion was abruptly ended by a bombshell from the Navy, who told the Cabinet that it was "no good thinking about what would happen next year; there would be no next year of war, for the Navy could not keep going unless the Germans were turned out of the Belgian coast!" No one really believed this rather amazing view, but it had sufficient weight to make the Cabinet agree to our attack going on.

D.H. gave the definite opinion that if the fighting was kept up at its present intensity for six months Germany would be at the end of her available man-power. This is going rather farther than the paper I wrote for D.H. on the 11th of June (I.A/35273). It depends on Russia. The Germans have 157 divisions on the Western front, 66 in Russia, 9 on the Danube, and 2 in Macedonia. At present she cannot spare more than twenty from Russia for the Western front, arriving at the rate of two divisions every six days. Of the 157 divisions now on the Western front, 105 have recently passed through the mill of battle. Germany has only two more annual contingents to call on, one (1919) is now at the depots, the other (1920) is already being examined prior to being called up. That is to say, if fighting goes on at its present intensity of wastage on the German man-power, in six months she will be unable to maintain the strength of her units at even their present reduced establishment. But my words were, " it is a fair deduction, given a continuance of the effort of the Allies, etc., etc." That includes Russia, but it does not differ materially from D.H.'s bolder statement. One thing he has stipulated, which is to the good, that our resources are all to be concentrated in France to the fullest possible extent.

D.H. tells me that Lloyd George was thinking of making Robertson First Lord of the Admiralty! That would fairly put the Naval fat in the fire, and probably bring Nelson toppling off his Trafalgar Square perch.

July 5. B.I. is killed—my closest friend. I was in Paris when my office rang me up to tell me, just going to attend a conference with General Pershing, and then had to go to see the American Ambassador. General Pershing took me with him in his car. We drove through cheering crowds, and through that tomfoolery I had to smile, while all the time my brain was throbbing, " Bob is dead." Oh, curse those Germans! I had another conference in the evening, but between times I got an hour's walk in the Bois, and calmed myself down; then at 11 p.m. I got away in my car and travelled all night to B.I.'s grave. It is at Lissenthiek, no different from all the other graves—why should it be? I stayed there an hour, and got back here in time for my work.

It is wrong that one should feel one death so much in all this holocaust. Indeed, I thought I had lost the power to feel. I almost wish I had.

July 11. I have been out all day, up to the coast where we have taken a very nasty knock. It is the first German success against us since the Loos counter-attacks. We had taken over some trenches from the French a short time ago, and the Germans, with complete justice, thought we were going to do something there and decided to forestall us. They attacked with great determination and we have lost practically the whole of a battalion, a real bad affair. Fortunately it does not affect the general situation, but it does show that the Germans have still plenty of kick left in them. The German attack was admirably planned and carried out.

July 20. Just back (from home). General Pershing is up here with some of his Staff, and I have had them with me most of the day, explaining to them the ramifications of the Intelligence show. I think Pershing will do well. He has determination and goes at everything very thoroughly. Both he and his Staff are, of course, just beginning where we were in 1914. We had to learn by experience, often pretty bitter experience. The Americans can benefit by what we have learnt. All the same, it will be a very difficult job for them to get a serviceable Staff going even in a year's time. They have very few trained officers, and those who are trained have nothing like the knowledge that our Staff College officers had in 1914.

All the Americans tell me that since they arrived in France, they have had to revise their ideas of what our army was doing. They left America quite convinced that the French were doing all the work, and that we were neither willing nor able, or either unwilling or unable, to do more than play a very poor second fiddle to the French. Generally they were enthusiastically pro-French, and not very much pro-British. Now the pendulum is swinging the other way. When the Americans arrived our stock in Paris went down to nothing. Naturally enough, the French people were falling over one another to honour the Americans, and did so rather at our expense. Pershing and his Staff thought them unjust. That is what made him take me with him in his car at the triumphal procession [1] in his honour last week, a very fine action which D.H. greatly appreciated. D.H. and Pershing get on very well together, and the Staffs are on excellent terms. When all is said and done, Americans do speak our language, and think our thoughts, and should be much easier to deal with than either French or Belgians.

July 22. I went to church this morning and heard a very fine sermon from a young Scots padre on Hope. I wish all those who scoff at optimism could have heard it, though probably they

[1] General Pershing was paying an official visit to the French President and then going on to a reception at the American Embassy. His route through Paris had been notified and great crowds had assembled in the streets to do him honour. General Pershing insisted that I should accompany him in his car, as a compliment to the British Army.

would only have scoffed at the sermon as well. If it were not for hope and faith who could go on in this war?

It has been a glorious summer day and it seems such utter absurdity to be devoting all one's time and thought to the destruction of other human beings, just because their leaders and teachers have deluded them and made brutes of them. Yet it has to be done, so that our children and children's children may spend their days in peace. And that, after all, is only a hope, it cannot be a certainty.

July 23. Sir W. Robertson arrived yesterday, and I was haled to a conference with D.H., Pershing and W.R. It was continued this morning. There will be a great deal of talk and discussion and possibly friction before a decision is reached as to the employment of the American Army. It has begun already, but the first thing is to "catch" your army. It cannot possibly develop into anything big within six months, probably not for a year. Ours took two years, and the Americans have the Atlantic to cross instead of the Channel.

July 25. I have been dining with a very distinguished brother Scot, Cosmo Lang, Archbishop of York. His father and my uncle were fast friends in the Scottish Church, and I remember Cosmo from my boyhood days. He did not remember me, of course, and I did not disclose the fact of our kinsfolk's friendship until he was just going to say good night. Up till then he had been very much the Archbishop; one almost felt the want of incense, but then he became very human, and we sat down again and talked for another hour. He had an admirable fund of anecdotes, both Scottish and English.

Our bombardment has commenced, but time is passing. We should have attacked by now. All our weather statistics show that we cannot expect much dry weather after this month.

July 30. Before this reaches you we shall have attacked again, the most important attack and, indeed, the only one that now matters for this year's fighting on this theatre. It is impossible to forecast the result. The only thing that is certain, is that most unfortunate of all things, a big casualty list. All the preparations are, I think, as good and as well advanced as those of our other two big attacks this year, and if we get as much success in this as in the others, great things will happen. My one fear is the weather. We have had most carefully prepared statistics of previous years—there are records of eighty years to refer to—and I do not think that we can hope for more than a fortnight, or at the best, three weeks of really fine weather. There has been a good deal of pretty hot discussion, almost controversy, as regards the time of attack.

We cannot hope for a surprise; our preparations must have been seen, and even if not, our bombardment must have warned the Germans, and no doubt they are already moving up troops towards our battle area. I had urged D.H. to attack on these grounds some days ago in spite of the fact that our preparations were not fully completed; it was a choice of evils. The Army Commanders wanted more time; the last conference was definitely heated. The Army Commanders pressed for delay; D.H. wanted the attack to go on at once, and in the end he accepted the Army Commanders' view. He could, indeed, do nothing else, for they have to carry out the job. I came away with D.H. from the conference when it was all settled, and reminded him of Napoleon's reply to his marshals, "Ask me for anything but time." D.H. was very moody, but once a decision is made he will not give it another thought. With reasonable luck it will make little difference, but we have so often been let in by the weather that I am very anxious.

We are all rather at sea about Michaelis, the new German Chancellor; neither the French, nor ourselves, nor the War Office know very much about him. A padre got a letter from the general secretary of the Student Christian Movement of Great Britain and Ireland which gave us quite a lot of information about him. I sent this on to the War Office and they have replied that it agrees with a little of what they have been able to find out, and that Michaelis will stand for:—

(1) True German freedom, taking account of the needs of the time to preserving a God-given monarchical constitution.

(2) Peace which will be German Christian, i.e. preserving Germany's honesty, rights and power, but also promote Christian brotherhood throughout the world (quite compatible in the eye of a Prussian conservative with all sorts of chauvinism).

(3) It would be a mistake to think of Michaelis standing for a pan-German peace, though it would be highly dangerous to think that he stands for anything but an undefeated Germany.

One of the things which led to the war was the fact that the industrial pan-German played upon the piety and self-interest of the old-fashioned Prussian Junker. The pious Junker holds the view, quite seriously, of Prussia that she need fear God and no one else.

The German newspaper, *Vossische Zeitung* quotes a speech made by Michaelis in 1914, much the same as his speech in the Reichstag; the necessity for a regenerated Germany, not desiring to terrorize over the world by the sword, but strong and peaceable.

To-day it has been raining the whole time, a bad outlook for to-morrow.

July 31. The attack so far has gone very well, but it is too soon yet to hang out the flags and cheer. The weather has been damnable, with rain and mist where we wanted sun and dry ground.

August 3. You ask for news of the progress of the battle.

The chief peculiarity of the fighting on the 31st was, of course, that owing to the weather we could make practically no use of our aircraft. This was most disappointing. The Flying Corps had worked for weeks for superiority in the air, and they had obtained it, only to find that owing to the bad visibility their efforts were in vain. To show what this means, it is enough to say that during the Messines battle in June we received two hundred of what we call "N.F." calls. These are calls sent down by the aeroplanes of fresh targets not previously identified, and which are then taken up by our artillery under direction from the air; on the 31st of July we did not receive a single call of this nature, owing to the bad visibility.

In spite of this the attack on the left, on the centre and on the right centre, was a complete success up to the ultimate objectives. It was, in fact, too much of a success; the troops obtained their objectives without much loss, and almost in advance of time. In consequence, they attempted to move forward to fresh objectives, and in doing so suffered a very considerable loss of life on the extreme right. The full result of the lack of aircraft visibility was felt at once. The rain had made the ground heavy. You will remember that near "Dumbarton's lakes" there are a lot of springs, and even one afternoon's rain makes this area sodden.

The artillery barrage went on at the normal rate allowed on these attacks, but the ground was so heavy that the infantry either could not, or did not (I am not quite sure which), keep close under it; the consequence was that some machine-guns, reinforced by concrete emplacements, came to life after the barrage had passed. They were able to hold up the attack on the centre division of the right corps, thus influencing the division on the right flank, and at this point the attack did not succeed in reaching its objective. It is noteworthy that the division which failed here is the one which did so during the battle of Arras. The hostile artillery fire was not heavy. On the other hand, although the volume of fire was little, the enemy used an instantaneous fuse, and the effect of a barrage with this fuse is far greater than an equal number of shells with the old delay-action fuse. Still the casualties in the advance were remarkably small.

Three things are now perfectly clear, viz. :—

(1) The Germans deliberately evacuated their front lines, except for sentry groups, and were only prepared to offer resistance at the Stutz-Punkt line.

(2) The divisions in the front were organized in groups of two regiments in the defence line and one regiment for immediate counter-attack. In each group of divisions one or more divisions were held back and specially trained for counter-attacks. This is precisely what we anticipated (see I.A/31733a).

(3) The rotation of divisions in Germany is as follows :—
(a) The front line is relieved by the counter-attack divisions; the counter-attack divisions are relieved by the division drawn from another area, which in turn is replaced by the division relieved from the front line.

The German artillery was quite deliberately withdrawn to a position well behind the ridge. This, again, is what we foresaw, and I think will now prove to be the normal organization in the German defence.

The divisions in the front line are relieved generally after five days of bombardment, or two days of attack, but this rotation will, of course, depend on whether suitable divisions are immediately available for relief, and this should not be the case when we go on again.

Actually, the counter-attacks delivered by the Germans were not very serious, except on the 1st of August. On that day they succeeded in turning back our centre by attacking on the right flank in considerable strength. Had our own right been able to make good its hold on its ultimate objective this counter-attack, I think, would not have succeeded. Since the 31st numerous massings of troops for counter-attack have taken place, and counter-attacks are reported from the front line; these are all considered to have been successfully dealt with by our artillery.

Personally, I cannot help being very sceptical about these counter-attacks. We had a well-known case at Monchy le Preux, where we claimed that the 3rd Bavarian Division had been annihilated in a counter-attack. The claim was made in all good faith, but subsequently captured documents showed, without doubt, that although the division was actually prepared for the counter-attack it was countermanded by the Germans for reasons quite unconnected with our operation. It is, of course, natural that the troops in the front line should call for artillery support as soon as they see any massing for assault. The artillery duly answers the appeal. No counter-attack develops. The result is, the report that the massing for attack has been broken up by our artillery fire. You will see the sequence of ideas, and will realize why I am sceptical about it all.

With regard to the enemy's casualty list, I do not like very much giving an official estimate which, as you know, can only be academic, and the Germans have always six to four of the best of us in making official estimates of their casualties. But there is no doubt, from the evidence of reliable, competent and independent observers, that the number of German dead, anyhow on the left flank of our advance, was greater than in any of the previous advances this year or last year. The reason for this is that we have a better organized artillery bombardment, and that owing to the nature of the ground the Germans had not proper dug-outs to take refuge in.

General Headlam,[1] who makes a point of wandering over each battlefield, and in the path of the infantry, tells me that this is the only one in which he has seen a remarkably greater number of German than British casualties, and he certainly does not err on the side of being optimistic.

The weather, of course, has been most disappointing. When we go on again we are really beginning the battle afresh, and although we have been able to move up our artillery into a better position, the bad visibility has also enabled the Germans to relieve almost all their divisions in the front line. The delay, too, will no doubt have enabled them to reinforce their air service, so that the first thing we shall have to do, as soon as the weather allows of it, is to fight again for the mastery of the air.

We are seeking to mislead the enemy as to our plans, and have succeeded in making him anxious about the possibility of an attack at Lille. We can, of course, never hope absolutely to mislead him

[1] Now Lieut.-General Sir John Headlam.

right up to the actual moment of assault; the bombardment gives away the whole position of assault, though the enemy cannot deduce, and should not be able to deduce, what direction our offensive is going to take after we have captured the front-line system of defence. This is the story of the battle as far as I can give it to you now.

We have been compiling material required for Lloyd George's speech to-morrow, and the telegram has just gone off. I do not know what form the speech itself will take, but I hope it is not too much of a Georgic; all that is really necessary is to keep Britain in the limelight and the Germans in Limehouse.

August 4. All my fears about the weather have been realized. It has killed this attack. Every day's delay tells against us. We lose, hour by hour, the advantage of attack. The Germans can reorganize and reinforce. We can do nothing but wait. Even if the weather were to clear now, it will take days for the ground to harden, if indeed it ever can, before the winter frost. It is very difficult to keep from saying, "I told you so." But I am glad that I fought as hard as I did against that delay of three days in our attack. I went up to the front line this morning. Every brook is swollen and the ground is a quagmire. If it were not that all the records of previous years had given us fair warning, it would seem as if Providence had declared against us. It is terribly disappointing for us at G.H.Q., but it is much worse for the men. Yet through it all they are cheerful, amazingly so. One good thing is that our organization is now so good that wounded men have seldom to lie out long. It is so easy to think what might have happened had we attacked on the 26th or 28th and got the high ground before this monsoon had burst on us. But that does no good. We cannot break off the battle now, even if we would. We have to fight forward here to keep the Germans from attacking the French. This afternoon there are signs that it may clear up for a spell.

Jack Cowans has assailed me to find a place for John Simon. He writes as if we had never even heard of Simon; says "he has quite a superior brain," has "extremely nice manners and is very tactful," and is "quite a possible future Prime Minister." Very amusing to read. Simon was Home Secretary in 1914 and was of the very greatest assistance to "I" in those early days. All the same, Simon is difficult to place, just because he is such a big man. None of the administration people will take him, so it lies between Trenchard and myself. I think he will do well in Intelligence with the Air people. That is a new show and developing rapidly.

A swarm of Allied Military Attachés from London have arrived. I presided at a dinner for them, and took the chiefs of our own foreign missions with me. It was a strange assortment of uniforms and of views on the war. They pressed me to give a forecast of the duration and vowed they would keep it secret and not even report it to their Ministers. I gave them two alternatives. (1) December, 1917, *if* the sun shone for the next six months, which it will not do, and (2) December, 1918, if it did not shine for the next six months. But I refused to give any reasons, though they were obvious enough. If we win through in this battle, we can force peace without the Americans. If we can't win through in this battle, we must wait until the American Army comes in to counteract the breakdown in Russia, and that means twelve months at least.

August 6. No rain, but dull, no sun and no drying wind, and more rain forecast. We had a visit from some extremist pacifist Labour "leaderettes"—quite pleasant, nice fellows, hugely ignorant about anything outside their own little shows. Their visits do a great deal of good. I do not think any of them go back without amending their views. They come here thinking we soldiers revel in bloodshed and bully the men. They find we loathe war as much as they do, that men and officers are comrades, not enemies, and the whole atmosphere of comradeship and goodwill and the determination to win impresses them. One cannot help sympathizing with these Labour pacifists even when one disagrees with them. To them war is simply senseless slaying: they cannot conceive any cause in which employer and employed can be united. Their highest ideal is increased personal comfort for their own class; they measure contentment in terms of well-filled bellies and full pockets. It is all so human and natural. You cannot argue against their view: for they would not understand the arguments: you can only let them feel the weight of the general view out here.

Sometimes we find among the officers and men here, one or two whose nerve has broken, and no wonder, and these are in complete agreement with these Labour leaderettes. These are very rare. When we find them, we either send them home or down to the Base, and they are happy again. The trouble is when the nerve half goes and they stay on. The curious thing, but perhaps it is not so curious, is that almost always these are from what, for want of a better name, we can call "the intelligentsia"—highly strung, vivid imagination, educated up to the teeth with all that books can teach and with so little real knowledge.

Leo Maxse is coming out again. He announces his acceptance of an invitation in a characteristic letter: "I do not think we can stand much more of Lloyd George, who is making a mess of everything and will lose the war if he can. It is becoming a fellow's duty to attack him. . . Churchill's appointment is a real danger to Army and Navy."

August 9. The rain keeps on and with each day's rain our task gets more difficult. There is only one good point—and that a very small one—about the rain; while we cannot attack and our chances of a great success in this battle steadily diminish, yet the rain itself is achieving one of our purposes for us. So long as we are here waiting to attack and the Germans know it, they cannot move away troops to attack the French. And so the French are getting time to recover their fighting powers. But the front area now baffles description. I went up again yesterday towards dusk. It is just a sea of mud, churned up by shell-fire. There was very little firing, and indeed nothing of what we call in the *communiqués* "activity," only the endless toil of moving reliefs and rations and ammunition under incredibly difficult conditions.

August 12. The stream of rather uninteresting visitors was broken by two interesting ones. Yesterday, Duncan brought Dr. Kellman to dinner, a man of great ability, eloquence and humour, and a most welcome guest. We sat over the dinner-table discussing the universe and the war and finally exchanging Scottish stories until midnight, when I had to go back to my office to clear up some work. To-day I went to hear him preach —a wonderfully eloquent and touching service in that little wooden hut on the ramparts. His fame had preceded him and the hut was crowded. He hit the note of high ideals and held us all spellbound for half an hour. The last hymn, "Fight the Good Fight," splendidly sung by a crowd of men and a few clear-voiced nurses, took me, and I think all of us, right away from France and war and work back to the real business of this life of ours, to develop ourselves so that in the end we can look back and think and believe that we have done our best.

After lunch I had an interview with Ian Hay who goes to America on propaganda work. So far the day had gone well.

But just after Hay had left and I was settling down to work, B. staggered into my room, looking like nothing on earth and shaking with fever. He was quite played out. He had been slightly gassed with this new devilry of the Germans and said he had had no sleep for a week. I sent him off to hospital at Boulogne in charge of Ryan, and wrote a note to his wife. I hope he will get all right again, but it makes one wonder whether one should not insist on getting out of G.H.Q. and up to the front line. I have tried twice already and been refused. As long as D.H. wants me I suppose my job is here. But one would feel so much more justified in being alive if one were up with the troops.

August 14. Three years to-day since I landed in France, and at least another year to go before we can celebrate peace. Ryan and I dined together to-night, the only two who came out with D.H. and have been with him all the time. We broached a bottle of champagne to mark the anniversary.

Leo Maxse has been here to-day painting a most disquieting picture of politics at home. He says things are far worse under L.G. than under Asquith. L.G., according to Maxse, is virtually dictator and refuses to accept any advice, even on the most technical points; full of wild-cat schemes to win the war without fighting, and utterly unscrupulous in his methods of downing those who disagree with him. As soon as Maxse had left I had a visit from Ian Malcolm (Balfour's secretary) so I am steeped in home political news. The sum total of it is not a pleasing or edifying picture. It seems a welter of intrigue and self-seeking. So long as they leave us alone out here and give us men and munitions, it does not much matter. The danger is that if L.G. gets his way, we may get neither or anyhow not enough of either. If so, and if Russia goes finally out of the picture, we are in for a very stormy time before many months are past.

August 15. The weather is improving and there are indications that we may have a few days clear of rain. The centre of gravity has shifted, very temporarily, I am sorry to say, to the old Loos area, where the Canadians brought off a very successful little attack this morning. It is only preparatory to another attempt here, but it gained ground and captured a couple of thousand prisoners. If only we had enough troops to attack *hard* in two places simultaneously we could accomplish much. To-day's attack found the Germans unprepared and with tired troops. To-morrow we go on up in the north, without much expectation—at least so far as " I " is concerned—of doing more than gain some ground.

August 16. We attacked at dawn. I was up with the Corps H.Q. We did fairly well on the left, but failed elsewhere. Got back late in the evening for a conference between D.H. and Robertson. Then back to office at 11 p.m. to write a report on the German methods in this battle, which have changed greatly, and concerning which some wild rumours are getting about in our own army.

A letter from home exactly crossed the " T"s " and dotted the " I's " of Robertson's view at the conference. My correspondent is very emphatic. He writes that the soldiers in France "work much harder than the politicians, who, as Asquith says, mistake bustle for business." The letter continues :—

" I only wish one saw one's way clearer as to what should be done to establish even tolerable conditions at the Back, so that the C.-in-C. may be given a fair chance of winning the war, as he certainly could do if we could only install a decent Government in London. It is maddening that a country which has proved itself so great in so many respects should fail in this vital particular, but the personnel of our politics appears to be as feeble as that of the Army is strong and competent."

The letter contrasts the pleasure shown by Australian and Canadian troops at the tributes they have received during the war, with the aloofness of the more phlegmatic English and Scotsmen. He is right. Australians and Canadians both like to get much well-deserved praise in *communiqués* and correspondents' dispatches. The British certainly don't get, and I don't think they want, proportionate measure of publicity. All the same, Australians and Canadians are only a small fraction of the Army, and it is the units from Great Britain that are necessarily bearing the brunt of the fighting and winning through.

The German casualties from official German sources show up to June 1 a total of 4,356,760, made up of $1\frac{1}{2}$ million final casualties (killed, died of sickness, prisoners and missing), half a million seriously wounded and two million, approximately, " other " wounded. Unless all our calculations are incorrect, that definitely limits their effort to another year and a half of war, if fighting goes on at the present intensity.

August 18. Just finished a report for D.H. on German

tactics in recent fighting. The principal changes are: no attempt made to hold a line of trenches; defence organized in strong points and immediate counter-attacks, first by regiments in immediate support, and second, within twelve hours by a reserve division. Artillery rely for protection on a number of alternative positions. Although the Germans have made full use of the time since the first attack, their defence system is still incomplete. The main group of German guns total about 500 in the area under attack. The morale has been very uneven. In some divisions it has been noticeably low, e.g., 119th and 3rd R. Division. We expected good morale in 6th Bavarian R. Division and 3rd Guards Division. Both of them proved to be suffering from bad morale. On the other hand the 38th Division and the 52nd R. Division fought better than was anticipated. On the whole the morale was about as expected, not noticeably lower than at Arras. German losses appear to have been about 3,000 per division engaged, or say 90,000 in all, of whom about 25 per cent. are final casualties.

The German trench lines are badly constructed; dug-outs are rare and communication trenches barely exist at all. This is, of course, due to ground and weather. The idea, that groups remained behind "shamming dead," and then reappeared to resist our mopping-up parties, is not borne out by investigations, but the shell-holed area has enabled small parties of Germans to dodge our mopping-up parties from one shell-hole to another.

The Fifth Army reports "the general morale of the Germans is undoubtedly lowered" since the commencement of the attack. Several captured orders seem to indicate that the German Higher Command is much exercised about the fall in morale.

I summed up the report :—

The two vital factors which from a military point of view will be decisive in this war are :—

Morale, of which the evidence shows a steady deterioration in the German Army, and

Man-power, of which calculations given above show that even the resources of the German Empire cannot stand the strain of war on its population for more than a limited number of months (a maximum of twelve months) *provided the fighting is maintained at its present intensity in France and Belgium.*

August 18. You ask me for a detailed account of a typical day for your records and the family archives. Here is my secretary's record for yesterday, though I don't know why it should interest anyone.

9.0	a.m.	Interview with D.H.
10.0	a.m.	Conference with heads of sections.
11.0	a.m.	Interview with mission from Rumania.
11.30	a.m.	Interview with Italian Military Attaché.
12.0		Interview D.G. transportation.
1.0	p.m.	Lunch.
1.30	p.m.	Interview with correspondents and heads of sections.
2.30	p.m.	Conference on ciphers with French.
3–4	p.m.	Correspondence.
4.5	p.m.	Exercise.
6.0	p.m.	Interviewed L.G.'s private secretary.
6.30	p.m.	Interview with C.S. from Lord Northcliffe.
9.0	p.m.	Conference with C.G.S.
10.0	p.m.–midnight.	Office work.

That is a fairly typical day when I am not out to see one or other of the armies.

August 21. Fifth Army reported a rather remarkable instance of low German morale. One whole regiment of the 75th R. Division is reported to have "fairly taken to its heels on the 16th and seven officers of the same regiment, found hiding in a dug-out, surrendered without even showing fight." The report seemed so extraordinary that I questioned it, and eventually went myself to Army H.Q. to sift the evidence. It seems completely true. Even as an isolated incident it is very remarkable.

D.H. has not only accepted *in toto* my report on fighting up to 16th, but has gone much farther. He has reported to W.O. that "time is fast approaching when Germany will be unable to maintain her armies at their present numerical strength." "In front of the XIVth Corps a large portion of their defending troops are reported both by our own men and by prisoners to have run away." "For all these reasons, although the struggle is likely to continue severe for some while yet, there is good reason to hope that very considerable results will then follow and with more rapidity than may seem likely at present." "If we are favoured with a fine autumn, therefore, I regard the prospects of clearing the coast before winter sets in as still very hopeful, notwithstanding the loss of time caused by the bad weather during the first half of August. At the least, I see no reason to doubt that we shall be able to gain positions from which subsequent operations to clear the coast will present a far easier problem than we had to cope with at the outset of this offensive, and in which the losses and hardships suffered round Ypres in previous winters will be much reduced. In these circumstances the right course to pursue, in my opinion, is undoubtedly to continue to press the enemy in Flanders without intermission and to the full extent of our powers, and if complete success is not gained before winter sets in, to renew the attack at the earliest possible moment next year. Success in clearing the coast may confidently be expected to have such strategical and political effects that they are likely to prove decisive."

August 22. For the time being operations here are at an end. For one thing, the weather has broken. For another, a new system of attack to meet the altered German system of defence has to be perfected, and for a third, we are going to shift the weight of our attack and use the Second Army as well as the Fifth Army. The newspapers at home have made a bad blunder with huge headlines, " Plumer's Great Thrust," which has aroused Plumer's wrath, quite rightly, for he has not attacked at all. The correspondents here are proved " not guilty "; apparently some ass at home has been exercising his imagination. I have telephoned home to prevent recurrence, but it is very annoying, as it may lead the Germans to anticipate our intentions. Harington's letter is very characteristic. " Sir Herbert Plumer hates publicity of all sorts," and hopes " that it may be made quite clear to the public that it is not his Army that is attacking."

By the same letter-bag comes another wail from the Australian people in London that *they* are not getting enough publicity, and suggesting that either D.H. or I should grant a special interview to an Australian Pressman to extol the Australians for their home consumption only. They undertake that the interview would not be allowed to leave Australia in any form! How can people be so foolish!

August 31. More trouble in the Press world. Esher writes that Burnham's henchman, B., has been hinting that Burnham is offended because the French Government have asked him officially to go to their front and our Government have not done the same as regards our front. I am writing to ask Burnham out here, but I do not expect he will accept. There is probably some newspaper feud on between him and the Press war-lords.

CHAPTER XXIII
PASSCHENDAELE

September 1. D.H. has called for a minute on German man-power. The results of the twelve months, September '16 to September '17, are very interesting.

September 1916.	*September* 1917.
Class 1916 Finishing as a source of drafts.	Class 1918 Finishing as a source of drafts.
Class 1917 Just commencing to be identified in front line.	Class 1919 Just commencing to be identified in front line.
Class 1918 Not yet called up.	Class 1920 Partially called up throughout Germany (?).

The 1916 class comprise men of 21
,, 1917 ,, ,, ,, 20
,, 1918 ,, ,, ,, 19
,, 1919 ,, ,, ,, 18
,, 1920 ,, ,, ,, 17

This means that in one year Germany has expended two years of her income in man-power. *At the same rate* by this time next year, she would be calling up her boys of 15 or, alternatively, she would not be able to maintain her present number of units at their present strength.

Actually even now her *company* strength has fallen from 230 in September, 1916, to an average of 175 now.

A "profit and loss" account of German divisions shows:—

Fresh Divisions on Western front, April 1, 1917.	146	Tired Divisions to Russia [1]	15
		Tired Divisions on Western front . .	122
Fresh Divisions from Russia since April 1, 1917	15	Fresh Divisions	8
		Fresh, but inferior material	16
	161		161

[1] "Tired divisions" are those that have been engaged in battle during last two months and suffered heavy casualties.

The comparative strength of German and British guns on British front shows: British 5,533; German 2,546.

During the battles, since April 1 of this year we had engaged against the British force 82 divisions (Arras 38, Messines 12, Lens 4, Ypres 28). The French have had 45 engaged at the Aisne and Champagne and 10 at Verdun. The total is therefore 137 on the whole Western front since April 1, while 15 have gone to Russia.

Our next attack cannot take place for at least three weeks, and already shortage of ammunition has caused the curtailment of our artillery expenditure, especially in 6-in. howitzers. We have had to stop all further efforts in the Lens area, and concentrate everything on the capture of the Passchendaele Ridge, which D.H. has designated of overwhelming tactical and strategical importance in his report to the W.O.

September 3. There is a suggestion to take away 100 heavy guns from the French Army fighting on our left, and send them to Italy. D.H. has written to-day, very strongly, against the proposal. He has written: " It is my conviction that it would be both unsound and unwise to send troops, guns and ammunitions from the Western front to Italy, and that the War Cabinet will incur a very heavy responsibility if they decide to do so."

It is quite probable that the Austrians will attack the Italians; it is practically certain that Germany cannot spare any considerable force to help the Austrians in their attack.

The whole tone of the letters from London show a very marked weakening of trust in D.H., combined with the fatal wish to transfer our strength to side-shows. It is confined to a few persons, but those few are in power. Neither the Press nor the public share the view at present. Apparently the discontent is due to dissatisfaction in the new Government at not being able to justify themselves by parading big results before the public, combined with a genuine belief that " old-fashioned methods " will not win, and that strategical knowledge reposes in their brains. The difficulty is bringing facts home to them, and when we do we only get resentment. Probably that is natural. It is the slaughter of the theory begotten of their brains, and someone once said the only real tragedy in life is the killing of a theory by a fact. Robertson is a master of hard facts, but I do not know whether his slaughter of theories is done tactfully—if slaughter can ever be tactful. Certainly the dislike in the Cabinet of the soldiers seems just as much against Robertson as against D.H.

Our line here is to keep clear of it all, for if we gave any handle to the present powers that be, they would seize it to sack D.H. and Robertson, or both, and Wilson is always lurking in the background to squeeze his way back to power. I get the brunt of it all, for D.H. turns all the politicians on to me as soon as he can get rid of them himself. Esher writes from Paris that F. is greatly dissatisfied with the "want of consideration" shown to him at G.H.Q. The facts are that I did not think it wise [1] for him to see D.H. and that his visit coincided with one from Morganthau, ex-American Ambassador with Turkey. Morganthau had much of interest and importance to discuss, and I had only the time available after dinner one night to give to both Morganthau and F. Morganthau's interview lasted from 9.0 p.m. to midnight, and F. had to wait until I had finished with Morganthau. I admit it was irritating for him, but Morganthau was much more important. F.'s interview was, after all, only solace to his vanity.

September 11. L. Maxse writes rather alarmingly about " another devilish intrigue by politicians to weaken the Western front in the interest of one or other side-shows." We know all about that already. More important is his view that munition workers are not working at full pressure. He gave an instance—a tank factory in the Midlands turning out 40 per week, that could in his opinion double their output if the men were really interested in their work, and wants arrangements made for the workers to be told of the great effect of tanks on operations. Boyd Cable is already doing a similar work for aeroplane factories. It is a W.O. business and we are sending the suggestion with our recommendation to them.

The weather is good now, and all looks well for our next effort. A captured German document shows ration strength of a German unit 50 per cent. of establishment.

September 14. An awful day of politicians. F. E. Smith before lunch; Churchill after lunch; Carson at tea and dinner to meet Asquith. F.E. very friendly and generally seemed to agree with our views, very satirical and amusing about the intrigues at home, which he says will do no harm and indeed keep "them" busy fighting one another and let "us" fight the Germans. I

[1] The purpose of his visit, I suspected, was to get material for some political manœuvre.

hope he is right. Churchill, very concerned about losses in attacks, said, " if French had remained I would have run the war for him ! " He has a great brain but very little judgment, great vision and little practical knowledge of war, most adept at twisting facts to fit his somewhat wild theories. Carson very charming, and quite straight. Anyhow, he did not seem to be trying to trap one all the time. Nor does he seem to have any object except to win the war. All three spoke of impending peace proposals from Germany, and seemed to indicate they thought they might be acceptable. Their whole visit seemed to me to be to find out what are the real prospects of success out here so that they decide how to deal with the German proposals. The scales are weighing down so steadily on our side that it would be folly to accept any compromise now. The whole argument is whether, in being *minus* Russia and *plus* America, we gain enough to be certain of ultimate decisive victory. There can only be one answer to that. If Russia were to crack so utterly that Germany could bring all her forces from Russia to France, we could still fight on until America readjusted the balance decisively within a year. But Germany cannot possibly bring all her forces westward this year.

In the evening I went to one of the visitors' châteaux to give Asquith dinner. We sat very late afterwards. The more I see of Asquith the greater becomes my admiration for him. He is, to my mind, the greatest of all the politicians and perfectly straight. If he were P.M. now, with the same powers and the same organization that L.G. has devised to make the P.M. virtual dictator, the outlook would be far more cheerful. Certainly he would never let down anyone serving under him, and the soldiers would not have to fight on two fronts. One very noticeable thing about Asquith is that he never permits himself to say anything bitter about his political opponents. He did not in any way refer to the present Government's conduct of affairs—except express great sympathy for Robertson. He was greatly concerned about developments in France and possible sources of danger there. He spoke much, and very highly, of Kitchener and was rather contemptuous of Wilson. He went out of his way to say some nice things about Hubert Gough. I asked him whether we could safely rely on the determination of the people at home as a nation to see the war through. His answer was very emphatic. " The only thing that would be certain to bring any Government down, would be any sign of weakness of will to win the war." He made one remark that stuck : " The war has demanded sacrifice of some sort from everybody—their own lives, or the lives of their sons, their fortunes, their position, their future or their fame, but the greatest loss of all would be the loss of our own self-respect." Let us hope the profiteers feel that loss—but I doubt it. Asquith comes tomorrow to stay with D.H. and will hear Wallace Williamson preach. He is very anxious that we should fix up a job for Sir J. Simon, and I told him this was being arranged.

September 16. A glorious day, bright sun and very warm. If only we had had this weather last month, but even now it may not be too late. There was a very full congregation to hear Wallace Williamson, and perhaps to get a glimpse of D.H. and Asquith; nearly 30 nurses and as many officers and over a hundred men crowded into a small schoolroom—a fair but not inspiring sermon, which obviously bored Asquith, and strenuous singing which seemed to astonish him.

Winston had started a hare about stick bombs when he was here. As they had been discarded on this front for the last two years, I set the machine working to know the source of his information. Apparently it all started with a lad fresh from Egypt and now with the Second Army, who had seen stick bombs there and thought them a new thing. Rather a typical case of how " information " gets about at home.

Gwynne of the *Morning Post* has written a very interesting letter. He begins, "Nobody knows better than you do that the critical period of the war is at hand .   the Germans know that it is only a question of time with them .   and will use all their wiliness to get a peace which will leave them undefeated. The pacifists, cranks and the politicians will be appealed to in every kind of way. That is the dangerous moment and the date of it will be at the beginning of this winter. Now it is a fact that the nation at home is as sound as a bell. There is a disgruntled and cranky minority who would like the war to end on almost any condition. . . This is the argument of the pacifist: ' You can't break the Boche; you've tried at Neuve Chapelle, at Loos, on the Somme, Arras, Messines and Ypres, and though you drive him back a bit he is still undefeated. The honour of the British Armies is amply satisfied. We have done wonders and have proved ourselves a magnificent race. But why continue this appalling bloodshed when this time next year you will only get the same terms that you can get now.' . . The answer to the pacifist contention about the military situation is not easily supplied by the man in the street because he does not know. The weak-kneed politicians *do* know but won't believe. In consequence there comes every now and then, a wave of depression." Gwynne goes on to urge that we here must counteract this through our correspondents and finishes, "Above all let the C.-in-C. see the correspondents from time to time. The C.-in-C. is the only man who can beat the Boche and win us the victory, and so save the Empire. We must make him a national hero, not because he would like it or dislike it, but because it is necessary, in order that the people in England will learn to trust him. At present they know too little about him."

This is all quite true and Northcliffe, and even Beaverbrook, have said much the same from time to time. But if we begin using the Press to crack up D.H. we shall have L.G. outing him at once. If we let correspondents have an interview with him, we shall have a repetition of last February's episode. If we check Philip Gibbs writing his "horror-mongering stuff" we shall have his paper down our throat. If we say the Boche is being beaten, or even that his morale is being lowered, we shall have the W.O. itself saying we are over-optimistic and thus making it harder for Robertson to screw the necessary men and munitions out of L.G. All the same I have taken steps to do what I can to give some effect to Gwynne's views, for they are right and it is worth taking the risk.

Meantime, Repington has apparently smelt out the exact date of our next effort, and proposes himself for a visit on that very day.

September 19. Our attack goes on to-morrow—the weather has been very heavy; steady rain all the evening, but a fair day promised for to-morrow by the weather experts.

September 20. The attack has gone very well. We have advanced the line up to the whole of the high ground overlooking the Menin road and taken over 3,000 prisoners and about 50 guns. The Germans fought well by all accounts. But I shall know more to-morrow when I have been out to the armies.

September 23. The fighting during the last three days has been more severe than was expected. The German methods were precisely as predicted; no attempt to support the front line but well-organized immediate counter-attacks. In all, eleven separate counter-attacks were delivered within 11 hours on the 20th. All except one were driven back. One succeeded in recapturing a stretch of the line, involving further fighting on 21st and 22nd to eject them.

All Corps and Divisional H.Q. except one, report a deterioration in fighting power of the Germans, but this is difficult to estimate.

French G.Q.G. report the conclusion, from evidence with them, that the Germans have prepared down to the last detail a plan for retirement along their whole front. All we have in this direction is a captured order dated June 1 giving minute administrative details for evacuation of the St. Mihiel Salient.

A comparison of German strength on the Western front between this year and last shows:

		Heavy artillery
September, 1916.	119 Divisions	420 guns in line
,, 1917.	145	617 ,,

So far only one German division is reported as now moving from Russia westward, and a second under orders to move shortly.

September 25. A day of distinguished visitors. Two Press war-lords, Rothermere and Beaverbrook, in the morning, and the P.M. and Robertson in the evening. The Press people were agreeable and pleasant, apparently well content with all arrangements for their people at the front. The P.M. is concerned about results of the breakdown in Russia and has called for a paper on the strategical situation if Russia, as now seems probable, makes a separate peace. He was also critical of progress made in the last attacks, and more than sceptical about fall in German fighting power.

The hostile strength, in divisions, in the European theatre is:—

	Western	Russian	Italian	Danube	Macedonian	Total
German	145	82	—	9	2	238
Austrian	—	34	40	2½	2	78½
Bulgarian	—	—	—	3½	8½	12
Turkish	—	—	—	2	—	2
	145	116	40	17	12½	330½

There are railway movements now in progress from East to West, probably of two divisions, one of which is heading for Verdun.

If Russia makes a separate peace, movement from East to West could proceed at the rate of 2 divisions per week, with a possible temporary acceleration of 4 in one week. Probably not more than 34 divisions fit to fight could be moved from the Eastern front, requiring 16 or 17 weeks to complete, i.e. available for next spring.

Clearly Germany's most urgent need must be to obtain a peace before the drain on her man-power becomes irretrievable, and before the Americans can get their armies into action.

To sum up, it appears probable that German action will be forced to the following, viz.:—

(*a*) Sending to the Western front such troops as are necessary to stiffen her resistance and enable her to make headway against the joint Anglo-American-French attack next year.

(*b*) Commence an active offensive against Italy in conjunction with Austria as soon as the season of the year admits of it.

The immediate problem for the Allies' strategy resolves itself into :—

(*a*) Whether a temporary defensive should not be assumed and maintained until such time as the full force of the American armies can be developed ; or,

(*b*) Whether continuous pressure should be maintained and developed from now onwards, increasing and developing as the greatest man-power becomes available.

In favour of (*a*) is the argument that it is in the national interest to husband our resources in man-power so that the nation is not so exhausted that even victory in the field may spell catastrophe in the future. Against this, great though the effort of Great Britain has been, it has not involved her so far as loss in her manhood goes, in any way proportionate to that of France and Germany. But still more important is the argument that if we stop the offensive, Germany will recover and France may give way. The relative advantage of a breathing space is greater for Germany than for her enemies. We are fighting the will-power of the German nation as much as, if indeed not more than, the German armies in the field. That will-power is being steadily undermined by the drain on Germany's manhood. It will rapidly recover if the pressure is relaxed. Quite apart, therefore, from any actual progress that we may hope to make this autumn, in terms of ground captured, we must keep up our pressure in order to :—

(1) Protect our Allies.
(2) Facilitate our task next year.

(3) Prevent the recovery of the power of resistance of the German people and the German Army.

Only if there were a danger that the will-power of our own people would not suffer the strain of the casualties involved, would we be justified, in view of all the circumstances, in relaxing our pressure so long as neither conditions permit and suitable occasion offers?

September 27. While our minds have been turned on the theoretical discussion of future policy, the armies attacked again yesterday towards Passchendaele. Again the fighting was very heavy, with numerous counter-attacks. We gained ground but did not reach the ridge. Nevertheless our position is improved, and there is now no reasonable doubt but that we can secure the whole ridge next month. That is the minimum. If the weather holds fine we may do much more. But the weather is now the dominant factor. As the sun loses power, it necessarily takes much longer to counteract each fall of rain. The general situation as regards the battle is strangely like the Somme. Now, as then, we had worn down the German resistance to very near breaking-point; then, as now, the weather went against us. It is a race with time, and a fight with the weather. One thing is certain, no other army but ours could fight on as we are fighting. D.H. is asking for the last ounce from it and getting a wonderful response.

The casualties are awful; one cannot dare to think of them. The temptation to stop is so great, but the obviously correct thing for the nation is to go on. I would not have believed that any troops would have faced what the Army is facing. But the Army knows it is winning. It is easy enough here for us, with all our information about the Germans, to count the cost coldly, to strike a balance sheet and see what is right to do. But for the men, and even more so for the regimental officers, it must seem a pretty hopeless outlook. Yet it is not at the front, but in England, that the calamity of casualties affects resolution.

September 30. There was a sharpish air-raid last night; bombs fell close, but did no damage. These air-raids have been so harmless, that we begin to look on them rather as a joke.

October 1. I was premature in my reference to the harmlessness of air-raids. A raid here last night did a good deal of damage and killed a round dozen, including four women.

October 4. A letter has come from Sir E. Carson saying that he has been asked by the Cabinet " to supervise arrangements for publicity at home in order to strengthen the morale of the people and counteract pacifist activities." He wants public speakers to visit the front and get first-hand information. He says " so great is the need of heartening the people over here, that some risk must be taken of giving information to the enemy." This is in rather sharp contrast to Gwynne's view that it is the Government, and not the people, that want heartening; but anyhow Carson's request is easy to comply with.

Repington writes from Paris, that the Paris politicians are very urgent that we should take over more front line, using all the old arguments, measuring the length of line held proportionate to the number of British and French troops, without any consideration of the nature of the line held or the number of German troops opposing them. Repington reports that Painlevé told him our Cabinet had already agreed to the French view. If it were not for the Calais Conference experience this would be incredible, but I would not like to gamble on it.

October 5. The attack yesterday was only just in time to forestall an attack by the enemy with their fresh divisions. We did not know of the Germans' intended attack and they did not know of ours. We, by great good fortune, started a quarter of an hour before they were due to do so. We had some 10 divisions attacking and the Germans had 5. Our barrage fell on their divisions for attack. None the less they fought exceptionally well. We won the day, and gained much very valuable ground.

Although we did not know of the Germans' intended attack yesterday, I had warned D.H. of the possibility of attack " before the 8th " and we did know that they had moved up troops. I was out all day going round to H.Q. of the Corps and Divisions engaged. It was a very anxious time. The reports coming back were very conflicting. It was not until late in the afternoon that we knew we had made good.

There was a conference late in the afternoon—D.H. and the Army Commanders. We are far enough on now to stop for the winter, and there is much to be said for that. Unless we get fine weather for all this month, there is now no chance of clearing the coast. With fine weather we may still do it. If we could be sure that the Germans would attack us here, it would be far better to stand fast. But they would probably be now only too glad to remain quiet here and try elsewhere. Anyhow, there are reasons far more vital than our own interests here that give us no option. But it is a tremendous responsibility for D.H. Most of those at the conference, though willing to go on, would welcome a stop.

October 8. We go on again to-morrow, and yesterday and to-day there have been heavy downpours of rain, a last effort. Documents taken on the 4th show that the Germans are very hard pressed to hold their ground. They have given up their new plan of thinly held front lines and gone back to their old scheme, which is all to the good; but unless we have a very great success to-morrow it is the end for this year so far as Flanders is concerned, and next year the Germans will have their troops from Russia. With a great success to-morrow, and good weather for a few more weeks, we may still clear the coast and win the war before Christmas. It is not impossible, but it is pouring again to-day.

October 10. I was out all yesterday at the attack. It was the saddest day of this year. We did fairly well but only fairly well. It was not the enemy but mud that prevented us doing better. But there is now no chance of complete success here this year. We *must* still fight on for a few more weeks,[1] but there is no purpose in it now, so far as Flanders is concerned. I don't think I ever really had great hope of a big success yesterday, but until noon there was, at least, still a chance. Moving about close behind a battle, when things are going well and when one is all keyed up with hope of great results, one passes without much thought all the horrible part of it—the wounded coming back, the noise, the news of losses, the sight of men toiling forward through mud into great danger. But when one knows that the great purpose one has been working for has escaped, somehow one sees and thinks of nothing but the awfulness of it all. Yesterday afternoon was unutterably damnable. I got back very late and could not work, and could not rest. D.H. sent for me about 10, to discuss things. He has to bear the brunt of it all. He was still trying to find some grounds for hope that we might still win through here this year, but there is none.

October 11. A letter from Mrs. Humphry Ward, telling me

[1] The French were still appealing for the protection provided by our attacks.

that her book "Towards the Goal" is making a great impression in America and wanting to come out here again to get more material, chiefly for a popular explanation of the terms of peace. A little premature, and I am asking her to come out next spring.

We are attacking again to-morrow. It is the weather and the ground that we are fighting now. We have beaten the Germans, but winter is very close, and there is now no chance of getting through.

October 19. Gwynne writes that "the good people of this country still want another buck-up . the public want to know if all their exertions are bringing them nearer victory. Some of them are doubtful whether we are winning. The Russian debacle, in their opinion, puts off the end of the war farther than ever, and they want now a good tonic under the influence of which they will, I believe, put forth their full strength. . We have forced our governors and rulers to acknowledge the work of the British Armies in France." The difficulty is to state a case convincing to those without full expert knowledge, to show how much has been accomplished. It would be easy enough if we had big gains of ground or capture of cities to record. But the wearing down of the German man-power cannot be shown to the public by any newspaper article or any speech. Also the War Office, for reasons of their own, do not want to make much of German loss of morale and the Government is not out to extol the Army! It is a fight now between the man-power and morale of the nations. We have positive proof that Germany must now choose between reducing her strength in the field and using her boys of 18 years of age. The War Office has committed itself to the opinion that the morale of the German troops in the field is, on the whole, good, and gives no cause for anxiety to the German Higher Command. We have direct evidence to the contrary, which the War Office, however, does not accept. We do not know on what it bases its opinion. Obviously, however, some people at home are looking for an excuse to give up the main effort in France and try to win the war by a side-show, and if the War Office does not stiffen its back, they will succeed.

D.H. has sent home some of the evidence of lower morale of the Germans, but it will not have much effect. If they are not prepared to accept D.H.'s opinion, no amount of written evidence will convince them. The real trouble is that no one at the War Office has had personal experience of fighting out here since 1915, when we had only a miniature army.

October 20. Just back from a visit to Paris, and G.Q.G. and American H.Q. On the whole the situation in Paris is satisfactory. There is a considerable defeatist party, but the general will is strong. G.Q.G. gives a much better impression than expected. Apparently Pétain has re-established confidence wonderfully quickly. By next spring everything should be in good order again. American G.H.Q. is more than satisfactory. Everyone from Pershing downwards is confident and sound and tremendously in earnest. Their Intelligence show has prospered quite marvellously and will be excellent within a few months. They are working independently of both us and of the French in all deductive work, which is all to the good. They bring fresh minds, and very competent minds, to the Intelligence problems. They will be very valuable next year. They have adopted throughout our system and organization as regards " I," after careful study of both ours and of the French. I saw some of the American troops, which are first class material, very serious-looking men, of excellent physique, well found and apparently very keen. The discipline is exceedingly strict. Their weak point will be inexperience of regimental officers and of the Staff in lower formations. There is a marked change in their outlook as regards the British Army. They have been following events very closely, and are very genuinely appreciative now of the British.

French G.Q.G. have information pointing to an early Austrian attack on Italy, but agree that no large number of German troops can have been detached to Italy. We have no confirmation of this impending attack, either from Italy or London. Our own sources of information do not cover Italy or Austria. American G.H.Q. has no confirmation. G.Q.G. thinks Italy can deal with any Austrian attack.

October 22. Another small attack this morning gained a little ground. It had no particular strategical purpose. We have to keep up pressure here. But plans are on foot now for another final effort elsewhere before winter sets in.

There were two visitors to-day. The Cardinal Archbishop of Westminster and Sir Walter Laurence. I met them both at dinner with D.H. The Archbishop has not the dignified bearing generally associated with great clerical statesmen. He was totally ignorant of, and apparently quite uninterested in, the military side of the war. It is not a matter for undue wonder. After all, his whole interests and outlook must be in his Church, and that has probably rather more adherents on the enemy's side than on ours. Our French friends are fond of telling a story attributed to a highly placed R.C. cleric in Paris who said, " I am telling my people that undoubtedly God is on their side ; my revered brother of Cologne is telling his people the same thing at the same time, only *le bon Dieu* knows which of us is lying ! " Anyhow, perhaps as a staunch Presbyterian I am biased.

Sir Walter Laurence is a very different type of man, very able and cultivated, with very broad views. He is going to America for propaganda work, and goes on from us to American G.H.Q.

October 25. The storm has broken in Italy and the news is very alarming : but we have not full information yet and often first reports are unduly pessimistic. The Italians have a great numerical superiority both in men and guns, and should be able to hold. But as D.H. caustically observed, " It is the spirit that quickeneth."

We attack again to-morrow ; the weather to-day is good, with a strong drying wind, and the forecast for to-morrow not unfavourable.

October 28. The full reports from Italy are worse even than the first. The Italians apparently panicked and put up no fight at all, and are going back everywhere. One report says " running like hares ! " Apparently not more than half a dozen German divisions were employed—the rest all Austrian. D.H. has called for a paper on the possibilities of the new situation. Germany's object is clear enough :—

1. To induce the Allies to detach troops from France and Belgium, and thereby ease the pressure here, and make a favourable situation for either peace proposals or an attack next year if Russia goes altogether out of the picture.

2. To reinforce the failing war spirit of Austria-Hungary.

3. Possibly to get supplies of foodstuffs, to ease the blockade stringencies.

L.G., with Henry Wilson in his pocket, is off to Italy. Fortunately, Robertson goes also. Foch goes from the French side.

Obviously France or Britain, or both, will have to send troops to Italy to bolster her up. But they should go if possible (i.e. if time permits) from the minor theatres. We could spare troops from either Salonika or Egypt. The great thing is not to weaken our forces in France and Belgium, unless it is absolutely unavoidable, and if unavoidable, replace them either here or in Italy by troops from the minor theatres forthwith.

But this Italian debacle will give a tremendous stimulus to all opponents of our policy and plans here.

October 30. The Munitions Department have issued a typically carping document, leading to the deduction that we must sit still for at least another year. It is full of the most amazing ineptitudes, so far as my own branch is concerned. It estimates fighting resources of the country by adding up and comparing the number of divisions. It ignores the impossibility of concealing front-line dispositions from the enemy, and thinks we could have great numbers of trench mortars in front line and keep them supplied without the Germans knowing anything about it. It sets great store on the bombing from the air of German bases, and throws doubt on the effect of the bombing of German towns. Actually, so far, all our efforts at bombing of bases, aerodromes, bridges and depots, have met with very little success, and certainly have never influenced the course of any battle, far less any campaign. The only two successes we can claim are the destruction of a depot and damage to Ledeghem junction, which threw out of joint part of the German railway system for two days. There may be political reasons against the bombing of German towns, but there can be no doubt that it would be most effective in lowering the will to fight of the German people. The Germans have no scruples about bombing French towns, or London, and it is difficult to see why we should not bomb theirs, if it is going to help to win the war.

The pundits in London are also sceptical about much of what both G.Q.G. and ourselves now regard as almost axiomatic. They question whether a German division, after having been heavily engaged in battle, is rightly considered as of lower fighting value. We know that Germany does not engage a division after it has been withdrawn from battle for at least two months, and we also know from actual experience that when re-engaged after two months it is of less fighting value. They question our calculations that Germany can only withdraw 32 divisions more from Russia. There can be no proof. French G.Q.G. put the maximum number at 40. I still think 32, or at most 35, will prove the correct figure.[1] They

[1] Actually between November 1 and the middle of March, 40 divisions (including 5 *en route* in March) were withdrawn from Russia and Rumania. But 2 divisions were sent from west to east in replacement during December.

question our estimates of German casualties. The official casualty lists of Germany showed 50 per cent. of their infantry engaged as casualties before a division was withdrawn. This year the fighting has been at least as hard, and we have based our estimates, as does G.Q.G., on the same scale, with allowance for lower establishments. As regards man-power, we calculate that Germany has only 300,000 more men to draw on for 1918. According to home authorities we have 637,000. France has 130,000, and American G.H.Q. says, we can count on 300,000 Americans by next May. From this total of $1\frac{1}{4}$ million we have to deduct requirements of the minor theatres. If they are kept reasonably low (but that is a big " if ") there can be little doubt that we have ample men to give us decisive superiority next year. This is making no allowance for Belgians or for Portuguese !

The paper from home finished with the definite recommendation that we should postpone all offensive operations until the Americans can develop their strength, i.e. late in 1918 or even 1919. The experience of 1916 and 1917 should be sufficient answer. It was only the Somme offensive in 1916 that saved Verdun. Russia on the defensive in 1917 became an easy prey to the German attack. Italy, stopping in the middle of a successful offensive, was herself assailed and beaten in a very short time. The defensive attitude adopted by France during the latter part of this year has resulted in 25 German divisions being brought from her front and added to the very large number operating against us.

However much we may wish to adopt a passive defensive in 1918 to avoid casualties, we should either be forced to retreat in front of a German onslaught, or ourselves take the offensive elsewhere than on the point selected by the Germans for their attack.

All this may be put to the proof.

The Munitions Department expresses the definite opinion that we shall not be able to assemble sufficient forces to defeat Germany in the field in 1918. It gives no figures to support its view, which is certainly at variance with the experience of 1917, and with which I, personally, entirely dissent.

November 1. The Cabinet are in full cry against D.H. and against our strategy. The P.M. has called for papers from French and Henry Wilson. Both are very critical. D.H. has replied in a very dignified and trenchant paper reminding the War Cabinet that the consideration of any strategical problem divides itself into :—

(1) The setting forth of the essential facts.
(2) A considered judgment based upon true facts.

It can never be wise to allow an opinion, however eminent may be the authority advancing it, to provide such evidence as is susceptible of the proof of ascertained facts. . . Even the setting forth of the essential facts is a task requiring a highly trained and experienced Staff and it is quite beyond the power of any individual, however eminent, to form, in a short period of time, a valid and reliable opinion of their bearing on the problem.

Henry Wilson's paper resolves itself into a recommendation for an International Board of Control of politicians, with military advisers, to co-ordinate the decisions of the Cabinets of the various countries. Admirable in theory, but no committee ever gives prompt decisions and no Council of War has ever yet won a war. D.H.'s criticism is that this will only provide machinery for further discussion and delays. John French wants us to sit still until 1919. D.H. is most strongly of opinion that to adopt a defensive attitude in defiance of the teaching not only of history, but also of the present war, would have elements of possible disaster in it as to be unjustifiable, except under the pressure of the most severe necessity. This necessity does not, in his opinion, exist.

All the same, the fact that L.G. has even called for these papers shows that he is out again to interfere, to try to win the war without fighting. Wilson will do anything and say anything to get back into power, and L.G. will probably have his way. If he does, heaven only knows what may happen next spring. Meantime, we are hard at work for our next big show, the last this year.

November 5. We are sending 5 divisions to Italy from here. The position there has been very bad, but seems to be steadying a bit. We are getting very full reports now from our own people who have gone there. They say the prisoners lost are nearer the German figure (180,000) than that given by the Italians (80,000), but there are many deserters who are being rounded up. It was a complete rout, with much looting by the Italian troops. Italian officers were shot in many cases by their own men, and many brigades, especially Piedmontese, surrendered *en masse*, under the impression that they were thereby hastening the end of a war which they loathed. The curious thing is that these same troops fought very well in the offensive earlier in the year. All the same, our people, some of whom saw the Russian rout in the spring, report that this is not so hopeless as it sounds. There is a feeling of confidence that the Italians can be pulled together again, when they have our troops with them. The Italians are very impressionable. Turin is reported to be quite normal and the military staff there functioning well. While our people have this amount of hope, the French are very pessimistic. They say that all the lower classes in Italy want an end of the war at any price. Anyhow, Plumer is the very best man we could have sent to pull them together. His departure makes a very big difference as regards our next operation, which, however, may not now come off.

News from Paris is mixed. The Ministry there is very shaky. Clemenceau is said to be first favourite as successor to Painlevé. He would stiffen up the French nation greatly. Rumour has it that it is only by the threat that Clemenceau will succeed him that Poincaré can make Painlevé carry on. Clemenceau would have the support of the whole French Army, owing to his frequent visits to the front. But Poincaré both hates and fears him. The bad news is that Albert Thomas is said to be going round the French munition works lecturing on the immediate need of peace.

November 7. We attacked again yesterday and captured Passchendaele, which means the whole of the ridge is now in our hands. We have now got to where, with good weather, we should have been in early September, and with two months in front of us to carry on the operation and clear the coast. Now, from the purely local point of view, it is rather a barren victory, and if the home people decide on a defensive next year, it will be almost altogether lives and labour thrown away. We have beaten the Germans nearly to breaking-point. The Russian debacle will give them some help; but the Americans will far more than outweigh that. If we keep all our strength in the West we must win next year. If we distribute it, we may still be fighting in 1919 or even 1920.

November 8. Full news is now in about the fighting on the 6th of November. The enemy appear to have made every effort to hold on to the ridge. They sent in five counter-attacks. Their artillery fire was very slight early in the day, but became intense in the afternoon and died away altogether in the evening. Apparently, the Germans only got warning of our attack one hour before we began. There are at present no indications that the Germans will attempt to retake the ridge.

CHAPTER XXIV

CAMBRAI AND ITS AFTERMATH

November 12. The Henry Wilson scheme has been adopted. There is to be a Supreme War Council—the P.M.s of France, Britain and Italy, with military advisers (Foch, Wilson and Cadorna), at Versailles, charged with the duty of " watching over the general conduct of the war," and apparently to co-ordinate the military scheme, but with no executive powers. It is utter rubbish so far as fighting is concerned. It will mean delay in any attack on the Germans and will break down at once if the Germans attack us. But it also means that the Cabinet is going to oust D.H. or Robertson, or both.

D.H. wishes to know what difference the debacle in Italy and the withdrawal of divisions from our Army to Italy will make in enemy plans now. It will make none this year. Germany cannot get divisions from Russia before winter; she cannot attack either us or the French without these divisions; she cannot take away divisions from our front as long as she is uncertain whether we are going to attack or not. She must know that next year's fighting is bound to finish her. The conclusion I have arrived at is that an offensive by Germany on the Western front would only be justified if the hope of speedy and decisive success were considerable. Germany cannot afford to fight another Verdun battle, and lose another half-million men even if, at the end of the time, she could claim a considerable tactical victory, unless she succeeded in delivering a knock-out blow. Therefore what Germany will try to do now is to make another attempt to obtain peace.

Meantime, preparations for our next attack are proceeding. There are no signs that the Germans have any suspicion of the attack, so we should get surprise, but we are taking on a big job with 5 divisions less than we expected to have. The whole situation is more complicated than usual. The news from Italy, though less bad, is still not fully satisfactory. Russia seems on the verge of a second revolution, and no one can have any hope of improvement there. The best we can hope for is that change for the worse does not come rapidly. It is inevitable that change will come, and that it will be for the worse. The situation in France is unstable, though not at present dangerous. At home, L.G. has opened his attack on the Army generally and on D.H. and Robertson in particular. I am told he will go for individuals on the Staff here, as the easiest way of hitting D.H. I discussed this with D.H. to-night and again offered my resignation, if he thinks it would strengthen his own position. He will not have it. He says, which is quite true, that when Joffre let his Staff be altered from Paris he only precipitated his own downfall.

Meantime, our own big attack is heavily prejudiced by the withdrawal of the divisions to Italy. We shall have no reserves. We shall be all right at first, afterwards is in the lap of the God of battle.

In church this morning I heard again, " Christ in Flanders." It is amazingly fine. I enclose a copy.[1]

November 15. There is a lull in the attack from home on G.H.Q., but it is only a lull. If we have a big success next week the whole thing may blow over. If we fail, or have only a modified success, it will blow up again worse than ever. The mainspring of the attack is the P.M. himself, and he has willing helpers in French, Churchill and Wilson. The War Office is so uncertain of its own

[1] CHRIST IN FLANDERS.
By L.W.

(From *The Spectator*, September 11, 1915.)

* * * * *

Now we remember, over here in Flanders—
It isn't strange to think of You in Flanders.
  This hideous warfare seems to make things clear.
We never thought about You much in England,
But now that we are far away from England
  We have no doubts, we know that You are here.

* * * * *

Though we forget You—You will not forget us:
We feel so sure that You will not forget us,
  But stay with us until this dream is past.
And so we ask for courage, strength, and pardon—
Especially, I think, we ask for pardon—
  And that You'll stand beside us to the last.

security that we cannot expect any support there, especially as X. is frankly sceptical about our results and pessimistic about the future. If the War Office prevent side-shows and keep all our efforts concentrated in France, they will have done their main job. If they allow us to be weakened here, they will have failed. I wish I could think that all those who are attacking D.H. are doing so solely on patriotic grounds. The only consoling thought at present is that D.H.'s position is so strong that his enemies have not yet dared to attack him openly. But the attack on the Staff is only a means of getting at him. There is an alarming similarity between all these intrigues and manœuvres against him and those against Joffre in 1916. They ended in the Nivelle disaster in 1917. I hope these do not bring a similar catastrophe in 1918. Austen Chamberlain was here last night. He was not very optimistic about things at home.

November 17. Just back from a visit to Third Army. Everything is well for the attack. We should have complete surprise.

On the way I passed through Albert where the Virgin still hangs downward from the church spire, an extraordinary phenomenon. The superstitious may take it either as a good omen that she is still there at all, or as a bad omen that her head hangs towards the ground. Omens loom larger in men's minds before a battle like our next, where margins are small. We shall have a big success at first, that is reasonably certain, but we are very short of troops to develop it.

I passed through Bapaume and part of High Wood where C—— is buried—an awful scene of desolation. Even now, though there is a good deal of rank vegetation, one sees nothing but yawning shell-holes half-filled with water. Two years ago it was " a green and pleasant land." If this war was indeed brought about by any human agency, no punishment on this earth or in Hell would be severe enough for its instigators. Yet in twenty years it will be all forgotten.

November 19. To-morrow we attack. The last conference is just over. The secret has been well kept. Very few of our own people knew the plans until the last moment when the troops were moved up. I am confident we shall get complete surprise with all its advantages, and we shall have 48 hours before the Germans can reinforce. But within 64 hours they can have as many troops as we have. It is a tremendous responsibility for D.H. and for the first time in the war "I" has been for holding back and "O" has been all for going on. D.H. gives us his final and conclusive reason for going on—that success here will greatly help the situation in Italy, where the last Italian retreat, to the Piave, is serious. He intends to stop short after 48 hours, unless by that time the situation is so promising that we can take further risks. On the "home front" things seem to have quietened down, but they will break out again very soon.

November 21. The attack yesterday was as nearly completely successful as any attack can be. We went in without any artillery preparation and using tanks to destroy the wire. We got complete surprise. All the same, at some places the Germans put up a very stiff fight. One very gallant German gunner officer served his gun single-handed until killed, and knocked out several of the tanks. The total of prisoners will work out about 8,000 with 100 guns, and we have gone forward some 4 miles on a broad front. For the first time, the cavalry (only a small body) did get through. We have still to-day and perhaps to-morrow before the Germans can get up reinforcements. We held up all Press messages yesterday so as to keep the Germans in the dark as long and as much as possible. Their wireless messages showed them to be hopelessly at sea. We had all French papers and the Eiffel Tower wireless similarly censored. To-day's operations are vital. If we get Bourlon and the wood there we are well placed.

November 22. We did well yesterday but did not take Bourlon. If we had fresh divisions all would be easy, but we have none. There was a conference this morning and D.H. has decided to go on with the attack. The first German reinforcements are up this evening. I went out to the Corps and Divisional H.Q. The troops are tired but full of fight.

November 23. All at home seem to have gone crazy about the last success. It was, of course, a very fine effort, but it was no greater than other shows and does not deserve hysterics. When the really big decisive victory comes, it will be time enough to ring church bells and sing the National Anthem. Meanwhile what we have to do is to work on and win the war, surely if slowly.

November 25. Things have not gone well. Our troops are tired, and the Germans are getting up large reinforcements; we have none available.

November 28. Another attack yesterday gained no ground. The enemy are strengthened in force and are registering artillery on the north of our Salient and to a lesser extent on the south. An attack is inevitable, but we should be all right.

November 30. The Germans attacked both sides of the Salient this morning and have driven deeply into the southern side. They were held on the north. We had ample notice of both attacks and special warnings had been sent out. All the same, four German divisions overran three of ours. The situation was saved by a very fine counter-attack by the Guards Division and no very great harm has been done. There is no explanation yet of how the 3 divisions were caught. Probably the real reason is that our troops were exhausted with the fighting last week.

It may be the beginning of a long battle, but I do not think the Germans have enough fresh troops to go on for long.

December 2. Yesterday we regained some of the ground lost on the 30th. To-day the Germans attacked again and made a little ground, and the battle is petering out. Neither we nor the Germans have enough fresh troops to go on.

The " home front " is getting very active. All D.H.'s enemies there will make a lot of the German counter-attack and forget about our success last week. The crazy bell-ringing on the 22nd makes them look rather foolish now.

I have to write an appreciation [1] of the whole situation for D.H. We still have plenty of winning cards, but shall we play them skilfully ? The margin is none too great.

The whole situation is depressing. The Russian news is the worst possible. We must now count them finally out. Italy is not much better at present. This battle will be the last before spring and by then the Germans will have many fresh divisions from Russia. The Americans fought well in a show a few days ago, but their G.H.Q. says they will not have more than 10 divisions ready by June. Our Government at home are certain to try to divert troops from here to anywhere else where some wild-cat scheme may point. The French Army has recovered wonderfully during the last six months, but France has no more men and none too strong a Government. L———, a very acute observer, has sent me some interesting views of the situation in France; he says :—
" I have been on the look out for any signs of apathy or antipathy

[1] Appendix A.

on the part of the French, but have never been able to hear of any. The inquiry has not, however, been nearly methodical enough, hitherto, to guarantee that there is none. I don't think the French think much about us, one way or the other, they have a sort of business appreciation of our honesty and generosity (things foreign to themselves) but our national lack of a quick, you might almost say 'flash,' intelligence, which always seems to me to be their great characteristic, makes us a matter of indifference to them.

"By the insistence on 'intelligence,' I mean that I have never yet met a French fool, among the people I have had to work with, nor a French 'lout' or 'dolt' as one knows and meets very many English fools, louts and yokels. At its best, I imagine that the English intellect is every bit as good as the French: but man for man, I should say that there is no doubt the French are far the most intelligent race there is. . . . Our Intelligence systems are very much more thorough, carefully thought out and industriously worked, but they don't seem to me to catch many spies. . . I don't think the French attempt anything at all on the same lines, and if ever a hostile element grew in France, the French armies would suffer from it, as the Italian armies have just done. That could never happen with your armies: hardly a prostitute can get into the area upon her normal business!

"France says what it is thinking at the moment very much more precisely and accurately than we do in England, but then it never thinks the same thing for two minutes together. When France says a thing, it means it: but that is very different from the English forte of saying a thing and sticking to it.

"I venture a last impression. In Lyon, typical of the country where the great French fighting men come from, the name of our Commander-in-Chief is permanently revered, as typifying the Army which is doing its best to see the French where they burn to be, in Germany. Our Prime Minister they watch with a sort of amused approval: the minute he stops being interesting, they will cease being interested. In Paris, they have no sort of affection for, or interest in, the Commander-in-Chief or our Armies. The Prime Minister is just the man for them: thunder and lightning.

"In harping on Lyon, I don't mean to say, nor do I think, that it is different from the rest of France. I would much sooner say, so far as my chance of seeing extends, that it is typical of the rest of provincial France. It is the second biggest city in France, hard-working, solemn, and much more like London than is Paris."

December 7. I had to review the whole general situation to a C.-in-C. conference to-day. Not a very cheerful task. Last week was a black week for us. But looking at the operations since the 20th of November as a whole, we have not done badly. We have taken 11,000 prisoners, 145 guns and some 8 miles of German extended line. We have certainly helped the Italians far more than we should by sending more troops to Italy. I believe if we had let the French retrieve the situation in Italy and kept all our forces here we should have had a really great success without any set-back.

The hard facts are that we face the new year without Russia, with Italy almost on her knees, with France exhausted, with America of little help until June, and with the initiative again with Germany.

I summed up my forecast as an attack by Germany in great strength in the spring, not later than March with choice of eight objectives. We shall know long before then which she selects.[1]

We shall win through, but we have a very anxious time in front of us, made much more anxious by uncertainty of sound leading at home. Northcliffe was here to-day very strong in his condemnation of the Government, much impressed with American methods as opposed to ours, and bubbling over with the importance of his own mission and of himself. Unfortunately, D.H. was too preoccupied to respond and Northcliffe was rather wounded in his self-esteem.

December 12. The attack on D.H. is in full swing. All our information is that L.G., Curzon and Churchill are out to down him, and will try to do so by attacking him through his Staff. I do not think they will succeed. The really important thing is that the Government should be forced to develop the man power and concentrate here in preparation for next year.

Rumour has it that both Allenby and Plumer have been offered the reversion of D.H.'s job. I do not know whether this is true. Both are good men, but neither is in the same category as D.H. If D.H. were to go, I personally think there is only one man with the strength necessary to succeed him, and he is Trenchard.[2]

December 16. D.H. does not agree about the German strategy for 1918. He says that the correct strategy for them is to play a waiting game and not commit themselves to a big attack. He does not think they will make a mistake which must lead to their com-

[1] See Appendix, Ia/42762, December 6, 1917.
[2] Now Lord Trenchard.

plete collapse. While this would obviously be their corect strategy, their internal troubles will outweigh strategy. At least I think so. Anyhow, we shall know during January. It makes no difference to our immediate plans, which are to get every man we can over here. If we do not, they will certainly attack and have a fair chance of a big success. If we do, we can only pray that they will attack, and already information both from agents and air observations, seems to show they are getting attacks ready. Our danger is at home. D.H. has told the Cabinet that we must expect casualties at the rate of 100,000 per month next spring. We have plenty of men for even this if the Government care to make them available. But L.G. does not believe either Robertson or D.H., and nothing is being done.

December 20. G.Q.G. agrees about a big German attack in the spring. There is no definite proof yet, but indications accumulate. We shall know by the middle of next month.

News comes from London that L.G. is determined to kick out Robertson and put in Wilson. If Wilson gets into the saddle, D.H. will follow Robertson within a few months.

If the Germans do attack, and if we have all our strength here, it is so easy to see what we should do. The battle of Cannae over again. But Hannibal was fighting in hostile country and we are fighting in France, so that is impossible. If the Germans were not so stupid, they could have tried this game on us all last year. But Ludendorff is no Hannibal—just an honest, very efficient organizer who always does exactly what you expect him to do. That is why I am certain he will attack in March.

December 23. Duncan preached to-day on the text, " If thou wilt, O God, let this cup pass from me. Nevertheless, Thy will not mine be done. . . And an angel came and ministered to him." D.H. was much comforted. He is as certain as Gough was in 1914, that God is on our side. So, no doubt, is Hindenburg, if all we hear of him is true! Napoleon was right: God is on the side of the big battalions. We have them somewhere, and the best ministration we could get would be some sign that the P.M. was going to give them to us. Unfortunately, everything we hear points the other way. All the same, we can't help winning, as one can count the chances. The only question is *when*, and *how*. One very good thing in our favour is old Clemenceau in Paris. Nothing will make him give in and he is just as determined to get his own way as L.G.—and far more sound. Both of them will try to use the Supreme War Council as their instrument. It will serve as their battle-ground and no other useful purpose.

Christmas Day. The fourth Christmas at war, and though the outlook is so black, yet still I think it will be the last War Christmas. How different each Christmas has been. In 1914, even with so many of our friends dead, we had the joy of victory at Ypres and the knowledge that the great crisis was over. 1915, with Loos behind us and just going to G.H.Q. and full of hope that with the new team and fuller forces we were on the eve of great things. 1916, just cheated of victory on the Somme, yet with everything so strongly in our favour. 1917, the year wrecked by the Calais Conference and still with these great battles won, with all the cards in our hands and our only real anxiety lest they should be wrongly played. We cannot fail to win. Each year inevitably shows success more certain, but for the next few months the prospect is the most gloomy since 1914.

D.H. has called for another appreciation [1] from the German point of view. There is not much to add. Germany has 10 divisions either moving or already here from Russia. There are 20 more to come, perhaps 30, but not more than 30. She can afford to expend some 900,000 casualties, which is not more than nine months' hard fighting. Czernin, who wishes to fight on, is more powerful in Austria-Hungary, who will not, therefore, now make a separate peace. Turkey is played out, and Germany is anxious lest she should make a separate peace. The Bulgarian Government had only a majority of nine on a vote of confidence. She now holds all she wanted to get from the war and is therefore not anxious to fight more.

Germany is very short of food, though the last harvest has eased the situation. The whole political situation there is dominated by the fight between civil and military authorities. The present Chancellor (Hertling) is an astute parliamentarian, apparently charged with the task of making concessions to the democratic parties. He will not last and will probably be succeeded by Kuhlmann, or by some nominee of the General Staff. There is great war-weariness in Germany itself. It is probable that the military party hopes that a great military success will govern the home situation.

[1] Appendix B.

Germany will fight her battle with 179 divisions available on the Western front. A few Austrian divisions may be added but will not be used in fighting. The possibility that either Bulgarian or Turkish troops will be brought to the Western front is so remote in any circumstances as not to merit serious consideration. As the American resources develop, i.e. by midsummer, even with 179 divisions and 1,600 heavy guns and reinforcements of drafts up to 1,000,000, Germany will be left with an inferiority in almost every particular. But in the early spring she will have superiority in numbers of men, though less artillery than the Allies.

Consequent on the victories in Italy and Russia, German morale is probably higher now than at any time since 1915. But their access of morale is not permanent, and will not stand the strain of an unsuccessful attack with heavy casualties. On the other hand, a successful attack, even with a limited advance, would maintain and possibly even enhance the morale.

The reason why Germany will attack in the spring is that the military situation is, on the whole, more favourable to Germany than any with which she has been faced during the past three years. It must change to her disadvantage by summer. Without a decisive military success Germany will be ruined by internal dissensions. If Germany could count on Austria-Hungary, Bulgaria and Turkey standing firm for another year, and if internal Germany could stand another year of war, then undoubtedly Germany's correct course would be to await our attack, trusting in the power of the defensive to stave off decisive defeat as in 1916 and 1917, in the confident hope that war-weariness in France and Britain would bring a compromise peace. She cannot count on any one of these factors, and therefore she must attack. It is playing into our hands if we concentrate our strength here—but that is the big *IF*.

December 26. D.H. has called for a paper on the German Peace proposals.[1] They are certainly interesting. They show that Germany has very little real hope of winning in 1918. If we were certain of the Government giving us the men we need here these proposals would not be worth a minute's consideration. But we are not certain. Anyhow, I have pointed out [2] that before giving any recommendation D.H. must insist on knowing what we in Britain can, and will do, if it is decided to fight on until we win.

[1] Appendix C.   [2] Ia/43382.

December 31. I am handing over charge of the Intelligence to General Lawrence.[1] I asked to go to a brigade or a division out here, but D.H. tells me he will not let me leave G.H.Q., so I become Deputy Inspector-General of Transportation, when I come back from leave. It is a disappointment, but is softened by the verdict of the doctors that in any case they could not have passed me as fit for front-line work.

[1] General Sir Herbert Lawrence, G.C.B.

PART FIVE—1918
G.H.Q.

CHAPTER XXV

THE SUPREME WAR COUNCIL v. G.H.Q.

January 26. There have been strange developments in the situation all this month. I know of them only by hearsay,[1] but I can piece it all together fairly completely. Apparently, the Prime Minister had decided in December to remove Robertson, and it was only Derby's threat of resignation if either Robertson or D.H. was moved that prevented him doing so at the New Year. That, of course, is only a respite. I fancy L.G. has probably quite made up his mind to get rid of both of them. Meantime, he has been gushing over D.H. at home, complimenting him on the fact that in 1915 it was only the First Army defences that were in good order—I suppose with the intention of sowing dissension between Haig and Robertson. D.H. tells me that at a luncheon party, Derby bet L.G. a hundred cigars to a hundred cigarettes that the war would be over in 1918. L.G. disagreed, and D.H. supported Derby's view on the grounds that the internal trouble in Germany would force her to peace. L.G. tried to get D.H. to commit himself to the opinion that the German Army was down and out, and that therefore there would be no German offensive, in spite of the fact that all the Intelligence reports show conclusively that the Germans are staging an attack. D.H. refused to commit himself, but the Cabinet seem to have made up their minds that there will be no attack.

Bonar Law tackled D.H. on the same point later, and asked him point-blank what he would do if he were commanding the German armies. To this D.H. replied that a limited attack would be wiser from the German point of view, because if a big attack failed, it would mean catastrophe for the Germans; but that they must attack in some form or other because of the situation in Germany, and that all indications showed that their attack would be on a very big scale, and that we must expect to lose ground and suffer casualties at the rate of a hundred thousand a month. The

[1] I had been on leave during the greater part of the month.

whole inner meaning of this is the *man-power* problem. We are far below establishment. The Government either cannot or will not bring us up to strength, and is trying to unload its responsibility on to G.H.Q.

Meantime the new Supreme War Council, with Foch and Wilson in charge, have decided that we have to extend our front by taking over more ground from the French. So that we are confronted with:—

(1) A longer front to hold.
(2) Reduced establishment to hold it.
(3) No hope of reinforcements.
(4) A German attack in greater strength than anything we have yet experienced.

Not a cheerful prospect. The only bright point is that D.H.—who saw Pétain and Pershing last week—says that both of them realize the situation and will help when the crisis comes. It seems impossible to convince the Cabinet of the danger that threatens, and make them call up more men at once. We shall have 130 miles of front, with Belgians on our left and Portuguese in the centre, and only 57 divisions; of these 57 divisions, only ten [1] are anything near establishment.

On the top of all this the Supreme War Council has just sent a proposal to the War Office advocating a campaign in Palestine. Robertson has objected and says he will resign if ordered to take it on. The only result of his objection will be to hasten his own replacement by someone more docile. But he was, of course, perfectly right to object. It was the only course open to him. To send troops to Palestine now, when every man is required in France, would be criminal folly. The whole idea shows L.G. at his very wildest and worst.

The devil of it all is that D.H. cannot take any effective part in all this welter of controversy. He can only give his opinion when asked. If he were to threaten to resign unless our strength is maintained, L.G. would jump at it, and put in someone else. Then L.G. and Wilson would embark on an adventure in Palestine, and we would be beaten to a frazzle here in the spring. As it is, we can just see it out. I do not think the Germans are strong enough to drive right through in the spring, and by the autumn the Americans will be fighting, and Germany will give in.

The Director-General of Transportation's camp, where I am now, is a most cheery place. It is staffed mainly by civilians,

[1] The Dominions divisions.

with a fair proportion of Royal Engineer regular officers. Altogether there are some 2,000 officers and over 50,000 men employed on transportation work. Most of the heads of the various branches are men with overseas experience, either in India or South America or Canada. The D.G.T. has a pretty free hand to carry out his work in his own way, though there is a permanent feud on with the Quartermaster-General branch. The Inland Water Transport Department is controlled by an old Indian marine officer, a jovial soul who has fitted out a barge as a sort of state galley, and goes bumping up and down the canals in great style. The head construction engineer is a very fine type of Scottish engineer, who never minces his words or conceals his opinion. There is a story going the rounds that when Sir Eric Geddes returned from the Admiralty on a visit to G.H.Q., and came out to see how his old job was progressing, he met our Scottish friend and asked him genially: " Well, how is the work getting on since I left ? " To this he got the unexpected reply: " Vary much better, Sir Eric, vary much better."

Graphs are the recognized method of illustrating progress in the various departments. There is much rivalry between the light railways and the standard gauge in the forward areas. Each seeks to justify its supremacy by graphs showing the number of men and tons carried every day. If rumour is to be believed, the light railways will stop any of their trains whenever a body of troops appears and almost beseech them to take a lift anywhere up and down the line, so that they can record them on their graph.

But there is great keenness everywhere, and the whole show is very efficient; without it the army could not fight, or even live.

February 6. I have been for a tour round the back areas— Havre, Rouen, Boulogne and Dieppe. It was very interesting to see the mechanism of all the supply services for the first time in four years. All these back areas live a life almost entirely detached from the battle side of war. If it were not for the hospitals with their wounded men, and the reliefs constantly passing up and down the lines, there would be very little to remind them that their sole purpose is to help a million men fighting for their lives in the trenches. The sound of the guns only reaches them as a very occasional and distant rumble. The staffs on the lines of communication know very little more of the actual events at the front than they read in the newspapers. Each mess is a hotbed of rumour. It is easy to realize how false impressions get about at home.

There have been further moves in the squabbles between the Supreme War Council and G.H.Q. The Supreme War Council had a full meeting in Paris last week. Nothing of any great value came of it. The Council decided that we had to take over a little more line, but left the date to be settled between D.H. and Pétain. It decided on the creation of a General Reserve at its own disposal; but as neither D.H. nor Pétain can set free any troops to form the reserve, it will exist only on paper. L.G. produced figures to show that "we were over-insured on the Western front" to avoid sending us more men, and then the Council proceeded to decide to "extend the military operations in Palestine," which, if it means anything, means sending more troops there. Ultimately, however, Clemenceau intervened and got a two-months' respite from the Palestine futility, and unless all the indications are wrong, by that time Germany will have settled the point by her attack. Robertson put in a minute of dissent from the Palestine operations. D.H. was not asked for his opinion, and did not volunteer it. I think he should have backed up Robertson: it might have helped, and could not have made matters worse. D.H. described the proceedings tersely as: "Much talk by civilians on problems of the basic principles of which they know nothing."

Meantime the Supreme War Council—or its British Military Section—has been amusing itself by a War Game, as a result of which it has finally given its opinion that the German attack will take place in July between the La Bassée Canal and the Bapaume-Cambrai road, with 100 divisions. I cannot imagine any reason why the Germans should wait until July. I still think the date I gave in December (viz. March) will prove correct. I am quite sure they will not attack between La Bassée and the Bapaume road. It would lead them nowhere, and bring them up against a very strong part of our line. But we shall know soon enough. If I am right, then the two months' grace that Clemenceau obtained for us will save the situation. If Wilson is right, I suppose all our spare men and ammunition will be sunning themselves in Palestine when we are attacked here, and our only hope of help will be from the Americans. Even then I do not see how the Germans can win a decisive victory, but there will be very little left of the British Army at the end of it.

February 13. All the evidence is accumulating that the German attack will take place next month, near the old Somme area. The Germans are improving their rail and road communications and putting down great dumps of ammunition and supplies.

I have just been on a very peaceful two-days' inspection tour round our waterways. I did most of it from a launch, and spent the night most comfortably on the Director of Water Transport's barge. The barge is fitted up like a private yacht, with very nicely finished saloon and cabins. It was originally intended to be suitable for touring the canals; but its top structure is so high that it catches every breath of wind, and unless the day is perfectly still the barge is quite unmanageable. It cannons from one side of the canal to the other with every gust, so it is generally safely tied up to the side, and used as an inn.

D.H. has been home, and has been definitely told of L.G.'s determination to remove Robertson. L.G. seems to have been anxious about D.H.'s action when Robertson's removal was made public, and threw out hints that Haig might be made Generalissimo of all the Forces, with a subordinate G.O.C.-in-C. of the British Armies in France.

Apparently the whole Army Council, after the last meeting of the Supreme War Council, sent a resolution to the Government pointing out that the position of the Commander-in-Chief in France was now impossible, and that the Army Council itself was deprived of the responsibility given to it by the Constitution; so now the British Military Representative at the Supreme War Council will be made a member of the Army Council, and the whole situation becomes even more absurd and Gilbertian than it has hitherto been. The Chief of the Imperial General Staff remains the military adviser of the Government; the Army Council issues orders to the Commander-in-Chief; the Military Representative at Versailles represents the Government on the Executive Committee, which in turn also issues orders to the Commander-in-Chief. It is all so absurd that it cannot last; but it may do infinite damage even in a short time, and nobody knows what will replace it. Nothing but a miracle could win a battle with such a fantastic organization.

Meantime, our divisions (except those of the Dominions) are being reduced from twelve battalions to nine battalions, which means a reduction from 741 battalions to 600 battalions—nearly 10 per cent.

February 20. Robertson has gone and Wilson rules in his stead. It has been inevitable for the last four months, but it is the worst possible thing that could have happened. Except for a small circle of personal friends, Wilson is universally distrusted throughout the Army. He will never stand up either to L.G. or to the French. It would be far better to have a French Generalissimo—who would at least be responsible—than have the British Army harried on the one hand by L.G. and Wilson, and on the other by the French, *without* responsibility.

D.H. tells me he did all he could to have Robertson retained. So apparently did Derby, so much so that there was some talk of Derby himself being replaced by Northcliffe.

The whole intrigue stinks in one's nostrils. The final moves were the nastiest of all. The Prime Minister wanted to make out that D.H. had approved the Supreme Council fantasy, and went the length of having a document prepared for Bonar Law to read in the House of Commons stating that D.H. thought the new scheme was workable. Bonar Law showed the document to D.H., who had it altered to read that he (D.H.) " would do his best to work under the new scheme." I think it would have been better if D.H. had not given even this qualified semi-approval of the scheme, which everyone knows is utterly unworkable: but even that would not have stopped L.G.

It is of course quite true that L.G. is well within his rights in choosing his own military adviser. The trouble is that he wants an adviser who will obey his orders and not venture on either advice on, or criticism of, any of L.G.'s own favourite strategical schemes. I am afraid he has now got the one man in the army who will play that rôle—our only military black-leg.

February 21. Butler has left G.H.Q. for a command. The old team round D.H. has now been altogether broken up. Kiggell, Butler, Rice, Maxwell have gone. Lawrence, who is now Chief of the General Staff, seems admirable. He has had great experience in the front line. He has one very strong asset. He has a very big job in civil life to go back to whenever he may wish to go, so he is absolutely independent. It is difficult for any regular professional soldier not to be influenced to some extent by considerations of his own future prospects. Lawrence has the independence of a civilian and the training of a soldier. He gives the impression of great strength of character and very clear judgment.

L.G.'s speech in the House of Commons on the differences between the Cabinet and Robertson is almost diabolically clever. Anyone reading it who does not know the facts would think Robertson a pig-headed theorist, and L.G. a marvel of long-suffering patience and forbearance, and there is no one in the House of

Commons who can, or dare, state the facts. Even if there were, it would not help much. L.G. has the House of Commons and the bulk of the Press in his pocket. Anyhow, you cannot have a General Election in the middle of a war.

The mere fact of a change of Chief of the Imperial General Staff is not in itself so important. The trouble is what lies behind it all. Robertson's offence is that he pointed out the unsoundness of L.G.'s military schemes. If he is sacked for that, it is difficult to see how his successor will be able to prevent L.G., or the Cabinet, embarking on any folly that may appeal to them at any moment. One would have thought that the Dardanelles story and the Nivelle disaster would have taught the Cabinet the danger of flying in the face of the advice of their experts. The Palestine folly of this year is far more dangerous than either of its predecessors.

It is fairly certain now that the German attack will open within a couple of months at latest. They have staged their onslaught —Lille, Somme and Rheims. The French think the big attack will be at Rheims. The most dangerous to us would be a simultaneous attack at all these places, with the greatest weight developed wherever the greatest initial success is obtained. The Germans have brought 28 divisions from Russia and 6 from Italy since November. This is pretty well what we had calculated in our November forecast. What we did not then foresee was the reduction in our own strength. All the same, I do not see how the Germans can win a decisive victory, unless Palestine takes all our men and the French give way.

Rawlinson goes to Versailles to be military representative on the Supreme War Council in place of Wilson, and Plumer is being brought back from Italy.

February 25. Clemenceau was with D.H. yesterday. Apparently the Supreme War Council is already almost defunct. Foch and Pétain are at loggerheads. Pétain says he has no troops available for the General Reserve which Foch wants to control. Neither has D.H. We have altogether only 6 divisions not in the front line or close up. Clemenceau is suspicious of Rawlinson, and more than suspicious of Wilson, but believes in Foch. D.H. tells me that Clemenceau has warned him that Rawlinson would turn against D.H. if things went wrong.

Now that Wilson is C.I.G.S. he seems all out to scrap the Supreme War Council and get control transferred again to London. He has apparently now shifted right round to the view that Robertson urged, and he himself opposed, two months ago, with regard to the Versailles machinery.

According to D.H., Wilson still seems enamoured of the Palestine adventure, and D.H. thinks he may even try to send troops there from France.

D.H. is delighted with Clemenceau. He thinks he is single-minded, with only one object—to smash Germany.

I was in the Ypres area yesterday, inspecting some units, and went up to the front line. There was some desultory German shelling, but no sign of any big attack. Our positions there are very strong, and I do not think there is the least chance of the Germans attacking in that area again. I came back through Béthune. There are signs of an attack there, but no great activity. The weather has been splendid—bright and dry—just what we wanted last year and did not get.

I see Balfour is again coquetting with peace in the House of Commons. Meantime we shall have our big attack on this front!

CHAPTER XXVI

THE GERMAN ONSLAUGHT

March 4. There is definite information that the German attack will be in the Somme area, and in all human probability it will be delivered during this month. The French are inclined to disagree. They think the attack will be later, and report that some German divisions are leaving their front and being sent back to Russia.

The weather broke yesterday, and we had a miserable, cold, wet Sunday. I went to a little church near Amiens. There was excellent singing—quite the best I have heard out here, mainly due to the choir. The service was a joint Church of England and Presbyterian one, and the church was packed. The sermon was the ordinary type of thing, but good of its kind. It is pathetic to see how, whenever a big action is in prospect, the churches are crowded, and when things are quiet, how they empty. This will probably be the last service many of the men will attend on this earth.

March 8. I have just returned from a visit to the Fifth and Third Armies. I spent the night at Amiens where things were normal, then went on to the Somme area and our new front. The Fifth Army is hard at work preparing a defensive position—still very imperfect, but all communications are good. There was a good deal of shelling going on in the front line, and swarms of aeroplanes—mostly our own—out reconnoitring. I went through all that remains of Delville Wood—just a tangle of bare boughs of trees, and a few naked skeletons of trunks—and then to Péronne. Afterwards I went north to the Arras area, where there was also a good deal of shelling. Our front there is pretty strong, and should give a good account of itself if it is attacked.

The Third Army is rather concerned about some new marks on air photographs in the fields by the roadside of the German back area. The tracks leading to them mean some form of German tank. I think there are too many of them in one place to be tanks.

The Fifth Army has something of the same sort on its photographs of areas near St. Quentin, and thinks it is ammunition brought up on caterpillar tractors. I am not sure that they are not large handcarts for the supply of small arms ammunition, but if so they must have particularly broad wheels. Whatever they are, they point pretty conclusively to a very early offensive.

Everyone is quite alive to the certainty of some form of attack in the near future, so there should be no chance of surprise. But almost every unit is below establishment. There are plenty of guns and ammunition.

March 15. It seems reasonably certain that the attack will begin within a week or ten days against the Fifth Army—and possibly the Third as well. D.H. has gone to London to put the whole situation before the Cabinet.

March 18. D.H. tells me that L.G. again tried to get him to admit that in January he had said the Germans would not attack in strength, and would only make limited efforts against small portions of the British front. I suppose the idea is, that if things go wrong he will be able to say he has been misled by G.H.Q. Anyhow D.H. has now warned him definitely that there will be an attack on a very large frontage of not less than 50 miles, and has also reminded him that we were short of men; he has been told we will not get many reinforcements.

The Germans have now 185 divisions on the Western front—possibly one or two more, so that they should have something like 60 divisions available for one great attack, or from 20 to 30 at each of their simultaneous attacks. It is now reasonably sure that they will not attack simultaneously at Lille and on the Somme, and the French are fairly confident that there will be no attack in the south this month. We have only 57 British divisions available on the whole front, but there is an arrangement with the French that they will send early reinforcements if we are attacked and they are not.

March 19. It is certain that the attack will be launched either to-morrow or the day after. And my W.A.A.C. typist has decorated my office table with daffodils! The first of the new spring flowers and very beautiful, but such a grotesque prelude to the battle. I am going off early to-morrow to see Sir Henry Horne at the First Army, unless the attack begins before dawn.

March 20. I have been out all day with the First Army. Everything is very quiet in that area, and there are troops ready to move to the Third Army or the Fifth Army fronts if required. I got back to First Army Head-quarters for dinner, and came back here afterwards.

The Duke of Teck, down from the King of the Belgians' Head-quarters, was lunching with me yesterday, and gave an excellent account of the Belgian Army.

March 21. The attack broke this morning against the Third and Fifth Armies. There was plenty of warning—a very heavy bombardment in the early hours, and then a general attack in great strength about 8 a.m. There was nothing to be done at G.H.Q., so I went forward in the forenoon towards the Fifth Army front. There was very little information to be gathered. The morning had been very foggy, so that little could be seen, and most of our telephone lines had been cut by the bombardment; but when I left at noon to come back here, the battle had been going pretty much as had been anticipated. Our thinly-held front line had been driven in, and the enemy was up against our real defensive line, and seemed to be held. But it is only the beginning. It will be a long battle.

March 22. The fighting to-day has gone badly for us. It seems pretty certain that the Germans are putting all their available strength into one great effort against us, and they have pressed us back much quicker than we expected. It is very serious. We have practically no reserves. It is not a question of a breakthrough. The German attack will peter out long before that becomes even a possibility, but the enemy will penetrate very deeply into our lines, and may reach Amiens. It is all a question now of man-power, and we are very badly off in that respect. The brightest spot in the picture is that the Germans seem to have struck with every available division yesterday and to-day, and cannot have many fresh divisions to send up. The battle front is nearly 60 miles long, and if we are driven back even a few miles on all that front, it will make a very deep re-entrant, and greatly extend the line we shall have to hold with our exhausted divisions. To-morrow and the next day will really decide the final result of the battle. If the Germans do not break through in those days—and I do not think they can—then we are safe enough. By the 26th, the French reinforcements should begin to arrive.

Your telegram with the news about Cyril[1] has just arrived. The telephone message was so faint that I had almost hoped there was some error until I saw the telegram. I had already asked for full news of him through a man on the Staff at Cairo.

March 25. The situation is very serious both in the battle and behind it. The right of the Third Army and the whole of the Fifth Army have been driven back right through their defensive areas, and the Germans are still pressing on. The Péronne bridgehead and the line of the canal were given up yesterday, and we shall soon be back to our old line of 1915.

Apparently the French reinforcements will not arrive until the end of the month—another five days. Pétain still thinks the Germans are going to launch a big attack at Rheims either this week or next, and will not send his reserves from there. So the French divisions that are promised will be from Alsace, and will not begin to arrive before the 30th. There was to have been a counter-attack this morning by the French on the right, but it did not materialize. The bulk of the few French reinforcements that have arrived have only fifty rounds S.A.A., and no guns, and are, of course, quite useless. Worse than that, Pétain met D.H. last night at Dury, and told him that if the German attack were pressed on on our right, he had ordered the local French commander[2] to withdraw south-west and cover Paris. That would leave a clean gap between our army and the French, and the Germans would get right through. D.H. has telegraphed home asking that a Generalissimo for the whole Western front be appointed at once as the only possible means of having Pétain overruled.

It is doubtful if there will be time even for that action to be effective. Meanwhile we are getting a few divisions from our own Second Army. D.H. has also appealed direct to Clemenceau and Foch to try and get one or other of them to take action. Pétain must have lost his judgment. The whole basic principle of the Allied strategy since 1914 has been for the French and British Armies to keep united. The one thing the Germans must most desire is

---

[1] My brother-in-law, Captain C. A. G. Hodgson, invalided from Palestine, died in Cairo on March 20. His brother, Captain C. B. M. Hodgson, had been wounded at the fighting on the Jordan, and was lying dangerously ill at the time in Cairo. He died on April 1.
[2] General Fayolle.

to separate them. Pétain must know that the Germans have used almost all, if not actually all, available reserve divisions in this attack, and cannot possibly attack elsewhere until this battle is over.

The only other possible course that D.H. might have adopted would have been to refer to the Supreme War Council, which would probably have meant at least a week's delay and argument, with Pétain and Haig each upholding his case at Paris, while the battle went on here.

March 26. These are sad days. It is small consolation to know that we soldiers always realized the risk the Cabinet were forcing the country to run, and did what we could to prevent it. Our casualties are enormous. There is not yet a complete return of them, but they exceed by far what we suffered during any of our great attacks in 1916 or last year. That also was what we have always urged—that attack, even when not fully successful, was less costly in lives than imperfect defence. The Cabinet would not believe it; but it is unfair to blame the whole Cabinet, for the Prime Minister is virtually dictator.

The reports to-day are so confused that it is almost impossible to get any clear idea of the position in the front line. The deepest advance yesterday was made against the Third Army, whose right is now driven in beyond the Fifth Army line. At one time there was a clear gap between the armies, but that has been made good. Now the main pressure is coming against the Fifth Army, which is giving ground and losing heavily. The only good news is that every account says our men are fighting splendidly; there is no running away, and their morale is as high as ever.

Lord Milner and Wilson arrived yesterday, and are meeting Clemenceau and Foch to-day.

March 27. The news this morning is a little better, and it looks as if we were at the end of the worst period of the battle: but it is too soon to be sure. Anyhow, it is practically certain that the Germans will not get through, or even get as far as Amiens. But the Fifth Army has almost ceased to exist. It is all so like Ypres in 1914, only on a far bigger scale. Yesterday Hubert Gough organized a force of stragglers, camp-followers and odds and ends into a sort of division—just as Johnny Gough did in the dark days of 1914—and put them into some old trenches in case the Fifth

Army broke down entirely. Our right is now fairly secure, and even if the French send us only half a dozen good divisions, we shall be all right on the left.

It is all so sad and so entirely unnecessary. If the home people had only kept us even up to last year's strength, the German attack would have been held up on the Canal and thousands of lives saved. Now it will be months before the army is fit to fight again.

If only the truth were known in England of the way we have been starved of men and made to increase our commitments with dwindling resources, how every protest was fobbed off with fine phrases, there would be some free hanging in England. But no doubt shortly the politicians and the L.G. peers will turn and rend the soldiers.

The misery of it all is to *know*, without any manner of doubt, that we should have done to the Germans last year what the Germans have been doing to us these last few days, if we had been given the men we pleaded for, and if there had been no Calais Conference in February, 1917.

March 28. The situation is very much better. The Germans shifted the weight of their attack up to the northern flank, and were soundly beaten this morning. That in itself is not so very important, but it means that the really dangerous thrust towards Amiens has come to an end, at least for the moment. It is not so much our resistance during these last days that stopped them, as the fact that their attack had advanced as far as any attack could without a halt to bring up supplies, ammunition, and men. We learnt the same lesson in almost all our own attacks. It will take them at least a week before they can get going again against the Fifth Army, and by that time we should be able to put up a reasonable resistance, and have fresh troops ourselves, either from the French or our own Second Army. I think we can safely say now that this great German effort has failed.

I have heard something of the conference on the 26th. All the Army Commanders were haled to Doullens to meet Milner and the C.I.G.S. Plumer has, as usual, played up, and is managing to set free at least 3 divisions, which will arrive at Amiens in the next week. Then there was a meeting with Clemenceau, Foch, Pétain, D.H., Milner and the C.I.G.S., at which it was eventually decided to make Foch Generalissimo in France. The whole and sole object is to override Pétain and get the French to send reinforcements to prevent the British and French Armies being separated.[1]

March 29. Things are distinctly better. The Germans seem to have made a most determined effort yesterday towards Arras and to have suffered a very heavy defeat. They attacked all out in very close formation, and must have had enormous losses. It was a clear, bright day, and our artillery got magnificent targets of German infantry massing for attack.

All our returns of losses for the first few days are now complete and are very serious. The really vital question for the next few months is man-power, and we are now suffering for the lack of judgment and decision of the Government. A telegram from the War Office yesterday said that the 4 divisions in England were

[1] Sir Douglas Haig subsequently told me further details of the proceedings at Doullens. There were in reality three separate conferences. The first one was an ordinary Army Commanders' conference between Sir Douglas Haig and his own Army Commanders. At this conference orders were given for the Second Army to send as many divisions as could be spared to the Fifth Army, and General Plumer promised 3 divisions complete within ten days. As the extension of the German battle front, which actually took place on the 28th, was foreseen, the call was not made on the First Army, which might be attacked. After the Army Commanders' conference was over, there was a meeting between Lord Milner, the C.I.G.S. and the Army Commanders, at which the whole situation was explained to Lord Milner and the C.I.G.S. Afterwards the meeting with Clemenceau and Foch took place. Monsieur Poincaré was also present. The meeting first decided that Amiens must be covered at all costs, and the union between the British and French armies maintained, with the corollary that French divisions must be hurried up at all speed possible. Then Clemenceau drafted a resolution that Foch should be appointed to co-ordinate the operations of the British and French troops in the Amiens area, with the specific task of covering Amiens and keeping the French and British armies united. Sir Douglas Haig regarded the suggestion as ineffective, as it would mean that Foch would really be in a subordinate position to both himself and Pétain, either of whom need not necessarily conform to his orders. Accordingly Sir Douglas Haig urged that Foch should be given command of all the British and French troops in France and Flanders, and this was accepted by the conference, with the proviso that Foch should take over his duties forthwith. Sir Douglas Haig hoped that as a result of this decision, the French divisions would arrive in the course of a few days to take the place of, or to reinforce, his exhausted and depleted divisions in the Fifth Army. As events developed, this hope was not fulfilled.

entirely composed of boys under eighteen, and that every fit man had already been ordered to France. It is not clear whether this means that large reinforcements are now on the way, or only that the men have not been called up, but most probably the latter. The hard fact is that on March 21 we had 100,000 fewer infantrymen than twelve months ago, and had three times as many Germans on our front. By the order of the Home Government our line had been lengthened by one-third in the last four months. The French divisions who were relieved in the front line were, by arrangement, to have remained ready to support the point of junction of the two armies, but for some reason they had been dispersed.

March 30. The King is out on a visit to the Army. He will do much to hearten the men, and it is well that His Majesty should get first-hand information of the state of affairs, and learn G.H.Q.'s side of the story of the reverses we have had. He is not likely to hear it at home.

The attacks are still going on, but in rather a desultory manner. If we had fresh troops there would be no difficulty in stopping them, or even in counter-attacking; but the troops that have been through the ordeal of the last fortnight are utterly exhausted. There is no particular sign that Foch as Generalissimo is able to get French troops moving up to us.

March 31. (*Easter Day.*) I suppose Easter will always mean for us who may survive, the memory of those who have gone. I went to church this morning. It was crammed, and the service was very impressive. The padre—a young man, hardly more than a boy, but one who had been two years in the trenches—broke down.

Yet the promise holds. This afternoon, as if to remind me of that, as I drove towards the east where the battle lies, there gleamed before me the most glorious rainbow I have ever seen.

April 2. The battle is at a definite pause. It is far too soon yet to think of its being over; but all we now hear shows that even in the worst days of last month our men fought magnificently. That is great news. The Fifth Army was given a task bigger than it could bear. Had we had the men to keep our divisions at full strength, the story would have been very different. The German attack would have been held, and by now we should have been looking forward to an early end to the war. For in reality this attack is suicide for the Germans. But with our losses, and no great hope of early reinforcements, it will be a long time before we can expect to take advantage of it.

One result of the new regime is, of course, that the Supreme War Council disappears, at least so far as its military components are concerned. Rawlinson comes back here to take Gough's place, and Gough goes to a skeleton reserve army. One cannot help—even in these days—being amused at the rapidity with which the only forecast adventured by the Supreme War Council has been disproved.[1] Its forecast of attack by the Germans has been totally and circumstantially incorrect in every particular—date, strength and place of attack. Even a random guess by a newspaper correspondent would probably have been right in at least one of these factors. The members have hastily sent out to recall all the maps issued to illustrate the forecast, and will, of course, try to have them all destroyed.

Conferences are now the order of the day—all with the hope of hastening French action, but so far without any result. Apparently Pétain is still sticking his toes in against Foch's orders. There is hardly a shot being fired along the whole French front. It is quite impossible now for the Germans to attack them in any strength for at least another month. The position is almost ideal for a French attack somewhere to relieve the pressure on us, but either their preparations are incomplete, or they either do not wish to attack at present, or to send troops here to support us. A French attack would be far more effective help to us than any reinforcements they can send—if they were to send them. Meantime there are signs that the Germans are coming on again in a few days, against our right and the French left this time. It cannot possibly be anything like as big an effort as on the 21st or even the 28th; all the same it is serious.

April 4. The Germans attacked again this morning and gained some ground both from us and the French, but at a very heavy cost, and there is no material change in the general situation, except that every unsuccessful German attack improves our prospects.

[1] See page 284 (February 6), and "Field-Marshal Earl Haig," by the author (pp. 310–311).

The Prime Minister was out yesterday for a conference, at which it was decided to give Foch formal control of the strategical operations of all the Allied Armies in France. D.H. says L.G. is now thoroughly frightened. He says a good deal more than that about him that will not bear repeating. L.G. is apparently expecting to be attacked in the House of Commons about manpower, and for ordering divisions to Palestine—as indeed he should be—against the opinion of his military advisers. He is, of course, looking for a scapegoat for the disaster to the Fifth Army, and has apparently decided to go for Gough. D.H. is furious about this. It would certainly be most unfair if Gough were held responsible. He had a dozen divisions to hold a front of 42 miles, and was attacked by 50 divisions. The whole weight of the German attack fell on his army. The fault lies with the Government, whose refusal of men made it impossible to strengthen Gough's army. The only thing Gough did that may be criticized when all the facts are known, was to give up the Péronne bridge-head. But no one can possibly say yet whether that was right or wrong. In any case, it is a matter for D.H. to deal with and not the Prime Minister.

One good thing has resulted from yesterday's conference. Foch and Pétain have promised to launch an attack near Montdidier in a few days' time. That will finally ease the pressure on us.

April 6. The battle is, I think, over, and even with all our losses, that brings the end of the war much nearer. For it is quite certain that the Germans will not be able to launch another attack on anything like the same scale again. They made a final effort on the 4th and yesterday, and were definitely held up. To-day has been quite quiet.

The news that the Americans are lending their men to fill the gaps in our ranks is good, and makes the final issue perfectly safe. It is sad for us to have come to this pass owing solely to the dilatoriness of the Government. It is humiliating to us as a nation, but perhaps out of that there may come great good both to us and the world. For it may bind Britain and America closer together in the post-war years. If we ever fall seriously apart, the world will have to face another conflict which will make this one seem trivial. Repington told me last year that he was certain that this was only the first of a series of world-wars which will follow in fairly close succession during the next century. The only chance I see of the fulfilment of his prophecy would be if America and Britain were at enmity.

Although this attack is over, the Germans are sure to try another attack in some other area. They will not admit themselves beaten yet. I think it is certain to be against us, for they know they have weakened our army dangerously. I am anxious about Flanders and the Channel ports. I hope that Foch has his eyes open, and will not rely too much on the French Intelligence. Their efforts at divining the German intentions for the last two months have been rather laughable.

April 8. There is a definite lull in the fighting. The March battle is undoubtedly over; but it is only the first round of the German effort. The Germans win it on points; but they bought their success very dearly. I told D.H. in February that there would be three German efforts—unless either of the first two was decisively successful. There is no reason yet to change that view. Each succeeding one will be less fierce. The fiercer they are, the nearer comes our inevitable victory.

The Generalissimo business is not proving all that was hoped from it. It fulfilled its primary object of getting Pétain overruled and avoiding a very threatening danger, though, as events have now proved, we staved off this German attack without any French assistance either direct or indirect. Foch seems quite at sea as regards where the next German blow will fall. He thinks they will go for Paris next, or renew their last attack. I do not think they will do either. The first would be grotesquely incorrect strategy: the second is not, I think, possible without a very long delay, which the Germans cannot afford. Our First Army says a big attack has been mounted against them for the last two months, and I am sure it will be the next to be attacked. But others think otherwise.

L.G. will, of course, use the Generalissimo arrangement to hide the shortcomings of the Government, but that does not matter if only it helps to win the war quickly. The bright spot is the American offer and action—both generous and prompt. I am personally very glad, for I am almost alone here in my belief in both American intentions and possibilities.

An American general discharged rather a good phrase to me a day or two ago. After a survey of the situation as impartial as one could make it, he said: " It looks to me as if some of your Allies were only attached to you for rations." At least I am convinced of one thing, the Americans are men of their word. If they say they will do a thing they do it, or as near it as is humanly possible. It is not always so with the French. They always seem to be able to produce a very plausible reason for getting out of their promises when they want to. The last example is the big counter-attack which Foch and Pétain promised on the 3rd would take place "within a few days from the Montdidier direction." It has never materialized, and will not now. The pity of it is, that there was a definite chance of interfering with the German plans, and possibly regaining the initiative. Now we have just to wait for the Germans to strike at us again.

The casualty lists for the fighting on the 4th and 5th are in. They are nothing like as heavy as in the March days, but they are very serious. I suppose we all out here seem to have grown callous about casualties. Perhaps we have to some extent. One can only measure casualties against the cause for which we are fighting. Yet sometimes they make one almost sick with sadness. I like Sir Sidney Low's lines in the *Daily Chronicle* to-day so much. They are really the thoughts we all feel.

> To you, our Dead, beyond the sea,
> Who gave your lives to hold us free,
> By us, who keep your memory,
>   What can be said?
>
> We cannot sing your praises right,
> Lost heroes of the endless fight;
> Whose souls into the lonely night
>   Too soon have fled.
>
> We can but honour, cherish, bless,
> Your sacred names; no words express
> The measure of our Thankfulness,
>   To you our Dead.

After all, we out here have as much right to feel the losses as those at home—probably more, for each one of us here loses his personal friends in each successive casualty list, as well as his relatives.

April 10. The battle has begun again, almost exactly where predicted, and we have lost heavily both in men and in ground.

The attack is on a much smaller scale than in March, but we have no men to meet it. The French are doing absolutely nothing. They seem to be still obsessed by the idea of a big German attack towards Paris, and definitely refuse either to send troops to our front, or to take over some of the line and set free our own troops. So far, Foch as Generalissimo has been useless—except for overruling Pétain. Actually he has done very little more than Pétain promised. I do not think this attack can get through—certainly it cannot, if even now the French take action; but we are reduced to the last man—which means the Portuguese, who are quite unable to stand up to the Germans. The Portuguese were to have been relieved to-day—just three days too late. The Germans have been lucky in the weather; the marshy ground in front of the Portuguese has hardened up during the dry spell last month, and there was again a thick mist when they attacked. But all that is no excuse. We have been caught more unprepared than we should have been. Foch is coming to G.H.Q. to-night. If he acts promptly, there is no danger. If he does not, it may become very serious.

I have only seen telegraphed extracts from L.G.'s speech in the House; but so far as I can make out it is full of the most amazing statements—very cunningly devised—to turn from himself the blame which is quite certainly his.

I have been asked to-day whether I will stand for —— in Parliament after the war. That must wait until the war is over, but I shall certainly leave the Army as soon as I can. Peace-soldiering after all this would be mere drudgery.

April 12. The news from the battle is not good. The Germans are making a big effort, and the French are doing nothing. Foch said two days ago [1] that he had at last made up his mind that the big German attack was against the British Army, and that he would send a large French force to take part in the battle, but so far nothing has happened. It looks as if we should have to fight out this battle alone, and we have no reserves. It will decide the war. God grant the decision is not against us! Everything else fades into insignificance. We are paying in blood for the follies of professional politicians. I pray that our payment in the lives of the Army may suffice and that the whole nation be not strangled.

[1] At Beaurepaire on April 10.

D.H. has issued a very finely worded appeal [1] to the Army to fight to the last, saying that French troops are hurrying to our assistance. I wish they were. It is all so like 1914 when we told the 1st Corps the French were coming, and they did not come. Yet then we won alone, and I believe we shall now. All the same I wish D.H. had *not* issued his order. It will immensely hearten the Germans when they hear of it, as they must. I do not think our own men needed it to make them fight it out. If the French are really hurrying to our assistance, they should be here in a few days, almost as soon as the order will reach the front-line troops. If they are not, it may have a really bad effect to raise false hopes in the troops' minds.

Although the position is serious, I do not think this attack can possibly get through. It will outrun its supplies and come to the end of its momentum just as the March attack did. So far there is no sign of a check. Our men are fighting well, but are hopelessly outnumbered, and practically untrained owing to the enormous front we have had to hold all winter when the divisions should have been training. Our losses are huge, and we are still being steadily pushed back. It is all so sad. Recriminations are

[1] TO ALL RANKS OF THE BRITISH FORCES IN FRANCE

Three weeks ago to-day the enemy began his terrific attacks upon us on a 50-mile front. His objects are to separate us from the French, to take the Channel Ports, and destroy the British Army.

In spite of throwing already 106 divisions into the battle, and enduring the most reckless sacrifice of human life, he has as yet made little progress towards his goals.

We owe this to the determined fighting and self-sacrifice of our troops. Words fail me to express the admiration which I feel for the splendid resistance offered by all ranks of our Army under most trying circumstances.

Many among us now are tired. To those I would say that Victory will belong to the side which holds out the longest. The French Army is moving rapidly and in great force to our support.

There is no other course open to us but to fight it out! Every position must be held to the last man. With our backs to the wall and believing in the justice of our cause, each one of us must fight on to the end. The safety of our Homes and the Freedom of Mankind alike depend upon the conduct of each one of us at this critical moment.

D. HAIG, F.M.

Thursday,
11th *April*, 1918.

useless. After all, the real judges are those of history, and the Army has little cause to fear the verdict.

This northern attack was, of course, a gigantic strategic surprise. Probably it was meant to be the real effort of the Germans, to have followed immediately after the first March attack.[1] The success in the early days then tempted the Germans to develop it, and now they have not enough men left to drive this one through. The Channel ports are, of course, the vital point to the British Army, and the Germans know it very well. If the French act, there should not be the least possibility of the Germans driving us back to the coast. Even if the French do nothing, I still think the German man-power will be exhausted before the enemy succeeds in driving us back to the coast—but that is not a certainty.

April 14. The battle is still in full swing, and I see no immediate prospect of relief. I calculate now that the Germans are well past the half-way stage of their whole effort. The slaughter has been enormous. The whole question is now one of man-power. At the front, both our men and the Germans are utterly exhausted and fall asleep within full view of one another. It has turned bitterly cold to-day with a very high wind.

I managed to get to church this morning. There was quite a big congregation. I wish padres would not always choose " appropriate " hymns. We had " For all the Saints " and " Fight the good Fight." It would be right if we were in the firing-line or in any greater personal danger than from a stray air bomb.

I had a long interview with D.H. He tells me that Foch has at last ordered French troops to move, and that they will begin to arrive to-day or to-morrow. D.H. asked for 8 divisions—4 behind the First Army, and 4 near Albert. He has not a very high opinion of Foch, and thinks he is not really looking ahead—just waiting on events and trusting that our men will stick it out as they did in 1914. It is easy to criticize. If Foch is doing this with the intention of sending in at the right moment a smashing attack by the French on, say the Aisne or at St. Mihiel, his strategy, if bold, may be perfectly right. If we were a homogeneous army under our own Commander-in-Chief, one could only admire the boldness of the strategy and pray for its success. But we are not a homogeneous army. By all reports the French Army is not yet

[1] Actually, it is now known that this was the proposal of Lieut.-General Wetzell, who was in charge of the strategical section of the German General Staff. He was overruled by Ludendorff.

sufficiently recovered from 1917 to be able to deliver a smashing offensive. The Americans cannot be ready before the autumn. It looks as if Foch were playing for a defensive all this spring and summer and probably autumn, and then give the *coup de grâce* in 1919. If so, it is very unfair to let the British Army take the whole weight of this spring effort unsupported. It shows the difficulty of a Generalissimo system with allied armies.

The irony of it all is that the Germans, now pretty well exhausted after two big attacks and in two deep salients, are simply asking for a vigorous counter-attack against one or other of their salients, and we have no troops available. If we had another 15 divisions, we could easily get a decisive victory. But it will be months before the men can come, however energetic the home authorities may at last be. By all accounts they are now really stirring themselves. Troops are being brought back from Palestine and Egypt, and England is at last being combed for men.

April 18. The attack is following fairly closely the lines of last month's effort. The Germans are now trying to extend their flank northwards. They attacked Kemmel yesterday, but were driven back, though they made a little ground at Wytschaete; but I think it is now nearly over. We are expecting another attack on the Amiens front in a day or two, but it cannot be anything very big. Probably it is only intended to prevent reinforcements being moved northwards to the new battle area.

There is one very noticeable and encouraging thing. The censor reports that ever since the 21st of March the whole *tone* of the letters from the troops has improved. All grousing has stopped, and has been replaced by a spirit of great confidence. This is very remarkable, considering what the troops are undergoing: but it was much the same in the early days of each of our big attacks. The grumbling begins when the fighting dies down, and the men have time to think over things.

April 21. There is a distinct lull in the battle. I think it is practically over. The Germans still have enough reserves for one more effort, probably of about the same strength as this last battle, but it will take them a month to get all their preparations made. They may make some small attacks in the meantime.

The French have taken over the Kemmel section of our line—the first active assistance they have given us since March 21.

Foch is said to be now quite convinced that the next German

attack will be on the Amiens front, and that there will be an attack south of Montdidier. He has not been very successful so far in his deductions, but he may be right this time. He is back at his old idea of an "amalgam" of the British and French armies, and now wishes our tired divisions to go into line on the French front, and withdraw fresh French divisions to form a strategical reserve. This has upset the Government very much, and a wire has been sent hoping that D.H. is refusing to comply. And so they make their "get-away" secure again. If D.H. does comply and things go wrong, they will put the blame on him. If he does not comply, they will get him for refusing to play up to Foch. Pleasant people, our civilian war-lords! Anyhow, D.H. is sending the IXth Corps to the French, and Foch is sending a number of divisions to the Amiens sector to be in reserve for the big German attack which he thinks is coming there.

April 27. The fighting has begun again, but on a comparatively small scale.[1] On the Amiens front a small attack was made on the 25th with about 5 German divisions. It made a little progress during the day, but a counter-attack on the same night regained it all and took over 1,000 prisoners—a very successful little show which actually marks the end of this battle.

At Kemmel the Germans captured Kemmel Hill, which the French had taken over from us—and still hold it. Though the attack was not a big one, the loss of Kemmel is serious as it overlooks much ground on our side.

I see Bonar Law has been making some remarkable statements in the House concerning the extension of our line before this battle. I am quite sure D.H. was never so ill-advised as to say anything—even in private conversation—that could possibly justify the Cabinet stating he favoured the fatal extension. Bonar Law makes out that it was arranged in France by the Commander-in-Chief without interference from home. This is absolutely untrue. The decision was made at a council at which no one from G.H.Q. was present. D.H. says Milner[2] now admits this, and also that he knew D.H. always objected to any extension.

April 29. The Germans attacked again yesterday rather unexpectedly in the north, and were very definitely beaten. There may be a few more of these expiring efforts, but the big battle is

[1] Actually, 4 divisions were engaged.
[2] Lord Milner had succeeded Lord Derby as Secretary of State for War.

certainly over, and we have won through again. It is a huge relief; but it has been at an awful price—not only of dead but of suffering. I went to-day to see some of the wounded in hospital at Étaples. The wards are terribly sad now, full of maimed boys, scarcely out of their teens. There was one with a bullet through his brain. He seems to recognize people, and to understand something of what is said, but he cannot talk and is paralysed. His wife, a mere girl, about to have a baby, is with him. Alongside of him was another paralysed boy with a bullet through his spine, and quite close, a lad who had lost both legs was moaning incessantly. There are worse things in war than being killed. War is so monstrously cruel. Nothing can justify it, except the freedom of a nation. For that, I suppose we would all fight again, and rightly. These wounded men make one feel very strongly that one should be out with them at the front. I am afraid it is quite impossible for me ever to hope for that: my ailment is rather worse now. Everyone tells me I should have an operation as soon as possible, but I hope to see the war out in France. Now that we have won through this battle, the end will be very soon. I do not see how Germany can fight on until the end of the year unless we make some awful blunder.

I see everyone at home is very excited about Zeebrugge. It was a very gallant affair, but I saw the air photos a few days ago, and it is quite certain that it has not blocked the harbour against submarines. Still, its moral effect is good from every point of view, both at home and in Germany.

May 3. Fighting is at a standstill, leaving a very interesting strategical problem as to what will be the next move, and when. It rests with the Germans or the French. For the time being we are out of the picture and so are the Americans. Neither can attack. Foch seems convinced that the Germans will launch another big attack at Amiens. I cannot see why they should. It would be a far more formidable task for them than it was in March, and they have already run through most of their available troops. D.H.'s view is that the next attack will probably be in Flanders or away in the south, where we know their preparations are well advanced.

I have been on an inspection to Boulogne, Calais and Dunkirk, which are all becoming normal again. I saw some American units on the march—very fine-looking fellows, but strangely stern and silent, and almost sad-featured. Our own men—and indeed the troops of all the other nations that I know—talk and sing when marching. The only time I have ever seen British troops marching in silence was during the retreat in 1914. Apparently the Americans are the exception to the rule. In the units I saw, there was only one man with a mouth-organ, and he was a Jew. All the same, these Americans look very formidable troops. They are, of course, the first-fruits of the nation, and naturally their physique is far better than any in our units, or in the French units now. They are every bit as good as the first Kitchener divisions were. Each company was at full strength, and the march discipline was excellent.

Our own units are a sad sight now. Almost every company is below strength and full of very young men. More than half a dozen divisions have had to be practically disbanded. Five have gone to the French to rest and get ready again. Foch is putting them into the Aisne front somewhere, and for the time being we lose them altogether.

I saw the Air people at Dunkirk. They are patrolling regularly over Zeebrugge, and although the port is not blocked effectively, the Germans seem to be using it much less, so that the naval show there has been of more use than we thought at first.

I did to-day's trip in a 12-cylinder Packard, which is faster than my Rolls but none too strong. Going about sixty downhill, one hind wheel came off and rolled along in front of us. Luckily the car kept the road and no damage was done.

May 5. I went to church this morning—quite a cheery service. Nothing now about "Saints resting" or "good fights," but already somewhat premature thanksgiving for victory! We are by no means out of the wood yet. There is still much hard fighting to be done, though the position is certainly infinitely better than at any time since last November. We are all so easily influenced by our own day-to-day situation here. Now that the worst of the attack is over, we are all perfectly happy and cheery. We forget so easily—and perhaps it is as well. You at home remember and mourn. Our feelings here are swamped in the gigantic drama of the operations. What will it all be like when it is over? Somehow one can hardly imagine a world at peace. The whole mainspring of one's life will be loose. What will wind it up again? I shall make the change myself quietly in hospital. Then I have only one resolve—to leave the Army and look for something else to interest myself in.

May 6. There is still no attack from the Germans, though they must be hard at work preparing for it. Every day's delay is, of course, to our advantage. We are absorbing such reinforcements as are coming, and the day of the Americans gets nearer. Wagstaff[1] tells me they are being rushed over much quicker than was originally intended.

A heavy bombardment has just begun—it may be the beginning of another attack. If so, it is coming in the north again, towards the Channel ports.

May 7. The German attack has not developed so far. It is too soon to say that it is definitely off, but it does not now seem probable, as the bombardment has entirely ceased.

Reuter's telegram tells of Freddy Maurice's[2] letter to the papers giving the lie direct to Lloyd George and Bonar Law. It is very plucky of him to publish it, and whatever other effects it may have, it should go far to bring about a more wholesome atmosphere in the Cabinet and Parliament. There are strange rumours here that L.G. had intended to move D.H. to succeed Lord French as Commander-in-Chief at home, and that Maurice's letter has at least stopped that scheme, and D.H. remains here for the time being. General —— came to see me to-day, full of admiration for Maurice, and anxious to write himself and endorse Maurice's facts. ——'s letter would of course be authoritative, for he deals with that side of the question here; but it would bring D.H. into it, and unless L.G. falls, that would inevitably mean D.H.'s removal. I am afraid Maurice will have to stand alone.

D.H. thinks Maurice's letter very ill advised. It offends all his ideas of discipline. That is quite true; all the same I admire Maurice for writing it. It will be a salutary check on the Cabinet's fixed belief that they can publish any misstatement they like without any danger of contradiction from the Services.

May 15. Poor Maurice! This latest development seals his fate. All the same, his letter has done much good. His facts were strictly correct, and he was fully justified in everything he wrote, and also, I think, in writing it. He has plenty of moral courage. Whatever happens to him, I do not think the Cabinet will wish a repetition.

[1] Liaison Officer at American G.H.Q., now Major-General C. M. Wagstaff.
[2] Major-General Sir Frederick Maurice.

May 17. I went for a ride with the First Lord (Sir Eric Geddes), who has been out here for a day or two. He is most optimistic. He thinks the submarine menace is definitely over, as ship-building now surpasses sinking. This is the best of good news, especially in view of the Admiralty's view in June of last year. He told me some rather tall yarns about submarine warfare. A delightful one was about a ship carrying a deck cargo of motors which was shelled by a submarine on the surface. The ship blew up and projected one of the heavy motors into the air. It fell on the submarine and sank it. Let us hope it is true.

You will be glad to hear that the 2/24th Londons are coming to France from Palestine. I will see them as soon as possible and get details about B. I shall also see the North Devonshire Yeomanry as soon as they arrive and hear what I can of C. Neither unit will be here until the end of the month.

There is still no news of the anticipated German attack. I do not think it will develop before the 22nd at the earliest. The delay makes it very possible that it will not be against us at all.

May 20. The German aeroplanes gave us rather a dose last night—much noise that kept us awake, but very little damage. All the W.A.A.C.s were bundled in their night attire into shelters. Some of their huts, with all their garments, were destroyed by bombs, and the young women presented rather an amusing appearance next day in all manner of borrowed clothes. They were not in the least panicky. I went round during the raid to see how they were getting on, and found them running quite a good impromptu concert, apparently entirely unconcerned.

The German attack is still hanging fire. I think the date will now be the 24th. The weather has changed: it is blowing hard now, but still bright and sunny. I went yesterday to the American area, and saw a great number of the troops. They impressed me very favourably. The young officers look splendid material—keen and intelligent, and the men are a very fine lot. The weak point is the Staff and senior regimental officers, who are, of course, quite inexperienced; but a few weeks' fighting will change all that. The Americans are pouring in now, and in a very few months they will have as many men in France as we have.

Altogether things look very well for the ultimate issue this year, though I am afraid Great Britain may not be the predominant partner in the final battles. According to the newspapers, France has rather taken advantage of us in the arrangements she has made for the interchange of prisoners; but one cannot judge without seeing all the negotiations.

It is curious how the general tendency here is to view very critically any arrangements made with, or by, the French. They have brought this on themselves. They are so accustomed to regard themselves as the monopolists in brains that they think any little piece of sharp practice will pass unnoticed. Now everyone searches as with a microscope for the sharp practice, and the Generalissimo arrangement has intensified the suspicion. In sharp contrast, all our negotiations with the Americans are on a basis of complete mutual trust.

I believe that most Britishers out here have by this time precisely reversed their opinions of these two allies of ours. We were accustomed to consider the French generous, chivalrous and strictly straight, and the Americans grasping, self-opinionated and rather keen in doing others down in negotiations. I think we have now revised these estimates of the national characteristics. According to my American friends, they have also had reason to reconsider their preconceived notions of both the French and ourselves—to our advantage.

May 25. No German attack yet, and it now seems reasonably sure that there will be nothing big on our front for some time. I feel fairly certain that Foch has been wrong again in his idea that the Germans' next effort would be towards Amiens. I am beginning to wonder whether they may not be transferring all their weight against the French. We have had some indications already—nothing very definite, but enough to make D.H. send a warning to the French.

May 28. The Germans have fairly caught Foch napping, and have scored heavily in their last attack; but it cannot go far or last long. They attacked yesterday on the Aisne in great strength against the very part of the line where our exhausted IXth Corps had been sent for a rest! We have very little news yet, but what we have got is serious.

May 29. This attack is developing into a big battle much on the lines of the March one. It was an absolute surprise. The French knew nothing of the German intentions until a few deserters came over on the eve of the attack. Our Secret Service agents had given some warning, and on the 26th D.H. sent a message to warn the French that an attack was impending. The French replied that their aeroplane service did not confirm the statement. Their reply came within sixteen hours of the actual attack. Real bad work.

May 30. I dined with D.H. last night. There was a long discussion on the situation with him afterwards. Lawrence, and Du Cane from Foch's H.Q., were present. There is no doubt but that Foch has been precisely wrong in every attempt he has made to forecast the German intentions ever since he became Generalissimo. He would not believe in March that the attack on us was the big German effort, and would do nothing to help us. Then when he was at last convinced of that, he sent French divisions to Kemmel as the quietest part of our line, and Kemmel was attacked and captured within a week of their arrival. Then he made up his mind that the next German effort would be towards Amiens, and collected most of his reserves there, sending tired British troops to the Aisne as a nice quiet part of the line for them to rest in. That sector has been attacked now, and I am afraid what was left of our IXth Corps has had a very rough passage. Foch is now all for sending more British troops down to help the French, as well as taking back all the French troops from our own part of the line. That is probably right enough, for this must be the last big German effort; but one cannot help wishing he had been equally prompt and energetic in sending French help to us in March and early April.

Foch apparently does not think the war can be finished this year. D.H. thinks it can and should. The Americans are coming in so quickly, and the Germans will be absolutely at the end of their tether as soon as their offensive stops. Our own army should be ready to attack by August, unless Foch uses it up piecemeal on the French front.

D.H. tells me the Staff think there will be another attack after this one in the Flanders and Lille area. It all depends how big their present attack is, and how long it keeps going. The information makes it look as if it is intended for a very big effort, in which case I do not think there is the least chance of another serious German attack. This makes the last of the three efforts which we had always considered the maximum Germany could do this year.

The Cabinet are now apparently thoroughly alarmed about the possibilities of the Generalissimo arrangement. They think D.H. should have refused to send any British troops to the French armies, and if anything goes wrong D.H. will certainly be superseded. He tells me Wilson has already more than hinted that he will be sent to the Home Command, and D.H. says he "may be wearing a blue suit" in London any day.

Meantime Foch and L.G. have been quarrelling. Foch apparently let fly at L.G. for not having kept the British Army up to strength before March and since; and L.G. insisted that the greatest possible effort had been made to increase the numbers of the British Army before the battle of March 21 ! Foch can be outspoken in his dealings with L.G., as he is in no way under his orders and can say what he thinks.

D.H. is wonderfully well. He looks harried and worn, but says he is perfectly fit. He seems to have lost confidence in Foch and in the French Army, which he does not think will be able to do much attacking this year.

CHAPTER XXVII

THE BEGINNING OF THE END

June 11. The Aisne battle is over rather sooner than seemed probable. It made a deep indentation in the French line, and then petered out just as the other two German attacks did. Our IXth Corps, by all accounts, fought very well. There was also an attack two days ago on a much smaller scale near the Montdidier sector.

There have been difficulties between Foch and D.H. about the movement of British troops. Foch has taken to issuing orders direct to British units without consulting D.H., who raised objections with the Home Cabinet, and Foch was overruled by Milner and Clemenceau in consultation with one another. Technically, Foch is right. If there is a grave emergency, he must obviously be allowed to order any troops by the most direct method. The trouble is that by the constitution, D.H. is responsible to the British Cabinet for the safety of the British Army, which may be prejudiced if troops are moved without reference to him.

I was in the Belgian area for a few days, and came across some "Fannys"[1] under rather curious circumstances. A town had been shelled, and everyone had gone to ground when I was driving through. Suddenly a motor ambulance with two young women in charge came up and proceeded to load up with wounded. I spoke to them. They seem to be used by the Belgians right up to dressing-stations, very close to the front line. Their Headquarters is at Calais where they have been coming in for a good deal of air bombing; but they seemed very happy and full of zeal. All the girls provide their own ambulance vehicles. It must be much more exciting war work than that done by the girls with our Army, who are kept as far as possible well out of the shelled area.

June 18. Things are very quiet now, not only at G.H.Q.,

[1] First Aid Nursing Yeomanry.

but all along the front. I have been doing a good deal of inspecting. I should have liked to have done more, but my ailment has been worrying me more than usual, and I have had to lie up for a day or two.

Our divisions are beginning to take shape again, and the general outlook is daily improving. There is some chance of one last final effort by the Germans, and it may come in Flanders, though I think that very unlikely. Next month, or the month after, should be our turn to do some attacking, and to test how far the Boche has really exhausted himself.

There has been a mysterious epidemic of influenza at G.H.Q., which has run through the whole camp of some 700 people. It is not at all dangerous, but causes five or six days' acute discomfort with high temperature and great pain. D.H. escaped. He looks less worried now, but still shows signs of the harassing time he has been through. I wish I could think his troubles were all over, or even that they will only be those that the Germans can cause; but I am sure the home people will be at him again. He has very few friends now, either in the War Office or in the Cabinet.

Wilson was out here yesterday. He says that the Government "at present" have no wish to replace D.H. as Commander-in-Chief. It is an utterly impossible situation for a Commander-in-Chief to be in—to know that he has only the temporary support of his Government, and that the politicians are only waiting for an opportunity to turn him out. Curiously enough, D.H. does not let it worry him much. He has become almost fatalistic in his outlook on life, and very deeply religious. He seems to acquire great comfort from the Sunday services at the kirk, and is, I think, quite convinced that he has the especial favour of Providence. I hope he is right. Providence in Heaven and princes on earth are valuable allies!

Jack Cowans was out last week and gave us all the home gossip—very interesting, but not very encouraging. He says—what everyone knows—that Wilson is not a patch on Robertson; but that, under the new Generalissimo regime, does not much matter. The real work now required at the War Office is in the administrative branches, with which Wilson never meddles. Apparently Wilson takes great pleasure in attending Cabinet conferences, and lecturing the politicians on strategy. The Lord knows they need it.

There is much talk here of further reductions in the Army as soon as the Americans are ready in sufficient numbers to take up the task of beating the Boche. I hope it is incorrect. The speeches in Parliament dealing with the present offensive are really amusing. Even Bonar Law had to confess that it came as a complete surprise—the second in six weeks. I see some enterprising members are pressing the point home, goodness knows for what reason, for no good can come of it now. The C.I.G.S. told us that the Cabinet had made up their minds to support Foch in everything he may want or do during the present crisis, but that as soon as the crisis is over, they mean to get the "arrangement altered." Presumably that means there will be some curtailment of Foch's power over the disposition of British troops. I hope it does not mean the disappearance of the Generalissimo, who is an admirable safeguard against the vagaries of the Cabinet. I do not think it matters much now who is Generalissimo. As soon as the Germans are definitely at the end of their offensive, it means they will crack at the first hard blow, and with the Americans coming in at the present rate, we shall have plenty of men to make a really heavy attack all along the line.

Cobbe [1] has asked me to go to Mesopotamia with him. A year ago I would have jumped at it; but the war is too near its end now. I want to see it through, and anyhow I am sure my health would not stand "Mespot" until I have my internal economy put right, and that means an operation.

July 1. Everything is still very quiet. I have had a week of dinners. The "I" staff insisted on my dining as their guest, and gave me a very cheery evening. A lot of the "I" men from the armies and corps had come in for the occasion. It is interesting to see how almost all our predictions made in December last have already come true. I hope the biggest and most important of them all—peace before the New Year—is also fulfilled. The Press correspondents also entertained me to dinner. There have not been many changes among them. They complain that they have nothing to write about now. There will be plenty soon!

The news from Italy is good, if true. The Italians seem to have done well against the Austrians, and Austria is in no state to stand mishaps. If we get through the next two months, there will be a very big change in the situation everywhere.

D.H. tells me that L.G. is now very angry because the French Press, people and politicians, are attributing too large a share of the success in the war to themselves, and not giving enough credit

[1] Sir A. S. Cobbe.

to Britain for what she has done. Rather amusing, considering that a year ago he was publicly comparing our efforts with those of the French—much to our disadvantage. I wish I could hope to be alive fifty years hence to read the criticisms of the historian of the future on all these great events and the people who took prominent parts in them. I think it will be found that Asquith and Joffre get more credit than L.G. and Foch. Certainly Robertson will be far ahead of Wilson, and the greatest of all will be Kitchener. D.H.'s reputation will depend entirely upon whether he survives until the end as Commander-in-Chief. If he were to go now, I fear he would be adjudged an unsuccessful Commander-in-Chief, quite wrongly, but whoever commands in the final battles will get all the credit.

D.H. wants me to go home next week. He himself is going on leave either on the 5th or 6th.

July 13. Back again. There has been some conflict of views between G.H.Q. and Foch. The latter is now convinced that the Germans are going to attack again in strength on the Rheims front, and thinks this will be in such strength as to be more than serious. Our G.H.Q. thinks that the attack at Rheims will only be a small affair, and that the real big German offensive will come from the Lille area.

I do not see how the Germans can possibly stage even one more big attack on anything like the scale of the previous ones, unless all our calculations of their strength are wrong. Anyhow, Foch has at last got a definite plan. He has taken every one of the French divisions from our area and sent them to Rheims. He also wants 4 more British divisions for the Rheims front, and has made up his mind to use his whole available force to counterattack, if the Germans do attack, and if they do not, in the next few days, to send in an offensive at Château Thierry.

July 15. Foch has asked for a further 4 British divisions to be kept in reserve near Amiens to secure the junction of the armies. D.H. has ordered Rawlinson to prepare schemes for an attack on the Germans, if things go well with the French effort.

Everything looks well. The only possible flaw is if the Germans attack at Lille and not at Rheims, in which case Foch may hold up his attack, and we should certainly have to stop ours.

July 16. Foch has scored. The Germans attacked yesterday

THE BEGINNING OF THE END 1918

at Rheims—apparently in great strength. It is too early to speak definitely, but it looks as if it had already been held up.

There are great reductions in contemplation for our army in France, but they will not come into force before the end of these next operations.

July 18. The news from the French is very encouraging. Their counter-attack seems to have made a great deal of progress. I hope it will continue. It brings the end of the war much nearer.

The Cabinet have been very frightened about the dispatch of the XXIInd Corps to Rheims, and sent out orders to get them brought back! It is what one would expect from them. When there was no Generalissimo, they were tumbling over one another to fall in with every French plan—however wild, and however much D.H. might protest. Now that there is a Generalissimo, they are all for interfering with him. Probably what is at the back of it all in their minds is to register a protest, so that if things go wrong, they can lay the blame on Haig. Heads-we-win,-tails-you-lose attitude again!

July 21. The battle is still going well on the French front. I dined with D.H. last night. David Henderson and Lawrence and the A.D.C. were the only others there. D.H. has drafted a paper giving his general plans. If the Germans attack at Lille (which is now very improbable—almost impossible), he will counter-attack there and retake Kemmel. If they do not, he will push in Rawlinson's attack in the Amiens area early next month. He is going to meet Foch and Pershing for a conference to-morrow or the next day.

July 28. Things are moving much more rapidly than appears from the published reports, and far more decisively than seemed possible a month ago. The German retirement before the French is the beginning of the end. It is a pity they were able to get away with so little loss; but any retirement now will take the whole sting out of their army. It brings the end of the war much closer. It is quite certain that there will be no attack from Lille, and D.H. is putting every possible effort into Rawlinson's attack at Amiens. Foch has promised him a French army to co-operate.

Make no plans for the winter, anyhow for another month. We shall know then whether it will be peace or war.

August 4. It is the fourth anniversary of the war. We began with a service out of doors. A Bishop from home officiated. It was all very impressive, but I fancy very few of us had our minds on the service. It let loose such floods of memories, of hopes and of disappointments, all the host of one's friends who have been swept away in this avalanche of horrors, of one's own escapes—all the might-have-beens. I think that none of us dared, or wished, to look forward. Fate has played such strange tricks with us during these last four years. Yet as one looks back, I do not think our success was ever really imperilled except in the first few months. After them, we might not win, but we could not lose. I do not believe that the danger this year was ever as great as in 1914. It looms larger in our minds, because it is closer. 1914 is almost forgotten. One thinks of it only on anniversaries.

It is hard to picture a world at peace, and almost impossible to imagine oneself living in it. Will all our minds be obsessed with memories of war? Will those of us who survive it all, live our lives in a world that will forget? Will any of us have the strength to throw it all aside like a bad illness, and live healthy lives and think healthy thoughts again? One thing is sure. The dread of war will be with us so long as we live, like the fear of the plague, or even of death. And that, I think, will be strongest with those who win. I can well imagine the vanquished losing their dread of war in their dislike of the stigma of defeat.

August 6. We are on the eve of another battle—nothing like as big as those of 1916 and 1917, but it will be the test. The news from Germany is very satisfactory. She is feeling the pinch. I think the end is very near. Both the German Army and the German nation will go very quickly when they begin to crack.

August 9. The attack yesterday was a complete success. For once the weather helped us enormously. There was a heavy ground mist. We sent in only 11 divisions, and by nightfall had made more than 100,000 prisoners and advanced our line more than 5 miles. I was out all day and got back about midnight. Before I started back, the Germans were in full retreat, blowing up dumps of ammunition all along the line. The break-through was made by the Canadians and Australians in the centre, as the German counter-attacks were directed against the British IIIrd Corps and the French on the flanks of the attack.

The attack is going on again to-day, and the last reports are that the cavalry are at last through. There is no doubt now that there is a real crack in the German Army.

The tanks are apparently irresistible. The Germans cannot face them, and the infantry follow them in fine fettle.

I saw one very extraordinary sight. Our artillery fire had fallen on a German howitzer battery very well placed in a large gravel pit, and had slaughtered the whole of the battery before the men could get away. Some had been trying to get their guns away—some had apparently been trying to make their own escape —all were dead. It was very horrible, but a great tribute to our own men's shooting.

August 12. These are great days. We are pushing the Germans back steadily and rapidly. At some places they are still fighting well, but on the whole they are showing unmistakable signs of collapse. We have advanced over 10 miles and captured nearly 20,000 men and 300 guns, and we have not engaged anything like our whole available force. A few more weeks of this sort of thing, and the war is over. The French are coming on well on our right.

I went up again early this morning, and spent most of the day with an attacking division commanded by an old Indian friend. The German guns are not firing much; but their aeroplanes are pretty active. I saw one of our observation balloons brought down. The observer escaped by parachute quite unharmed, and with great presence of mind had brought with him his whisky and sandwiches. The balloon observers have a dull time, cooped up in a small basket and swaying about with every breath of wind. They do very long spells without relief, and although it is not especially dangerous work, they have no means of hitting back at anything that attacks them.

It is four years to-morrow since I left Aldershot for France. It seems so long ago. I hope it will only be a few months before it is all over, and we can settle down and get some rest and peace.

The whole of the Transportation Branch is being broken up. B. goes to Mesopotamia to the job that was offered to me, and others have already gone to jobs in England. The French and Americans are taking over much of the railway work. We had a visit to-day from the American Director of Railways, who is here on a flying visit from the States. I took him to see one of our big Handley Page machines start on a long-distance bombing expedition. It was commanded by an old friend of mine who was one of my air observers on the Aisne in 1914, and has been out here all through the war.

August 16. There is a lull in the fighting. The German resistance has stiffened a bit in front of the Fourth Army, and D.H. is going to put in the Third Army. There have been some sharp discussions between him and Foch about it. Foch wanted us to press straight on. D.H. refused on the ground that it was not the best method. In the end Foch gave way.

I am afraid my own time out here is coming to an end. I was medically examined to-day by Ryan. He says no Board would pass me as fit. He wanted me to go into hospital here, but I do not want to do that. I would rather have whatever is necessary done at home. It is rather maddening not to see the last few months out in France, but I am at the end of my tether. I am getting a few weeks' leave.

August 23. The Third Army attack is in full swing and going extraordinarily well. It began with some small attacks on the 21st, and to-day the big attack went in. The reports so far say that everywhere there has been complete success. There is no doubt that the Germans are beaten. It is only a matter of a few more weeks now. I lunched with D.H. yesterday and said farewell.

September 14. (*At St. Thomas's Hospital, London*). Here I am, very comfortable. I have been rather better these last few days, and the doctors have not yet decided what to do with me, but it is sure to be a pretty big operation. It is strange to have nothing to think about except oneself, and to get all one's news of the war from the newspapers. My main interest is when your attack of influenza will allow you to come to London.

APPENDIX A

NOTE ON GERMAN INTENTIONS

I. THE GENERAL SITUATION

The recent speeches of the German Chancellor and the interview of Field-Marshal von Hindenburg with the Austrian Press representatives both indicated the view held by the German authorities on the general situation.

The note struck is one of optimism, but in both it is noticeable that, while a successful issue of the war is foreseen, it is expressly stated that this issue will not be the result of feats of arms so much as of other forces.

There appears to be a considerable amount of foundation for the optimism of the German authorities. Russian military opposition is broken, and, whatever the result of the armistice negotiations, it is unlikely that Russia will be able to materially affect the military situation for some time.

Inevitably this will free a considerable number of both formed units and men as drafts, and also artillery and other material for other theatres of war.

At the same time, there is evidence that the whole of Germany does not view with unmixed satisfaction the anarchy at present reigning within Russia: the danger of the revolutionary spirit spreading to Germany is recognized. It is also apparently accepted that Germany would not be able to exploit Russian resources to her own advantage for a considerable number of months, and probably not until next year's harvest.

The Italian menace to Trieste has been definitely removed. The fighting efficiency of the Italian Army, although it appears to be recovering in some measure, is not likely to be sufficiently restored during the present war to exercise serious pressure on either Austria or Germany. At the same time, the fact that Italy is short both of coal and grain commodities, of which Germany has not a superfluity, renders it improbable that Germany will seek an independent peace with Italy. Information from our Foreign Office indicates that Austria-Hungary is not anxious to push Italy to extremities.

In the Near East the situation is not so favourable to Germany.

APPENDIX A

There are repeated reports that Bulgaria is seeking to enter into peace negotiations with the Entente. On the other hand, there is no military menace at present exerted by our force in Salonika, nor can it be held that even the participation of the Greek Army in hostilities in that theatre is likely to exert great pressure on the Central Powers in Macedonia.

The exhaustion of Turkey appears to have proceeded far. She has suffered an unbroken series of military defeats during the present year, and there are constant reports that both her governing classes and the people themselves are tired of German domination and would willingly obtain peace.

The last of Germany's colonies has now been torn from her.

On the sea, except in the Baltic, Germany has made small effort to restore her fortunes during the present year.

There is not enough evidence to enable a reliable opinion to be formed of the extent of the menace which the submarine is exerting.

Documents captured in the recent battles show conclusively that, until the present harvest eased the situation, the German Empire was suffering acutely from shortage of food, and that this had spread even to the armies in the field. The shortage in Austria-Hungary is believed to be even more acute. It is doubtful whether the resources of Rumania, of the captured portion of Italy, and such help as Russia may be able to give, will make good this shortage for the ensuing year.

The situation as regards man-power, from the point of view of the army, has, of course, been materially eased by the Russian situation. Evidence in the recent battle showed that drafts had been brought from the Eastern front into units on the Western front. In addition to this, it is clear that, in the near future, a considerable number of divisions —variously estimated at from 30 to 40—will be able to be moved to the Western front.

Nevertheless, the situation as regards man-power is still serious for Germany. In each of the preceding years of the war she has had to use two annual classes, and for the campaigns of 1918 she will only have available such troops as she can bring from the Russian front, together with not more than one annual class, unless she elects to put into the firing-line boys of 17 years of age.

The man-power of the nation at large, as opposed to the military problem, is also not satisfactory for Germany. Reliable statistics appear to indicate that the fall in Germany's birth-rate is as much as 48 per cent. from the peace figure, and in Austria-Hungary the figure quoted is 51 per cent.

A survey of the general situation, therefore, from the German point of view, leads to the conclusion that, although there does not appear to be any immediate danger of her being defeated in the field, still, the country is exhausted, both as to its military power and as to its productive possibilities.

NOTE ON GERMAN INTENTIONS

II. AGENTS' REPORTS OF GERMAN INTENTIONS

During the past few months rumours of a possible German offensive have been rife. Similar rumours have reached us in the winter and spring of all the previous years of war.

In those years varieties of objectives have been mentioned, but in each year the bulk of the reports has indicated the two extreme flanks as the most probable objectives, viz. Flanders or Alsace.

These reports are probably put about by the German agents, but, in the meantime, it must be uncertain whether the German intention is to conceal the preparations for an attack elsewhere than against the objectives mentioned, or whether she will be content to rest and train her troops in preparation for a campaign next Spring.

It is noticeable that there is a considerable number of reports of agents which mention the dates of December 10 to 25 as a possible period during which the Germans will commence an offensive.

III. ACTUAL INDICATIONS ON THE WESTERN FRONT OF GERMAN INTENTIONS

(*a*) *Location of Troops.*—The comparative density of the Germans on various portions of the front is shown in the attached graphic. It is noteworthy that, except in the Flanders area and, to a lesser degree, at Cambrai, there is in no place a sufficient concentration to justify the conclusion that an immediate offensive on a large scale is probable.

The concentration in the Flanders area is less than it was during the period of our offensive operations; the concentration at Cambrai is, of course, due to our attack on November 20 and the German counter-stroke on November 30; but even now it is nowhere near the intensity of an offensive battle front.

(*b*) *Defensive Works.*—On the British front, such works as have been noted have been markedly of a defensive nature.

During the progress of our operations in Flanders the enemy traced out hurriedly the Wercken—Hooglede and Roulers lines. Since, however, weather conditions and the state of the ground have stopped operations on a large scale in that area, he has devoted his energies to his forward defences.

A considerable number of new projected lines in rear defences is shown on a captured map of the Cambrai area.

Reports to-day indicate a deepening of the defensive area in the neighbourhood of Lens. But the whole of the defensive works on the British front are such as would be expected for the continuation of the so-called " elastic defensive " advocated and adopted by the Germans in the campaigns of 1917.

(*c*) *Artillery.*—Weather conditions have not been favourable to observation of hostile artillery during the last few weeks. So far, however, as it has been carried out, and so far as other evidence goes

APPENDIX A

(with the exception of the weakening in the Flanders area), there does not appear to have been any material alteration in the location of German artillery on the British front. French General Head-quarters state that their observations of the French front are giving similar results.

(d) *Wireless.*—During the progress of the Cambrai battle the German wireless stations were hurriedly packed up and moved from the Houthulst Forest area down towards Cambrai. During the last two days stations in the Armentières and Lens area have been packed up and moved away to some destination not yet known.

This rapid movement of wireless stations indicates rather an anxiety to discover our intentions than any offensive policy on the part of the Germans.

(e) *Train Movements.*—Observations of train movements in Belgium and Northern France during the past two or three months have been remarkably complete. A study of these justifies the conclusion that not more than 2 divisions can be moved from Russia to the Western front without our knowledge up to the present date. Thus, the total number of divisions on the Western front cannot be more than 152.

In the immediate vicinity of the front, aerial observation during the past two days has reported a considerable amount of activity, both in Flanders and in Artois.

IV. THEORETICAL CONSIDERATIONS OF THE GERMAN PROBLEM

The German problem at the present moment is to decide between :—
(a) An immediate offensive ;
(b) An offensive in the spring of 1918 ;
(c) An " elastic defensive " campaign during the whole of 1918.

If an offensive on a large scale is intended anywhere it may be accepted that it will take place on the Western front. Germany is not likely to expend her forces at the present state of the war in subsidiary campaigns which, as the German Chancellor said, cannot affect the final issue of the war.

The arguments in favour of an immediate offensive may be summarized as follows :—

Germany is probably aware, by means of her agents and by evidence contained in the British Press, that the state of the British man-power problem is unsatisfactory. She is also probably aware that this problem will probably be taken in hand by the British people in the course of the present winter, and that any deficiency will be made good before midsummer of 1918.

Germany is also probably aware of the exact number of troops sent by France and England to the Italian front. From the German point of view, 6 inferior German divisions have attracted to this minor theatre 12 British and French divisions.

Germany probably also calculates that the offensive and defensive military power of France, although better now than it was in the early stages of the present year, has not yet fully recovered.

NOTE ON GERMAN INTENTIONS

Finally, and most important of all, Germany must realize that, as 1918 passes, the United States will gradually develop an ever-increasing army on the Western front which, after midsummer, should more than replace any wastage which the Allied forces in the Western theatre are likely to suffer.

Moreover, Germany has taken into consideration the war-weariness of her allies.

The arguments against an immediate offensive and in favour of a deferred offensive in the spring of 1918 may be summarized as follows :—

So far, Germany has not been able to take advantage of the resources set free by the Russian situation.

It is calculated that divisions can move from Russia to the Western front at the rate of from 8 to 10 divisions per month. Thus, it will take Germany three to four months to move the divisions which would be set free. These divisions not only have to be brought over to the Western front: they have to be trained and equipped for fighting in this theatre.

The 1919 Class, although a certain number of them have been found in front line, were apparently considered too immature to be put into the battle during the present year. It is unlikely that this class will stand the rigours of a winter campaign. By the spring of next year, however, they would probably be ready to take part in the battle.

Germany's field army, in spite of the drafts which it has received from Russia, and in spite of the comparative quiet on the French front during the past three or four months, has suffered severely in the 1917 campaign, and, in common with the other armies of the belligerents, requires rest and training before it can take part in large movements such as would be required by an energetic offensive.

As regards the third of the alternative plans which Germany may adopt, viz., the "elastic defensive," the only argument in favour of this course must be a belief that other nations will be affected by the Russian situation. Germany is probably justified in believing that sooner or later, if Russia makes peace, Rumania will have to follow suit. If Rumania made peace, Italy and Greece would inevitably be affected, and it would be very probable that peace with these two countries would ensue.

If this were so, Germany might argue that a great impetus would be given to the pacifists both in France and in England, and if either of these countries gave way to the pacifist movement a general peace must ensue.

It must be remembered that Germany has probably now given up all idea of dictating peace and that therefore every life lost to her now represents a grave loss in the real wealth of the nation. Already her net casualties probably exceed 4,125,000 out of a total available male population of 13,600,000.

APPENDIX A

V. SUMMARY

A careful study of all these considerations appears to justify the conclusion that, although the dominant feature, viz., the economic situation in Germany, must be to a large extent shrouded in mystery, still, it can hardly be in Germany's interests to precipitate the decisive battle of the war in the immediate future.

To have full advantage of the varying factors as they present themselves at present, Germany's plan would appear to be :—

(*a*) To spend the winter in as much quiet on the front as she can, evading all offensive operations, and where an offensive against her is contemplated evading it in so far as she can by the " elastic defensive." During the winter she can bring over from Russia such of her best troops as can be spared from that theatre, and from those which remain on the Eastern front she should seek drafts for her Western units.

(*b*) She should seek to conceal her real point of attack on the Western front by various rumours, by camouflage works and other expedients.

(*c*) In the early spring (not later than the beginning of March) she should seek to deliver such a blow on the Western front as would force a decisive battle which she could fight to a finish before the American forces could take an active part, i.e. before midsummer.

For such a battle it is essential that Germany should choose a battlefield where the Allies are defending some objective of vital importance to them. By this means alone can Germany ensure that the Allies do not escape the blow by short retreats and delaying actions. Numerous objectives of this nature are offered on the Western front, e.g. Verdun, Nancy, Châlons, Rheims, Amiens, Béthune, Hazebrouck, and Dunkirk.

J. C.,
Brigadier-General, General Staff.

General Staff (Intelligence),
    GENERAL HEAD-QUARTERS,
    December 6, 1917.

APPENDIX B

NOTE ON THE SITUATION FROM A GERMAN POINT OF VIEW AT THE END OF 1917

The ruling factors in the situation for the Germans are :—
1. Man-power.
2. The stability of existing alliances.
3. The economic situation
4. The internal political situation.
5. The military situation.

Man-power.—The successes in Russia and Italy will enable Germany to transfer a considerable proportion of her armed forces from the Eastern and South-Eastern theatres to the Western theatre, but will not increase the annual resources available for next year's campaign. During previous years, Germany has required to spend two annual classes together with the equipment of about half a class obtained by combing her industry. At the present moment she has called up the last class which can be claimed by law this year. The situation as regards classes at present is :—

1918 Class : Finished as a source of drafts.
1919 Class : Partially in front-line units on the Western front.
Partially in front-line units and depots on the Eastern front.
Partially in frontier units.
Considerable number in depots in Germany.
1920 Class : Being called up, and will soon be in depots in Germany.

The 1918 class proved to be bad fighting material in 1917. The 1919 class, therefore, was not considered sufficiently trustworthy to take the field on the Western front.

It is noteworthy that the same reasons which prevented the Germans using the 1919 class in this year's campaign will equally, if not to a greater extent, prevent the use of the 1920 class during the campaign of 1918, unless forced to do so by the most urgent necessity.

Ultimately, then, to meet the casualties which she will suffer in 1918, Germany can rely on :—

(*a*) The 1919 class.

APPENDIX B

(b) Men combed from industries and returned wounded.
(c) Units transferred from the Russian front, either as complete units or as drafts.

German industry has already been combed six times and it is improbable now that very much strength can be obtained from this source, except in so far as Italian prisoners and Russian labour may prove able to replace German labour in her factories. An estimate of the extent to which this can be done cannot be made here, but it seems fair to allow an additional 100,000 men as available for combing during 1918.

With regard to the transfer of complete units from Russia, recorded train movements do not at present show any intense or continuous movements on a large scale from East to West. Possibly this may be due to anxiety as to the situation in Russia; equally possibly, however, it may be owing to that fact that already over 85,000 men have been transferred from East to West, and those remaining on the Eastern front are now immature and old men.

It was estimated in August that approximately 30 divisions would be available for transfer from East to West. Of this number some 10 have already been transferred, but there seems no reason to alter the estimate of a possible transfer of the remainder, viz., 20 in the course of the next few months.

The maximum rate at which such transfer could take place is 10 divisions in any one month from Russia, or 8 divisions per month over a space of 2–3 months, in addition to 1 or 2 from Austria or Italy.

It will be seen, therefore, that the situation of the Germans with regard to man-power for the campaigns of 1918 is not, in fact, materially better than was the situation at the end of last year for the campaigns of 1917. This is, however, regarding the problem solely from the German point of view and without reference to any fluctuations which may have occurred in the Allied man-power problem.

Summing up, it may be stated that Germany can afford to expend from 900,000 to 1,000,000 casualties during 1918.

The Stability of Existing Alliances.—For some time past we have had continuous reports that Austria-Hungary, and particularly the Emperor, regards an early peace as a vital necessity. The last reports indicate that the Emperor has weakened slightly in his views and has fallen more under the influence of Count Czernin, who now apparently wishes to fight on until a military decision is reached. On the other hand, information from Vienna shows that both the food situation and the health of the country must be causing great disquiet to the Austrian Government. There is no reason to anticipate that under any circumstances Austria could be induced to make a separate peace with the Entente. On the other hand, there is small doubt that all her influence with Germany will be exerted on the side of an early peace, even if only moderate terms were secured.

Information from Palestine definitely states that Turkey is denuded of her male population and that the troops now fighting there are immature.

A well-informed American source, dated from Constantinople as late as the middle of November, states that there is a rising tide of feeling against both the Germans and their principal agent in Turkey, Enver Bey. The same source states that Turkey has undoubtedly been influenced by the removal of the threats against Constantinople. It seems probable, therefore, that the attitude of Turkey and the possibility of her forming a separate peace has been causing anxiety to the German Higher Command.

As regards Bulgaria, information from a well-informed French source states that the Government, in a vote of confidence on October 29, only obtained a majority of nine votes. Bulgaria is now in possession of all that she started in the war to obtain. She has shown no inclination to waste her man-power in further attacks on the Allied Armies in Salonika. She has never professed any affection for her German allies. As in the case of Turkey, therefore, so with Bulgaria, the possibility of a separate peace must be causing anxiety to the German authorities.

As against these influences tending to detract from the stability of Germany's alliances must be set the influences of the continued successes of Germany's policy, both in Russia and Italy.

On the whole, it would seem to be unduly optimistic to expect the breaking up of the alliance in the immediate future, although the possibility of such event would necessarily weigh heavily in the German scales if peace proposals were negotiated either by the Central Powers or the Entente.

The Economic Situation.—Reports which reach G.H.Q. regarding the economic situation continue to show that, although there is no immediate prospect of starvation, the pressure of the shortage of food and other necessaries is telling on the will-power.

There appears to be no reason to anticipate that the food situation will improve materially before the harvest of 1918 is gathered. Even if Germany were able to take over possession of South-Eastern Russia, it is unlikely that she would obtain and be able to transport to Germany supplies on a sufficiently large scale for the danger months, viz. June and July.

Apart from food, the most noticeable shortage of necessaries appears to be in leather, linen fabrics, copper, paper and rubber.[1]

---

[1] With regard to rubber, it is interesting to note that during the last few weeks the Germans have been sending over propaganda wrapped up in rubber packets, made apparently of good natural rubber. Probably this was only to impress us. It is possible that, although answering to the tests we were able to make locally for rubber, it is in fact a synthetic. We have had records here of synthetic rubber being manufactured.

APPENDIX B

In the course of the Cambrai battle one of the first definite indications that the shortage of food had extended to the German Army itself was obtained. A captured order showed that for the few weeks immediately before October 3 the German front-line troops had been placed on reduced rations, on the ground that the food saved was necessary for the maintenance of the home country. The order continued that the necessary diminution in the ration of the field troops had ceased when the 1917 harvest became available. But it is a fair deduction that a similar necessity for reducing the ration of the front-line troops will occur even earlier in 1918 than it did in 1917.

The Internal Political Situation.—During the whole of 1917 the political situation in Germany has been dominated by the fight between the civil and the military parties. The Civil Party is led by Kuhlmann, at present the Foreign Minister. Hertling, the present Chancellor, is not popular, and it is believed that in due course he will give place to Kuhlmann as Chancellor.

The Military Party is led by Ludendorff and Tirpitz. Hindenburg is stated to have refused to allow himself to be mixed up with politics.

The Kaiser appears to have wavered during most of the year between the two parties, now inclining to the one and then to the other.

The fall of Bethmann Hollweg was almost certainly due to a conflict of opinion between him and the Military Party.

Michaelis, who succeeded him, was believed to be a ready tool of the Military Party.

Count Hertling, the present Chancellor, is an astute parliamentarian, apparently charged with the duty of making concessions which will appear large, but which will, in fact, be small, to the democratic parties in the Parliament. In due course he will give place to either Kuhlmann, if the civil authority in Germany becomes predominant, or to some nominee of the Military Party, if that party should obtain supreme power.

It is a remarkable fact at present that although the Socialist Majority Party has conformed to the Government requirements and is now in no sense independent, the Minority Socialists who were independent and anti-war, although a small party in the Reichstag, appear to be acquiring increased support in the country. Recent Municipal Elections have shown that the sympathies of the peoples of the larger towns are predominantly with the Minority Socialists.

In close connexion with the political situation in Germany must be considered the question of the freedom of the Press.

When Hertling came into power there were great promises of the removal of the political censorship. So far, however, this has not materialized into any great independence on the part of any of the more important newspapers. It seems probable that the increased liberty of the Press, if there is any increase in its liberty, will be more than counteracted by the restrictions imposed by the lack of paper, and a strict control over the news which issues from the Government offices.

NOTE ON THE GERMAN SITUATION, 1917

Captured correspondence, although showing a great deal of suffering within Germany itself, and a very large amount of war-weariness, has displayed little anti-monarchical, or even Socialistic, tendencies. There is, therefore, no reason to believe that in the immediate future there will be any such Socialistic movement within Germany itself, as to force the Government's hand to a premature peace. At the same time, the wiser heads in Germany must realize that although the reckoning will not probably come during the war, it will follow rapidly on the conclusion of peace, and it will be the more bitter the longer peace is deferred.

It is possible that the Military Party may entertain hopes that the political reckoning may be displaced by a great military success and a victorious peace, but it is unlikely that the Emperor or the Civil Cabinet can share this belief.

The Military Situation.—The military situation has been summed up so often in recent papers that it is only necessary to summarize it briefly.

It is calculated that, with the present situation in Russia and Italy, Germany can raise her forces in the Western theatre to a total of 179 divisions, and can increase the present number of her guns by some 1,600 heavy artillery, brought from the Eastern front.

Although a certain number of Austrian troops may be brought, and probably will be brought, as a concession to political principles, to the Western theatre, it is unlikely that these Austrian troops will be there in such numbers as to affect the strategical problem. Nor is it likely that Austrians will prove formidable adversaries under the conditions obtaining in France and Flanders.

It is so unlikely as not to merit serious consideration, that either Bulgarian troops or Turkish troops will be brought in any numbers to the Western theatre.

It has been shown at the beginning of this paper that the ultimate resources upon which Germany can depend for next year's campaign amount to approximately 1,000,000 men.

Even with 179 divisions on the Western front and artillery increased by 1,600 heavy guns, and reinforcements amounting to 1,000,000 men, Germany will be left with an inferiority in almost every particular to the Allies when the American strength has been developed to the extent anticipated by midsummer of 1918.

In the early spring, however, Germany will have a superiority in numbers, although an inferiority in artillery, on the Western front.

German morale at the present moment, consequent on the German successes in Russia and in Italy, and on the hope of an early peace, is higher than it has been at any time in the campaign in France since 1915. This access in morale is, however, not of a very permanent character, and it is not likely to stand the strain of an unsuccessful attack, with the consequent heavy losses.

APPENDIX B

On the other hand, a successful attack, even when the success is only a limited advance, would maintain, and probably enhance, the morale of the German Army.

The alternatives, then, before the German Higher Command are :—

(1) To deliver an attack, or attacks, on a very large scale in the Western front, with a view to knocking out either England or France, or both, before American power can develop;

(2) To await our attack in its present situation, trusting to war-weariness and pacifism in England and in France, and the effect of the submarine campaign, bringing about a state of mind in which the German peace terms would be accepted;

(3) To take advantage of the present opportunity to offer peace terms.

The main arguments in favour of the first of these (an attack or attacks on the Western front) are :—

(*a*) The morale of the French Army was known to be bad in the month of June, 1917. The German Higher Command has never regarded the French fighting qualities as being such as are likely to be capable of resisting a determined effort by the Germans in full force;

(*b*) The present military situation is on the whole more favourable to Germany than any with which she has been faced during the past 3 years of the war;

(*c*) Without a decisive military success to finish the war, the Military Party in Germany will inevitably lose position and power, as it is probable that Germany will be ruined by internal dissensions; indeed, the economic conditions at present obtaining in the world are such as will not enable Germany to recover readily her commerce unless she is able to dictate terms of peace to her enemies.

The arguments in favour of the second of these courses (to await our attack and trust to the effect of war-weariness in France and in England) will appear to be :—

(*a*) The course of the war during the last 2 years has shown the great strength of the defensive. If Germany, fighting on three fronts, was able to resist the attacks of the French and the British in 1917, then she can look forward with confidence to be able to resist the attacks of even the French, British and the Americans in 1918;

(*b*) The waste in Germany's man-power in an attack without being successful, will be fatal to her future prosperity, and it would therefore be better to minimize this loss by accepting a defensive attitude for the next year;

(*c*) German propaganda in Italy and Russia had met with great success; opportunities already exist for propaganda in France, and with the conclusion of peace in Russia, these opportunities will become much greater;

(*d*) The attitude of the Scandinavian powers appears to be steadily

NOTE ON THE GERMAN SITUATION, 1917

changing in favour of Germany. If, however, Germany becomes again the aggressor, then, likely, there will be a reaction in Scandinavia, as in all the small neutrals, against the predominance of any one power in Europe.

The arguments against this course are :—

(1) However willing Germany might be to accept a defensive attitude for another year, it is to the greatest extent improbable that Austria, Bulgaria and Turkey would agree to be partners in such a course. Austria, in particular, is known to regard an early peace as almost a vital necessity to her Empire. All the evidence which reaches us from Palestine shows that Turkey is nearing the end of her resources, as of her patience. Bulgaria has in her possession all that she went to war to obtain ;

(2) Although another year would probably produce a considerable increase in pacifism in France and in England, it would equally make stronger the independent Socialists and the pacifists within Germany itself ;

(3) The financial burden of Germany is probably now as great as she can ever hope to meet. This burden would be materially increased by another year of war.

(4) A peace after a year's defensive war, however unsuccessful the Allies' attacks may be, would inevitably be a compromise peace, in which Germany could have no hopes of dictating terms. Even if and when the Allies' offensive failed, Germany in 1919 would not be able herself to take the offensive.

The arguments in favour of the third of these alternative courses, viz. the offer of favourable peace terms at the present juncture, are the converse of the arguments given above.

Although the Military Party in Germany would not be able to claim the war as a decisive victory for Germany, still they would be left in a position so favourable as they might hope to retain sufficient influence within Germany to enable them to risk again a trial of war within the next few years, and before their power had entirely disappeared.

Germany has probably taken due note of the reception which Lord Lansdowne's letter received in the Press in England.

Generally, this was favourable throughout the provinces, and unfavourable in London.

Germany is probably also well aware of the general strike which was threatened by the industrials in France at the time of the fall of Malvy, and she is also probably aware that the danger of such a strike is never long absent from the mind of the French Government.

It is impossible to say what estimate Germany has put upon the effect of the submarine campaign. The claims which she makes in the Press must be well known to her authorities to be false.

On the other hand, she cannot be blind to the increasing shortage of provisions now apparent in Great Britain.

APPENDIX B

Above all it seems certain that the great fear which Germany now has is of an economic war after the conclusion of peace. The surest method of avoiding this economic war must be a peace by negotiation and compromise, in which neither side can claim decisive victory.

J. CHARTERIS, Brig.-General.

December 28, 1917.

APPENDIX C

THE GERMAN PEACE PROPOSALS

The history of the initiation of the present German peace proposals has become somewhat obscure. It is well to recapitulate.

When Russia asked Germany to meet her representatives at a peace conference she did so, so far as is known at present, with the intention of making a separate peace. The various Labour parties throughout the Allied countries apparently then addressed representations to the Soviet urging that no separate peace should be made. Russia, however, did not officially change her view. Her attitude towards her Allies was rather one of a threat. The Allies could join her if they cared to, but if they did not care to, then she would proceed alone with her task.

It is interesting to remember that Kerensky, as far back as August, said that Russia would be unable to fight on through this year under any circumstances.

To the Russian peace proposals—which were, in fact, contained in the principle "no annexations and no indemnities"—Germany replied by saying that she was prepared to accept these principles as the basis of a general peace, but not as the basis of a separate peace with Russia.

The reason of this is not far to seek. One of Germany's greatest assets at present is the Russian territory which she holds. This she would use to bargain with at a general peace conference. If she makes a separate peace with Russia prior to the general peace conference, then she loses thereby several of the cards which she hoped to play; particularly so if the separate peace with Russia is on the basis of "no annexations."

Although the German offer does not at present go as far as was laid down by the British Prime Minister and President Wilson in their various speeches, it is noteworthy that the only points of difference at present are :—

(a) The Prime Minister said that the disposal of the colonies would be referred to the peace conference. The Germans say at present that their colonies must be given back unconditionally.

(b) President Wilson and the British Prime Minister have, at one

APPENDIX C

time or another, stated that reparation must be made to Belgium. The Germans expressly exclude this from their present offer.

(*c*) The British Prime Minister has expressly said that Palestine, Armenia and Mesopotamia will, under no circumstances, be given back to Turkey, but states that the future of these countries must be decided by international agreement at the conference. The German peace terms imply that the fate of these lands cannot be a matter for the conference, and accepts, anyhow, the possibility of their being restored to Turkey.

It is noteworthy that the main points of difference here are chiefly words. Thus, the question whether or not the German colonies are returned to Germany is clearly one of bargaining and of money. Germany obviously, in her present financial circumstances, would be prepared to sell some or all of her colonies. Equally obviously it would be cheaper for us to buy the colonies now than to fight on for a year and then obtain them by right of conquest. Similarly, the question of the restoration of Belgium is not, in point of fact, a practical difficulty. At the present moment, if Germany were to make peace she could not restore Belgium by a cash contribution, because she has not got the cash to do so. She could start a credit with Belgium, but this, in fact, would put Belgium under her domination, and would, therefore defeat more than ever the Allies' aims. Equally would it be undesirable for German workmen to penetrate into Belgium and to do the actual work of restoration. Therefore, if Belgium is to be restored ultimately the cost of restoration must come from the Allies. The amount in any case would not be comparable with the cost of a year's war.

Similarly, the questions of Mesopotamia, Armenia and Palestine do not present a serious ground of difference, because Turkey, in her present state, would obviously be prepared, and more than prepared, to sell her rights in one or all of these countries, and would probably prefer to do so to the other alternative, which would be internationalization.

It is quite clear that the Allies cannot, at the present moment, refuse to consider seriously the German peace terms, although they may decide to refuse them. Such a consideration at the present juncture should be clear of sentiment, and the following main points in forming an opinion should be borne in mind, viz. :—

(*a*) The terms as they stand as offered by the Germans can, in no sense, be interpreted as a German victory. They are not the terms which Germany set out the war to obtain. Equally certainly, however, they are not the terms of a wholly defeated country determined to obtain peace at any price.

(*b*) Theoretically, the terms of peace, as they stand, leave Germany free to renew the struggle at any time she may desire to do so. Actually, however, the question of whether any country will renew the struggle is one of natural laws and chiefly of human nature. No treaty can render the struggle impossible or even defer it indefinitely if the peoples of the countries are determined to continue to settle their quarrels by force. While it is impossible to prophesy, there are certain indications that a peace formed on the present lines would be shortly followed by such a movement towards democracy in Germany as would probably render very distant the chance of Germany renewing the struggle in the next fifty years. Beyond that it will, under no circumstances, be possible to look.

(c) The alternative to a peace by negotiation at the present moment would appear in all probability to be another year or two years of war. At the end of this time it is reasonably certain that Germany would have to accept the terms of a defeated belligerent. On the other hand, it is also equally certain that France, already nearly completely exhausted, in two years' time would be so exhausted that she would have little chance of recovering her productive power. England at present is in good condition relative to her immediate neighbours, viz. Germany, France, Austria and Italy. At the end of two years of war, even if victorious, her man-power would have been so affected that she would be in a very little better position than France. England at the present moment is solvent. At the end of two years she would probably be bankrupt to America.

(d) The situation of America alone among the Allies justifies her in her determination to continue the war. For her this will have two main results :—

1st: The unification of her varied peoples into one homogeneous nation;

2nd: Supremacy of wealth and influence throughout the civilized world. It is probable, in fact, that, in two more years of war, begun to prevent Germany obtaining the hegemony of Europe, Europe would have to accept the hegemony of the United States.

(e) Against all these arguments, which admittedly tend towards the acceptance of the principle of peace by negotiation at the present juncture, there must be set the following :—

(1) A peace by negotiation at present might well result in the colonies breaking away from the mother country, and would almost certainly result in Belgium deciding that her future security would be better ensured by a close alliance with Germany than by treaties with her present Allies.

(2) One of the most beneficial results which can be anticipated from the war, both from the point of view of Great Britain and from that of mankind, would be a strong alliance between the United States and Great Britain. This would inevitably result, if the war continues during 1918 and 1919 and if America and Great Britain fight as Allies during these years, but it will then be an alliance in which Great Britain will occupy the position of the junior partner.

APPENDIX C

If peace by negotiation should ensue now it is doubtful whether an alliance between the United States and Great Britain would necessarily result, but if such alliance did result, it would be one on which the two countries would meet on terms of equality.

(3) It is noteworthy that, at the present moment, with the exception of small portions of Turkey, Austria-Hungary and Persia, which are in the hands of Russia, and with the exception of a very small portion of Haute Alsace which is in the hands of France, Great Britain is the only one of Germany's present enemies which holds German territory, and which, therefore, will enter the conference room with something to bargain.

Thus, at the conference, while our Allies will be those who will require something from Germany, even if that something is only the evacuation of their own territory, Great Britain on the other hand will be the only one of the Allies from which Germany will have to require the evacuation of her territory.

It is clear, therefore, that negotiations on the basis as at present enunciated would be likely to lead to great probabilities of friction between ourselves and our Allies. The formula of "no annexations and no indemnities" cannot then be accepted as in itself a solution of the present problems of the peace conference. On the other hand, it may form a basis of discussion from which a formula of more general application and in greater consonance with the needs of Great Britain may be evolved. For example, if instead of "no annexations" is read "no annexations of the home territory of any of the belligerent powers," and if for "no indemnities" is read "no punitive indemnities," a basis of discussion which we could clearly accept is at once reached.

It might be possible to submit frankly to the belligerent powers the definite proposal that the following questions will be submitted for consideration at the conference without any prejudice to the decisions which would be arrived at there :—

1st: The question of the colonies;
2nd: The question of German shipping in Entente hands;
3rd: The question of compensation for damage done to territories owing to the occupation by an opposing belligerent power.

It is noteworthy that this is in conformity with the memorandum of the Trade Unions Congress in England and also of the resolution of the workers of France, and apparently also of the Soviets of Russia.

The final decision as to which of the policies is most in our interests must depend upon a consideration, not only of the arguments given above, but also of such even more important ones as :—

(1) The present state of British man-power and the possibility of maintaining units at strength;

(2) The submarine campaign and its probable effect in six months' time on the food supply of Great Britain and her Allies, and on the transportation of man-power from America to Europe;

(3) The possibility that pacifism may spread through the Allied powers to such an extent as to force peace before military victory has been obtained.

The first necessity at the present moment is to estimate clearly what we can do if it is decided to continue the struggle until a decision is arrived at by force of arms. The history of the campaigns in France and Italy of 1916 and 1917 shows very clearly that if one or other of the Allies is pressed by the enemy to breaking-point, then relief cannot be given by the other Allies sending troops to fill the gap but only by these Allies themselves attacking. This is a strategical principle clearly realized before the war, but apparently sometimes forgotten in the course of the war. If England should have to help France, and if this help should be necessary to prevent the French front being broken, then that help can only be given by an attack by British troops. Unless the man-power in Britain is to be so exploited as to render feasible an attack in the case of necessity by the British troops, then it should be clearly realized that Great Britain cannot in 1918 render efficient assistance to France. The converse is equally true as regards assistance which Great Britain might demand and France might seek to give in the case of a German attack coming against the British front.

Similarly, it is essential before deciding on what, if any, answer is to be given to the German proposals, that the food situation should be estimated and placed clearly before the Military authorities, who will have to give an opinion on the strategical situation. For the question of food, both to the actual men in the front line and to their relatives at Home, affects vitally the fighting power of the troops.

There is a big range between well-fed troops, secure in the confidence of their relatives being well provided for at Home, and troops receiving insufficient nourishment and anxious about the food supplies of their relatives at Home.

Finally, it is essential that the attitude of the great unions and of labour generally in the Allied countries should be very clearly estimated and placed before the Military authorities.

Pacifism at Home must inevitably affect the fighting efficiency of the troops in the field.

J. CHARTERIS,
Brigadier-General, General Staff.

General Staff (Intelligence),
  GENERAL HEAD-QUARTERS,
    December 30, 1917.

INDEX

A

ADMIRALTY, and propaganda, 167
Aeroplanes, direction of artillery fire by, 36, 39
African troops, in fighting round Ypres, 88
Air photography, 77, 82, 88, 155, 289, 290
Air-raids, 257, 263, 309
Air reconnaissances, good work by, 163
Aisne, the, orders to seize the crossing of, 31; battle of (1914)—and after, 34 *et seq.*; lesson of first battle of, 48; lack of reinforcements, etc., recalled, 155; German attack (1918) on, 310–313
Aitken, Max, and Press interviews, 194 (*see* also Beaverbrook, Lord)
Aldershot, precautionary orders received at, 5; departure from, 8
Allenby, General (afterwards F.-M. Viscount), nickname and a characteristic of, 210–211; rumoured offer of reversion of Haig's command to, 273
Allied Military Attachés, visit from, 242
Allies, and German peace proposals, 335–338
Alsace-Lorraine, as reported German objective, 198, 199
Alsatian deserters, 123

America, Lord Bryce and, 160; suggested propaganda for, 171; enters the war, 207
American characteristics, as compared with those of the French, 310
American G.H.Q., visit to, 261
American journalists, Northcliffe on, 196 (note)
American troops, fill gaps in British ranks, 298; physique of, 307, 309
Americans arrive in France, 235; author's faith in intentions of, 299–300
Amery, L. S., association with, 50; important Intelligence information from, 55
Amiens, conference with Pétain at, 225; a joint church service at, 289; German thrust towards (1918), 291 *et seq.*
Amiens Cathedral, sketched under difficulties, 171
Ammunition Committee, visit from members of, 101–102
Ammunition, shortage of, 55, 59, 81, 82, 92, 93, 98, 99, 250 (and *passim*)
Ancre, the, German attacks on driven off, 195; enemy retirement from, 197
"Angel of Mons," story of, 25–26; probable source of, 75
Antwerp, fall of, 45
Army Commanders, conference at Doullens, 294, 295 (note)

341

INDEX

Army head-quarters, life during lull of battle at, 77–78
Army in the field, difficulty of appreciating vastness of organization of, 208–210
Arras, plans for attack near, 132, 191; battle of (1917), 207 *et seq.*; German onslaught near (1918), 295
Artillery (heavy), lack of, 40–41, 45 (and *passim*); superiority of German, 36, 59
Artists' impressions of the war, scheme to secure, 176
Artois attack by the French fails, 116
Asquith, Right Hon. H. H. (afterwards Earl of Oxford and Asquith), convenes Council of War (3 Aug., 1914), 7; visits the front, 95, 164; Haig's interview with, 124; as politician, 133; supports Kitchener, 137; fall of his Government, 179–180; author's opinion of, 180, 252; and Caillaux, 229; on politicians, 245
Asquith, Raymond, joins Intelligence Staff, 131
Attachés (foreign), rule regarding, 62
Aubers Ridge attack, overruled, 104
Australians, their success in Somme battle, 161, 163; their desire for publicity, 245, 246
Austria, a reported impending attack on Italy by lacks confirmation, 261; attack materializes: Italians ingloriously defeated, 262
Austria-Hungary, separate peace by considered unlikely, 275; food shortage in, 322, 328; reported desire for peace, 328, 333

B

BAIRD, D., appointed to Staff of Indian Cavalry, 63
Baird, J. (afterwards Lord Stonehaven), 50
Balfour, Right Hon. A. J. (afterwards Earl), visits the front, 87; a probable "philosophic doubt" of, 174; and Press interviews, 194; "coquetting with peace," 288
Balkan War (1912), 3
Balkans, the, Government "terrified by," 124
Bankers, alleged vindictive action towards a former employé, 154
Banning, Lieut., killed by a shell, 56
Bapaume, reported capture of, 202; aftermath of war in, 269
Barges, as "hospital ships," 89
Bavarians, tribute to fighting by, 170
Bazentin le Grand, capture of, 166
Bazentin le Petit, capture of, 166
Beaurepaire, Foch at, 301
Beaverbrook, Lord, insists on more publicity for work of Canadians, 211; favours interviews by correspondents with Haig, 254; visits G.H.Q., 255
Belgian area, women's ambulance work in, 313
Belgian coast, proposals for attacks along, discussed, 74
Belgian frontier reported to be closed, 203
Belgian G.H.Q., author at, 150; and the German peace proposals, 224
Belgians, and the Channel ports, 38
Belgium, conscription conditions in, criticized, 47; rumours of

Belgium—(*continued*)
possible German offensive in, 203
Beresford, Lord Charles, impressions of, 231–232
Berlin, an epidemic in, 186; strikes in, 217
Bethmann Hollweg, Lord Haldane's view of, 102; fall of and what ascribed, 330
Béthune, incident at a tea-shop in, 123; signs of enemy activity at, 288
Billeting, as a "lucky bag," 22
Blackwood's Magazine, article on incidents at Ypres in, 80
Boesinghe, 190
Bols, Lieut.-Col. (afterwards Sir Louis), prophecy of war by, 3
Bone, Muirhead, war pictures by, 153; Haig impressed by, 171; sketches Amiens Cathedral during imprisonment, 171; his sketch of author, 229–230; author's tribute to his picture of Haig, 230 (note)
Bonnet, head-quarters at, 15, 16
Boulogne, inspiring spectacle at, 63; tours of inspection to, 283, 306
Boulogne Harbour, British collier sunk in fairway of, 107
Bourg, incident at, 36
Bourlon, lack of reserves prevents capture of, 270
Bourne, Cardinal, visits G.H.Q., 261
Briand, M., presses for better film propaganda, 159; and de Castelnau's appointment, 204
British Army in France, handed over to Nivelle, 200; Haig, responsible for safety of, objects to Foch's action, 313; talk of further reductions in, 314

British Cabinet, rumoured trouble in, 121
B.E.F., plan of operation for discussed at War Council (3 Aug. 1914), 7; reception in France, 10, 11; intended grouping into Armies of, 65; again reorganized, 101
British G.H.Q., composition of criticized by Haig, 10
Bruhl, M. (French Socialist), visits the front, 97
Bruyère, G.H.Q. conference at, 15
Bryce, Lord, visits the front, 160
Buchan, Col. John, as war news official, 147, 149, 153, 170; speaks at a St. Andrew's Night dinner, 179; Northcliffe and, 196 (note)
Bucquoi-Loupart Wood line, enemy retirement to, 198
Bulfin, Brigadier-General, and first battle of Ypres, 39, 48, 49
Bulgaria, question of neutrality of, 99, 100; Germany apprehensive of a separate peace by, 275, 276; reported peace negotiations by, 322, 329, 333
Bulou, von, "Experiences of the Somme Battle," by, 214
Bülow, Count, rumoured object of his mission to Rome, 64
Burgess, Captain L., 172
Burnham, Lord, visit to G.H.Q. during battle of the Somme, 157; takes offence at not being officially asked to visit the front, 248
Bury, Howard, political news from, 65
Butler, Lieut.-Gen. (now Sir R. H.), visits Haig, 100; report on weather prospects at Loos taken to, 113; Haig's desire for services of as C.G.S., 125, 126;

Butler, Lieut.-Gen.—*(continued)* at a New Year's dinner (1916), 129; leaves G.H.Q. for a command, 286
Byng, General, takes Vimy Ridge, 213–214

C

CABINET, and Haig, 223, 250, 273, 281, 290, 308 (and *passim*); alarmed at possibilities of the Generalissimo arrangement, 311–312; and Foch, 317
Cable, Boyd, 251
Cadorna, General, and Supreme War Council, 267
Caillaux, M., and French finances, 229
Calais, scenes in prior to and after Britain enters the war, 10; conference at (Feb. 1917), 199–200; question of responsibility for proposals at conference, 204; tour of inspection to, 306; head-quarters of First-Aid Nursing Yeomanry, 313
Cambrai, battle of, 270 *et seq.*
Canadians, in action, 210, 211, 244; their desire for publicity, 245
Capper, General (formerly Staff College Commandant at Quetta), 58
Carson, Lord, visit from, 252; asked by Cabinet to supervise arrangements for publicity at home, 258
Cassel, conferences at (1914), 57; (Dec. 1916), 181
"Caterpillar" tractor, experiments at Aldershot with, 165 (note)
Cavalry in war, author's opinion on, 29

Cecil, Lord E., proposal *re* Press work for, 225
Cecil, Lord Robert, author's impressions of, 224
Censor, the, encouraging report from regarding letters from troops, 304
Censorship, 94
Chamberlain, Rt. Hon. Austen, pessimism *re* home affairs, 269
Champagne, success in, 116; German attack in, of no strategical importance, 199
Channel ports, German push for forestalled, 46; reported intention of Government *re*, 100; author's anxiety *re*, 299, 303, 308
Chantilly, visit to G.Q.G. at, 111
Charrier, Colonel (commanding Munster Fusiliers), death of, 23
Charteris, Brigadier-General John, relinquishes Staff appointment in India, 3; *re* possibility of war, 3–4; "Field-Marshal Earl Haig," by, 7 (note), 297 (note); sees Joffre for first time, 23; on change of command in 5th French Army, 26; Legion of Honour for and appointed G.S.O. for Intelligence, 28; on duties of British Intelligence service, 37–38; on a week of crises, 51 *et seq.*; and Sir Henry Wilson, 65, 73, 87 (and *passim*); appointed G.S.O. of "Operations Staff," and transferred to charge of "Intelligence" work, 67, 71; talk with Lord Esher, 85–86; D.S.O. awarded to, 99; brevet lt.-colonelcy for, 106; introduced to Joffre, 125–126; at

INDEX

Charteris, Brigadier-General John
—*(continued)*
memorial service for Kitchener,
147; chairman of St. Andrew's
Night dinner in Paris, 179;
gazetted full Colonel, 185; conference with General Pershing,
234; a typical day's work of,
246; offers Haig his resignation, 268; hands over charge
of Intelligence and becomes
Deputy Inspector-General of
Transportation, 277; resolution to leave Army as soon as
war circumstances permit, 301,
307

Chemin des Dames ridge, attempts at advance to, 34–35;
British objective on not secured, 41; successful attack
on, 223

Choques, head-quarters at, 96

" Christ in Flanders " (poem published in *The Spectator*), quoted,
268

Churchill, Right Hon. Winston,
leaves the Admiralty, 95;
author on, 95, 252; resignation of, 121; at G.H.Q., 123;
topics discussed, 130–131; and
Haig, 226, 268, 273, 274; appointed Minister of Munitions,
243

Cinematograph films, censored,
204

Circular letter to Trade Unions,
and its signatories, 226, 227

Clemenceau, M., visits the front,
172–173; Poincaré and, 266;
and Supreme War Council,
274–275; and Palestine scheme,
284; suspicions of Rawlinson,
287; Haig and, 287, 288; at
Doullens conference, 294, 295
(note); overrules Foch, 313

Clyde workers on strike, 80

Coalition Government formed,
179

Colonial troops (French), 37,
39

Combrie Castle, departure from
Southampton on, 9

Communiqués, German, misleading, 165–166

Compulsory Service Bill, Sir J.
Simon and, 131

Connaught, Duke of, visits the
front, 175

Conscription, need of suggested
to Asquith, 95; and pressed
on Kitchener, 105–106

Co-ordination, Wilson's scheme
for, 265, 267

Copper shortage in Germany,
221, 329

Correspondence (German), captured and what disclosed by,
152

Counter-attacks, author sceptical
regarding, 240

Cowans, Sir John (Quartermaster-General), 138, 241; visit from,
314

Crauford, Lord, joins Intelligence
Staff, 148–149; promoted to
Cabinet rank, 152–153, 158

Crewe, Lord, and Lloyd George,
148

" Crucified Canadian " story,
source of, 75 (note)

Cuirassiers sent to assist British:
their appearance, 49

Curzon, Lord, visits the front, 87;
at G.H.Q., 135; and the attack
on Kitchener, 137; administrative ability of, 185; and the
D.H. interviews, 194, 195, 196;
pessimism at a Cabinet meeting,
233; and Haig, 273

Czernin, Count, his power in
Austria-Hungary, 275; views
on peace, 328

D

"DAILY CHRONICLE," Sir Sidney Low's poem in, cited, 300
Dammartin, G.H.Q. deserted at, 28
D'Annunzio, Gabrielle, visits the front, 221
Danube theatre of war, hostile strength in (Sept. 1917), 255
Dardanelles scheme, question of responsibility for, 95 ; opinion of British and French on, 98–99 ; Cabinet and War Office desire more troops for, 100 ; failure of, 120, 231
Davidson, Major-Gen. Sir J. H., 67, 126
De Castelnau, General, attends conference at G.Q.G., 138 ; appointed by Lyautey as Chief of Staff, 204
Delville Wood, capture of, 166
Deputy Inspector-General of Transportation, author becomes, 277
Derby, Lord, visit to G.H.Q., 134 ; problem of the Press discussed with Haig, 155 ; sends miners' agents to visit the front, 191 ; sympathetic attitude *re* change of command, 203 ; threatens resignation, 281 ; and Robertson, 286
D'Espérey, General Franchet, takes over command of 5th French army, 26
Devonshire, Duke of, visits the front, 173
Dieppe, tour of inspection to, 283
Director-General of Transportation and his staff, 282
Dispatch riders, 78
Donald, Robert (of *Daily Chronicle*), and Press arrangements, 157

Doullens, conference at, 294
Doyle, Conan, account of Loos battle by censored, 191 ; visits to the front, 221
Dubois, General, and first battle of Ypres, 48 ; tribute to help by, 52
Du Cane, Major-Gen., visits Haig, 311
Duncan, Rev. J., 243, 274
Dunkirk, tour of inspection to, 306
Duration of war, various forecasts as to, 7, 22, 74, 84, 95–96, 98, 104, 311
D'Urbal, General, sees Haig, 52 ; author and, 53 ; ordered by Foch to retake lost line, 57
Dury, meeting of Haig and Pétain at, 292

E

EDINBURGH, Lord-Provost of, at G.H.Q., 143
Egypt, Kitchener and, 123 ; Government and, 124 ; troops transferred to Western front from, 304
England, man-power trouble in hand, 304
Enteric fever, outbreak of, 42
Enver Bey, feeling in Turkey against, 329
Ersatz Divisions (4th and 5th), at Ypres, 163
Esher, Lord, visits Haig, 85 ; visits to the front, 98, 99, 101, 145, 153, 172, 207 ; résumé of daily operations telephoned to, 153 ; presses for better film propaganda, 159, 161 ; desires to produce a "Chronicle of the Somme," 174 ; aspirations to be made Lieu-

Esher, Lord—*(continued)*
tenant-General, 187; presses for interviews by Haig with foreign correspondents, 192; and Wilson's appointment at G.Q.G., 203–204; on political situation in France, 224–225
Estreblanche, a war-time horse show at, 99–100
Étaples, visit to hospital at, 306
Eugénie, Empress, gift to author, 95
European theatre of war, hostile strength in (Sept. 1917), 255
"Experiences of the Somme Battle," a captured copy of, 214
"Eye-Witnesses," official, names of, 79

F

"FANNYS" (*see* First Aid Nursing Yeomanry)
Faunthorpe, tribute to Somme film by, 166
Fayolle, General, instructed to cover Paris, 292
"Field-Marshal Earl Haig," by author, cited, 7, 297 (note)
Fifth Army, report on German morale, 246, 247; and the German onslaught, 289 *et seq.*; disaster to, 291, 292, 293, 298
Figaro, the, a fictitious interview with Northcliffe published in, 196 (note)
Film propaganda, lack of interest in, 166
Findlay, Brigadier-General, death of, 32
First Aid Nursing Yeomanry ("Fannys"), war work of, 313
First Army, constitution of, 65, 67; a projected offensive in conjunction with the French,

First Army—*(continued)*
discussed, 101; and battle of Neuve Chapelle, 81 *et seq.*; and first battle of Ypres, 88 *et seq.*; and battle of Loos, 113; last visit of author as Staff officer to, 126; and battle of the Somme, 151 *et seq.*; and battle of Arras, 212 *et seq.*; and second battle of Ypres, 238 *et seq.*; and battle of Passchendaele, 257 *et seq.*; and battle of Cambrai, 270 *et seq.*; and the German onslaught (1918), 291 *et seq.*
First Army Corps, and retreat from Mons, 14 *et seq.*; and battle of the Marne, 27 *et seq.*; battle of the Aisne, 34 *et seq.*; and first battle of Ypres, 46 *et seq.*; 7th Division attached to, 51
First Army H.Q., distinguished visitors to, 87
Fisher, Admiral, and the Dardanelles scheme, 95
Fitzgerald, Colonel (Kitchener's Staff Officer), 106, 136, 137
Flammenwerfer, new form of, 190
Flanders, as a possible theatre of war not investigated by the French, 88; plan for final big attack in, 132; as reported German objective, 198; German reserves at, 199; anxiety regarding, 299; considered by Haig as next probable objective of Germans, 306
Fletcher, Alan (A.D.C.), 63, 113, 129
Foch, General, author and, 54; Haig's conference with French and, 57–58; visits First Army H.Q., 87; on plight of French fantry, 169; stories *re* German movements by, 170; appointed

INDEX

Foch, Gen.—*(continued)*
C.G.S., 225; goes to Italy, 262; and Supreme War Council, 267, 282; at loggerheads with Pétain, 287; appointed Generalissimo in France, 294, 295 (note); formal control of strategical operations of Allies in France given to, 298; promises a counter-attack near Montdidier which does not materialize, 298, 300; Haig's estimate of, 303; falsified forecasts of German intentions by, 304, 311; quarrels with Lloyd George, 312; orders movement of British troops without consulting Haig, 313; Cabinet and, 315; conflict of views with G.H.Q., 316, 320

Food rations of German army reduced, 218, 221 *(see also* Germany, food shortage in)

Football matches, 63, 65

Foreign attachés visit the front, 138

Foreign correspondents, interview with Haig, 192

Foreign Office, and propaganda, 157, 158, 167; and war films, 161

Fourth Army, and battle of the Somme, 151

Fowke (Chief Engineer at G.H.Q.), 85

France, first days in, 9 *et seq.*; as decisive theatre of war, 111; views of situation in, as observed by a correspondent, 271–272; strike danger ever present in, 333

Frederick Charles, Prince, and a British Intelligence officer, 205

French army, morale of affected by memories of 1870, 22; their lack of "punch," 37; com-

French, army—*(continued)*
missariat of, criticized, 39; a day with, 124; trouble in, 225

French Cabinet, rumours of trouble in, 121

French Government, fall of, 121; vacillating policy *re* command, 220, 225

French G.Q.G., visit to, 261

French Intelligence, author on efforts of, 299

French Press correspondents, arrangements for, 153; Northcliffe on, 196 (note)

French, Sir John (afterwards F.-M. and first Earl of Ypres), at War Council (Aug. 3, 1914), 7; author invited to lunch with, and congratulated, 12; at Bruyère conference, 15; and G.H.Q. Intelligence service, 28; underestimates German strength, 46, 48, 50; conference of Corps Commanders at head-quarters of, 56; Haig's conference with Foch and, 57–58; favours Wilson as C.G.S., 65; and Intelligence Staff, 76; dispatch on battle of Neuve Chapelle resented, 83; suggests that Haig be sent to India as C.-in-C., 87; friction with Kitchener, and reconciliation, 99, 100; and reserves at Loos, 107, 111, 113, 114, 116; reported wish to take first opportunity of concluding peace, 116; succeeded as C.-in-C. by Haig, 125; advocates a defensive attitude, 265; and intrigues against Haig, 268

French, the, characteristics of, 124, 310

Fricourt, King George V at, 162; British capture of, 165

G

GALICIA, Russian successes in, 147
Gallieni, General, 121
Garvin, J. L., criticizes Lloyd George, 231
Geddes, Sir Eric, as General and Admiral, 187; a story concerning, 283; optimism *re* submarine menace, 308
Gemeau (French liaison officer), and Kitchener's prestige in France, 86; report on return from Switzerland, 190
G.H.Q., friction at, 50, 55, 64, 101, 111, 117; rumours of changes at, 64; dispatch *re* battle of Neuve Chapelle criticized, 83; distinguished visitors to, 87; and the Indian Corps, 89; and the Loos dispatch, 121; author takes over at, 126; attack from home on, 268; epidemic of influenza at, 314
G.S.O. for Intelligence, duties of, 28; what is expected from, 37-38
George V, King, destroyer escort on return from first visit to France, 63; secret visit to the front—and accident to, 119-120; another visit to the front, 162; visits the Army (March, 1918), 296
George, Right Hon. D. Lloyd, becomes Minister of Munitions, 93; and Kitchener, 100, 121, 137; interrogates author on Intelligence work, 133; as probable successor of Kitchener at War Office, 148; visits the front, 164; becomes Prime Minister, 179; Strachey's opinion of, 180; disparages efforts on the Somme, 189;

George, Right Hon. D. Lloyd—(*continued*)
and Haig, 194, 195-196, 267, 273, 281, 286, 290 (and *passim*); at Calais conference (Feb. 1917), 199-200; author on fascination of, 223; pessimism at a Cabinet meeting, 233; Leo Maxse on, 243, 244; visits G.H.Q., 255; goes to Italy, 262; calls for papers from Sir J. French and Wilson, 264, 265; opens his attack on the Army, 268; disagrees with Derby's view of duration of war, 281; determines to remove Robertson, 285; speech in House of Commons on Cabinet differences with Robertson, 286; after the disaster to Fifth Army, 298; a statement by contradicted by Maurice, 308; quarrels with Foch, 312; angry with the French, 315-316; speech on German peace proposals, 335-336
Gerard, J. W., speculations as to his mission to America, 186-187
German Corps Commander, a, unwittingly aids Intelligence Staff, 50, 60
German "frightfulness," a new form of, 102-103
German gunner officer, a gallant, 270
German Intelligence, their knowledge of British dispositions, 86
German intentions, author's appreciation of (1917), 321 *et seq.*
German man-power, report on, 249
German onslaught, the (1918), 289 *et seq.*

German prisoner, on folly of Great War, 15

German Reservists, a Press notification of recall of, 4

German tactics in warfare, report on, 246

German withdrawal, the, 197 *et seq.*; probable strategical reasons actuating, 201

Germans, reported atrocities by, investigated, 38; skill as military engineers, 98

Germany declares war, 5; how news of death of Kitchener was conveyed to, 146 (note); an appeal for peace circulated in, 161; food shortage in, 186, 206, 213, 217, 218, 221, 251, 275, 322, 329; reported riots in, 204; peace proposals of, 224, 252, 276, 335-339; war-weariness in, 275, 331; probable separate peace with Italy, 321; loses her colonies, 322; internal political situation (1917), 330; fear of economic war after conclusion of peace, 334; prepared to accept Russian peace proposals as basis of general peace, 335

Gheluvelt, fall and recapture of, 52, 53

Gibbs, Sir Philip, War Office desire for special articles by, 157

Glasgow, Lord Provost of, at G.H.Q., 143

Gold (meteorological expert of Intelligence Staff), 109, 113

Good Hope, sunk, 65

Gough, General Sir Hubert, and battle of Loos, 114; Asquith and, 252; the German onslaught (1918), and disaster to Fifth Army, 289 *et seq.*; goes to a skeleton reserve army, 297

Gough, General John, farewell to author (Aug. 13, 1914), 8; and the retreat from Mons, 17, 21; wishes to conceal news of ill-health from Haig, 37; indignant at author's request for additional material for Intelligence work, 40; how he described French Cuirassiers, 49; promoted to Divisional Command at home, 74; killed on farewell visit to his battalion, 76-77; C.B. awarded to, 77

Gramophone in German trenches, 86

G.Q.G., conferences at (Feb. and Dec. 1916), 138, 181

Great Britain, revolutionary tendencies in, instanced by a circular letter, 226, 227

Grierson, General Sir James, at War Council (3 Aug. 1914), 7; author's conversation at Havre with, 10; death of, 11

Griffiths, Sir J. Norton, exploits in Rumania, 215; and the Messines mines, 232

Guards, in action at Landrecies, 20; war-time discipline of, 61; attack to readjust line near Loos, 115; counter-attack at Cambrai, 271

Gwynne, H. A., forecasts pacifists' peace procedure, 253; on public demand for fuller news, 260

H

HAGUE CONVENTION, breach of by Germans, 88

Haig, Sir Douglas (afterwards F.-M. Earl Haig), attends first Council of War (3 Aug. 1914), 7; at Wassigny conference,

INDEX

Haig, Sir Douglas—*(continued)*
13; at Cassel conference, 57–58; sent on mission to Kitchener, 61; asked to be C.G.S., declines, 65; constitution of First Army under, 65, 67; reorganization of army proposals adopted, 73; and the Neuve Chapelle dispatch, 83; as probable C.-in-C. vice French, 86; suggestion by Sir J. French *re* India to, 87; recommends author for a brevet Lieut.-Colonelcy, 99; and reconstitution of War Office Staff, 100; official visit from Kitchener, 105–106; presses for reserves and G.H.Q. objections, 107, 111, 113, 114, 117; reports on the reserves, 116; urges that Robertson be made C.G.S. and to advise Cabinet direct, 121–122; becomes C.-in-C., 125; daily routine of, 169, 209–210; at Cassel conference, 181; Northcliffe's remark concerning, 189; attends meeting of War Council (Jan. 1917), 191; interviews foreign correspondents, 192; intrigues against, 194–196, 267, 273, 281, 286 (and *passim*); refers " impossible demands by Nivelle " to London, 203; at Paris conference (April, 1917), 219; attends Cabinet meeting (June, 1917), 233–234; protests against denudation of Western front, 250; intrigues against compared with those against Joffre, 269; description of a meeting of Supreme War Council, 284; telegraphs home asking appointment of a Generalissimo for whole of Western front, 292; appeals to

Haig, Sir Douglas—*(continued)*
Foch and Clemenceau against Pétain's instructions to Fayolle, 292; at Doullens conference, 294, 295 (note); appeal to the Army (April, 1918), 302; strange rumours as to future career of, 308; considers supersession probable, 312; difficulties with Foch *re* movement of British troops, 313; " almost fatalistic in his outlook on life," 314

Haldane, Lord, Haig's esteem for, 50; talks of his recent visit to Germany, 102; investigates question of reserves in battle of Loos, 117–118

Hamburg, an epidemic at, 186

Hankey, Colonel, visits the front, 224

Hanover, reported preparations for war at, 5

Harington, General, and battle of Messines, 226, 228; on a newspaper report, 248

Havre, arrival at, 9; tour of inspection to, 283

Hay, Ian, interview with, 243

Hazebrouck, amusing experience at, 61

Headlam, General (now Lieut.-Gen. Sir John Headlam), on German casualties at Ypres battle, 240

Henderson, Lieut.-Gen. Sir David, 317

Hertling, Count (German Chancellor), unpopularity of, 274, 330; and censorship of the Press, 330

High explosives, British lack of, 36; defective, 41; wounds caused by, 42

High Wood, ravages of war in, 269

Hill 70 (near Loos), as objective of First Army, 104

Hindenburg, F.-M. von, and offensive against Russia, 199; interview with Austrian Press representatives, 321; refuses to mix himself up with politics, 330

Hindenburg Line, probable withdrawal of Germans to, 195; reported German intention to retire to, 197; probable strategical reasons for such retirement, 198

Hinges, unexpected arrival of Kitchener at, 111

Hobbs, General (senior administration officer), and author's medal of Legion of Honour, 54; an attack of appendicitis, 72; and brevet lieut.-colonelcy for author, 99

Hodgson, Captain Clarence, wounded at Loos, 116; killed on the Somme, 116 (note)

Hodgson, Capt. C. A. G., invalided from Palestine dies in Cairo, 292 (note)

Hodgson, Capt. C. B. M., wounded at fighting on the Jordan and death of, 292 (note)

Home Office, and propaganda, 167

Hooge Château, liquid fire in attack on, 102

Horne, 56

Horne, Sir Henry, 290

Hospital train, a well-found, 42

Houthulst Forest, 48 (note)

Hughes, C. E. (Prime Minister of Australia), personality of, 145–146; an American and, 177

Hunter-Weston, Lieut.-Gen. Sir Aylmer, visit from, 136

Hutchinson, Colonel, 129

I

IMPERIAL GENERAL STAFF, Haig's suggestion of formation of, 122

India, Government concern regarding, 87; probable effect of breaking off Dardanelles scheme on, 120

Indian cavalry, horse show staged by, 99

Indian Corps, criticism of H.Q. of, 63; heavily attacked, 65, 66; lack of training as reason of failure of, 66–67; in fighting round Ypres, 88; difficulties with, 107

Indian division arrives at the front, 47

Infantry, tribute to work of, 61

Influenza, outbreak of at G.H.Q., 314

Instantaneous fuse, enemy use of at third battle of Ypres, 239

Intelligence service of G.H.Q., criticized by Haig, 28; Gough and, 40

Intelligence Staff, author's tribute to helpers on, 62; growth of, 82; additions to, 100, 108–109

Intelligence Staff (French), criticism of, 104

Intelligence work, how handicapped, 50, 55

Ireland, comments on divisions and people of, 211

Italy, hesitating attitude regarding entry into war, 64; falls out of combined offensive plan, 205; Haig and suggestion to transfer troops to, 250; reported impending attack on, 260; attack materializes, 262; divisions from Western front transferred to, 265; German troops trans-

Italy—(*continued*)
ferred from, 287 ; independent peace with Germany deemed unlikely, 321
Italian theatre of war, hostile strength in (Sept., 1917), 255

J

JOFFRE, GENERAL, author's impressions of, 23 ; his criticism of kilted warriors, 26 ; and battle of Neuve Chapelle, 84 ; dismisses a French general and a staff officer, 85 ; opposes First Army scheme for attack on Aubers Ridge, 104 ; introduction to and a present from, 125–126 ; and plans for Somme attack, 131 *et seq.*, 152 ; and Verdun attack, 140, 141 ; "sniped at," 153 ; fall of, 181 ; intrigues against likened to the attack on Haig, 269

K

KAISER, tribute to British 1st Corps by, 85 ; Haldane's visit to, 102 ; wavers between Civil and Military Parties, 330
Kearns, 37
Kellman, Dr., meeting with, and a sermon by, 243
Kelvin, Lord, recollections of a lecture by, 211
Kemmel, German attack at (1918), 304
Kemmel Hill, taken over by the French, 304 ; captured by Germans, 305
Kennington, E., suggested as official artist, 176
Kerensky, and Russia's inability to fight on through 1917, 335

Kiggell, Lieut.-Gen. Sir L. E., appointed C.G.S., 126 ; succeeded as C.G.S. by Lawrence, 286
Kipling, Rudyard, a quotation from blue-pencilled by the Censor, 94
Kitchener of Khartoum, Earl, at first War Council (3 Aug. 1914), 7 ; Haig presses necessity of expanding B.E.F. into a great army on, 7 ; his " New Army," 7, 59, 72 ; Haig's mission to : questions to be discussed with, 61 ; intrigues against, 65, 100, 121, 137 ; attitude towards French and Wilson, 94 ; friction with Sir J. French, 99 ; Haig discusses conscription with, 105–106 ; impresses political importance of success, 111 ; "full agreement" with Haig, 124 ; instructions to Haig as C.-in-C., 129 ; points emphasized by regarding Somme attack, 137 ; death, 146 ; memorial service at St. Paul's, 147 ; Asquith and, 252
Knox, Major-Gen. Sir A., disquieting reports *re* Russia from, 136
Kuhlmann, as probable successor of Hertling, 275 ; leader of Civil Party in Germany, 330

L

LABOUR pacifists, visit from, 242–243
Labour Party, and peace proposals, 335
Labour Party Conference, Manchester, resolution proposed at, 191

INDEX

La Grande Fère, head-quarters at, 20
Lampson, Sir Miles, and film propaganda, 166; urges that Haig sees foreign visitors, 193
Landrecies, a wearisome march to and fighting at, 17–19
Lang, Cosmo, Archbishop of York (*see* York, Archbishop of)
Langemarck, fierce fighting at, 49
Lanrezac, General, and retreat from Mons, 23; superseded by D'Espérey, 26
Lansdowne, Lord, views on peace communicated to the Press, 333
La Tretoire, 1st Army Corps bivouac at, 29
Laurence, Sir Walter, visits G.H.Q., 261, 262
Law, Right Hon. Bonar, Haig's impressions of, 124; and Lloyd George, 133; and Lord Crauford, 153; pessimism at a Cabinet meeting, 233; questions Haig on German tactics, 281; a document prepared for altered by Haig, 286; statement in House of Commons *re* extension of line, 305; Maurice contradicts a statement by, 308
Lawrence, General Sir Herbert, charge of Intelligence handed over to, 277; as C.G.S., 286, 311, 317
Leather shortage in Germany, 329
"Leave" trains, pathetic scenes on departure of, 8
Le Boissel, British capture of, 165
Le Cateau, battle of, 26, 36
Ledeghem junction, damaged by British air-raid, 263
Leipzig Redoubt, capture of, 166
Le Touquet, author in hospital at, 142

Lewis, Captain Donald, directs artillery fire by aeroplane, 36
Lille, rumours as to taking of, and their object, 151 (and note)
Lillers, head-quarters of First Army at, 67, 71
Limoges, as French military equivalent to Stellenbosch, 85
Linen fabrics, shortage in Germany, 329
Liquid fire, first use of, 102
Lissenthiek cemetery, a night visit to, 234
Lomax, General (G.O.C. 1st Division), 13; retirement postponed, 5; and battle of the Aisne, 35, 36; and first battle of Ypres, 48; wounded, 50, 53; offered reserves, refuses, 51
London, rumoured passage of Russians through, 38
London conference (March, 1917), decision that British Army remains under Haig, 203
London Scottish in action, 60
Loos area, successful Canadian attack in, 244
Loos, battle of, 111 *et seq.*; Haig demands correction of a dispatch on, 121
Low, Sir Sidney, lines by quoted, 300
Ludendorff, General, as organizer, 274; overrules proposal of Wetzell, 303 (note); leader of Military Party in Germany, 330
Lumsden, Major, joins Intelligence Staff, 108
Lyautey, General, fall of, 204
Lytton, Lord, to what he compared the Taj Mahal, 192
Lytton, Major the Hon. Neville, and presentation of foreign visitors to Haig, 192; interview with War Cabinet on the subject, 194

M

MacDonald, Right Hon. J. Ramsay, and munition workers, 84
Macdonogh, Gen. Sir G., head of Intelligence at G.H.Q., 28, 125, 217
Macedonian theatre of war, hostile strength in (Sept., 1917), 255
Macready, General, 129
Malcolm, Ian (Balfour's secretary), home political news from, 244
Malcolm, General Neil, 37
Malvy, fall of, and a threatened strike in France, 333
Mammetz, British capture of, 165
Man-power, question ever to the fore, 74, 282, 294, 295, 303 (and *passim*)
Man-power problem of Germany, 322, 325, 327, 329, 331 (and *passim*)
Marker, 37; death of, 56, 57
"Marmalade cancer," 186
Marne, battle of the, 27 *et seq.*
Marquion, reported prisoners' camp at, 207
"Marraine" advertisement, a, and the Intelligence Department, 132–133
Masefield, John, Lord Esher's opinion of a work by, 174
Masonry forts as targets for heavy artillery, 48
Masterman, Rt. Hon. C. F. G., and propaganda, 161, 167
Maubeuge, fall of, 31; air reconnaissance work at, 163; enemy reserves at, 199
Maud'huy, General, asks assistance to round up retreating enemy, 30; Haig's interview

Maud'huy, General—(*contd.*) with on a decision of Joffre *re* extension of British line, 79
Maurice, Major-General Sir Frederick, contradicts a statement by Cabinet Ministers, 308
Maxse, Leo, author and, 188; characteristic letter from, 243; discusses political situation at home, 244; on "another intrigue to weaken Western front," 251
Maxwell, General, 286
Medical service, tribute to, 42, 116–117
Merville, head-quarters at, 66, 91
Mesopotamian campaign, discussed with Sir Harcourt Butler, 100; author and, 231
Messines, mining at, 143; battle of, 226 *et seq.*; services of Flying Corps during battle of, 238
Michaelis, Dr. Georg, and peace ideal of, 237; a speech by recalled, 238; succeeds Bethmann Hollweg as Chancellor, 330
Military situation in Germany summarized, 331
"Milking" by Germans, 152
Milner, Lord, administrative ability of, 185; pessimism at a Cabinet meeting, 233; at Doullens conference, 294, 295 (note); becomes Secretary for War, 305 (note); and difficulties between Foch and Haig, 313
Miners' agents, visit the front, 191
Mobilization ordered, 5
Monaco, Prince of, visits war front, 160
Monchy le Preux, unsuccessful attack at, 212; 3rd Bavarian Division at, 228, 240; capture of, 229

Monro, Gen. Sir Charles, in command of Third Army, 101
Mons, the retreat from, 14 *et seq.*; air reconnaissance work at, 163
Montauban, British capture of, 165
Montague, C. E., joins Intelligence Staff, 158; his articles objected to by War Office, 175
Montdidier, French promise attack near, 298; which does not materialize, 300; a small attack near (June, 1918), 313
Montenegro, King of, visits the front, 176
Montgomery, General Kerr, visit to, 65
Monthuis Sart, head-quarters at, 40
Montmédy, enemy reserves at, 199
Montreuil, head-quarters at, 143, 210
Morganthau (ex-American Ambassador to Turkey), interview with, 251
Morris, killed in action, 24
Motor-buses from London, a convoy of, 72-73
Moynihan, Sir Berkeley, operates on Gough, 76, 77
Munition-making, slackness in the factories, 84, 251
Munitions Department, "a typically carping document" issued by, 263-264
Munro, General, 13; wounded, 53
Munsey, Mr. (American publicist), visits the front, 172
Munster Fusiliers, 23
Murray, Gen. Sir Archibald, 11; ill-health causes resignation as C.G.S., 65
Murray, Sir Malcolm, equerry to Duke of Connaught, 175

N

NAPOLEON, a reply to his marshals quoted, 237; a dictum of, quoted, 274
Napoleon's tomb, Haig's visit to, 141-142
Navy, the, launches a bombshell at a Cabinet meeting, 233
Near East, situation in (1917), 321
Neutrals, and duration of war, 84; author on a visit from, 134-135
Neuve Chapelle, preparations for attack on, 71 *et seq.*; battle of, 81 *et seq.*; estimated German losses at, 82; G.H.Q. dispatch *re*, resented by the Staff, 83; unexpected results of, 84; Indians in action at, 89
New Army, Haig's suggested reorganization adopted for, 73; author's opinion of, 95; in battle of Loos, 114 *et seq.*; in Somme battle, 178
New Year dinner (1916), 129
Newspaper proprietors, demand special correspondents for each paper, 153, 155
Newton, Lord, question of censorship and propaganda discussed with, 146-147; and Northcliffe, 173; ridicules a report from Belgian Intelligence, 190; presses for interview by Haig with foreign correspondents, 192, 193
"N.F." cells, explanation of, 238
Nicholas, Grand Duke, opinion of a Russian Attaché of, 205
Nicholson, Sir W., dictum of, quoted, 224
Ninth Corps, sent for a rest, are attacked on the Aisne (1918), 310

Nivelle, General, succeeds Joffre in chief command, 181; tentative agreement with Haig, 193; British Army handed over to, 200; insistent for appointment of Wilson as head of mission at G.Q.C., 203; uneasy time with French politicians and generals, 203, 208; rumours of his probable replacement, 216, 220, 225; fall of, the initial cause, 269

Nolan, General, of American Intelligence Staff, visit from, 232

Northcliffe, Lord, 155, 273, 286; telegram from counter-signed by author, 156; and Kitchener, 156; visits G.H.Q. during battle of the Somme, 156, 157; and Repington, 157; and propaganda, 167; claims credit for putting Lloyd George in power, 182; warns Lloyd George of withdrawal of support, 188; compares Asquith with Lloyd George, 189; and the D.H. interviews, 194; and intended repudiation by Government of the D.H. interviews, 195–196; on effect in America of boosting of Canadians, 211; telegram from, *re* Press work, 213

Nurses, work of, after battle of Loos, 116–117

O

OBSERVATION BALLOONS, 149, 155
Official *communiqués*, writing of, devolves on author, 170
"Oil-cans," explained, 228 (note)

Onslow, Lord, joins Intelligence Staff, 100
Orleans, Prince of, 41
Orpen, (Sir) W., suggested as official artist, 176

P

PACIFISTS, and their views, 242
Padres, tribute to work of, 148
Pagan, Gavan, object of author's visit to, 148
Painlevé, M., 258, 266
Palais de Justice, Ypres, 47
Palestine, campaign in advocated by Supreme War Council, 282, 284; British troops recalled from, 304, 309
Palmer, Frederick (American war correspondent), visits the front, 80, 193; situation in America discussed with, 82
Paper shortage in Germany, 329, 330
Paris, aspect in war-time of, 109; conferences in, 140, 217, 219; St. Andrew's Night function in, 179; and Gerard's mission to America, 186–187; cause of trouble with the Embassy at, 188; political convulsion in, 204; strikes in, 229
Passchendaele, battle of, 254 *et seq.*
Peace proposals (*see* under Germany)
P. and O. liner mined, 139
Péronne, taken from the Germans, 204; bridge-head given up by Gough, 292, 298
Pershing, General, reception in Paris, 234, 235; a graceful compliment to British Army, 234, 235; ramifications of Intelligence Staff explained to, 235;

Pershing, General—(contd.)
 confers with Haig and Robertson, 236
Pétain, General, 261, 282, 284; appointed French C.G.S., 220; replaces Nivelle as C.-in-C., 225; impressions of, 225; at loggerheads with Foch, 287, 297; meets Haig at Dury, 292; at Doullens conference, 294, 295 (note); a promised attack near Montdidier does not materialize, 298, 300
Photographs from aeroplanes (see Air photography)
Piave, the, Italian retreat to, 270
Picture post-cards, brisk trade in, 64
Piedmontese brigades surrender *en masse*, 265
Pigeon service, value of, 214
Plumer, Major-General, successful attack at Messines, 226, 228; Haig's tribute to, 228; his dislike of publicity, 248; sent to Italy, 266; rumoured offer of reversion of Haig's command to, 273; brought back from Italy, 287; at Doullens conference, 294, 295 (note)
Poincaré, M., and Clemenceau, 266; at Doullens conference, 295 (note)
Poison gas, used by Germans, 88; sufferings of victims of, 89; British use of determined on, 107, 113
Polish deserters, 123
Politicians, peace parsimony of, criticized, 59; versus Army, 250, 251
Politics, to what likened by Churchill, 130–131
Poperinghe, description of, 47; head-quarters moved to, 56

Portuguese, in the German onslaught (1918), 301
Press correspondent, captured as a spy, 33
Press correspondents, at the front, 79; facilities for special telegrams by, 149, 151, 155; Staff officers and, 173; the Chief Censor and, 177
Press, the, official *communiqués* issued to, necessarily incomplete, 146; question of freedom of in Germany, 330
Primrose, Neil, "Eye-Witness" with Indian Corps, 94
Prisoners, interchange of, negotiations for, 309, 310
Propaganda, 44, 139, 145, 157, 158, 163, 165, 166, 329 (note), 332 (and *passim*); essentials for British, 167
Prussia, an epidemic in, 186
Przemysl, captured by Russians, 83

Q

Queen's, the, in first battle of Ypres, 49
Quetta, story of a dentist at, 39

R

Rawlinson, General, meeting at Poperinghe with, 47; opinion of author of, 87; takes over First Army, 125; surprise attack by succeeds, 154; succeeds Wilson as military representative at Versailles, 287; comes back to take Gough's place, 297; ordered to prepare plans for attack at Amiens, 316; co-operation of Haig and Foch with, 317

INDEX

Ray, a claimed wonder-working, proves a fraud, 178
Reading, Lord, visits the front, 164
Recruit, story of a grateful, 6
Redmond, John, visits the front, 122
Reinforcements, need of stressed, 59, 60
Repington, C. A. C., 254, 258; confirms a report concerning Wilson, 73; an uncensored article by, and a consequence, 94; Kitchener and, 94; author and, 152, 153; Northcliffe and, 157; and the submarine menace, 215–216; prophesies more world-wars, 298
Rheims, enemy attack at, 316–317; Cabinet orders XXIInd Corps to be brought back from, 317
Ribot, M., impressed with notes prepared for Haig, desires to use them in a state paper, 219
Rice, General (one-time senior Sapper at Aldershot), a story of, 27; an original forecast by, 38, 40; brings news of recapture of Gheluvelt, 53; returns from Salonika, 168
Rifle-bullet, wound of, 42
Roberts, Lord, at War Council (Aug. 1914), 7; death of, 61
Robertson, Sir W. R., 65, 134; appointed to succeed Murray as C.G.S., 73; on uselessness of a pessimist in war, 77; concerned at proposal to send more troops to Salonika, 119; appointed C.I.G.S., 124, 131; and the D.H. interviews, 194; Lloyd George's mimicry of, 223; and Wilson, 225; conferences with Haig, 236, 245;

Robertson, Sir W. R.—*(contd.)*
Asquith and, 252; goes to Italy, 262; Lloyd George and, 274, 281; threatens resignation *re* Palestine scheme, 282, 284; superseded as C.I.G.S., 286
Robinson, Geoffrey (editor of *The Times*), visits the front, 172; suggestions for improvement in Press work by, 173
Robinson, Perry (Press correspondent of *The Times*), 158
Rocket signals, German, new form of, 37
Romer (of Intelligence Staff), 108
Roosevelt, President, and Mrs. Humphry Ward, 139
Rothermere, Lord, visit from, 255
Rothschild, Leo, and sound ranging, 168
Rouen, tour of inspection to, 283
Royal Engineers, remove a wrecked collier, 107 (note)
Rubber, synthetic, German, 329 (note)
Rumania, rumours concerning her entry into war, 64; question of joining Allies, 99; adventures of Norton Griffiths in, 215; German divisions withdrawn from, 263
Russia, bad news from, 72, 102, 108, 202, 205, 213, 271; collapse of predicted by Esher, 99; corruption in, 140; revolution in, 202; falls out of combined offensive plan, 205; German troops withdrawn from, 255, 263, 287; on verge of a second revolution, 267; anarchy in, how viewed in Germany, 321; separate peace proposals of, 335
Russian Army, ammunition shortage in, 136
Russian C.G.S. visits Haig, 154

Russian officers, official visit from, 136
Russian Staff officer, disclosures by, 154
Russian theatre of war, hostile strength in (Sept., 1917), 255
Russians, rumoured passage through London of, 38, 75; German defeat in East Prussia by, 42; defeated in the Carpathians, 92
Ryan, Colonel E., 18, 39, 56–57, 72, 116–117, 142, 148, 169, 244, 320

S

SAARBRUCKEN, enemy reserves at, 199
St. Davids, Lord, suggestion by, resented by G.H.Q., 123
St. Mihiel Salient, a captured order with details for evacuation of, 255
St. Omer, head-quarters at, 130
Salonika, proposed expedition to, comments on, 73; ammunition from Western front sent to, 82; uselessness of the scheme, 231
Sapper and Miner Company, visited by author, 124
Sarajevo tragedy, 3
Sargent, J. S., suggested as official artist, 176
Sassoon, Sir P., 129
Scotland Yard men, and Secret Service of Army H.Q., 84
Second Army, and second battle of Ypres, 100; and battle of Messines, 226, 228; and German onslaught (1918), 292
Second Army Corps, and retreat from Mons, 14 *et seq.*; and battle of the Aisne, 34 *et seq.*
Secret Service system, a temporary breakdown in, 159
Secrett, Haig's personal servant, 17

Seely, Major-Gen. Right Hon. J. B., an experience at Dammartin related by, 28; as attaché to G.H.Q., 50; becomes Brigadier-General of Canadian Corps, 123
Senlis, visit to, 138
Serbia, problem of, 120
Shaw, George Bernard, visits the front, 192, 202; questions in House of Commons regarding the visit, 221
Shell-fire, a curious result on troops of, 56
Siege howitzers, auctioned among Corps Commanders and obtained by 1st Corps, 40
Simla, a scheme prepared at, considered "dangerous and useless," 47
Simms, Rev. Dr., an extension of service for granted, 5; becomes Principal Chaplain to the Forces, 6; enters Parliament as member for County Down, 6; at a New Year's dinner (1916), 129
Simon, Sir J., opposes compulsory service, 131; request from Cowans to find a post for, 241–242; Asquith anxious that a post be found for, 253
Sloggett, Lieut.-Gen. Sir Arthur (Head of Medical Services in France), 129, 130
Smith, Right Hon. F. E., Official "Eye-Witness" with Indian Corps, 79; is replaced, 94; tells author of an interview with Kitchener, 74; visits the front without a pass and is arrested, 135; on intrigues at home, 251
Smith-Dorrien, Lieut.-Gen., and the retreat from Mons, 16; criticized by Haig, 36

INDEX

Smuts, General, visits the front, 207, 208; pessimistic attitude at a Cabinet meeting, 233
Socialists, two prominent, visit the front, 97
Socialists, Majority and Minority, 330
Soissons, war-time appearance of, 25
Somme area, enemy reserves in, 199
Somme, battle of, plans for, 129 *et seq.*; battle begins, 151 *et seq.*; comparison of the battle with those of the Aisne and Loos, 155, 169; outstanding successes in, 164, 168
Sound ranging, value of and improvement in, 155, 168
Southampton, departure from, 9
Spectator, The, a poem entitled " Christ in Flanders " appearin, quoted, 268
Spies, unceremonious treatment of by the French, 33
" Spy-fever," 43
Spy-hunting with two detectives, 96
Stellenbosch, significance of word, 85
Steward, Sir H. Alan, 172-173
Stink bombs, investigation of a rumour regarding use of, 253
Stonehaven, Lord (*see* Baird, J.)
Strachey, J. St. Loe, on political crisis in London, 180, 181
Strikes, their effect on duration of war, 84
Submarine menace, the, 76, 88, 180, 215-216, 307, 322; optimism of Sir E. Geddes regarding, 309; false German estimate of effect of, 333
Supreme War Council, appointed and its constitution, 267; versus G.H.Q., 281 *et seq.*; Wilson

Supreme War Council—(*contd.*) and transference of control of, 287; incorrect forecast by, 297
Sweden, rumours of desire to enter the war, 64, 100
Swettenham, Sir Frank, and Press correspondents, 177
Swinton, Col. (now Sir) E. D. (" Ole Luk-Oie "), as official " Eye-Witness," 79; author discusses idea of the Tanks with, 165 (note)
Swiss frontier, reported concentration of German troops on, 199
Switzerland, alarm in with regard to intentions of Germany, 190
Sykes, Sir Mark, visits the front, 207-208, 229

T

TANK, a British, in German hands, 177
Tanks, evolution of, 165 (note); seen by M.P.s—and leakage of information, 165 (note); success in battle of the Somme, 164-165, 168; defects of, 168; German fear of, 319
Teck, Duke of, 129; reports favourably of Belgian Army, 291
Telephone messages, intercepting apparatuses for, 152, 159
Territorial Force, expansion of, urged by Haig, 7; in action, 60, 94
Territorials (French), their commander on discipline of, 20; an English public schoolmaster and, 27-28; in battle of Ypres, 88

INDEX

The Times, an uncensored article in, 94; bought by Lord Northcliffe, 157; on an epidemic at Hamburg, 186

Third Army, formed, Sir C. Monro in command, 101; visit to (Nov. 1917), 269; and the German onslaught, 291 *et seq.*; in action (Aug., 1918), 320

Third Army Head-quarters, conference at, 132

Thomas, Albert, pacifist lectures to French munition workers, 266

Tillett, Ben, visits the front, 97, 173

" Tired divisions," explained, 249 (note)

Tirpitz, Admiral von, Haldane on war views of, 102; and the German Military Party, 330

Tison, M., accredited French war correspondent, 153

Torpedo-boat destroyer, rough crossing on, 139

Trade Unions invited to a conference " to hail the Russian Revolution," 226, 227

Train movements, observations of, 324

Transportation Department, 282–283, 319

Transportation problems discussed at Calais, 199

Trench-life, adaptability of troops to, 123

Trench mortars, British lack of, 36

Trenchard, General (now Lord), 129, 242, 273

Trieste, Italian menace to removed, 321

Trois Tours château and its proprietor, 56; Haig's head-quarters at shelled, 58

Trones Wood, capture of part of, 166

Turkey, Germany's fear of separate peace by, 275, 276; and question of separate peace, 322, 329, 333

U

UHLAN, surrender of a, 25

Ulster, speech by Lt.-Col. Bols in —and a prophecy, 3

U.S.A. (*see also* America), attitude towards Allies discussed, 83

V

VALENCIENNES, enemy reserves at, 199

Verdun, fierce German attack at, the French surprised, 139 *et seq.*; regarded by Haig as a "wearing-out" battle, 143; continued German attempts for, 147

Vesle, bridge on the, 43

Villers-Cotterets, fighting near forest of, 24

Vimy Plateau, taken by the French, 115

Vimy Ridge, Canadians' surprise attack on, 211, 214

W

W.A.A.C.s (*see* Women's Army Auxiliary Corps)

Waddington, M., 24

Wagstaff (now Maj.-Gen.), C. M., and American reinforcements, 308

Wales, Prince of, 65

War Cabinet, and the D.H. interviews, 194; gist of Haig's paper prepared for, 219; "in full cry against Haig," 264
War correspondents, unofficial, visit the front, 79; Haig's orders concerning, 94; weekly official statements given to, 141
War declared (4 Aug., 1914), 5
War, horrors of, 22, 47, 52, 220–221, 233, 269, 306; waste as essence of, 109; effect on religion in France, 148; remarkable progress in scientific side of, illustrated by Somme battle, 155
War Office, concession to demand for more news, 79; politicians and, 93; and Dardanelles scheme, 99; and the Press, 154; and propaganda, 157, 158, 167, 174; and films, 161; Intelligence of, and the difficulty regarding dissemination of news, 161; estimate of Germany's man-power (Aug. 1916), 162; urge presentation of foreign visitors to Haig, 193; inquiries as to Shaw's visit from, 221–222; opinion on question of German morale, 260; and Q.H.Q., 269; and Palestine scheme, 282
Ward, Mrs. Humphry, visits the front, 139–140, 201; "Towards the Goal" by, 259–260
Warsaw, fall of considered imminent, 102
Wassigny, conference at, 13
Wells, H. G., visits the front, 221
Welsh coal strike, 101
Western theatre of war, hostile strength in (Sept. 1917), 255
Westminster, Cardinal Archbishop of, visit from, 261

Wetzell, Lieut.-Gen., of German General Staff, 303 (note)
Whigham, Lieut.-Gen. Sir R., 53
White Château, the, battle headquarters at, 52, 54
Wilkinson, on Intelligence Staff, 108
Williams, Valentine, spends a night in the trenches, 94
Williamson, Sir A., and Mesopotamia, 232
Williamson, Wallace, sermon by, heard by Asquith, 253
Wilson, Col. (afterwards F.-M. Sir Henry), at first War Council (3 Aug., 1914), 7; considered by Haig as a "politician," 11; appointed Liaison Officer with the French, 73; as conversationalist, 87; report on Russian re-organization from, 192; appointed head of British mission at G.Q.G., 203; Foch and, 225; Asquith and, 252; accompanies Lloyd George to Italy, 262; scheme for Supreme War Council, 265, 267; and Palestine scheme, 282, 284, 288; becomes C.I.G.S. vice Robertson, 286; at Doullens conference, 294, 295 (note); hints that he will be sent to the Home Command, 312
Wilson, S., appointed on "Operations" Staff of First Army, 67
Wilson, President, discussed with an American, 177; peace note of, 185, 186; and Germany's peace proposals, 335–336
Wireless stations, German, removal of, 324
Women's Army Auxiliary Corps, coolness during an air-raid, 309

INDEX

Wytschaete, heavy bombardment at, 203; Germans gain ground at, 304

Y

YARDE-BULLER, BRIG.-GEN. THE HON. SIR H. (Military Attaché with the French), 132
Yarmouth, bombardment of, 59

York, Archbishop of, visit from and talk with, 236
Ypres, first battle of, 46 *et seq.*; war scenes in, 47, 61, 89, 105, 125; second battle of, 88–94; third battle of, 238 *et seq.*

Z

ZEEBRUGGE, naval attack on, 306; effect on submarines of, 307

www.ingramcontent.com/pod-product-compliance
Lightning Source LLC
Chambersburg PA
CBHW040301170426
43193CB00021B/2969